PlyDesign

I would like to dedicate this book to all of the creative people whose work fills its pages, and to my daughter, Leigh, who began her official design work at age two, building ambitious structures with dozens of baby board books. I have no doubt that the parents of every one of this book's contributors have a similar story to tell. — PS

The mission of Storey Publishing is to serve our customers by publishing practical information that encourages personal independence in harmony with the environment.

Edited by Nancy Ringer and Lisa Hiley
Art direction by Alethea Morrison
Book design by MacFadden and Thorpe

Pencil renderings by Michael Gellatly
Technical drawings by Peter Sherratt
Cover photography by:
  Front cover, row 1, left to right: © Eric Bishoff, © Alexis Liu, © Chad Kelly, © Lightbox Images Photography, images by Thomas Cooper, © Steven Ewoldt; row 2, left to right: © Arthur Koch, © Lightbox Images Photography, images by Thomas Cooper, © Sara Schalliol-Hodge; row 3, left to right: © Maya Lee, Marcelino Vilaubi, © Eric Bishoff; row 4, left to right: © Adele Cuartelon, © Christy Oates, © Mark Bradley; row 5, left to right: © Ryan Mahan, © Beth Blair, © Marcus Papay
  Back cover, top to bottom: © Cezary Gajewski, © Dieter Amick, © James Scheifla, Marcelino Vilaubi
Interior photography credits appear on page 316

Indexed by Nancy D. Wood

Storey Publishing
210 MASS MoCA Way
North Adams, MA 01247
www.storey.com

Printed in China by R.R. Donnelley
10 9 8 7 6 5 4 3 2 1

Library of Congress Cataloging-in-Publication Data on file

PlyDesign

73 Distinctive DIY Projects in Plywood (and Other Sheet Goods)

Philip Schmidt

Storey Publishing

Contents

Preface

Like most people, I used to think of plywood as a strictly utilitarian building material. As kids, we used it to cobble together treehouses, or we'd lean a scrap of it over cinder blocks to make a bike jump. In our teenage years, we screwed thin sheets of it onto a lumber frame to make the curved faces for our skateboard ramps (which we promptly spray-painted with antiestablishment symbols; I wonder if real anarchists got in trouble for coming in late to dinner). Back then it never would have occurred to me that the finely shaped and artfully painted decks of our skateboards also were made of plywood.

Even when I worked as a carpenter I knew plywood only as subflooring, roof decking, and sides for concrete forms. And, of course, plywood is ideal for all those applications. But as this book shows, construction is just the beginning.

I can recall two discoveries that opened my eyes to the design possibilities of plywood. The first was a gallery space in Minneapolis that had every wall lined with full sheets of clear-coated maple panels. These were gapped about an inch apart and mounted with trimhead screws. Entering the room, I was entranced by the towering wood surfaces and the breadth of their luminous grained faces. And then, upon close inspection of the gaps, seeing the stratified core of the material: "Plywood! Yes! Why not?"

My other "plywood moment" was seeing one of Charles Eames's molded plywood leg splints for the first time, in a small art exhibition where I could get close enough to touch it with my nose. Modernists of all stripes know this piece as a seminal work of design, engineering, and mass-production technique, but at the time I was unfamiliar with all that, and I was completely enthralled by the work and its conception. As the story goes, Eames was told by a doctor in 1941 that the metal splints used in the battlefields of Europe were too heavy and lacked sufficient means for strapping limbs. With considerable effort and innovation, the designer created a plywood version that was strong and lightweight, had plenty of holes for strapping (thanks in part to cutouts necessary for production), and worked equally well for both right and left legs. The U.S. government ultimately bought over 1,500 of them.

Perhaps what's most remarkable about the Eames splint is its beauty. It is, in essence, a work of art in wood. And it had to be plywood; you certainly couldn't carve 1,500 splints out of solid wood blocks (especially in wartime). Today you could easily make the splints with plastics or carbon fiber, but they still wouldn't have the look and feel of real wood. That's what makes plywood such a great and unique material. It's a precisely machined, manufactured product that started life as a tiny seed in the ground — the perfect blend of nature and engineering.

This book features the creative work of dozens of design professionals, students, and enthusiasts (and at least one full-time writer: me), all of whom share a love of plywood and what you can do with it. These projects are built with ordinary shop tools and range in difficulty from downright easy to somewhat woodworkery. Not all of the pieces are made with plywood, or with plywood alone. Some call for MDF (medium-density fiberboard), some have glass or aluminum parts, and one particularly stylish work makes decorative use of construction-grade strandboard. In every case, you can rest assured that these designers know their materials, and you'll be amazed at what you can create using readily available, off-the-shelf supplies.

If you're a designer, woodworker, or experienced maker, I'm sure you'll be inspired and entertained by many of the fresh ideas presented in these pages. And if you're new to the shop or the drawing board, I hope this book or one of its projects becomes one of your own plywood moments.

— *Philip Schmidt*

Shop Talk

Buying, hauling, and working with sheet goods: an unhandyman's
guide to understanding plywood (and its woody cousins).

A Panel Discussion: All about Plywood

Plywood is the head of a growing family of wood-based panels generically referred to as sheet goods, or sheet stock. All of these fall under the category of *engineered wood:* building products that start out as trees and, after a good deal of industrial processing, end up as interchangeable products made to precise specifications. While solid wood has many undeniable merits, the beauty of the engineering is that it removes or counteracts some of wood's biggest drawbacks — namely, knots and other natural flaws, shrinkage and expansion, and warpage, plus the fact that you can't buy a nice solid-wood board wider than 11¼" without refinancing your house.

HOW PLYWOOD IS MADE

Plywood gets its unique blend of strength, stability, and economy from its layered construction. A plywood panel is made up of thin plies, or veneers, of wood glued together under pressure and heat. Each ply is laid perpendicular to the plies above and below. This process, called cross-graining, is key to plywood's strength and dimensional stability. Moisture causes wood to expand and contract mostly *across* its grain (a board gets wider and narrower rather than longer and shorter). Cross-graining effectively suppresses this movement. A plywood panel keeps its shape and doesn't constantly shrink and expand like solid wood.

Wood is by nature much stronger in line with its grain than across it. Cross-graining builds upon this strength, making plywood equally strong in all directions. This may be why ancient Egyptians used laminated wood to build caskets, some of which are still holding up today.

Cross-graining gives plywood edges a striped appearance, created by the alternating layers of end grain and face grain. In traditional styles of woodworking, the stratified edges are typically concealed by a band of solid-wood trim or other material, creating the illusion that the plywood is a solid plank. In the modernist style, not only are the plywood edges left exposed, they're often a major design element.

The plies for making plywood are cut by a big, lathelike machine that rotates a log by its ends while a long knife strips off the wood in a continuous thin layer, sort of like an old-fashioned apple peeler. For certain grades and outer veneers, some plies are cut across the log (called slicing). This yields a grain pattern more like that of solid lumber than does rotary cutting, which follows the wood's growth rings and produces wide, wavy patterns of grain.

The top and bottom layers of a plywood panel are called the face and back veneers, respectively. These are the plies that count, aesthetically, and they're usually the thinnest layers in the sheet (but thicker is always better). So that the grain of the face veneer runs in the same direction as the grain of the back veneer, all plywood is made with an odd number of plies, ranging from 3 up to 17, including the face and back. Generally speaking, the more plies, the better the plywood.

Workers make plywood at a wood processing plant in northeast China.

PLYWOOD GRADING

The language of plywood can be much more complex than you might expect when talking about big slabs of wood. And as with most building materials, the terminology is anything but universal. So even if you memorize everything explained here, don't be surprised if things aren't the same at your local lumberyard, and try not to feel belittled, as when talking to a computer support technician. The bottom line is that you'll know what you want when you see it at the yard (and don't be afraid to be choosy with the stock).

For furniture pieces or any decorative work where you want the edges to show, it's best to stick with Baltic birch (see page 12) or a general group of cabinet-grade, or furniture-grade, material generically called *hardwood plywood*. This plywood is made with all-hardwood plies and is much less likely to have voids within the plies than standard plywood, which often contains layers of softwood (Douglas fir, pine, et cetera). Also, the edges of hardwood plywood machine and sand more uniformly than those of standard plywood. Voids are a problem because they leave you with unsightly cavities in cut edges, and there's no way of knowing where they are before you make the cut.

A plywood panel gets two grades, one for the face veneer and one for the back. The most common standard grades for face veneers, from best to worst, are N, A, B, C, and D. With hardwood plywood, N and A grades should be "clear" or stain-grade, meaning they look good enough not to be painted. B-grade veneers are smooth and have only minor flaws but may contain patches; they are generally used for the back or less-exposed side of a piece. C-grade is used for fully concealed surfaces, like the back of a bookcase. D might as well be code for Downright Ugly; it's found only on construction-grade material.

For back veneers, some suppliers assign one of these letter grades, while others use a number, such as 1, 2, or 3. Typically, the number grades of 1, 2, and 3 are loosely equivalent to an A-minus, B, and C, respectively.

Veneer Matching

In addition to the general grading, the face veneers on cabinet-grade plywood can be categorized according to how they're made. A face made with a single sheet of wood, with no seam, is called single-sheet, or whole-sheet, veneer. When the face is made of two or more sheets butted together lengthwise, it's "matched" veneer, categorized according to how the grain pat-terns of the different pieces are arranged. *Book matched* veneers consist of two mirror-image patterns opened like a book and laid flat. *Plank matching* arranges mating pieces so all the grain runs in the same direction, but the grain patterns are random. This results in a look that's most similar to sawn boards that are edge-glued together. It's not quite as dramatic and interesting as book-matched veneer, but it looks more realistic to a discerning eye. Both book-matched and plank-matched veneers are arranged for consistent coloring. *Unmatched* veneers (typically rotary-cut) are arranged with no intentional order to the grain or color.

PLYWOOD SIZING

A standard "full sheet" of plywood is 4 feet wide and 8 feet long. Some suppliers sell sheets in smaller pieces, such as 2 x 4 feet and 4 x 4 feet, while online you can find such oddities as 12" squares of Baltic birch for about $2. And sometimes that's all you need. Length and width measurements are generally true to their named, or nominal, dimensions.

Sizing is not quite as simple when it comes to panel thickness. Standard thicknesses are as follows, in inches: 3/16, 1/4, 3/8, 1/2, 5/8, and 3/4. Some suppliers also offer 1"-thick material. Seems simple enough, but don't be surprised if you run into nominal (and actual) dimensions like 7/32", 15/32", and 23/32". The lumberyard staff will probably still call these 1/4", 1/2", and 3/4", respectively.

When working on projects, be sure to measure the actual thickness of your material, and always run test cuts for things like dadoes, rabbets, and slots. Assuming your stock is 3/4" when it really measures 23/32" could get you into trouble.

Book matching (left) results in a dramatic, if not particularly realistic, display of wood grain. Plank matching (right) is an assembly of typically narrower strips, with the grain aligned more or less vertically.

Other Sheet Goods You'll Find in This Book

While most of the projects here use hardwood plywood as the primary material, a handful of designs call for different engineered wood products. And you can make substitutions with a fair number of designs — for example, using MDF instead of plywood.

MDF

Medium-density fiberboard comes in 4 x 8-foot panels made of tiny wood fibers glued and pressed into a perfectly uniform, color-through material. The color happens to be a dull puttyish hue that can look pretty good with a clear finish, but most applications call for paint. MDF has no layers (and no voids) and cuts and routs like butta'. It's a good substitute for plywood on painted projects because it's cheaper, takes paint better, and is sanded smooth at the factory. MDF is also dead flat, with no surface deviations whatsoever.

The main drawbacks of MDF are important to note: When unfinished, this material is highly susceptible to water damage; imagine a roll of paper towels set down on a wet countertop. Its compressive strength (flat pressure) is high, but its tensile (bending) strength is much lower than plywood's. You also must be careful when screwing or nailing MDF: it splits or chips if you're too close to the edge, and screws can strip out fairly easily, especially on the edges. Always drill pilot holes for fasteners in MDF, and seal the edges before painting (see Finishing Plywood and MDF, page 20). Finally, be prepared for a blizzard of dust when cutting or milling MDF, and work outside whenever possible. The dust is superfine, and it gets *everywhere*.

MDF-CORE & COMBINATION-CORE PLYWOOD

Regular plywood, with all natural-wood plies, is technically called "veneer-core" plywood. You need to know this only to distinguish it from a group of plywoods made with one or more layers of MDF. *MDF-core plywood* is a nearly full thickness of MDF with face and back veneers of real wood. It's very flat, and it's void-free, but it has the same drawbacks as regular MDF.

Combination-core plywood has a center of three or more wood plies sandwiched by layers of MDF and finished with pretty wood veneers. The result is a panel that's stronger than

MDF

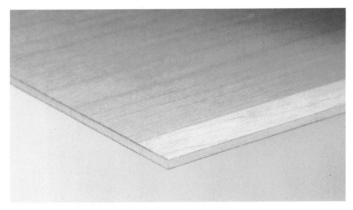

MDF-core plywood

MDF with ultraflat surfaces that you can't always get with conventional plywood. Both of these hybrids are a good option for large, flat panels that will have their edges covered (with solid wood, veneer edge tape, mating panels, et cetera).

BAMBOO PLYWOOD

This is the new kid on the block, and he's very proud of how green and cool he is. He's made with cross-grained layers of bamboo, which acts like wood but is really a woody grass. The layers consist not of thin plies but of narrow, edge-glued strips of solid bamboo, making for very distinctive edges and very beautiful faces. Bamboo is considered an environmentally friendly natural resource because of its rapid renewal rate —

Bamboo plywood

OSB

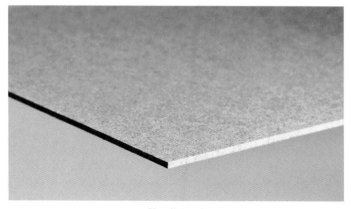

Hardboard

some species can be harvested and replenished every three to five years.

Bamboo plywood is a strong performer and comes in a limited range of colors, including natural blonde, carbonized (a dark brown created by boiling the raw material), and an eye-catching "zebra" whose pattern comes from a blending of light and dark layers. Panel thicknesses range from ⅟₄₀" to ¼" single-ply veneers to ½", ¾", and 1" laminated structural panels. As of this writing, the price of 4 x 8-foot bamboo panels can range from 30 to 100 percent more than that of hardwood plywood, but prices are trending downward as the material reaches a broader market.

OSB

Oriented-strand board is similar to plywood, but it looks like someone put the plies in a blender before gluing up the panel. It's made up of a few layers that are cross-grained, like plywood, and has two outer layers that share the same "grain" direction. OSB is cheap and reasonably strong. In specific applications, it can be a good plywood substitute, whether for economy or the interesting look of its surfaces; for example, it looks pretty cool with a semitransparent paint job.

HARDBOARD

Also known as high-density fiberboard or by the popular brand name Masonite, hardboard is commonly available in 4 x 8-foot sheets of ⅛" or ³⁄₁₆" thickness. It's dark brown and has one smooth side and one rough side, which has a slight waffle-grid texture. Hardboard is, literally, pegboard without the holes. You won't use it for any building projects (unless you really want to), but it's a good material for making templates for tracing and routing your workpieces. Hardboard is thin, void-free, and much easier to cut and shape than ¾" plywood, for example. It's also very cheap, so you won't mind messing up a template or two.

Where to Buy Sheet Goods

Now to apply all that we've learned to the real world: If you browse the aisles at a local "big box" home center, you'll likely find lots of construction-grade plywood (for things like roof sheathing and subflooring), as well as ¾" (²³⁄₃₂") plywood with red oak and birch face veneers. This is pretty standard seven-ply stuff and will

Baltic Birch — From Russia, with Love

Beluga caviar notwithstanding, Baltic birch plywood may be Russia's finest export. Made with all-birch plies from the Baltic regions of Russia and Finland, Baltic birch (or BB) has long been a standard choice for cabinetmakers, furniture designers, and woodworkers. In short, it's a good, cabinet-grade material, with thin, even plies and quality face veneers (typically single-sheet). It's also a good deal, starting at about $75 for a full 5 x 5-foot sheet of ¾" stock.

And you read that right: most BB plywood comes in a 5 x 5-foot sheet. It's an odd size, for sure, but it's really handy when you'd rather have a little more width instead of length. Some American suppliers carry 4 x 8-foot sheets, and many offer smaller sizes in a range of thicknesses.

As mentioned, some BB comes from Finland and is considered by some purists to be superior to "Russian birch," but you can't go wrong with either. For furniture projects, look for Baltic birch in B/BB-grade (not to be confused with the Baltic birch abbreviation). This has a clear, single-sheet face veneer and a nice, if sometimes patched, single-sheet back veneer.

Baltic birch plywood has consistently thin, virtually void-free plies that make for beautiful milled edges. The light-blonde face veneers are great for clear-coating, oiling, or staining.

probably have some voids inside, so it's not the best choice if really nice exposed edges are important.

Be very wary of 2 x 4-foot precut panels that are often sold in an aisle endcap. Sometimes these panels can have decent-looking face veneers, but always check the edges: if the plies are inconsistent and overlapping instead of flat, continuous layers, you don't want the panels, unless you're using them to hurricane-proof windows.

Other sheet goods, including MDF, OSB, and hardboard, are likely to be of the same quality at big boxes as anywhere else.

A better option for finding good plywood is a well-stocked lumberyard or hardwoods supplier. Lumber prices can vary widely even in the same town, so it's best to call around first. Always ask how many sheets they have in stock — you don't want to make the trip only to find that their "selection" is one sheet from the bottom of the bundle.

Lumberyards often carry a few sizes of hardwood plywood in birch, oak, maple, apple, and other common veneer species, as well as Baltic birch (see box at left). Hardwoods suppliers will carry all that plus cherry, walnut, alder, hickory, and things you've never heard of, like wormy maple, kewazinga, and afromosia. Prepare for severe sticker shock with some of these species.

Considering how much mileage you can get out of a full sheet of plywood, it's a real bargain compared to clear solid lumber. Try to keep this in mind when you're out shopping. It's almost always worth it to spend a little more for good plywood, both for the all-important void avoidance and for quality face veneers.

Hauling & Storing Sheet Stock

For beginners, trying to wrestle a full sheet of plywood to the top of a car can quickly turn into a Buster Keaton routine, spelling certain embarrassment at the lumberyard. The following tips can help you get your goods home safely with your pride intact.

First, here's the one and only proper way to lift a panel: Stand it upright on one of its long edges. Position yourself at the rear end of the panel, with one hand on the top edge and the other ready to grab the bottom edge. Lift the panel enough to grab the bottom rear corner with the lower hand, then raise the rear end of the panel while pivoting the front bottom corner on the ground. Move both hands (along with the rest of your body) to the center of the panel, then rock the panel back to raise the front end. Carry the panel with your hands in the same positions, tilting it against your shoulder at a comfortable angle.

If you're practical and nerdy enough to own a minivan (like this book's author), chances are you can lay down flat a full 4 x 8-foot sheet of plywood in the back, so that it sticks out only a couple of feet. The trick is to stack up a couple of shipping pallets (or a pallet and some 2 x 4s on edge) so the plywood rests above the seat brackets and the curve of the hatch door opening. The same thing works in many SUVs. Be sure to run a tie-down strap over the rear end of the panel to keep it from sliding out when your turbo boost kicks in (if only minivans came with turbo). For those of you with pickup trucks, you can stop snickering now and skip ahead a few paragraphs.

If you have a car, your only option for hauling a full or half sheet is to throw that sucker on the roof rack or the roof itself. Be sure to pad the roof or rack with a blanket, to protect the car and the panel. Center the panel on the roof. Open the doors, and strap the panel down through the doors, using ratcheting straps (webbing with come-alongs, or mini hand winches; you can buy a whole set of these for $10 to $15 at any home center) or strong rope. Don't use bungee cords, which are made to stretch, of course, and can't handle strong forces.

Next, run a strap or rope from the right front corner of the car over the panel crosswise, and tie it to the left rear corner of the car. Repeat with a crossing strap going from the left front to right rear. These are the most important tie-downs, because most of the wind uplift will come from the front. Drive home with care. And whatever you do, don't take the highway!

If hauling a full sheet just isn't feasible, you can have your panel cut into more manageable sizes right there at the lumberyard; see Making Straight Cuts, page 15. Or, if you're buying more than one sheet, you can probably have the panels delivered for free.

Once you get your material home, proper storage is key to protecting your investment. Above all else, remember to *keep it flat* and *keep it dry*. Stack panels flat, whenever possible, placing them back-face down on flat 2 x 4s or other scrap material to keep them off the floor. Stack multiple panels face-to-face, aligning their edges neatly. You can cover a stack to keep the material clean, but always allow for plenty of air circulation. If stacking is not an option, stand the panels up on their long edges, against a wall, and resting on top of some scrap 2 x 4s.

When you're moving panels around, be very careful to set them down gently, lest you ruin a perfect factory edge with a ding or gouge. As mentioned earlier, moisture will quickly ruin MDF, and it's not great for plywood either. That's the main reason to keep the panels off the floor or ground. All panels can start to sag if left upright for long periods, so find a place to lay them flat if you won't get to them for a while.

Essential Techniques

Many of the pieces in this book employ special techniques for cutting curves and custom profiles and for setting up your own production line to create multiple identical parts. The techniques are generally simple and relatively foolproof, but often it's important to remember that you're working with engineered wood and not solid lumber, which you're probably more familiar with.

VENEER: THE BEAUTY AND THE BEAST OF PLYWOOD

Plywood's pretty face veneer makes it possible to have a 32-square-foot panel of luxuriously grained hardwood, but it's also the Achilles' heel of the material. At an average thickness of about $1/32$", veneer is easy to damage with any kind of tool, and mistakes often can't be sanded out as they can with solid stock. That said, once the panel edges are milled or trimmed and the material is finished, veneer faces and edges hold up quite well in everyday use.

The first thing to avoid is splintering. This is most often caused by saw teeth exiting the material as they cut. Circular saws and jigsaws (with standard blades) cut *up* through material, resulting

---

Plywood to Float Your Boat

While you won't find any boat projects in this book, if you're building a piece for outdoors, you might want to consider springing for marine plywood. This high-grade material is made with water-resistant, exterior-grade glue, so it's very resistant to delaminating due to moisture exposure. Marine plywood also has solid plies — that means no voids. However, it is not chemically treated for rot resistance (like some exterior-grade construction plywoods), so be sure to give it a good finish rated for outdoor exposure.

in splinters along the cut line on the top face of the stock. Table saws and most handsaws cut *down* and therefore splinter the bottom face. The best way to prevent splintering with portable saws is to score the cut line with a sharp utility knife, effectively cutting through most of the veneer before the saw blade sets its gnashing teeth to the delicate wood layer.

For straight cuts, start by marking your cut line with a pencil or marking tool, then score down the center of the line with a knife, using a straightedge as a guide. Make one light pass first, then repeat with increasingly forceful passes — two or three total should do it. Set up a straightedge so one side of the saw blade is precisely aligned with the scored line, and make the cut (see Making Straight Cuts, page 15). Scoring usually is necessary only when you're making crosscuts (perpendicular to the grain). Rip cuts (parallel to the grain) typically don't splinter much.

Curved cuts aren't so easy to score, but the tools used for these — namely, jigsaws and routers — don't cause splintering as much as circular saws do. If splintering is a problem with a jigsaw, switch to a finer blade with less "set" (the side angle of the teeth), or use a special down-cutting blade if you must cut from the top face. The latter is often recommended for cutting panels veneered with melamine or plastic laminate.

One of the best ways to dress an exposed plywood edge is to round it over with a router and roundover bit (see page 20), and any reasonably deep roundover will eliminate edge splinters. Easing an edge with sandpaper is less effective at removing splinter damage.

On the topic of sanding, you might be surprised how easily you can mar a veneer with the gritty stuff. Very thin face veneers (less than 1⁄32") may withstand little sanding before showing through to the layer below or disappearing altogether. And don't assume that premium plywood has thick face veneers. As a general rule, sand faces as little as possible, and be especially careful along edges, where the veneer recedes surprisingly fast with sanding. Use only fine-grit paper (at least 150 grit or so) on faces, as coarse paper leaves scratches that can be risky to sand out.

Are Sheet Goods Green?

Ecofriendliness is a highly debatable subject no matter what you're talking about, but it's safe to say that sheet goods are generally green because they optimize the use of wood, a renewable natural resource. Engineered products like MDF and particleboard are particularly stingy in their material use, since they're primarily made with recycled sawdust and wood pulp from lumber operations.

Plywood is resource-efficient because the best hardwood grades are reserved for the thin outer veneers, while lower-grade woods (which are often unsuitable as solid stock) can make up the interior plies. However, the manufacturing resources required to make engineered products can be greater than those for solid-lumber processing.

Where sheet goods aren't so green is in the adhesives used to bind the wood together. Most sheet goods are made with glue containing formaldehyde, a naturally occurring carcinogenic gas that's used in many building materials and furnishings. Traces of formaldehyde can be released into the air (offgassed) from exposed surfaces of plywood, MDF, and other sheet goods, such as particleboard. While the health risks to the typical homeowner are largely unknown, there have been reports of chemically sensitive people suffering from headaches and other symptoms believed to be caused by formaldehyde offgassing.

Interior (standard) plywood, MDF, and particleboard typically contain urea-formaldehyde binders, which offgass more than the phenol-formaldehyde binders used in many exterior-grade sheet goods. Some manufacturers offer sheet goods made with "no added urea-formaldehyde" (NAUF) or "no added formaldehyde" (NAF).

Back on the resource side of things: Some sheet goods are available from suppliers certified by the Forest Stewardship Council (FSC) and other organizations that award certification for sustainable forestry practices. For a list of companies that offer certified and/or no-added-formaldehyde products, visit the website of the Green Building Advisor (see Resources).

Crosscuts made with a circular saw are notorious for splintering face veneers.

A careful cut along a scored line greatly minimizes splintering. Always use a straightedge guide to keep your saw straight during this cut.

MAKING STRAIGHT CUTS

The factory-cut, or "factory," edges of a sheet-good panel are your best friends in the workshop. These machine-cut edges are reliably straight and typically form perfect 90-degree corners (but always check your panel with a straightedge and a framing square just to be sure). This makes them ideal as references for laying out panel cuts and for using as critical edges and corners of a finished piece. For example, if you're building a desk with long, straight sides, use the factory edge for the front side of the desktop, and make the rip cut on what will become the back edge.

But, alas, a new panel has only four factory edges and corners (and sometimes they get dinged along the way, which just isn't fair). To make all of your other edges as close to factory perfection as possible, the best ordinary tools are a circular saw set up with a straightedge guide or, the woodworker's choice, a table saw. If you own a table saw, I'll assume you know how and when to use it, so I won't explain it here. For those of you with a circular saw who are new to working with large panels, read on.

Setting up a circular saw for straight cuts is simple and takes just a little practice to become second nature. Here's how it works: The rectangular metal (or plastic) base, or "foot," of the saw has perfectly straight sides that are parallel to the blade. Therefore, if you clamp a smooth, low-friction straightedge over your workpiece and run the saw's foot along the side of the straightedge, you'll make a clean, straight cut with minimal burning (see Ring of Fire, page 16) and saw marks.

Using a straightedge with a circular saw

The only thinking part is measuring between the edge of the saw blade and the edge of the foot, then using that dimension for setting the distance between the straightedge and your cut line.

You can use a lot of different things for a straightedge; it just has to be straight, flat, smooth, and rigid enough to resist flexing during a cut. For cuts up to 4 feet long, a 4-foot level works quite well. Longer cuts pose more of a challenge. You can use a 6-foot level, if you have one, or create a homemade jig, using a 12"-wide piece of ⅜" or ½" plywood or MDF for the base and a straight piece of stock for the straightedge, or fence: Snap a chalk line onto the base, a few inches from one long edge. Screw the fence to the base, using the chalk line to keep it straight. Then run your circular saw down the base, with the saw foot against the fence — the saw trims the base at the precise offset between the blade and the straightedge. To set up a cut, simply align the edge of the base with the cut line, and clamp the jig down to the workpiece.

The key to success with a homemade jig is a perfectly straight fence, something that's hard to accomplish with most off-the-shelf lumber. A better option is a strip of ½" or thicker MDF or good hardwood plywood that includes a long factory edge.

You can also buy fabricated aluminum straightedge guides in a range of lengths. Some include integrated clamping devices, while others are just tracks that you secure with standard clamps. These are great as long as they're straight — and beware of two-piece models of questionable quality; any movement in the joint results in a flawed cut. People who make a lot of long panel cuts often use a track saw, a circular saw with a special foot that rides along a track in a proprietary straightedge. These are ideal but certainly overkill for most hobbyists.

Another option for straight cuts is having them made at the lumberyard or home center where you buy the material. Lumberyards may charge for this service by the sheet or based on the time involved. Make sure you know exactly what sizes you need for each cut piece, and remember about the kerf — the material removed by the saw blade. The lumberyard may not guarantee accuracy greater than about ⅛", and you can count on some splintering in crosscuts. Therefore, this is a good option for ripping a full sheet down the middle for easy transportation, especially if the dimensions aren't critical. While home centers often will make a few cuts for free, the quality of the cuts depends on the employee's experience and the fitness of the home center's panel saw; in other words, you're taking your chances here.

HOW TO MARK & CUT CURVES

Finally, a real-life application for grade-school geometry! Marking and cutting curves in sheet goods is pretty darned fun, and this book gives you hundreds of opportunities to hone these skills. Let's start with a very brief refresher course:

Diameter is the distance across the center of a circle.

Radius is half of the diameter.

The standard method for drawing curves and circles involves a compass. The "radius" of any curve is the distance between

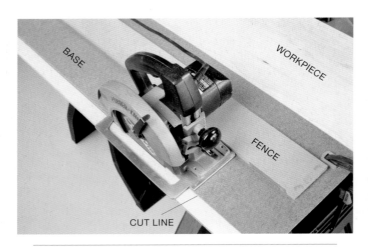

Using a homemade straightedge jig

Ring of Fire

It takes just a few seconds of cutting for saw blades to get hot enough to burn wood. Circular saws and table saws are the worst offenders, as are routers and their incredibly fast-spinning bits. To prevent unsightly burn marks on cut edges, keep the saw (or workpiece) moving during the cut. The slightest hesitation or errant movement can result in a dark brown or black streak. You can sand these out, for the most part (and even the best woodworkers have to do this sometimes), but heavy sanding can ruin your straight edge. So it's best to avoid burns in the first place.

the pivot point on a compass and the drawn line. A small pencil-type compass that you can buy in any school-supply aisle will make radii up to 5" or 6". For larger radii, you'll need to create a homemade version. This is the simplest tool you'll ever love:

1. Find a thin, straight board or stick (a wooden yardstick is ideal).

2. Draw a centerline down the top face of the stick, parallel to its long dimension.

3. Use a utility knife to cut a small V-notch in one end of the stick, with the V's point meeting the centerline; this is for holding a pencil point in place.

4. Measuring down the stick from the point of the notch, mark the centerline at the desired radius.

5. Drill a hole at the mark, and tap in a small finish nail; the nail should be snug in the hole. This is the pivot point of the compass.

Now you're ready to mark curves like an old-school draftsman.

To lay out and draw a curve on a piece of stock, first plot the location of the pivot point. This is always equidistant from the desired ends of the curve. For example, if you're rounding off a square corner of stock with a 3" radius, the pivot point must be 3" from both adjacent sides of the material, as shown in the illustration on the top right.

To mark a large radius, start by drawing a centerline down the stock at the midpoint of the curve or workpiece. The centerline must be at least as long as the radius of the curve; if you run out of room on the workpiece, simply butt up a scrap panel to the workpiece, and continue the centerline onto the scrap, as shown in the bottom illustration.

To mark the pivot point for your homemade compass, measure down the centerline and mark the line at the radius distance. Drill a pilot hole, and drive the finish nail through the compass and into the stock at this mark. Set a pencil into the V-notch, and pivot the stick and pencil on the nail to draw the curve.

To cut a curve of any size, you can use a jigsaw, a band saw (if available), or a router. The best method for cutting simple curves and circles is to make a rough cut with a jigsaw (or band saw), staying about ⅛" outside the cut line. Then come back with

a router set up on a trammel to clean up the edge; see Two Easy Ways to Cut a Circle, below. For complex curves and custom profiles, you can carefully freehand the cut with a jigsaw or band saw, then sand the edges as needed to smooth and refine the curves.

TWO EASY WAYS TO CUT A CIRCLE

With the right setup, cutting a disk from sheet material is a piece of cake (or, rather, a piece of *pi*). Again, the best tool for this, by far, is a router.

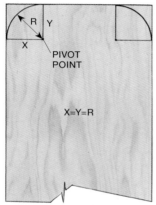

For a small corner radius, plot the compass's pivot point by measuring from each adjacent side.

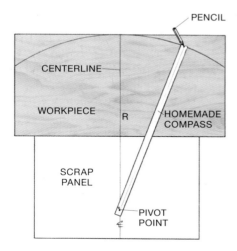

A compass made with a yardstick can draw radii up to about 36". Use an extra piece of stock material, if necessary, to draw a centerline for the compass's pivot point.

Router and Trammel

In woodworker's parlance, a trammel is a board that controls the motion of a tool. Here, a trammel works just like the homemade compass you'd use for marking curves (see the preceding section), except at the "business" end you have a router instead of a pencil.

You can make a trammel in about ten minutes: Cut a strip of ¼"- to ⅜"-thick sheet stock about the width of your router base and 1 to 2 feet long. Draw a centerline down the top face of the board, parallel to the long dimension. Bore a large hole (for bit clearance) near one end of the board, centered on the line. Drill counterbored pilot holes through the bottom of the trammel centered on the clearance hole and mount the trammel to the router base with machine screws and washers as shown at top right (remove the router's plastic subbase first).

Set up the router with a two-flute straight bit or a spiral bit. To establish the radius of the circle on the trammel, measure from the innermost projection of the bit out along the centerline on the trammel, and mark the centerline at the radius distance. Drill a small hole at the mark for a finish nail.

Mark the circle on your sheet material with a homemade compass (see previous page), and rough-cut the disk with a jigsaw, cutting it slightly larger than you want it. This initial cut with the jigsaw is to reduce wear on your router bit, and it allows you to clean up the edge of the disk with one smooth pass of the router. Then position the trammel over the disk, and pin it down with a nail tapped into the same hole you used for the compass.

There's one catch to using a trammel here, and this applies only to fixed-base routers (plunge routers can simply plunge into the cut): with the workpiece rough-cut slightly large, there's no free access for the bit to initiate its cut. Here's one way to overcome this obstacle (note: any method you try is done *at your own risk*): Hold the trammel down with one hand and the router body with the other. Tilt the router up and back slightly, flexing the trammel, so the bit is free when you start the router. When the router is up to speed, carefully lower the router to engage the bit into the work. Complete the cut, moving the router counterclockwise around the circle.

Jigsaw and Trammel

The same basic trammel setup used with a router works (almost) as well with a jigsaw. To make this jig, cut a strip of sheet stock a

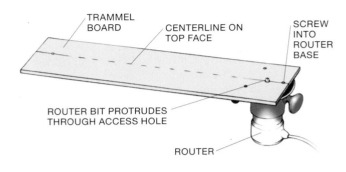

Remove the router subbase, and mount the trammel to the router base using machine screws with the same thread size as the subbase screws.

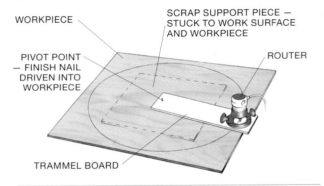

To cut a circle in one pass, use a spacer and double-sided tape or other hold-down to secure the spacer and workpiece. Otherwise, clamp the workpiece over the edge of the bench and move the setup once to complete the cut in two operations.

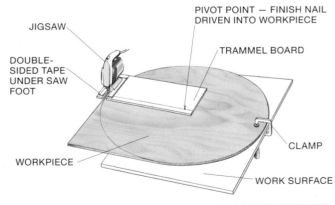

A jigsaw with a trammel makes an accurate disk, if not as cleanly or efficiently as a router.

little wider than the length of the saw's foot. Use a square to draw a line across the board, a few inches from one end and perpendicular to the board's long dimension; this is a reference line for the inside edge of the saw's foot. Cut a notch, centered in the front edge of the board, to provide clearance for the saw blade.

Draw a line parallel to the board's long edge, aligned with the blade location. Secure the saw to the trammel with double-sided tape, so the inside edge of the foot is on its reference line and the blade fits into the notch. Measure from the inside of the blade and mark the long line at the radius distance; drill a hole and tap in a nail here for the pivot point.

You can make the cut by starting with the blade snug against the edge of the workpiece, or drill a starter hole that just touches the edge of the circle.

TEMPLATE ROUTING

Template routing, also called pattern routing, is an important technique for many of the projects in this book. You'll use it to make exact copies of a shape or profile on multiple workpieces. If you don't have a router, you should know that there are two alternatives to template routing: 1) having the pieces cut on high-tech machinery such as a CNC (computer numerical control) router or laser cutter, or 2) cutting each piece individually (typically with a jigsaw or band saw), then ganging the pieces together and sanding their edges until their profiles match. Obviously the first option is far preferable, if you happen to know someone with access to an updated woodshop.

Template routing is simple and quite foolproof (as woodworking techniques go). You start by making a template — a precise prototype of the finished piece for your project. In most cases, it's best to use an inexpensive, easy-to-work material, like hardboard or MDF, for the template; these cut and sand easily and cleanly and have no voids in their edges. Plus they're cheap, so it's no big deal if you make a mistake. Sometimes, however, it makes sense to create the template from the project stock and ultimately use it in the finished piece.

Once the template is cut and sanded to perfection, you secure it to each workpiece and use a router and a flush-trimming bit to make the cut. This bit has a bearing that rides along the edge of the template, while the cutter trims the workpiece even with the template, creating an exact duplicate. The importance of getting the template just right can't be stressed enough: even the slightest imperfections in the template will transfer to each workpiece, where they will have to be sanded out; better to sand once than many times over.

Flush-trimming bits have the bearing either below the cutter or above it. Top-bearing versions are sometimes called "pattern" bits, while bottom-bearing versions may be called "laminate trimmers." With top-bearing bits, the template goes on top of the workpiece; with bottom-bearing bits, the template goes on the bottom.

As with cutting circles, it's a good idea to rough-cut the shape of the workpiece with a jigsaw before routing with the template. Use the template to trace the shape onto the work, then cut about ⅛" outside the lines with the saw. Next, adhere the template to the workpiece top or bottom, depending on the type of bit you have, using double-sided tape or small dabs of hot glue. Even if you clamp the template and work to your bench, the tape or glue may be necessary to prevent any shifting that could distort the finished product. Rout the workpiece in one full-depth pass, moving around the template in a counterclockwise direction.

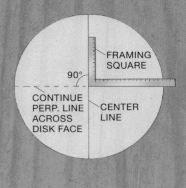

Marking Quadrants on a Circle

To draw reference lines on a disk that you've just cut, first draw a line through the disk's centerpoint, aligning a straightedge with the hole left from the pivot nail. Next, place a framing square (or other flat-sided square) on the centerline, with the corner of the square on the center hole; mark along the perpendicular leg of the square. Use the square or straightedge to continue the second line across the face of the disk.

FRAMING SQUARE

90°

CONTINUE PERP. LINE ACROSS DISK FACE

CENTER LINE

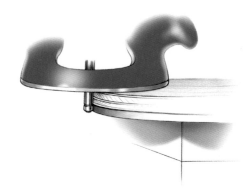

For template routing, set the bit depth so the bearing rides squarely along the edge of the template, and the cutter reaches the entire thickness of the workpiece.

A full or partial roundover made with a router and round-over bit adds a clean, finished look and feel to plywood edges and highlights its layered construction. Rounding over is also an ideal remedy for splintered saw cuts.

Finishing Plywood and MDF

Virtually any finish that works for solid wood is equally appropriate for plywood, MDF, and other sheet goods. This includes all the standards: polyurethane (and other varnishes), penetrating oils, paste wax, and paint, as well as wood stain for adding color before applying a protective finish.

Where finishing plywood and MDF differs from finishing solid wood is in the edge grain. Plywood edges may have voids that should be filled prior to finishing, while MDF edges are porous and, if finished directly, tend to absorb a lot of liquid, requiring additional coats of finish. Unless you're covering a plywood edge with veneer tape, fill any edge voids with a color-matched, nonshrinking wood putty (for stain and clear finishes) or auto-body filler, such as Bondo (for paint). MDF edges, once sanded smooth, need only a good primer/sealer to prevent excessive absorption of paint.

As with solid wood, if you're painting, you can fill screw and nail holes with nonshrinking putty or filler, sanding it flush with the surrounding surface. For clear (and stained) finishes, you can conceal exposed fasteners with precut wood plugs or dowel pieces glued into the hole, trimmed, and sanded flush.

Dressing the edge corners of plywood is important for a finished look and to prevent splintering of the thin veneer layers. If you prefer a square-edged look, simply bump, or slightly round over, the edge corners with fine sandpaper prior to finishing. For a rounded look and feel, the best treatment is to mill the edges with a router and roundover bit. Like the flush-trimming bits described earlier, roundover bits have a guide bearing that rolls along the material's edge, controlling the depth of the cut.

Roundover bits are sized for the maximum depth of roundover they can create: on a ¾"-thick panel, a ¼" bit can round-over about one-third of the edge; a ⅜" bit rounds half of the edge; and a ¾" bit can cut a full bullnose edge. For most applications, a ¼" or ⅜" bit is the best all-around choice.

One important note about roundover bits: the bearing needs a flat surface to travel along. If you're rounding over both corners of a single edge, you must leave ⅛" or so in the center of the edge uncut. Without this flat surface, the second roundover will be slightly deeper than the first, leaving you an asymmetrically rounded edge with an ugly little ridge running down the middle. It seems that the ridge comes from the sharp corner at the bottom end of the bit's cutter when it's allowed to get too close to the wood, thanks to the rounded bearing surface.

Surfaces I

Tables and desks: for dining, for work, for setting up on poker night
and knocking down when the guests have gone.

Florence Table

Designed by Cezary Gajewski

Perhaps more than any other piece in this book, the Florence Table celebrates the very best characteristics of plywood: strength, flexibility, uniformity, and beauty. Take a moment to study the table's leg structure and you'll see exactly what I mean. And you might be surprised to learn that this is also a knockdown design. The whole thing disassembles in minutes and packs flat into a 3-foot-diameter package. The shape and scale of the table make it ideal for small spaces, where it can seat up to four people — although you might have to look hard to find chairs that do the table justice.

MATERIALS

- ☐ One 36" x 36" sheet paper
- ☐ Two 35" x 35" sheets ½" MDF
- ☐ One 5 x 5-foot sheet ½" Baltic birch plywood
- ☐ Eight sets 1¼"-long Chicago bolts
- ☐ Finish materials (as desired)
- ☐ Four silicone bumpers (clear, low-profile, self-adhesive)
- ☐ One 36"-diam. tempered glass top, approx. 9 mm thick

TOOLS

- ☐ Quality HB pencil
- ☐ Framing square or T square
- ☐ Straightedge
- ☐ Scissors or utility knife
- ☐ Double-sided tape (non-foam-backed, clear)
- ☐ Jigsaw or band saw with fine-tooth wood blade
- ☐ Sandpaper (up to 220 grit)
- ☐ Router with ¼" and ½" flush-trimming bits
- ☐ Combination square
- ☐ Chisel
- ☐ Drill with straight bit(s) (see step 7)
- ☐ Screwdriver
- ☐ 4-foot level

Note: This project calls for a 36"-diameter round piece of glass with finished edges. The glass must be tempered for safety, so you have to order it from a glass fabricator (any glass shop can handle it). Tempered glass can't be cut — it's tempered after sizing — so this isn't a DIY option. Discuss your project with the glass dealer to be sure to get the right product for the application.

1. Trace leg templates.

Fold a 36" x 36" sheet of paper in half. Using an HB pencil, a framing square or T square, and a straightedge, draw a grid of 1" squares on one outer side of the paper, using the fold as the centerline of the grid. Carefully transfer the profile shown in the leg template illustration onto the grid. Using scissors or a sharp utility knife, cut the curves out of both halves of the paper at the same time. Unfold the paper. This is your paper template for leg A.

2. Create an MDF template for leg A.

Using a good-quality, non-foam-backed, clear double-sided tape, temporarily attach the paper template to one of the MDF sheets. Trace the profile onto the material, then remove the template. Cut the profile with a jigsaw or band saw, but do not cut the rectangular slots in the center portion of the leg. Carefully sand the edges of the MDF template to smooth the curves and remove any imperfections. Lightly sand all edges so they are smooth and flat. As you sand, keep the edges as square and flat as possible.

It's important to take your time with this step, as any imperfections on the template will transfer to all of the legs.

3. Create an MDF template for leg B.

Place the MDF template for leg A on the remaining sheet of MDF. Trace the entire profile of leg A onto the blank sheet. Remove the template. Cut out the template for leg B with the jigsaw, but this time stay about ⅛" outside the pencil line. Again, do not cut out the rectangular slots. You will trim the excess material in the next step.

4. Rout the template for leg B.

Using double-sided tape, temporarily attach the two MDF templates together, with the A template beneath the rough-cut B template, making sure the A template fits inside all of B's cutting lines. Set up a router with a ½" bearing-guided, flush-trimming bit so the bit's bearing rides along the A template (see Template Routing, page 19). Rout the edges of the B template to create two identical pieces.

Note: If you're using a router table, the A template goes on top of the B template, because the bit will be upside down.

5. Cut the interlocking slots.

Carefully cut the rectangular slots in the A template, using a jigsaw. When cut, the slots should provide a snug fit for your plywood stock, so be sure to measure your plywood and mark and cut the slots accordingly. Match up the two templates again, and transfer the slot locations onto the B template. Use a combination square or similar marking tool to extend the pencil lines on the B template downward, so that the slots are on the bottom half of the center section, opposite to the slots on template A (see the cutting diagram on page 25, noting that the B legs are oriented upside down).

Cut the slots in the B template. Test-fit the templates together at the slots, and make any necessary adjustments. Keep in mind that the slots must conform to the plywood stock, not the MDF.

6. Cut and rout the legs in plywood.

Repeat the process of step 3, above, to mark two A legs and two B legs on your plywood stock, orienting the pieces as shown in the cutting diagram. Cut out the pieces with a jigsaw or band saw, staying ⅛" outside the lines. Then rout each plywood leg just as you did with the B template in step 4. Rout the slots in the

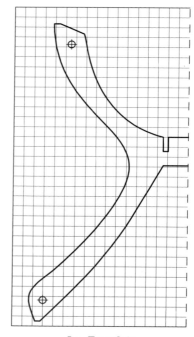

Leg Template

plywood using a ¼" flush-trimming bit for tighter inside corners. Test-fit the slots and make any necessary adjustments. You might need to clean up the inside corners of the slots with a sharp chisel.

7. Drill the hardware holes.

Select a drill bit that is slightly larger than the sleeve end of your Chicago bolts. Mark the centerpoints of the four holes on one A leg and one B leg, as shown in the leg template. Gang the like templates together — A with A and B with B — and clamp each pair with a backerboard (a piece of scrap wood set behind the bottom piece to prevent tearout). Drill the holes through both pieces of each pair.

Note: If you like, you can use a Forstner bit that is slightly larger than the head of your bolts to countersink the heads slightly on the outside of the legs. Just make sure to drill the counterbores before drilling the through holes.

8. Assemble the legs.

Slot the leg pairs together so the As are parallel to each other and the Bs are parallel to each other. Pinch the tops of the paired legs together, and secure them with the Chicago bolts, tightening

the bolts with a screwdriver. Confirm that all four leg ends stand firmly on the floor, and use a 4-foot level set across the leg tops, in different combinations, to make sure the assembly is level. Adjust for level by sanding the bottom ends of the higher legs. (However, keep in mind that your floor might be out of level, or it might have dips or high spots, so check it before sanding the legs.)

9. Finish the legs.

When everything fits properly, disassemble the legs and sand all of the surfaces (at least up to 220 grit). Finish the legs as desired. The table shown on page 22 was finished with clear polyurethane in semigloss on the plywood faces only. The edges of the legs were given two coats of dark brown acrylic paint for a decorative accent. Allow the finish to cure fully, as directed by the manufacturer.

10. Complete the final assembly.

Assemble the legs as before, and confirm a proper fit. Add clear silicone bumpers to the top ends of the table legs; these are to protect the glass top from being scratched by the legs. Set the glass on top of the legs, and measure straight out from each leg pair to the top's edge to make sure the top is centered.

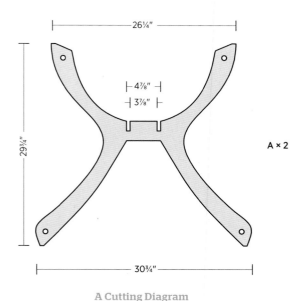

A Cutting Diagram

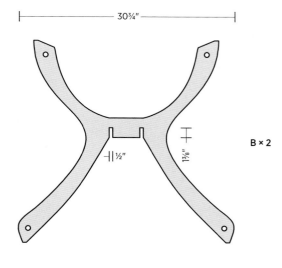

B Cutting Diagram

RTA Desk

Designed by Henry Boyle

"RTA" is designer's shorthand for ready-to-assemble. In most cases, it also indicates a knockdown design. This piece is a quintessential example of both concepts. For starters, all of the main parts are cut from a half sheet of plywood, and the waste pieces are small enough to get lost under your workbench. When assembled, the desk is secured with one of the coolest design features you'll find anywhere: all-plywood retaining rings, or C-clips, made from round cutouts in the desktop (which also create access holes for computer cables and cords). The desktop is removable for easy transport, and the whole assembly knocks down in a matter of minutes.

MATERIALS

- One 4 x 4-foot sheet ½" hardwood plywood
- One 36" length 1"-diam. birch (or other hardwood) dowel
- Sixteen ⅞" (overall length) exterior-grade coarse-thread drywall screws
- One 30" length ¾" metal L-angle
- Twelve $5/32$" x ½" (overall length) flat-head Phillips-drive lag screws
- Two 1½" x 8" piano hinges
- Twenty-four $3/32$" x ½" (overall length) flat-head Phillips-drive lag screws
- Finish materials (as desired)

TOOLS

- Homemade compass (page 17)
- Circular saw with panel blade and straightedge guide
- Jigsaw with thin, fine-tooth wood blade
- Miter saw or miter box and backsaw
- Sandpaper (up to 220 grit)
- Wood file (optional)
- Table saw with push tray (if available)
- Router with ¼" roundover bit
- Drill with:
    - 1" Forstner bit
    - ⅛" straight bit
    - Combination pilot-countersink bit
    - ½", 1", and 1¾" hole saws
- Square
- Clamps (trigger-style or C-clamps with min. 3" throat)
- Fine wood handsaw/backsaw or Japanese crosscut saw (pull-stroke cut)
- Small hammer (optional)
- Hacksaw or reciprocating saw
- Center punch or nail set

1. Lay out the main parts.

Lay out the parts on the half sheet of plywood, as shown in the plan drawings on page 29. First mark all the straight cuts, then mark the endpoints of the gussets. Use a homemade compass to draw the 28¾" radius for the convex curves on the desktop; the same line marks the concave curves on the gussets and legs and the convex curve on one of the ribs. Use the same radius on the opposite side of the panel to mark the concave desktop cutout and the other rib's curve.

Note: If you like, you can change the height of the desktop by making the legs taller or shorter. Keep in mind that this results in a one-to-one tradeoff with the desktop depth. For example, if the legs are 27" tall, the desktop will be 21" deep.

2. Cut the main parts.

Make the straight cuts with a circular saw and straightedge guide. Because the layout is a tight fit, use a thin blade (known as a "panel" or "plywood" blade) with the circular saw, and cut along the center of all cut lines to remove the same amount of material from neighboring parts. Carefully freehand the curved cuts with a jigsaw, or use a homemade circle jig, or trammel, as described on page 18. Sand the cut edges as needed to remove any saw marks.

3. Cut and mill the post.

Cut the post (the 1" dowel) to length at 24¼" (or ¼" longer than the height of the legs). To make sure both ends are square, cut the post with a power miter saw or a miter box and backsaw.

Make a mark on the post 3" up from its bottom end. Then use sandpaper or a file to round over the edges of the bottom end of the post. Set the table saw blade for a ⅛"-deep cut. Set the post on a sled or push tray and hold it against the fence with the reference mark in plain sight, then align the left side of the blade with the *inside* of the reference mark. Holding the post firmly in place and with the saw running, push the sled until the post center is just beyond the high point of the blade. With both hands on the post, slowly rotate it to cut a ⅛"-deep groove completely around the post.

Remove the post and make a reference mark ½" up from the bottom edge of the groove. Position the post on the sled and align the right side of the blade with the *inside* of the reference mark. Cut another groove, as before. Then make incremental, overlapping cuts to remove all waste material between the two grooves. You should end up with a continuous ½"-wide, ⅛"-deep channel around the post.

Repeat the same process to mill a second groove whose top edge is precisely 9" up from the top edge of the first groove.

Note: If you don't have a table saw, you can mill the grooves with a router and ½" straight bit. Set up a simple right-angle jig that can be clamped in place above the post, and use a stop block to keep the post in position as you rotate it to make the continuous groove.

4. Prepare the desktop and shelves.

Use a router and ¼" roundover bit to slightly round over all edges of the desktop. Also round over the following areas:

- All but the top edges of legs
- The curved edges of the ribs and gussets
- The long side (hypotenuse) of the shelves

Draw a centerline from front to back on the underside of the desktop. Measure in 6" from the rear edge of the desktop and mark the centerline for a 1"-diameter, ¼"-deep bore. Cut the bore using a 1" Forstner bit (see A Forstner Drilling Jig, page 30); you can't use a spade bit because the guide point would penetrate the top face of the desk.

On each triangular shelf, use a square to mark a centerline from the long front edge (hypotenuse of the triangle) to the rear point (90-degree corner). Mark each centerline 2" in from the 90-degree point. Cut a hole at each mark, using a 1" hole saw. Round over the edges inside the holes with the router and roundover bit.

5. Create the C-clips.

On the underside of the desktop, draw a line 3" from the rear edge of the panel and perpendicular to the original centerline (from step 4). Mark this line at 3" to either side of the centerline. Clamp the desktop to a sacrificial backerboard to prevent splintering of the top face, then make a hole at each of these marks, using a 1¾" hole saw. Round over the edges inside the holes on both faces with the router.

Clamp one of the cut-out disks from the holes to your work surface, and use the ½" hole saw to cut a hole through the center

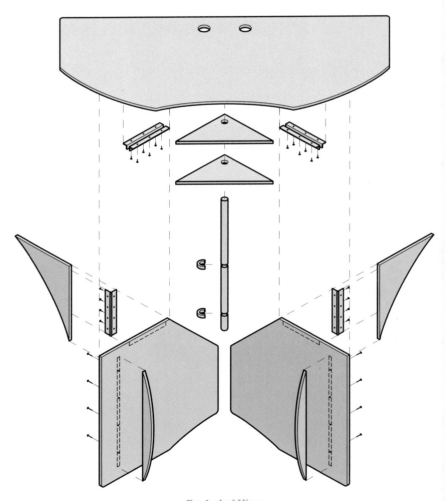

Exploded View

of the disk, creating a ring. Repeat with the other disk. Place each ring in a vise, and use a handsaw to cut out a ⁷⁄₁₆"-wide section, creating a C-shaped clip. Round over the edges of the clips with sandpaper.

6. Assemble the post and shelves.

Lightly sand the post with 100-grit sandpaper to smooth the edges of the channels and slightly decrease the post's overall diameter.

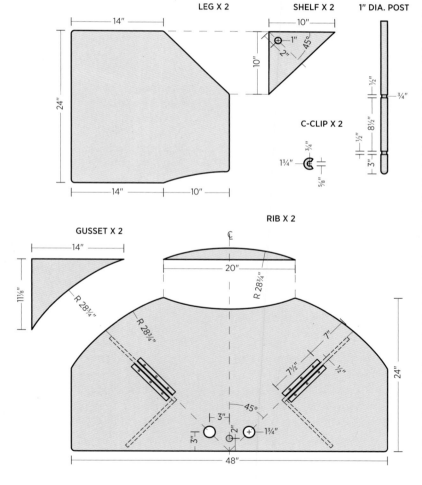

Cutting Diagrams

Secure the post on a hard, flat surface so it won't roll. Position a C-clip on one of the post grooves, wrap the fingers of both hands around the post, and place one thumb on top of the other behind the back of the clip. Snap the clip into the groove. If this is too difficult, you can tap the clip into place, using a *small* hammer and a wood block to protect the clip from damage. Repeat with the second clip.

Slide the shelves onto the post, one from the top and one from the bottom, until they rest against the clips.

7. Drill pilot holes for the shelves and ribs.

With a helper, hold one leg upright so it is plumb. Stand the post-shelf assembly next to the leg, holding the lower shelf up against its C-clip. Trace a line on the inside face of the leg marking the position of the top face of the shelf. Using a square set against the rear (short) edge of the leg, draw a second line ¼" down from, and parallel to, the first line. Measure up 10" from each of these lines and draw two more lines on the leg's inside face. The top lines of each pair represent the top faces of the shelves when installed; the bottom lines are for locating screws.

Measuring in from the rear edge of the leg, mark the lower lines at 3" and 6". Stack the legs back-to-back, with the marked leg on top, and clamp the pieces down to a backerboard. Make sure all outer edges are aligned. Drill a ⅛" pilot hole through both legs at each mark. Unclamp the legs, flip them both outside-face up, and countersink the holes on the outside faces to a maximum depth of ⁵⁄₁₆", using a pilot-countersink bit.

Drive drywall screws through the outside faces of the legs, turning them just until the tips emerge through the other side about ¹⁄₁₆". Remove the shelves from the post. Position the top shelf against its reference line so the screw tips mark each of the shelf's 10" edges along its center. Repeat the process with the lower shelf and remaining leg to mark the position of the screws along both 10" edges of each shelf.

Wrap tape around the ⅛" drill bit ¼" from the tip. Drill ¼"-deep pilot holes into the shelf edges at each screw-tip marking. Be careful not to drill deeper than ¼".

To drill the pilot holes for the ribs, draw a line parallel to and 4" in from the front (long) edge of each leg. Mark four pilot holes along each line, spacing them 4" apart. Repeat the same process used on the shelves to drill pilot holes on the legs and edges of the ribs.

8. Assemble the shelves and legs.

Slide the shelves onto the post again. Stand one leg up, and line up one shelf against the leg's face. Drive drywall screws through the two pilot holes, turning each just until the head prevents it from going any deeper. Be careful not to torque these screws, as they can easily strip in the edges of the shelves. Repeat to fasten the other shelf to the same leg. Then fasten the remaining leg to both shelves in the same manner. The legs, post, and shelves are now one unit.

9. Install the L-angle.

Cut the 30" piece of L-angle into four equal pieces, using a hacksaw or reciprocating saw. Drill and countersink three centered and equally spaced clearance holes for the $5/32$" screws along *one* side of each angle piece. Set the pieces aside.

Lay the desktop facedown on a flat surface. Place the leg assembly upside down on the desktop, fitting the flat end of the post into the bore on the underside of the desktop. Rotate the legs until their side edges are equidistant from the centerline penciled on the underside of the desktop. Trace a line on the desktop surface along the inner edges of both legs.

Position an L-angle against the inner face of a leg, 5" in from the long, straight (front) edge of the leg, as shown in the plan; the side of the angle with the holes should be against the desktop surface. Trace the outline of the angle on the desktop, and trace inside the screw holes. At each hole marking, deeply drive a center punch or small nail set into the desktop to create pilot holes for screws; you do not use a drill for these pilot holes. Fasten the angle to the desktop with $5/32$" x ½" screws, being careful not to overtighten the screws.

Repeat to install the remaining inner angle, then install the two angles on the outside faces of the legs.

Note: The desktop is not fastened to the leg assembly; it is simply held in place by the angles (which fit over the top edges of the legs) and the top end of the post fitted into the ¼" bore.

10. Add the ribs.

Remove the desktop and set the leg assembly flat on one leg face. Install the two ribs, using drywall screws and the pilot holes made in step 7.

11. Install the gussets.

Reposition the desktop on the legs, fitting the legs into the slots created by the L-angle pairs. Draw a straight, vertical reference line on each outer leg face so the line is perpendicular to the L-angle and 1" away from the rear end of the angle. Remove the desktop. Position one 8" piano hinge ½" below the top edge of a leg, as shown in the plan, so the hinge's holes are centered over the reference line. Trace inside the holes with a pencil. Center-punch the holes, as before (don't drill the holes). Fasten the hinge to the leg with $3/32$" x ½" lag screws. Repeat with the other leg.

Hold a gusset with its inside edge up to the leg face and its top edge flush with the top of the leg. Trace the holes of the free side of the hinge onto the gusset. Center-punch the holes, and install the gusset to the hinge with screws. Repeat the process to install the remaining gusset.

12. Finish the wood parts.

Finish-sand all exposed wood surfaces, then apply wax or another desired finish. In the project shown on page 26, Johnson Paste Wax was applied by hand, followed by burnishing with a wool pad attached to a wheel grinder. If you use polyurethane or another varnish or lacquer finish, it's best to completely disassemble the desk before finishing.

When the finish has dried, stand the leg assembly upright in the desired location, and set the desktop onto the legs to complete the project.

Shop Tip

A Forstner Drilling Jig

Unlike a spade bit, a Forstner bit doesn't have a guide point to start the hole and keep the bit from "walking" before the main part of the bit engage the material. This isn't a problem with a drill press, but it can be with a portable drill. Here's the solution: First drill a hole through a piece of scrap material, using the Forstner bit or a spade bit of the same size. It's okay if the Forstner bit walks a little at first; it will eventually engage and cut a straight hole. Place the scrap over the workpiece, with the hole at the desired location, and clamp the pieces together. Use the scrap to guide the Forstner bit to make the hole in the workpiece.

8 x 4 = 2 Tables

Designed by Barnaby Gunning

These nicely proportioned knock-down tables come from an architect who uses them as work benches in his studio. His studio has offices in both London and Milan, which explains why the tables are made with metric plywood — both complete pieces come from a single sheet of 24 x 1220 x 2440 mm material, the closet thing to a 1"-thick, 4 x 8-foot panel. While 24 mm stock is ideal for this application, you can also use ½" plywood in doubled thickness (yielding one table from a full sheet) or ¾" plywood in single thickness. You don't have to worry too much about converting the dimensions, because no matter what material you use, it's all relative; your pieces will be cut based on the precise thickness of your stock. And who knows . . . if more clever things like these tables had been around in the 1970s, maybe America would have actually succeeded in going metric.

MATERIALS

- ☐ One 24 x 1220 x 2440 mm sheet (4 x 8-foot sheet at ½" or ¾") hardwood plywood
- ☐ Finish materials (as desired)

TOOLS

- ☐ Straightedge
- ☐ Compass
- ☐ Jigsaw with straightedge guide
- ☐ Circular saw with straightedge guide (optional)
- ☐ Drill with ⅜" straight bit
- ☐ Sandpaper (up to 220 grit)
- ☐ Flat file

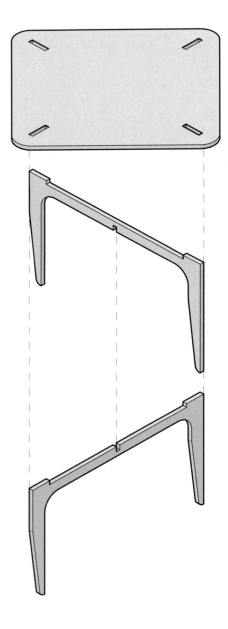

Exploded View

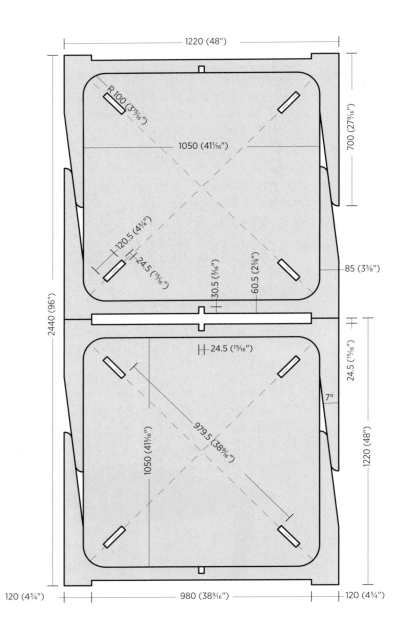

Cutting Diagram

1. Lay out the panel cuts.

The cutting diagram shows the dimensions and layout of the parts in both metric and imperial measures. Use this as a general reference to lay out the pieces for one table on half of your full plywood panel. As mentioned, you'll have to modify the dimensions shown to conform to the exact thickness of your material so that the following joint connections are accurate:

- The tabs in the legs must fit snugly into the slots in the tabletop, and the tabs should be flush with the tabletop surface upon assembly.
- The half-lap notch in the horizontal member of each leg must fit snugly into its counterpart in the other leg.

Also, to account for the kerf of your saw (the material removed by the blade), plan to cut down the center of each cut line except for any parts that will mate with other pieces — for these, you want to "leave the line" so that the finished dimensions match the thickness of the material.

Note: To make your own conversions, you can convert millimeters to inches by multiplying by 0.039. Convert decimalized inches to fractions (to the nearest 1⁄16 or 1⁄32" increments, as desired) using a free online calculator (search with keywords such as "converting decimalized").

2. Cut the parts.

Cut out all of the parts, using a jigsaw with a thin, fine-tooth blade and a straightedge guide to ensure clean, straight cuts. If you like, you can make any long straight cuts with a circular saw and straightedge guide. To cut the slots in the tabletop, first drill a starter hole with a drill and 3⁄8" bit (or larger, if necessary), staying inside the marked lines. Insert the jigsaw blade into the hole to begin each cut.

3. Test-fit the first table.

Assemble the table as shown in the exploded-view illustration on page 32. If any joints are too tight, sand and/or file the mating pieces as needed for a snug fit (a flat, square-edged file works best for cleaning up the corners of the slots, tabs, and notches). Make sure the table stands squarely on all four legs and the tabs in the legs are flush with the tabletop surface. Take the time now to make any necessary adjustments so the pieces fit just as they

should. Sand the cut edges of the pieces so they are flat and smooth, but be careful not to alter any mating parts.

4. Create the second table.

If you're making two tables, arrange the cut parts from the first table on the remaining half sheet of plywood. If you're using a standard 4 x 8-foot panel, you should have about 3⁄8" of play in the width and about 3⁄4" of play in the length of the remaining material. Trace around the cut parts to lay out the pieces for the second table.

Cut the parts for the second table, then test-assemble it and make any necessary adjustments, as before.

Note: If you're using 1⁄2" plywood, glue the matching parts together face-to-face with all edges perfectly aligned. Clamp the pieces together thoroughly, paying particular attention to the leg tabs, the area around the half-lap notches, and the area around the tabletop slots. After the glue dries, test-fit the table and sand the glued parts so all edges are flush and smooth.

5. Finish the tables.

Finish-sand all the parts for smooth surfaces and consistent appearance. Slightly round over the edges of the tabletop (but not the slots) and the legs (but not the tabs or half-lap notches).

Finish the tables as desired. Be aware that some thicker finish materials (especially paint) may make the joints fit tighter. Assemble the tables after the finish has completely dried.

Note: If you would like to fasten a table together, you can screw through the tabletop and into the horizontal members of the legs with a couple of screws per leg. Drill countersunk pilot holes so the screw heads will be flush or slightly recessed. Or you can drill counterbores and fill the holes with matching wood plugs glued in place; sand the plugs flush to the tabletop surface after the glue dries. You can also glue the legs together at the half-lap joints.

Bubbles (Desk & Drinks Trolley)

Designed by Elisa Williams

In the words of its designer, this piece is "the furniture equivalent of the little black dress. During the day, it's a fully functional laptop desk. In the evening, the unit is ready to party as a mobile drinks trolley." Several details give this simply constructed piece its unique styling. The trapezoidal shape breaks free of the boxy look and provides some extra room at the front of the desk surface, where you need it most. The little triangular side "wings" at the bottom add an unexpected mod touch. And the bubbles (hiccup) speak for themselves.

MATERIALS

- ☐ One 5 x 5-foot sheet apple, Baltic birch, or other hardwood plywood
- ☐ Biscuits (for joinery; optional)
- ☐ Wood glue
- ☐ Four 1¾" swiveling casters with mounting screws
- ☐ 1¼" coarse-thread drywall screws
- ☐ Finish materials (see step 7)

TOOLS

- ☐ Circular saw with straightedge guide
- ☐ Drill with:
    - ☐ ½" straight bit
    - ☐ Combination pilot-countersink bit
    - ☐ Hole saw set
- ☐ Biscuit joiner (if available)
- ☐ Clamps
- ☐ Sandpaper (up to 220 grit)

1. Cut the plywood panels.

Following the cutting diagram, lay out and cut the top, front, and two side panels using a circular saw and straightedge guide. The top is trapezoidal in shape and has square edges. The front is rectangular in shape, but its side edges are beveled outward toward the back at 15 degrees. The sides are rectangular and have their side edges beveled 15 degrees at parallel angles.

For a foolproof method, cut the top panel first, then confirm the angle of its corners; this is the angle at which you bevel the side and front panels. Cut one side bevel on the front panel, then fit the front against the top and mark the width for the front's other side edge. Dry-assemble the top and front panels to fit and mark the side panels.

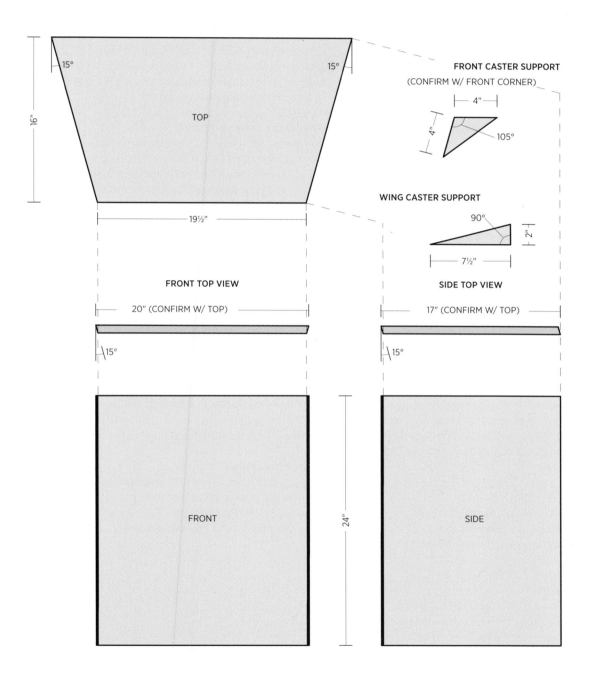

FRONT CASTER SUPPORT
(CONFIRM W/ FRONT CORNER)

4"
4"
105°

WING CASTER SUPPORT

90°
2"
7½"

TOP

15° 15°
16"
19½"

FRONT TOP VIEW

20" (CONFIRM W/ TOP)
15°

SIDE TOP VIEW

17" (CONFIRM W/ TOP)
15°

FRONT

SIDE

24"

Cutting Diagrams

Note: You can modify the width, depth, and/or height of your desk to accommodate your work surface needs and ergonomic proportions. The desk as shown is 27¼" tall. When calculating new dimensions for your project, be sure to measure from the floor to the top of the desk while sitting in the chair that you will use.

2. Create the bubbles.

Using various sizes of hole saws (or Forstner bits on a drill press), cut randomly spaced holes throughout the front panel, as shown in the project here. Begin with larger holes spaced closer together at the bottom, transitioning to smaller holes spaced farther apart as you move upward. Be careful not to cut any holes closer than ½" to the bottom edge or 1" to either side edge. Use a ½" spade or straight bit for the smallest holes, or go smaller, if desired.

To prevent unsightly tearout, start all the holes from the front face of the panel. Cut/drill about halfway through (far enough for the hole saw's mandrel or spade bit's guide point to penetrate the back side), then flip the piece over and complete the hole from the inside face. Let the hole saw cool between holes to minimize burn marks.

Sand the edges and interiors of the holes as needed for a finished look; you'll likely have to sand out some burn marks and small ridges from the hole saws.

3. Cut the biscuit slots (optional).

The best way to join the panels is with biscuit joints and glue. If you're not equipped for biscuits, you can simply glue the panels together. Cut the biscuit slots into the top and front edges of the side panels, the top edge and front face of the front panel, and the bottom face of the top panel.

4. Glue the panels.

Apply glue to the mating surfaces of the panels, assemble the parts, and clamp the entire assembly securely. Make sure all mating pieces are flush at the outside. Let the glue dry overnight.

5. Prepare the caster supports.

The casters will mount at the front to triangular supports installed inside the corners of the front and side panels and at the back to laminated "wings" fastened to the side panels.

Use the circular saw to cut the two front triangles from the plywood stock. Their sides are 4" long and meet at an angle that matches the inside angle of the front and side panels; see the cutting diagram.

For each rear wing, cut three triangles with 2" and 7½" sides that meet at a right angle (90 degrees). Glue and clamp the three pieces together, and let the glue dry overnight. Sand the edges of the wings so they are smooth and flat.

6. Install the caster supports.

As with the unit's panels, it's best to use biscuit joints for the caster supports. If you don't have a biscuit joiner, you can use glue and screws. Install the front triangles on the inside faces of the side and front panels, with the bottom face of each support flush with the bottom edges of the panels. If you're not using biscuits, drill two angled, countersunk pilot holes through the supports and into the side and front panels, being careful not to drill through the front faces of the panels. Fasten the pieces together with 1¼" drywall screws. Be careful not to overtighten the screws; small plywood edges like this can split easily.

Glue each wing to a side panel, flush with the back and bottom edges of the panel. If you're not using biscuits, screw through the inside face of the side panels, predrilling and countersinking, as before. Let the glue dry overnight.

7. Finish the desk.

Finish-sand all the surfaces, working up to 220-grit or finer paper. Finish the piece with a clear protective finish of your choice. The project as shown was finished with two coats of Arm-R-Seal (a wipe-on, oil-based urethane), applied with a clean, lint-free cloth.

8. Mount the casters.

Fasten the front casters to the front and side panels and the triangular supports, using the screws that come with them and driving them through pilot holes. Fasten the rear casters to the side panels and wings in the same manner.

One-Sheet Table & Benches

Designed by Ashley Schwebel

What do you see when you look at a 4 x 8-foot sheet of plywood? This designer saw a full-height table with an 8-square-foot top, plus two versatile bench-style seats that store neatly underneath. In use, the ensemble occupies about 4 x 4 feet of floor space. Constructing this project is a study in efficiency: All of the cuts are straight, and you can even have the longest cuts made at the lumberyard. As with a jigsaw puzzle, there isn't a single cut that affects only one piece. And the whole thing goes together with glue and screws. But what makes this design a true one-sheet wonder is the amount of waste: the biggest leftover piece measures about 1" x 6" — not a bad size for a paperweight.

MATERIALS

- ☐ One 4 x 8-foot sheet ½" plywood (AB or A-2 grade or better)
- ☐ Wood glue
- ☐ Fifty-two (or more) ¾" #8 wood screws
- ☐ Finish materials (as desired)

TOOLS

- ☐ Circular saw with straightedge guide
- ☐ Japanese saw (without a spine, such as Ryoba), standard handsaw, or jigsaw
- ☐ Marking knife (optional)
- ☐ Drill with combination pilot-countersink bit
- ☐ Bar clamps
- ☐ Sandpaper

1. Cut the parts.

Mark the layout of all the parts on a full sheet of plywood, as shown in the cutting diagram. If you need to have the long crosscuts made at the store so that you can fit all the plywood in your car, make them at 24" and 48", leaving you two 2 x 4-foot pieces and one 4 x 4-foot piece (see the warning about precutting material in Making Straight Cuts, page 16). At home, make the cuts with a circular saw and straightedge guide. To avoid overcutting at the triangular corners, cut just to the lines with the circular saw, then complete the undercut with a Japanese saw, a standard handsaw, or a jigsaw. When starting cuts at a corner, it helps to go over the lines first with a marking knife.

2. Assemble the bench legs.

Arrange two bench-leg triangles so they cross, as shown in the bench leg diagram. Choose the better-looking faces for the exposed side. Mark a light pencil line where the triangles overlap so you'll know where to apply glue. Clamp the pieces together, making sure their tops are flush. Use a pilot-countersink bit to drill pilot holes for screws, following the pattern shown in the diagram, or as desired (the screw heads will be exposed). Drill slight countersinks so the screw heads will be just flush with the surface. Glue the pieces together and secure with screws.

Repeat with the remaining three leg assemblies.

3. Install the bench supports.

On the inside of each leg assembly, make a straight cut to trim off ½" from the point of the inner leg triangle, at the top end of the leg. (Make this cut with the leg assembly flat on a work surface, keeping the saw blade parallel to the inner leg. Stop sawing as soon as you get through the inner leg to prevent cutting into the outer leg.) This cut makes room for the 6" x 9" triangular bench support on that side.

Each leg gets two supports. On each side of the leg assembly, hold a support so its 6" edge is against the inside face of the leg and the pieces are flush at the top. Drill a pilot hole at 1" and 4" down from the top and ¼" in from the side. Glue and screw the parts together.

4. Add the bench tops.

The bench tops are secured with glue only. Apply glue to the top edges of each leg assembly, and position a leg assembly along each 18" end of both tops, making sure the pieces are flush at all edges. Clamp the parts with bar clamps; you'll need to use scraps of sheet stock or lumber to sandwich the pieces, to provide even pressure and a means for clamping at the pointed ends of the legs. Let the glue dry.

5. Assemble the table legs.

Prepare the legs by installing three 6" x 6" triangular table supports along the top of each leg, using glue and screws. Locate one support flush with each side edge of the leg, and the third centered in between. Make sure the tops of the supports are flush with the tops of the legs. Locate the screws 1" and 4" down from the tops of the supports. Let the glue dry.

Note: When installed, the two Z-shaped table legs face in opposite directions (see photo, page 37).

6. Install the tabletop.

Like the bench tops, the tabletop is secured only with glue. With a helper (if available), stand the table legs upright, and apply glue to the top edges of the legs and table supports. Set the tabletop on the legs so the legs are flush with the outside edges of the top. Clamp the parts using two bar clamps on each leg, with a straight piece of scrap lumber set across the tabletop, parallel to the long sides. Let the glue dry.

7. Add the long table support.

Trim 1" from one end of the long (6" x 48") table support. On the inside face of each leg, make a vertical line across the diagonal section, 12" from the front edge of the leg; this is a reference line for the table support. Position the support between the legs so its front face is flush with the reference lines and its top edge is flush with the top edge of the diagonal support (the support extends a little below the bottom edges of the diagonals; you can rip it down if desired). Drill pilot holes through the legs and into the support at 1" and 4½" from the top of the support, and fasten the support with glue and screws.

8. Finish the project.

Sand all surfaces of the table and benches, and slightly round over all exposed edges to prevent splintering. Apply the finish of your choice.

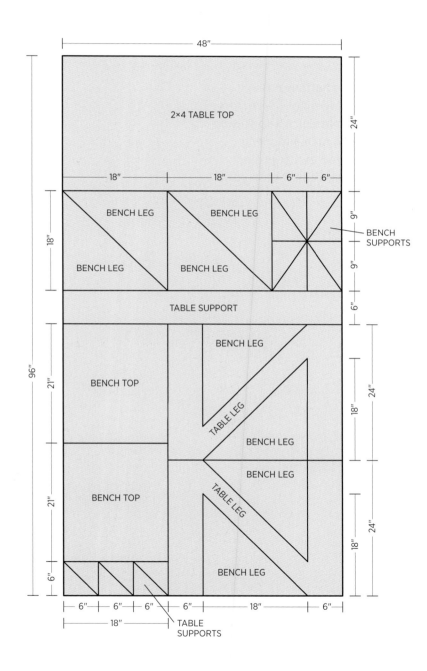

48"

24"

2×4 TABLE TOP

18"   18"   6"   6"

9"

BENCH LEG   BENCH LEG

18"   BENCH   BENCH
SUPPORTS

BENCH LEG   BENCH LEG

9"

TABLE SUPPORT

6"

96"   BENCH LEG

BENCH TOP

21"   TABLE LEG   24"

18"

BENCH LEG

BENCH LEG

21"   BENCH TOP   TABLE LEG

18"   24"

6"   BENCH LEG

6"   6"   6"   6"   18"   6"

18"   TABLE
SUPPORTS

Cutting Diagram

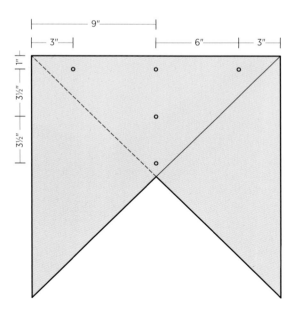

9"

3"   6"   3"

1"
3½"

3½"

3½"

Bench Leg Diagram

Lap Desk

Designed by Philip Schmidt

This simple piece was created as a gift for the designer's wife, who had searched
high and low for a suitable lap desk but found that all of the prefab versions were too
small or bore unnecessary features, like side baskets and flip-up panels. All she really
wanted was a good-size plank with a pillow — the perfect role for a nice, flat piece
of plywood with some simple routered details. The sewing involved in this project
shouldn't deter anyone; it's very basic stitching that can be done by hand or machine,
and the seams are mostly concealed in the finished product.

MATERIALS

- ☐ One 16" x 24" (or larger) piece ⅜", ½", or ¾" plywood
- ☐ Wood finish materials (see step 3)
- ☐ 1 sq. yard fabric
- ☐ Twenty-four (or more) upholstery tacks
- ☐ Fiberfill pillow stuffing

TOOLS

- ☐ Circular saw with straightedge guide
- ☐ Sandpaper (up to 220 grit) and sanding block
- ☐ Router with:
  - ☐ ½" straight bit
  - ☐ ⅜" or ¼" roundover bit
- ☐ Sewing needle and thread or sewing machine
- ☐ Scissors
- ☐ Clothes iron
- ☐ Hammer

1. Cut the desktop.

As shown here, the desktop measures 16" x 24", but you can make it any size you like. For those who like to sit cross-legged, the 24" width fits nicely atop crossed legs.

Cut the desktop to the desired size from your plywood stock, using a circular saw and straightedge guide to ensure clean, straight cuts. If necessary, sand the cut edges smooth and flat with coarse sandpaper and a sanding block.

2. Mill the pencil groove.

The desktop gets a 14"-long, ¼"-deep groove for storing pencils, pens, X-Acto knives, et cetera. This is an optional feature, but it's highly recommended for anyone who will use the desk for writing or crafts — the pitch and frequent movement of a lap desk means pens and other tools are constantly sliding and rolling away. You can experiment with different dimensions and depths for the groove, using scrap plywood. At a depth of ³⁄₁₆ to ¼", pens and pencils are held securely but are easy to retrieve.

Set up a straightedge guide to mill the groove so its leading edge is ½" from the front edge of the desktop. Cut the groove in two or more passes, using a router and ½" straight bit. If the finished depth ends up right between two plies (which doesn't look so good), cut slightly deeper to expose the next ply down (this is a good reason to test the depth first on some scrap pieces of the same plywood stock).

3. Finish the desktop.

Round over all the outside edges of the desktop with the router and a roundover bit. Finish-sand the entire desktop, working up to 220-grit or finer sandpaper. Carefully sand the edges of the pencil groove with fine paper so it is smooth and has a finished look, but don't round over the edges too much.

Finish the desktop as desired. As shown here, the birch plywood top was given three coats of standard, oil-based polyurethane in satin. This yields a smoother, harder surface than most paint and other clear finishes can offer, and it highlights the grain of nice face veneers. Let the finish cure completely, as directed by the manufacturer.

4. Sew the cushion cover.

Any soft, durable fabric will do for the cushion cover. Lay out the fabric cuts as shown in the pattern drawing, or as desired. The overall dimensions and the angle cuts don't have to be precise, but they should be consistent. A tip for beginners: Measure from the selvage edge (a factory-finished edge that's typically blank). Be sure to account for and cut off the selvage area (after laying out the pattern) so it's not part of the working piece of fabric.

Cut out the pattern with sharp scissors. Sew the edges of the fabric flaps together at each corner. If you're hand-sewing, use a basic stitch that binds the seam and raw fabric edges with each stitch. You will turn the fabric inside out, so the stitches don't have to be decorative.

Fold each top edge of the cover in on itself about 1", then iron the fold to create a straight hem, as shown in the drawing.

5. Attach and fill the cushion.

Turn the cushion cover inside out so the hem and stitching will be concealed on the inside of the cushion. Fit the cover over the bottom face of the desktop and center it in both directions. Starting at one corner, secure the cover to the plywood with two upholstery tacks placed close together, centering the tacks on the hems of the two adjacent sides of the cover.

Continue tacking the cover to the desktop, working down one side and then the other, keeping the fabric straight and taut as you go and spacing the tacks evenly at about 3½" apart. Secure the next two corners with pairs of tacks, then tack the remaining two sides to within a few inches of the last remaining corner, leaving enough of an opening that you can get your arm through to stuff the cover.

Fill the cover with fiberfill pillow stuffing to the desired fullness. Distribute the stuffing evenly so the cushion is uniform, with no lumps or voids. Secure the open corner of the cover to the desktop with tacks.

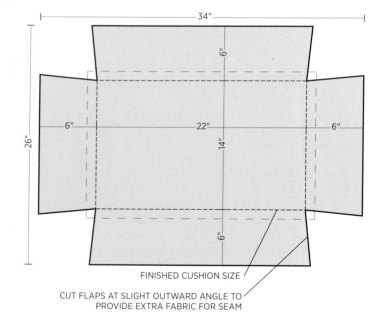

34"

6"

6"   22"   6"

14"

26"

6"

FINISHED CUSHION SIZE

CUT FLAPS AT SLIGHT OUTWARD ANGLE TO
PROVIDE EXTRA FABRIC FOR SEAM

Cushion Cover Pattern

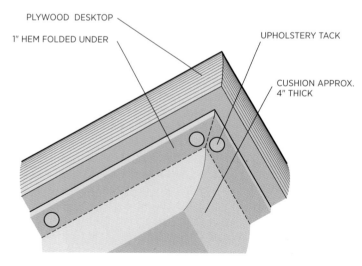

PLYWOOD DESKTOP

1" HEM FOLDED UNDER

UPHOLSTERY TACK

CUSHION APPROX.
4" THICK

**Cushion Edge Detail
(view from below)**

Plywood as . . .
A showcase of inspired pieces and
the stories behind them

. . . movement and form

Bentwood Table and Chair

by Megan Wright

Building a piece of furniture is a very fulfilling accomplishment. It is gratifying to be able to use your creation in your everyday life. My two pieces were inspired by movement and form. The design process began with the manipulation of paper: cutting slits into paper without cutting any pieces out. This helped achieve my goal of wasting as little material as possible.

By creating a form from MDF and birch bending plywood, I was able to make one mold that would create each half of the table. The table is composed of five layers of bending plywood — one ¼" sheet and four ⅛" sheets. I layered glue in between and then placed the layers in a vacuum-sealed bag and compressed them for about two hours. Formed steel legs complete the table.

The chair is designed as a child's rocker and uses the same bent lamination process as the table, with one mold making the whole piece. Its bottom is made with formed aluminum.

Today, the making of molded furniture has turned me to the love of ceramic molds. I am currently working on dinnerware and serving pieces, and I love creating new and innovative dining experiences. The dinnerware and serving pieces are the experience within the experience.

Birch Ply Dining Table

Designed by Brian Everett

If any designs in this book can be described as ingeniously simple, this certainly is one of them. It's a full-size dining table that's little more than a single sheet of plywood with legs. The key to its nice proportions and custom look is the built-up edges made with cutoffs from the panel itself. The legs are prefab, and you can use whatever style you like. Same goes for the plywood; the table shown here is Baltic birch, but alder, walnut, apple, you name it can work just as well. Keep in mind that the panel's edges and, of course, face veneer are critical to the finished product, so don't skimp on quality when choosing the plywood.

MATERIALS

- One 4 x 8-foot sheet ¾" Baltic birch or other hardwood plywood
- 1¼" coarse-thread wood screws or drywall screws
- Wood glue
- Three 8-foot poplar 1 x 2s
- Finish materials (see step 6)
- Four table legs with mounting plates and screws

TOOLS

- Circular saw with straightedge guide or table saw
- Utility knife and straightedge (if using circular saw)
- Miter saw (if available)
- Four (or more) clamps
- Drill with combination pilot-countersink bit
- Foam brush
- Belt sander or sanding block
- Sandpaper (up to 220 grit)
- Disk sander (if available)

1. Cut the tabletop to size.

Using a circular saw with a long straightedge guide or, preferably, a table saw, cut the full 4 x 8-foot panel of ¾" plywood to length at 80". Be very careful to prevent tearout when making the crosscut (with a circular saw, cut from the back face of the panel, and score the cut line with a utility knife and straightedge; see page 14).

Next, cut a 4"-wide strip from each side of the 48" x 80" piece, leaving you with a main tabletop panel at 40" x 72". Save these four strips; you'll use them for the built-up edges.

2. Miter the buildup strips.

Lay the tabletop panel facedown on your work surface. Using the top as a guide, mark one of the long 4" strips (for the table's side edge) to length for mitering the ends; the long points of the miters should be aligned with the top panel's corners, as shown in the bottom-view illustration.

Miter the ends of the strip at 45 degrees, using a miter saw or circular saw. Test-fit the strip on the tabletop. Adjust the cut(s) if necessary, then clamp the strip in place to facilitate measuring the adjoining strips.

Mark, cut, and clamp the other long side strip as with the first. Mark the short end strips for cutting to match the long points of the miters on the side strips. Make the cuts, and test-fit all four pieces. They should be flush with the tabletop's edge and meet tightly at all four corners (at least where they'll be visible in the finished product).

3. Install the buildup strips.

Leaving the side strips clamped in place, drill countersunk pilot holes through the strips and into the tabletop, spacing them about 1" from each end and every 12" in between, as shown in the bottom-view illustration. Be very careful not to drill through the top face of the tabletop. The countersinks should be only deep enough to set the screw heads slightly below the surface. Drive 1¼" coarse-thread wood or drywall screws into the holes, being careful not to drive too deeply and risk piercing the top. Clamp the two end strips into place and repeat the process.

To complete the glue-up, remove one of the end strips, use a foam brush to cover its top face with wood glue, set it back in position, and screw it down tight. Clamp along the outside edge of the strip and tabletop to make sure the joint is completely closed; any gapping here will be visible in the finished edge. Let the glue set, as directed by the manufacturer, before removing the clamps. Repeat the gluing process with one of the side strips, followed by the other end strip and the remaining side strip.

Note: The reason for installing the buildup strips one at a time is that the miter joints must be tight, and miters have a funny way of not fitting back together the way they're supposed to once you've taken them apart, especially during the pressure of a glue-up. If you have enough clamps, however, you can install one piece right after the other.

4. Add the stiffeners.

Cut two lengths of poplar 1 x 2 to fit between the side buildup strips, near each end of the table. Position the strips about 10" from the tabletop ends, making sure to leave sufficient room for the table legs' mounting plates. Drill countersunk pilot holes, as before, and fasten the strips to the underside of the table with glue and screws. The screws alone should provide adequate clamping force for the glue-up.

Cut two more 1 x 2s to fit between the installed stiffeners, perpendicular to them, and about 10" in from each side of the tabletop. Install them in the same way, with screws and glue.

Note: The poplar 1 x 2s installed on the underside of the tabletop add rigidity to prevent sagging over time (as well as a little extra "thud" value). Poplar lumber is recommended because it's generally the cheapest hardwood, and construction-grade (pine, spruce, fir, et cetera.) 1 x 2s would offer much less structural value here.

5. Sand the tabletop.

If you've carefully aligned the edges of the tabletop panel and buildup strips, your sanding job should be minimal. If not, a belt sander can save the day. Just be careful not to sand too much or to round over the top or bottom edges of the panel and buildup strips.

Sand the edges of the tabletop panel and strips so they are smooth, flat, and perfectly flush, using a belt sander or a sanding block. Hand-sand the four corners of the top and all edges to knock down the sharpness and prevent splintering. As an option, you can draw a radius with a compass and round off the tabletop corners with a jigsaw or by filing and/or sanding.

Finish-sand the entire top, the built-up edges, and the bottom faces of the buildup strips, working with up to 220-grit or finer sandpaper. A disk sander works well for the top surface, but don't use one on the edges, as it's likely to round them over. Wipe down the entire top with a tack cloth to remove all dust.

6. Finish the tabletop.

Apply the finish of your choice to all surfaces of the tabletop. The table shown here was finished with wipe-on polyurethane applied with a foam brush. With any polyurethane, you'll want at least three coats on the top and edges and two coats on the table's underside.

Note: Wipe-on poly is relatively thin, yielding a somewhat more hand-applied feel, while standard poly creates a thicker finish that's a little more durable and better at smoothing over slight imperfections. Given the abuse a dining table is subject to, a tough surface-type finish like polyurethane (or varnish) is recommended over penetrating finishes, like Danish oil, tung oil, and so on. Furniture wax simply isn't durable enough for this application.

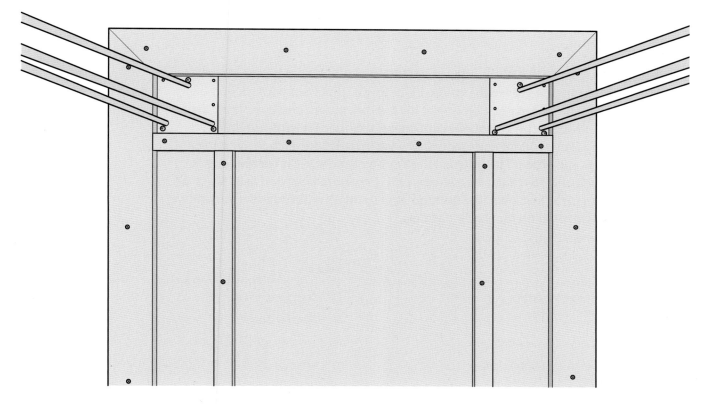

Bottom View of the Table

7. Install the legs.

Mark the positions of the legs' mounting plates, drill pilot holes, and mount the legs to the tabletop panel with screws (make sure they won't go through the top of the panel). For stability and looks, most types of legs should be located very close to the inside corners of the buildup strips, as shown in the bottom-view illustration.

Note: The legs shown here were purchased from a retailer but unfortunately are no longer available. You can find prefab legs from furniture retailers and from custom manufacturers. Vintage midcentury legs are available in custom sizes (see Resources).

Peninsula Workstation

Designed by Larry Finn

This piece comes from one of the world's great "handy dads," who has more than a few awesome handmade gifts to his credit, including a giant backyard half-pipe and an aluminum skateboard deck. Now that his kids are grown and have their own houses and busy lifestyles, he gifts them with pieces like this. It's a his-and-hers workstation that makes brilliant use of an otherwise problematic alcove, creating a high-functioning home office. The finished desk spans almost 10 feet across and is 2¼" thick, yet it uses only two and a half sheets of ¾" plywood. How, you ask? Much of the bottom layer of ply is just a narrow buildup strip to thicken the edge for decorative effect. So what have you built for *your* kids lately?

See page 208 for another work by Larry Finn.

MATERIALS

- ¾" hardwood plywood (quantity as needed)
- Wood glue
- 1¼" coarse-thread drywall screws or wood screws
- 1½" x 1½" galvanized angle (with holes)
- 2½" coarse-thread drywall screws or wood screws, with washers (for mounting angle to wall)
- Heavy-duty hollow-wall anchors (as needed; see step 6)
- 1⅝" coarse-thread drywall screws or wood screws, with washers (for mounting desk to angle)
- Materials for support post (see step 7)
- Finish materials (see step 8)
- Wood trim or caulk (as desired)

TOOLS

- 4-foot level or laser level
- Tape measure
- Architect's (scaled) ruler or standard ruler
- Compass
- Circular saw with straightedge guide
- Jigsaw
- Clamps
- Drill with:
  - Pilot bits
  - 2" hole saw (optional)
- Sandpaper (60 to 220 grit)
- Router with roundover bit
- Stud finder (wall scanner)
- Hacksaw or reciprocating saw

1. Plan your workstation desk.

The desk shown here is custom built, but you can easily modify the dimensions and configuration as needed to fit your own space. The actual dimensions of the original are included in the plan drawing to provide an example of a good working design.

To plan your project, first determine the desired height of the desk surface. As a general reference, standard typing surfaces are 26 to 27" above the floor, and standard desk height is 29 to 30". If you do a lot of drawing or other work away from the computer, you might prefer a height of 31 to 32". When sitting in your desk chair, you should have at least 8" of clearance between the tops of your legs and the bottom of the desktop.

Using a 4-foot level or a laser level, draw level lines along all three walls of the installation space at the precise height of the finished desk. Measure across the width of the space, holding your tape measure just below the level lines, to find the overall length of the desk.

Next, determine the depth of the desktop and length of the peninsula, based on your work needs and the size of the installation space. As shown in the plan, the original desk is 117" long and 71⅝" deep. The portion of the desktop along the back wall is 23⅝" deep, and the peninsula surface is 27⅜" wide.

2. Plan the plywood layers.

The goal of this step is to lay out the three plywood layers of the desktop: the top surface; the middle structural layer; and the bottom layer, which consists primarily of 2½"-wide buildup strips. The important part of the layout is deciding where the joints will go, considering aesthetics and the structural assembly, and making the best use of the plywood stock. It's a good idea to map out everything on paper before laying out the material and making any cuts.

Draw a dimensioned overhead view of the entire desk, similar to the plan drawing. If desired, you can use overlays of tracing paper to show each of the layers separately. Apart from aesthetics (which is primarily a concern for the top layer), the only requirement for joints is that they are offset from the joints in adjoining layers by several inches or more. This ensures structural integrity so that the assembly performs like a continuous slab of material.

Experiment with different joint configurations to find the best layout, and draw the final joint locations on your plan. On a separate sheet of paper, create scaled outlines of your plywood sheets. Use these to lay out the cuts of the various parts for the layers and confirm that everything will fit. If necessary, the buildup strips for the bottom layer can be narrower than the 2½" strips used in the original design.

3. Cut the plywood pieces.

Lay out the cuts on the plywood stock, following your drawings. Mark the 4" radii for the inside and outside corners of the peninsula with a compass. Cut the pieces from each sheet, using a circular saw and a straightedge guide for the straight cuts. Use a jigsaw to rough-cut the rounded corners, staying at least ¼" outside the marked line. You will clean up the rounded corners after the desk is assembled.

4. Assemble the desk.

You can assemble the layers of the desk and prepare it for finishing in any way that suits your space. Just keep in mind the weight and maneuverability of the desk once it's assembled.

One option is to assemble the layers upside down: Place the pieces of the top layer facedown on a flat surface. Apply glue to the top pieces, and set the middle-layer pieces into place. Clamp the parts, or tack them together with a couple of screws. Drill pilot holes into both layers, then drill larger clearance holes into only the middle layer pieces; this ensures the screws won't bind in the middle pieces so the two layers suck up tightly together. Fasten the layers together with 1¼" drywall or wood screws driven every 6" along the edges and every 8" to 10" in the field of the pieces. Make sure all joints are tightly closed before fastening, and check the exposed edges to make sure there are no visible gaps between the layers. Clamp along the edges as needed to close any gaps. Install the bottom-layer pieces in the same fashion.

5. Prepare the desk for finishing.

After the glue dries completely, flip the assembled desk right side up, and clean up the rounded corners with a jigsaw and a very-fine-tooth wood blade (to minimize splintering), cutting through all three layers at once; see the bottom view illustration of the inside corner. Smooth the radius cuts with coarse sandpaper to remove any saw marks and eliminate flat spots.

Use a router and roundover bit to ease all of the exposed edges on the top and bottom of the desktop. You can rout the top edge while the desktop is on the floor, but you'll have to tip or prop it up to rout the bottom edge.

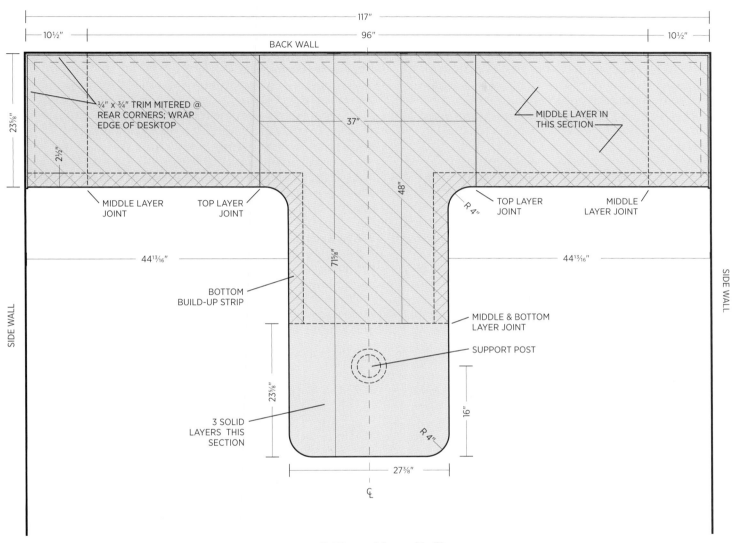

117"

10½" 96" 10½"

BACK WALL

23⅝"

¼" x ¾" TRIM MITERED @
REAR CORNERS; WRAP
EDGE OF DESKTOP

MIDDLE LAYER IN
THIS SECTION

2½"

37"

48"

MIDDLE LAYER
JOINT

TOP LAYER
JOINT

R 4"

TOP LAYER
JOINT

MIDDLE
LAYER JOINT

SIDE WALL

SIDE WALL

44¹³⁄₁₆"

71⅝"

44¹³⁄₁₆"

BOTTOM
BUILD-UP STRIP

MIDDLE & BOTTOM
LAYER JOINT

SUPPORT POST

23⅝"

3 SOLID
LAYERS THIS
SECTION

16"

R 4"

27⅜"

₵L

Cutting and Assembly Plan

If desired, cut holes through the desk for running cords for computers and office equipment, using a 2" hole saw. Cut halfway through the desk from one side, then complete the cut from the opposite side, to prevent tearout of the plywood veneer.

Finish-sand all exposed surfaces of the desk, working up to 220-grit or finer sandpaper. The plywood layers of the exposed edges should be flush and smooth to the touch as shown below.

6. Install the desk.

Following your level lines from step 1, mark the wall-stud locations in the installation area, using a stud finder or other method. Cut the 1½" x 1½" galvanized angle to fit along the back wall, using a hacksaw or reciprocating saw. Install the angle by screwing through the holes and into each stud with a 2½" drywall or wood screw and washer. The top of the angle should be flush with the level line.

Install a piece of angle on each side wall so it extends from the back-wall angle to the desk's buildup strip, as shown in the illustration of the bottom view at the wall on the right. Depending on the stud placement on the side walls, you may need to install heavy-duty hollow-wall anchors (such as toggle bolts) for securing the angle pieces.

Cut a temporary post from a 2 x 4 or other scrap material to support the peninsula end of the desk; cut this to length at the desktop height minus the thickness of the desk. Set the desk on the angles, fitting it tightly into the wall corners, and support the peninsula with the temporary post. Secure the desk to the angle with 1⅝" drywall or wood screws and washers.

7. Install the support post.

You can create a permanent post from any suitable material, including metal plumbing pipe, glued-up layers of plywood, or solid lumber. Black steel gas pipe (commonly called "black iron") is a good choice for an industrial look, and you can install the pipe with a threaded flange on each end.

Make sure the desk is level, and cut the post material to fit. Install the post so it is centered under the width of the peninsula and 16" or so in from the end. Secure the post at both ends, as appropriate.

8. Finish and trim the desk.

Finish the top and all exposed edges of the desk as desired. Polyurethane is a good option for a hard-wearing, moisture-resistant surface. Let the finish dry completely.

If desired, install wood trim along the top and front edges where the desk meets the walls. Or, if the desk fits tightly enough to the walls, you can simply caulk the joint with a color-matched caulk.

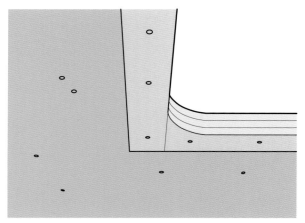

Bottom View at Inside Corner

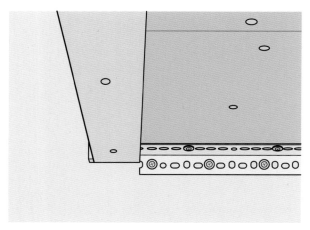

Bottom View at the Wall

Surfaces II

Tables of every other description: for reading by and for dancing around,
for ends and for occasions, for coffee and for tea.

Type A Coffee Table

Designed by Katherine Belsey

Combining a table surface, magazine rack, hidden storage compartment, drinks shelf, and padded footrest in one compact, rollable unit, this unique piece can best be described as a coffee table on a wicked caffeine buzz. It's a first-rate multitasker with stimulating extra features like two mirrored sides, which reduce the table's visual mass and provide entertainment for babies crawling about. The casters and storage bin also provide the makings of an excellent indoor race car for youngsters. But, as its designer advises, "This function should be discouraged. It is, after all, just a coffee table."

See page 236 for another work by Katherine Belsey.

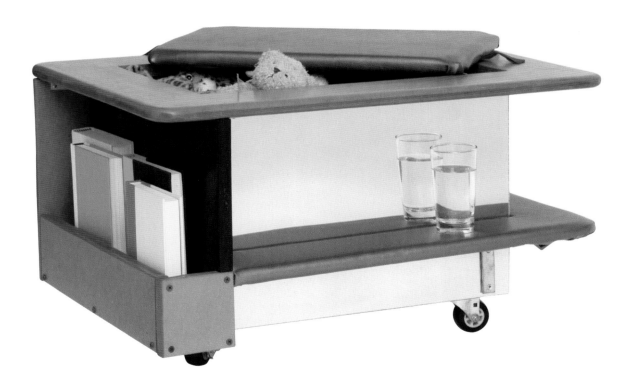

MATERIALS

- One 4 x 8-foot sheet ¾" MDF

- Two ⅛"-thick acrylic plastic mirrors (one at 12" x 12" min.; one at 12" x 18⅛" min.)

- One 36" length 1 x 1 or 1 x 2 lumber

- Wood stain in black (or other desired color)

- Polyurethane finish (clear, in sheen of choice)

- 1 sq. yard vinyl cloth (optional)

- One 12" x 18" (or larger) foam pad (optional)

- Staples (optional; for vinyl cloth)

- Ribbon or other material for handle (optional)

- 1¼" coarse-thread drywall screws (see step 7)

- Mirror adhesive

- Six 3" x 3" 90-degree metal brackets with screws

- 6d (2") finish nails

- Wood putty

- Four 2"-diam. casters with mounting plate and screws

Note: "Gold" screws, which have a brassy color, look better on this project than standard black drywall screws. If desired, you can use finishing washers and oval-head wood screws for all exposed fasteners.

TOOLS

- Circular saw with straightedge guide

- Jigsaw

- Compass

- Drill with:

    - ¾" spade bit (optional; see note in step 1)

    - Combination pilot-countersink bit

1. Cut the MDF parts.

Following the cutting diagram on page 57, lay out and cut parts A through I and parts L and M from ¾" MDF. Make all the straight cuts with a circular saw and a straightedge guide to ensure clean, straight cuts. Finish the inside corner cuts on parts A, E, and I with a jigsaw. Mark the rounded corners on parts B, I, and L with a 2" radius, and make the cuts with a jigsaw (see How to Mark & Cut Curves, page 16). To save material, you can cut piece M from the cut-out center of piece I.

Note: If you plan to cover parts M and/or L with vinyl (see step 6), cut the parts slightly smaller to account for the thickness of your vinyl cloth. If you won't cover M with vinyl, drill two ¾"-diameter finger holes through the piece, as shown in the cutting diagram, using a ¾" spade bit and a backerboard to prevent tearout on the bottom face.

2. Mill the wood parts.

Refer to the exploded-view drawing on the next page for help with orienting the table's parts for this step. Using a router and ⅜" or ¼" roundover bit, mill a slight roundover on the following edges:

- Outside edges of L

- All edges of I

- Both edges on bottom and exposed side of B

- Long top edge of G

- One long edge and one short edge of H, outside face only

- Exposed edge of E (not in notch area)

- Bottom and two side edges of F, outside face only

As an option, you can mill a deeper roundover on one side edge of F and H, using a ⅜" or ½" roundover bit, or use a ¾" bit for a full roundover (bullnose edge).

Be careful not to round over any edges that will butt against other parts. It might be helpful to preassemble some of the parts (without fasteners) to see which edges will be exposed and which will be joined.

3. Cut the mirrors.

If the two acrylic plastic mirrors (J and K) are not already cut to size, cut part J to size at 12" x 12", and cut part K to size at 12" x 18⅛" (the mirrors will be slightly larger than the base pieces). Follow the manufacturer's directions for cutting your specific material. Typically, acrylic sheets can be scored and snapped, much like cutting glass: Leaving the protective plastic film intact, mark the cutting lines on the film. Place a straightedge on each mark and hold it firmly. Score the line several times with a sharp utility knife. Position the sheet so the scored line just overhangs a straight, square table edge. Hold down the straightedge firmly, directly behind the cut line. Snap off the waste with a firm downward motion. File the cut edge as needed with a fine metal file.

4. Cut the corner supports.

The three corner supports are cut from 1 x 1 or 1 x 2 lumber. They install into three of the four corners of the storage compartment and serve as screw backing for the adjacent panel joints and as supports for part M, the lid/tabletop of the storage compartment.

Cut the three corner supports to length at 11¼" each, using a miter saw, miter box and back saw, or circular saw.

5. Finish the wood parts.

Finish-sand all the wood parts, as needed. Be careful not to round over any edges that will butt up to mating pieces.

Apply black stain (or another desired color) to all surfaces of parts B, L, and M. (If you plan to cover M and/or L with vinyl, you don't have to stain them.) Also stain the entire outside face and exposed side edge of part E; on its inside face, apply stain only between the exposed side edge and the nearest end of the notch on its bottom edge, as shown in the illustration on page 58. Let the stained surfaces dry.

Finish all the pieces with three coats of polyurethane, as directed, including all edges and stained surfaces. All surfaces must be completely sealed; unprotected MDF is highly susceptible to damage from moisture.

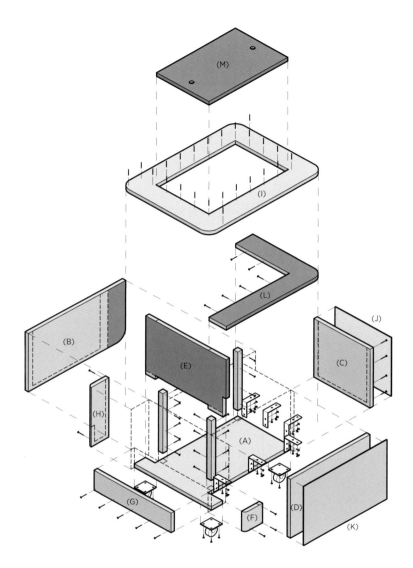

Exploded View

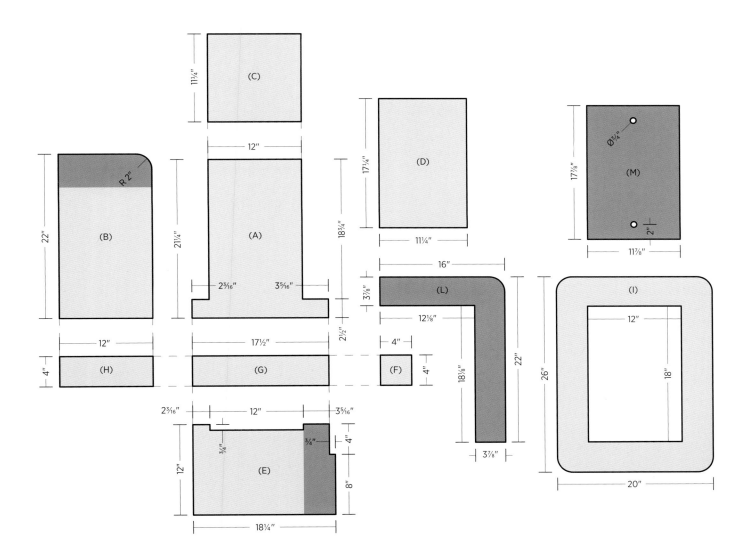

Cutting Diagram

6. Cover M and L with vinyl (optional).

Vinyl cloth over the exposed surfaces of M (storage lid/tabletop) and L (drinks shelf) adds extra water resistance and a nice, slightly cushioned place for setting down glasses and bottles. You can also add a layer of thin foam under the vinyl covering on M to create a padded landing for putting your feet up.

To cover the pieces, lay the vinyl facedown on a flat surface, and set each wood piece on top. Mark the cloth so it's about 2½" larger than the wood in all directions. Cut the cloth with scissors. If you will pad M, cut the foam to the same size as the wood, and increase the margin of the vinyl by the thickness of the foam on each side.

Tightly wrap the vinyl to cover the top faces and all edges of each wood piece, securing the edges of the vinyl to the underside of the wood with staples. Also staple tabs or loops of ribbon or other material at each end of M to serve as handles for lifting out the panel.

7. Assemble the table.

Assemble the parts as shown in the exploded drawing, using 1¼" drywall screws driven through countersunk pilot holes. Space the screws about 4" apart, keeping all outer screws at least ⅜" from the panel edges. Have a helper hold the mating pieces as you drill pilot holes, or use clamps as needed.

Start the assembly with A, and work your way around and up. All the screws are concealed except those on parts F, G, and H. To minimize the number of visible screws, you don't have to fasten H to G; H is adequately secured by the joint with E. Fasten B and E to the corner supports by screwing through the insides of the supports and into the back sides of B and E.

After assembling the base unit (parts A, B, C, D, and E) and the magazine rack (F, G, and H), glue K (large mirror) to C and J (small mirror) to B, using mirror adhesive, which won't damage the silver mirror backing. Temporarily secure the mirrors with tape; don't use clamps.

To attach the drinks shelf (L), mark its location on the mirror (the top of L should be aligned with the top of F), and drill five pilot holes (three for the longer leg of L and two for the shorter) all the way through to the storage area. Drill corresponding pilot holes on the inside edges of L, and screw it on from inside the base. Install six metal brackets underneath the shelf, using screws, spacing the brackets evenly along the length of both shelf legs.

Center part I over the base unit, and fasten it to the edges of B, E, and H with a few finish nails driven through pilot holes. Set the nails slightly below the surface with a nail set. Fill the nail holes with color-matched wood putty, then spot-finish the putty with polyurethane.

Install the casters at the corners of the base unit to complete the project.

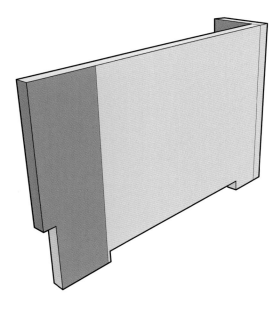

Staining part E

Striated Ply Table

Designed by Brian Hinz

Made from scrap strips of plywood salvaged from an architectural model-building company, the original Striated Ply Table was designed to embody the characteristics of plywood itself. Thus, it became a "laminated" piece created out of numerous thin layers. The table has a pleasing visual rhythm and a sense of lightness provided by the spacing between layers and the central openings, and these change with each different view. For example, when viewing the table straight on, you notice that the pieces crossing in the center actually extend below the lower horizontal slats, vaulting the table ends into a cantilever and giving the whole table the illusion of floating. The table shown here alternates strips of clear pine lumber with strips of plywood; you can do the same or make the entire piece with plywood.

MATERIALS

- ☐ One 5 x 5-foot sheet ¾" Baltic birch plywood (or scrap plywood; see step 1)
- ☐ Eleven 8-foot lengths 1 x 2 lumber (ash, poplar, white oak, birch, or "select" pine)
- ☐ Wood glue
- ☐ Ten 24" lengths ⁷⁄₁₆"-diam. dowel (in solid wood of choice)
- ☐ Finish materials (as desired)

TOOLS

- ☐ Table saw or circular saw with straightedge guide
- ☐ Miter saw
- ☐ Drill with ⁷⁄₁₆" straight bit
- ☐ Clamps
- ☐ Sandpaper
- ☐ Japanese flush-cutting saw or similar saw
- ☐ Palm sander

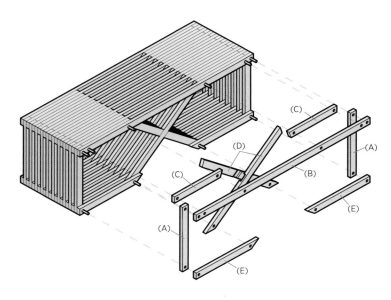

Exploded View

Note: Given the number of cuts (many of which are mitered) and the accuracy required, it's pretty much essential to use a power miter saw for all of the crosscuts. If you don't have access to a miter saw, you can rent one at any home center or rental outlet.

1. Rip the plywood strips.

If you're building the table as shown, you will cut pieces A, C, and D from plywood and pieces B and E from solid 1 x 2 stock; see the exploded-view drawing above and the cutting diagram on the opposite page. On a table saw, rip the plywood into 1½"-wide strips: you need a total of 22 strips at 60" long or 44 strips at 30" long. If you don't have a table saw, you can rip the strips with a circular saw and a straightedge guide to ensure straight cuts, but be very careful to cut the pieces at exactly 1½" wide.

2. Cut the plywood parts to length.

Set up a stop block for your miter saw and cut 22 A pieces to length at 15⅜", cutting one from each full-length plywood strip; cut these with square ends, as shown in the cutting diagram. Reset the stop block and cut 22 C pieces to length at 12⅝", mitering one end at 19 degrees; cut each from a different strip. Finally, cut a D piece from each of the remaining strips; you need 22 total. First, make all of the 19-degree end cuts, then set up a stop block and cut the remaining ends at 52 degrees. These pieces measure 27⅝" from the long points (toe to toe) of the miters.

If you cut your plywood strips to 30" in length in step 1, cut the A and C pieces from the same strips, and cut the D pieces from the remaining strips.

3. Cut the half-lap joints.

The 22 D pieces are joined in pairs with half-lap joints near their centers. Mill the dadoes for the joints on a table saw. Set the blade to a depth of ⅜" (half the thickness of the plywood), and set the fence 12⁷⁄₁₆" from the *outside* of the blade. Register the workpiece against a miter gauge set at 14 degrees off center, with the sharp mitered end pointing away from the fence, as shown in the illustration of the half-lap dado cuts. Run a test cut, and make sure it matches the dimensions shown in the cutting diagram. Run the 22 pieces. Move the fence to 10¹⁵⁄₁₆" from the *inside* of the blade. Run a test cut, then run the 22 pieces. Remove the waste material between the two shoulder cuts on each piece by making multiple passes, using the miter gauge.

4. Assemble the half-laps.

Apply glue to the dadoes of each pair of D pieces and compress and fit the pieces together to create a cross. Make sure the flats of the sharply mitered ends are aligned. Clamp each of the 11 pairs and let the glue dry.

5. Cut the solid-wood pieces.

Use the miter saw and a stop block to cut 12 B pieces at 46" from six of the 1 x 2s. Cut 24 E pieces at 16⁹⁄₁₆" from the remaining five 1 x 2s, mitering one end at 52 degrees.

6. Drill the holes.

Carefully mark and drill the ⁷⁄₁₆" holes on one of each lettered piece, as shown in the cutting diagram. All the holes are centered on the width of each piece. Dry-assemble the pieces, using dowels (see step 7), to make sure the holes are accurately positioned. Then use each piece as a template to drill the remaining pieces of each type. Clamp the template to each new piece before drilling, and use a backerboard to prevent tearout behind any pieces that will be exposed.

7. Complete the glue-up.

If necessary, sand the dowels lightly to facilitate the assembly – they should fit snugly but not so tightly that you have to fight every piece. Apply wood glue to 1" at the end of a dowel and slide it through one of the holes on a B piece, leaving a ½" nub to be cut off later. Repeat for the remaining holes in the B piece, then do the same with two E pieces. Let the glue dry.

Slide a D pair and two each of A and C pieces onto the dowels, following the orientation shown in the exploded-view drawing. Apply glue to all mating areas of the pieces, clamp all the joints, and let the glue dry.

Repeat to assemble the remaining layers. For best results,

clamp all of the joints in each layer, and let the glue dry before adding the next layer.

8. Finish the table.

After the last glue joints have dried, trim off the dowel nubs with a Japanese flush-cutting saw (or similar saw with no set, or outward angle, to the teeth), then sand the dowels perfectly flush to the surrounding surface. Sand the entire table with a palm sander and by hand, as needed. Stain and/or finish the table as desired. To retain the natural coloring, apply only a clear finish, such as polyurethane (some products will amber the wood slightly) or beeswax.

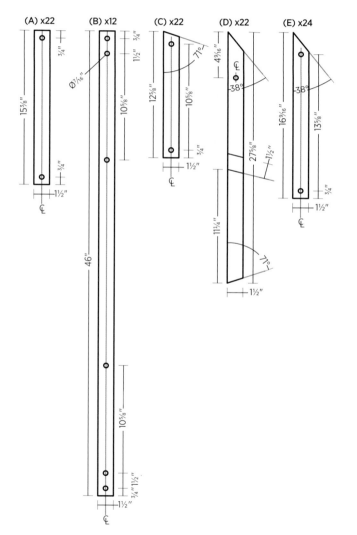

Cutting Diagram

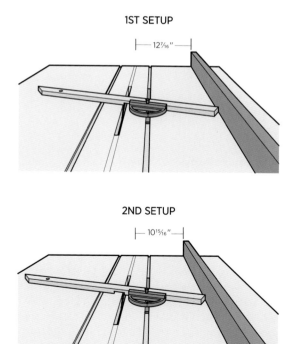

Half-Lap Dado Cuts

Alliance Table

Designed by Fawn Brokaw

Like many of the best knockdown designs, the Alliance Table is a clever assembly of parts that are cut out and fit together like a jigsaw puzzle. Here, cutting out the round tabletop forms the large, semicircular cutouts on the legs, while cutting the two smaller arches on the legs produces cutouts that become a stabilizing disk on the bottom of the tabletop. The entire work is produced from a single 2 x 4-foot piece of ½" plywood, a precut size commonly available in home centers and building supply stores. With a little bit of figuring, the design can be scaled up or down to accommodate different table dimensions or materials. And, as if this concept weren't clever enough, it's just as easy to create two sets of legs and add a large oval top to create a sofa table or console table.

MATERIALS

- One 2 x 4-foot piece ½" plywood
- Wood glue
- Finish materials (as desired)

TOOLS

- Straightedge
- Homemade compass (page 17)
- Jigsaw with thin, fine-tooth wood blade
- File
- Sandpaper

1. Lay out the table parts.

Start the layout by drawing a grid of construction lines on the 2 x 4-foot piece of plywood; these are the red lines shown in the cutting diagram. Make a horizontal centerline across the panel, then make three vertical lines (perpendicular to the horizontal) at 12", 24", and 36".

Set a homemade compass for a 10" radius (see How to Mark & Cut Curves, page 16). Draw a 20"-diameter circle around the centerpoint of the panel to mark the Top 1 piece. Then draw two semicircles (with 20" diameters) at each side edge of the panel, with the pivot point of the compass set at the very ends of the horizontal centerline; these semicircles are extra (or waste) pieces.

Draw four 8"-diameter semicircles, pivoting at the very ends of the two outer vertical lines on the top and bottom panel edges, to form the arched tops and bottoms of the legs. (Two of the semicircles you've just marked will become Top A and Top B.) Mark ½"-wide slots extending from one semicircle to the horizontal centerline on each leg, as shown in the cutting diagram.

Finally, mark the two 2" and one 4" cutouts with straight lines starting from the top edge of the panel, as shown in the diagram; these are waste.

2. Cut the parts.

Cut along the layout lines with a jigsaw. Be sure to cut on the inside (slot side) of the slot lines to ensure a tight fit during assembly. You can always sand or file the slots if the fit is too tight. Carefully freehand the curved cuts with the jigsaw, or use a homemade circle jig, or trammel, as described on page 18.

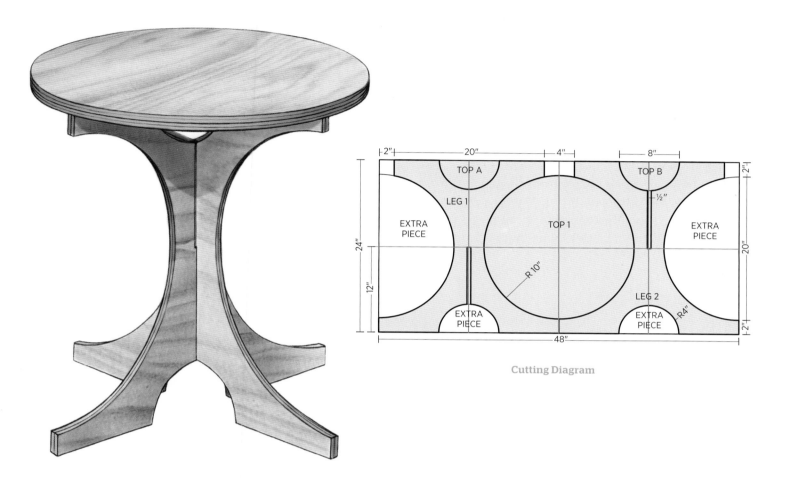

Cutting Diagram

When cutting out the legs, remember that you will use two of the small semicircles at the top and bottom and the adjoining Top 1 cutout, so make these cuts with extra care. Start the Top 1 cutout somewhere within the 4" waste piece between the two legs.

3. Add the top support disk.
The disk that serves as a cleat to keep the tabletop in place is made up of two of the small semicircles cut from the top and bottom of the legs. Find the two semicircles that fit together best and arrange them on the bottom face of the top, centering them perfectly. Mark the outer edges of the disk pieces for placement reference. Apply glue and clamp the semicircles to the top, following your reference marks. Let the glue dry.

4. Fit and finish the table.
Test-fit the legs by fitting their opposing slots together. If the fit is too tight, carefully file or sand both edges of each slot (to keep things centered) just until a snug fit is achieved.

Assemble the legs and test-fit the top (the cleat made by Top A and Top B should fit snugly into the semicircular cutouts in the tops of the legs). If you prefer a snugger fit here, you can glue small, thin strips of wood to the top inside edges of the leg cutouts, as needed.

Finish-sand all the pieces, and apply the finish of your choice. (If you like, you can glue the legs together, after sanding and before finishing the pieces.) To prevent sticking with surface-type finishes (polyurethane, paint, et cetera), make sure the finish cures before assembling the table.

Plane Table

Designed by Matt Wolpe

The Plane Table was one of the first works submitted for this book, and it remains among the quintessential examples of what we originally set out to find: simply constructed pieces of uncommonly good design. Its creator teaches a class in which each student designs and builds an original piece of furniture from a single 5 x 5-foot sheet of plywood. Of his own "class project" the designer says, "The Plane Table is a coffee table of proportions . . . a slightly asymmetrical intersection of complementary planes, also intended for putting your feet up, collecting magazines, or being completely clear of clutter." Now that's good plywood design, plane and simple.

MATERIALS

- ☐ One 5 x 5-foot sheet ¾" apple, Baltic birch, or other hardwood plywood
- ☐ Biscuits (for joinery; optional)
- ☐ Wood glue
- ☐ Six 3" lengths ¼"-diam. mahogany dowels
- ☐ Finish materials (see step 8)

TOOLS

- ☐ Circular saw with straightedge guide
- ☐ Straightedge guide for saw and router
- ☐ Router with:
  - ☐ ¾" straight bit
  - ☐ ¼" straight bit
  - ☐ Chamfer bit (bearing-guided)
- ☐ Wood chisel
- ☐ Handsaw or tablesaw with crosscutting sled
- ☐ Biscuit joiner (if available)
- ☐ Square
- ☐ Drill with ¼" straight bit
- ☐ Hammer or mallet
- ☐ Clamps
- ☐ Sandpaper (up to 220 grit)

1. Cut the plywood panels.

Cut all the table pieces to the following dimensions, using a circular saw and straightedge guide to ensure clean, straight cuts:

- 1 top at 22" x 40"
- 2 sides at 15¼" x 22"
- 1 stretcher at 32⅝" x 8"
- 1 shelf at 9½" x 12"

2. Cut the dadoes and notches.

The left side panel and stretcher fit together with dadoes, while the right side panel and the stretcher fit together with slots, as shown in the plan drawings on page 66. And the shelf gets a dado that fits over the top of the stretcher.

Using a router and ¾" bit set up with a straightedge guide, mill a ¾"-wide, ⅜"-deep dado into the inside face of the left side panel, centered along the panel's width (side to side), and extending 7½"

up from the bottom edge, as shown in the plans. After milling the dado, square off its top end with a chisel.

On the stretcher, mill a ¾"-wide, ¼"-deep dado on each side face of the panel, directly opposite each other, with the outside edges of the dadoes 3" from the panel end.

Next, mill a ¾"-wide, ¼"-deep dado down the center of the shelf's bottom face (parallel to its 9½" dimension).

Switch to a ¼" router bit, and mill a ¼"-wide, 7½-long *through dado* (slot) into the right side panel, centered along its width (side to side). Square off the top end of the slot with the chisel. (The remaining material between the opposing dadoes in the stretcher should match the width of the through dado in the right side panel.)

Finally, use a good handsaw (or a table saw with a crosscutting sled) to cut ½"-deep notches into the top edge of the stretcher, as shown in the plans.

Test-assemble the base pieces (the stretcher and two side panels) and make adjustments as needed for good-fitting joints.

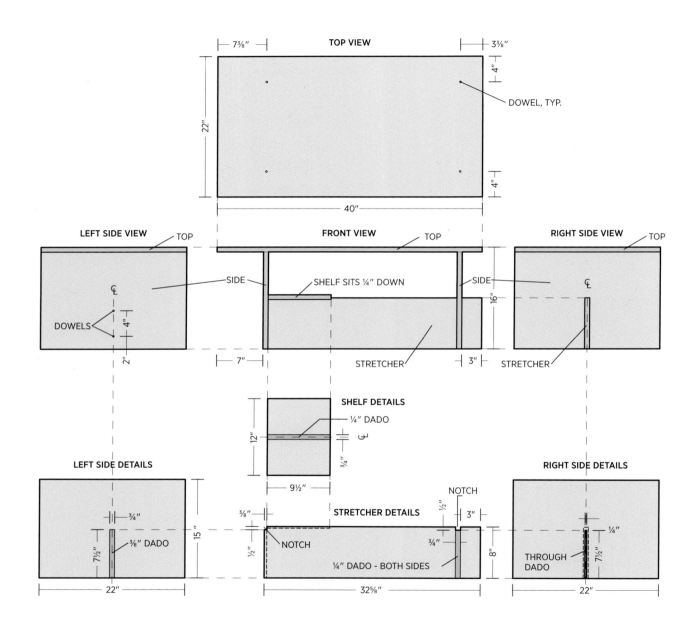

TOP VIEW

7⅜"   3⅜"

4"

DOWEL, TYP.

22"

4"

40"

LEFT SIDE VIEW   TOP   FRONT VIEW   TOP   RIGHT SIDE VIEW   TOP

SIDE   SHELF SITS ¼" DOWN   SIDE

℄   16"   ℄

DOWELS   4"

2"   STRETCHER   STRETCHER

7"   STRETCHER   3"

SHELF DETAILS

¼" DADO

12"   ℄

¾"

LEFT SIDE DETAILS   9½"   RIGHT SIDE DETAILS

NOTCH

¾"   ⅜"   ½"   3"   NOTCH

15"   ¼"

7½"   ⅜" DADO   ½"   NOTCH   ¾"   THROUGH   7½"

¼" DADO - BOTH SIDES   DADO

22"   32⅝"   8"   22"

Cutting and Assembly Plan

Note: The ¾" dado slots must equal the plywood's thickness. If necessary, use a smaller router bit and make the cuts in two passes.

3. Cut biscuit slots for the shelf.

In the table as shown, the shelf is secured to the left side panel with biscuits. Cut the biscuit slots into one of the shelf's 12" edges and into the inside face of the left side panel. If you don't have a biscuit joiner, you can simply install the shelf with glue — and dowels, if desired — after the base is assembled (see step 6).

4. Mill the panel edges.

Use the router and a piloted (bearing-guided) chamfer bit to mill a slight chamfer on all edges of the top and all but the mating edges of the sides, stretcher, and shelf pieces.

5. Glue up the base.

Apply glue to the mating surfaces of the dado joints and notches, and assemble and clamp the base. Make sure the sides are perfectly square to the stretcher and that all three pieces stand flat on their bottom edges.

Mark the locations for two dowels on the outside face of the left side panel, as shown in the plans. The holes are centered along the width of the panel and are 2" and 6" up from the bottom edge. Drill ¼"-diameter, 3⅛"-deep holes at the marks. Apply a thin layer of glue to two 3" lengths of ¼" dowel, and tap the dowels into the holes with a hammer or mallet. Let the glue dry overnight.

6. Install the shelf.

Apply glue to the mating surfaces of the dado joint and the left edge of the shelf (and biscuit slots, if you're using biscuits), and glue the shelf to the stretcher and the left side panel. Clamp the shelf carefully so there is no gapping between the shelf and the side panel.

If you're not using biscuits, you can reinforce the joint with a couple of dowels driven through the left side panel and into the shelf edge, as with the side panel and stretcher.

Let the glue dry overnight.

7. Install the top.

Set the tabletop on the base so it is centered from side to side. Use a straightedge to align the right-side edge of the top with the end of the stretcher below. The top will overhang the right side panel about 3" and the left side panel about 7". Use light pencil marks to transfer the precise locations of the side panels onto the side edges of the top.

Mark the four dowel holes on the top face of the top, as shown in the plans. Space the holes about 4" from the front and back edges, and center them over the side panel locations. Clamp the top in position, and drill a dowel hole at each mark, as before.

Apply glue to the top edges of the side panels, and set the top in place. Drive glued dowels into their holes, then clamp the assembly and let the glue dry overnight.

8. Finish the table.

If any dowels are protruding more than 1⁄16" or so from the surface, trim them as flush as possible with a handsaw (make sure the saw's teeth have no "set," or sideways angle, as this will scratch the surrounding surface). Sand all of the dowels flush with the surrounding surfaces.

Finish-sand the entire piece, working up to 220-grit or finer sandpaper. Finish the table as desired. If you'd like to paint the stretcher, as shown in the table here, use a high-gloss, oil-based (alkyd) enamel paint for the best shine and durability. Otherwise, you can use a pure acrylic (latex-free) paint on the stretcher and then clear-coat the entire table with a compatible acrylic polyurethane, applied as directed by the manufacturer.

Mind the Gap Table

Designed by Chad Kelly

One look tells you that Mind the Gap is no ordinary coffee table. Yet it takes more than a glance to see all that's going on here. For starters, its top is a full inch thick, created with two laminated layers of ½" plywood. The extra thickness highlights the edge strata and adds just the right mass to play against the top's gaps (which you don't really have to mind, since they're only a quarter of an inch wide). The dramatic inlay design is cleverly made with a walnut veneer set into a field of maple veneer (this is easier than it looks). A set of 1950s-style hairpin legs completes the look, clearly setting a wide gap between this and most other coffee tables.

See page 168 for another work by Chad Kelly.

MATERIALS

- ☐ One 5 x 5-foot sheet ½" Baltic birch plywood (or 4 x 4 feet min.)
- ☐ Wood glue
- ☐ One 2 x 2-foot piece ¼" MDF
- ☐ One 12" x 96" piece maple veneer
- ☐ One 12" x 48" piece walnut veneer
- ☐ Distilled water in spray bottle
- ☐ Finish materials (see step 7)
- ☐ One 56" length ¾" aluminum C-channel
- ☐ Black spray paint
- ☐ Thirty-two ⅝" #8 wood screws
- ☐ Four hairpin legs with mounting screws

TOOLS

- ☐ Circular saw with straightedge guide or a table saw
- ☐ Small trim roller
- ☐ Bar clamps
- ☐ Compass
- ☐ Jigsaw or band saw
- ☐ Sandpaper (up to 400 grit)
- ☐ Utility knife
- ☐ Straightedge
- ☐ Clothes iron
- ☐ Router with top-bearing flush-trimming bit
- ☐ Tack cloth
- ☐ Small foam brush
- ☐ Hacksaw
- ☐ Drill with:
    - ☐ ⅛" straight bit
    - ☐ ³⁄₁₆" straight bit

1. Cut the tabletop quarters.

Using a circular saw with a straightedge guide or a table saw, cut eight pieces of ½" plywood to size at 11⅞" x 23⅛". The grain orientation doesn't matter with these pieces because the top faces will be covered with veneer. However, it's critical that the cuts are straight and the corners of the pieces are square. The most important edges are those along the tabletop's gaps, so plan to use the panel's factory edges and corners for these as much as possible. The two outside edges of each quarter section will be trimmed about ⅛" with the router.

2. Glue up the quarters.

Arrange the quarter pieces into four pairs, placing them face to face and aligning their best edges for what will be the inside (gapped) edges of the tabletop. Open up each pair like a book, and wipe the face-up surfaces clean.

Apply glue to each face, using a small trim roller (small paint roller), and then sandwich each pair together. Stack up the four glued pairs, making sure the edges are perfectly aligned, and clamp the entire stack with several bar clamps.

Clean up any glue squeeze-out with damp paper towels, being careful not to let any glue drip onto neighboring quarter pairs (you don't want the pairs sticking together).

3. Create the templates.

Following the plan drawings, lay out the table quarter template on ¼" MDF stock. Use two adjacent factory edges of the panel for the completely straight edges of the template. Mark the roundover at the opposing corner with a 2" radius.

Cut the two outer edges of the template with a circular saw and straightedge guide, then cut the roundover with a jigsaw or

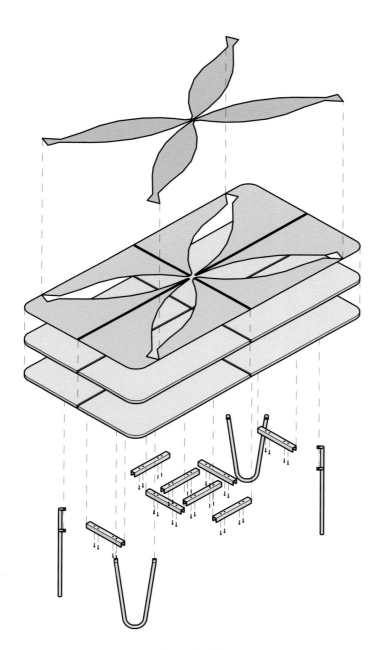

Exploded View

band saw. Sand the roundover smooth, then sand the straight edges with 220-grit sandpaper, as needed, so their surfaces are flat and smooth.

Draw the profile of the inlay template on the leftover MDF stock, as shown in the plans. You can copy the profile just as it's shown or modify the shape as desired. Using a flexible strip of wood or plastic helps create smooth arcs. Once you have a shape you like, cut out the template with a jigsaw, and sand the edges with 220-grit sandpaper.

4. Cut the veneers.
Using a sharp utility knife and a straightedge, cut four pieces of maple veneer to size at 11⅞" x 23⅛", with the grain running lengthwise. Then cut four pieces of walnut veneer to length at 5½" x 22", again with the grain running lengthwise.

Place one piece of maple veneer on one of the tabletop quarters, then place the table quarter template on top of the veneer. Align the inside (factory) edges of the pieces. Holding the template in place, trace along the outside edges of the template to mark the quarter outline on the maple veneer. Remove the template.

Position a piece of the walnut veneer on top of the maple veneer and plywood, following the positioning shown in the plans. Place the inlay template on top of the walnut veneer. The ½" "nose" of the template will overhang the inside corner of the quarter somewhat, and the "tail" end should just touch the penciled outline.

Use two bar clamps to secure the inlay template, two veneers, and plywood quarter to the work surface. With the utility knife, carefully cut through the two sheets of veneer at the same time, following the edges of the inlay template.

Repeat this process with each of the tabletop quarters. Arrange the quarters as you work to make sure the inlays and rounded corners of the plywood have the proper orientation, as shown in the project photo.

5. Apply the veneers.
Working on one table quarter at a time, spritz the faces of the maple and walnut veneers with distilled water. Use the trim roller to spread wood glue over the top face of the plywood and the backside of each veneer, then let the glue dry completely.

Once the glue has dried, arrange the veneers on the plywood in their finished positions; the inlay should fit inside the matching cutout in the maple veneer. Set a clothes iron to medium heat. Use the heated iron to apply firm pressure to the veneers, causing the dried glue to melt and bond with the plywood face. Let the assembly cool for at least 2 hours.

Repeat the same process to complete the veneers on the three remaining tabletop quarters.

Note: If the veneer needs some extra pressure to stay in place after being ironed, try dulling the edge of a brick chisel (or find a similar tool with a hard, flat, dull edge) and using it to press down firmly on the veneer, moving from the center to the edges.

6. Trim the quarters.

Position the table quarter template on top of each tabletop quarter, again aligning the inside (factory) edges of the template and plywood. Clamp the pieces to the work surface with a scrap spacer set underneath. Using a router and flush-trimming (top-bearing) bit, trim the outside edges of the plywood and maple veneer, rounding over the outside corner and cleaning up the straight edges.

Repeat this process to rout the remaining table quarters. Then sand all edges and faces of each piece with 220-grit sandpaper, and wipe them clean with a tack cloth.

Note: If your bit isn't long enough to cut the entire thickness in one pass, remove the template after the first pass and use the routed portion of the plywood to guide the bit for the second pass.

7. Finish the quarters.

Use a small foam brush to apply a water-based acrylic polyurethane (the project as shown was finished with Minwax Polycrylic in satin) to all the surfaces of each table quarter. Take the time to brush in the direction of the grain on all areas, including the walnut inlay. Once each piece is dry, lightly sand the surfaces with 220-grit sandpaper, and wipe them clean with a tack cloth. Apply two additional coats of finish, sanding with 400-grit paper after the second coat. Do not sand after the final coat.

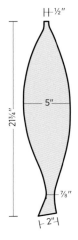

Inlay Template

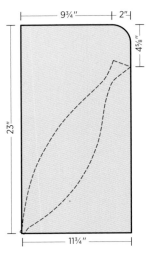

Table Quarter Template

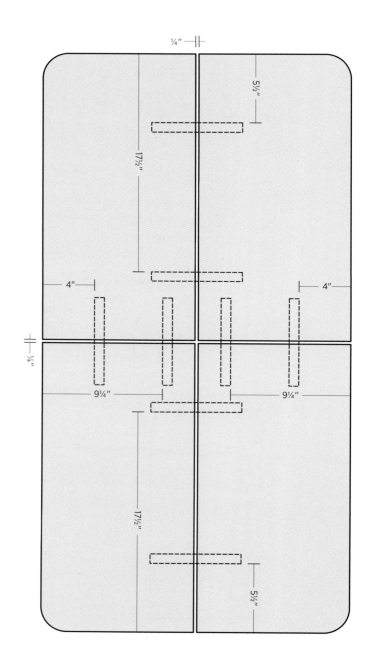

Bracket Layout

8. Prepare the tabletop brackets.

From the ¾" C-channel aluminum strip, cut eight pieces at 7" long, using a hacksaw. Mark each piece for four centered holes, 1¼" and 2" from each end. Drill the holes with a ³⁄₁₆" bit.

Paint the brackets on all sides with flat-black spray paint to match the legs (or, if desired, you can leave them unpainted and let the aluminum shine through the gaps).

9. Assemble the table.

Place the tabletop quarters facedown on a flat surface, arranging them with a precise ¼" gap between the pieces. Position the brackets over the quarters as shown in the bracket layout illustration.

Mark the brackets' holes on the plywood pieces, then drill a pilot hole at each mark with a ⅛" bit. Fasten the brackets to the plywood with #8 wood screws, making sure the table quarters are perfectly aligned.

Position each hairpin leg at a corner of the table, about 2½" from the long side of the table and 4" from the short side. Mark the hole locations for the mounting screws. Drill pilot holes, and fasten the legs to the table with the provided screws, or use ⅝" wood screws.

Note: You can order authentic hairpin legs in custom sizes (see Resources).

Tank Table

Designed by Rebecca Muyal

. . . *Fish* tank, that is. Designed especially for apartment dwellers who suffer from space constraints and, in most cases, a woeful lack of natural scenery, Tank Table is compact, rollable (on casters), and playfully decorated with a colorful underwater scene. Using all-thread (threaded steel rod) for its legs, the table's construction is exceptionally straightforward. And you can decorate your table however you like. For those who stick with the oceanic theme, the designer has this recommendation: "Add a couple of reclining lawn chairs, a painted floor cloth, and a scenic print (for background), and voilà: an instant vacation at home."

MATERIALS

- One 2 x 4-foot piece ¾" oak or other hardwood plywood
- Clear lacquer finish
- Stenciling materials (see step 4)
- Four 360-degree swivel casters with screws
- Nine 12" lengths ½" all-thread rod
- Eighteen ½" hexagon zinc nuts
- Thirty-six ½" zinc washers
- Eighteen ½" hexagon zinc lock nuts

TOOLS

- Homemade compass (page 17)
- Jigsaw
- Router with homemade trammel (page 18) and straight bit
- Straightedge
- Framing square
- Protractor
- Drill with:
  - ⅛" (or smaller) straight bit
  - ½" spade bit
  - Small pilot bit (for caster screws)
- Clamps
- Sandpaper (150 to 300 grit)
- Stenciling tools (see step 4)
- Wrenches or pliers (for nuts)

1. Cut the tabletop and shelf.

The table's top and lower shelf are both 16"-diameter disks cut from ¾" plywood. See How to Mark & Cut Curves (page 16) and Two Easy Ways to Cut a Circle (page 18) for detailed instructions on the following procedure.

To cut each disk, draw a 16"-diameter circle on your stock, using a homemade compass. Rough-cut the disk with a jigsaw, staying ⅛" outside the marked line. Then clean up the edge using a router and straight bit set up with a trammel.

2. Drill the leg holes.

The table has nine legs total, arranged in three even groupings. To lay out the holes for the legs, first draw a 14"-diameter circle on the bottom face of the tabletop disk, using the homemade compass and pivoting from the original centerpoint. Then draw a straight line through the centerpoint and across the entire face of the disk; this line should be parallel to the grain of the face veneers (the grain adds to the "water" effect of the finished piece, so it should run in line with the motion of the fish).

Use a framing square to draw a second straight line, perpendicular to the first, to map the quadrants of the disk (see Marking Quadrants on a Circle, page 19). The center leg of each grouping is at the intersection of the quadrant lines and the 14" circle line, as shown in the leg layout illustration.

Using a protractor and straightedge, draw a straight line from the centerpoint to the 14" circle line at 10 degrees to each side of the side and rear quadrant lines, as shown in the drawing. The two outer leg locations are at the intersections between the angled lines and the 14" circle. Circle each intersection now, so you'll know exactly where to drill.

Make a ⅛" hole at each location, using a drill and ⅛" bit. Flip the tabletop over and set it on top of the shelf so both pieces are top face up. Place both pieces on a sacrificial backerboard (to prevent tearout). Align the disks' edges perfectly and clamp everything down to your work surface. Using a ½" spade bit, drill down through both pieces, guided by the ⅛" holes, to create the nine leg holes. Be careful to keep the drill bit plumb as you work.

3. Apply the base finish.

Finish-sand the tabletop and shelf using 150-grit sandpaper and working up to 300 grit. Sand slight roundovers on all the plywood edges to prevent splintering and create a finished look. Alternatively, you can round over the edges of the disks with a router and roundover bit.

Wipe the disks carefully to remove all dust. Apply a single coat of clear lacquer, as directed by the manufacturer, then let the finish dry completely. Lightly sand the surfaces with fine sandpaper, as directed.

4. Paint the decorative scene.

You can create the oceanic (or other) scene using precut stencils or make your own stencils by transferring specific images to stencil sheets, using graphite paper. The best paint to use is oil-based stencil paint, which is formulated to cover in one coat and minimizes bleeding under stencils. You can use other types of paint, but be sure to test them out with the stencils on a plywood scrap. Having to stencil with more than one coat is problematic.

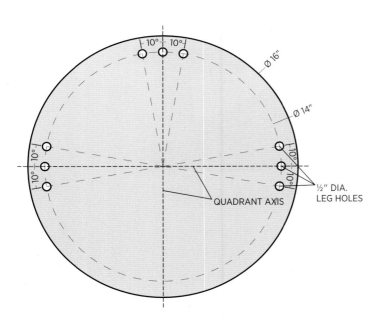

Leg Layout

Arrange and tape each stencil on the tabletop or shelf, making sure it is aligned with the veneer grain (and leg locations, as applicable). Paint the images with a good stencil brush, using one coat for each color. Let the paint dry between each color, and clean the stencils carefully between applications.

5. Complete the finish.

Apply three coats of lacquer to all surfaces of the tabletop and shelf, lightly sanding between each coat, as directed by the manufacturer. The lacquer protects the wood and paint and visually enhances the wood grain, adding depth to the underwater scene.

6. Install the casters.

Arrange the casters on the underside of the shelf, spacing them evenly from the disk's edge and from one another. Keep in mind that placing the casters closer to center will make the wheels less visible from above, but getting them too close will compromise the stability of the table; find the position that works best. Drill shallow pilot holes and fasten the casters with the provided screws.

7. Assemble the table.

On the bottom end of an all-thread rod, thread one standard nut about 1½" up. Add a washer, then insert the bottom end into one of the leg holes on the shelf and secure it underneath with a washer and lock nut. The rod end should be nearly flush with the end of the lock nut. Hand-tighten the nuts for now, leaving them a little loose. Repeat with the remaining eight legs.

Follow a parallel process to install the tabletop at the top ends of the rods: thread a nut and washer onto the rods, slip the rod ends through the tabletop, and then secure with a washer and lock nut. Fine-tune the position of the lock nuts so they sit slightly above the ends of the rods. If necessary, you can grip the rods with Vise-Grips or pliers protected by a leather work glove or similar material to prevent damage to the threads. Use two crescent wrenches, open-end wrenches, or pliers to tighten the nuts toward each other, locking the tabletop in place. Tighten the lower nut pairs to secure the shelf.

Swing Table

Designed by Ralph Stampone

Swing Table looks like one of those rarefied midcentury pieces you might see in an old Taschen sourcebook or on the set of *The Avengers* and think to yourself, "Man, I'd love to find one of those somewhere." Well, now you can have an original (or rather, an original *copy*). What makes this table really swing is the pivoting top, aided by a ball bearing hidden in the end of its leg. The fixed shelf is great for magazine storage, while the usable tabletop surface can be virtually doubled at any time — perfect for really big shindigs when you need lots of space for setting down martinis, smokes, and Blue Hawaiians.

MATERIALS

- One 4 x 4-foot sheet ½" MDF
- Finish materials (see step 4)
- One 66" length aluminum or steel tubing (2" outside diam.; 1¾" inside diam.), with four matching mounting plates
- Three 1" set screws
- Ball transfer (sized for 1¾" inside diam. of leg tubing; see step 5)
- Sixteen ½" wood screws
- ¾" brads
- 1¼" lag bolt

TOOLS

- Jigsaw or band saw
- Clamps
- Sandpaper
- Router with ¼" roundover bit
- Paintbrush or sprayer
- Drill with:
  - Straight bits
  - Tap (for set screws)
  - 2" hole saw
- Hacksaw, reciprocating saw, or metal band saw
- Metal file
- Socket wrench (for lag bolt)

1. Cut the tops and shelf.

The lower top, which is fixed, is identical to the shelf. The swing top has its own shape overall, but much of it matches the fixed top and shelf. Therefore, it's easiest to cut the fixed top and shelf first, then use one of them as a template for marking the majority of the swing top.

Draw the fixed top/shelf outline on the MDF stock, following the plan drawings. Rough-cut this piece from the sheet, staying ½" or so outside the cutting line. Set the cut piece on top of the sheet (positioned so you'll have plenty of room for the swing top) and clamp the pieces together. Carefully cut out the shape to the cutting line with a jigsaw, cutting out both pieces at once. (You could also use a band saw, in which case you should rough-cut both pieces first.)

Keeping the pieces together, sand the edges to smooth out the curves and remove any saw marks.

Place one of the cut pieces on the MDF stock and trace its profile to begin shaping the swing top. Remove the cut piece and complete the outline of the swing top, following the plan template. Cut out the swing top with a jigsaw or band saw, then sand the edges smooth, checking to make sure the matching curves are identical to those of the fixed top and shelf.

2. Mill the wood edges.

Use a router and ¼" roundover bit to mill a slight roundover on the top and bottom edges of all three wood pieces.

3. Drill the leg holes.

Mark the centers of the legs on the shelf, as shown in the plan template. Drill each leg hole with a 2" hole saw. To prevent tearout on the bottom face of the panel, drill only about halfway through the material, then flip the piece over and complete the hole from the opposite face.

Test-fit the leg tubing in the shelf; if it's very tight, you might need to sand the insides of the holes slightly so the tubing will fit after the shelf is painted.

4. Finish the tops and shelf.

Finish-sand the wood pieces with fine sandpaper. Apply a good primer/sealer to all surfaces; this is important for sealing the porous edges of MDF. Paint the pieces with at least two coats of quality gloss paint, using a brush (or better yet, a sprayer) for a smooth finish.

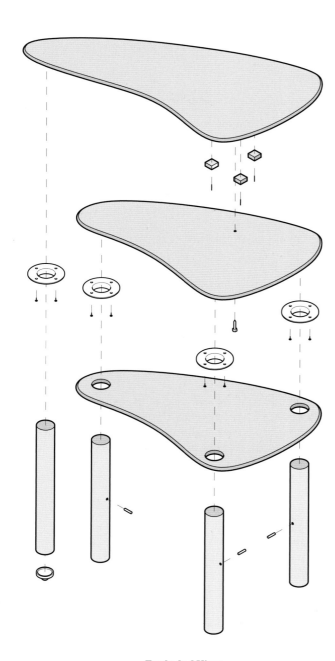

Exploded View

Note: The right paint colors really make this piece. You can use whatever colors you like, but it's best to go with at least two different colors, making the fixed top different from the swing top and shelf, as shown here (or use a different color for each part). You can try to find small samples of paint (3 ounces or so) in your desired colors, but make sure it's gloss in sheen, for a durable, washable finish.

5. Prepare the legs.

From the tubing, cut three legs to length at 16" (for the shelf and fixed top) and one at 17" (for the swing top), using a hacksaw, reciprocating saw, or metal band saw. File the bottom end of each leg to remove any burrs or sharp edges.

Measure up from the bottom end of each 16" leg and make a mark at 8½". Drill a pilot hole through the wall of the leg tube, using a straight bit sized for the set screw diameter. Tap (thread) each hole with an appropriately sized tap. Drive a 1" set screw into each tapped hole, leaving half to two-thirds of its length extending from the leg wall.

Insert a ball transfer into the bottom end of the 17" leg, pressing it in until it's fully seated.

Note: In the project shown, the ball transfer was purchased from McMaster-Carr (see Resources).

6. Prepare the tops.

Place the shelf over the bottom face of the fixed top so their edges are precisely aligned. Trace around each leg hole in the shelf to transfer the leg locations to the fixed top. Install a mounting plate at each location, using ½" wood screws. Install another mounting plate to the underside of the swing top as shown in the plan.

Place the fixed top over the swing top, both bottom face up, with their edges aligned. Drill a small pilot hole through the fixed shelf and partially into the swing top, at the lag bolt location shown in the plan; be careful not to drill completely through the swing top. Separate the pieces. Through the hole in the fixed top, drill a hole of a diameter slightly larger than that of the shank (smooth section) of the 1¼" lag bolt. Into the swing top, drill a ¼"-deep pilot hole that's the same size as the bolt shaft (screw diameter minus the threads).

Cut three 1"-square pieces from the MDF stock to use as spacers between the swing top and fixed top. Sand the spacers

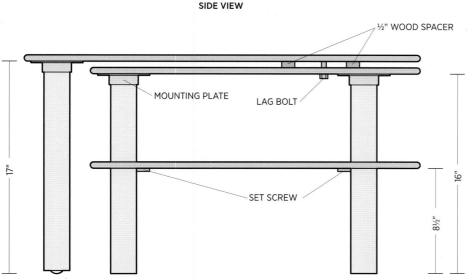

SIDE VIEW

½" WOOD SPACER

MOUNTING PLATE

LAG BOLT

SET SCREW

17"

16"

8½"

to round over their top edges. Position the spacers around the lag bolt hole on the top face of the fixed top, spacing them evenly around the hole; set them as far apart as possible for maximum stability but close enough to the hole that they will always be concealed under the swing top as it rotates. Drill pilot holes through the spacers, and fasten them to the fixed top with ¾" brads.

7. Complete the assembly.

Insert the top ends of the 16" legs through the holes in the shelf until the shelf rests on the setscrews, then secure the top ends of the legs to the mounting plates in the fixed top, as appropriate for the type of plates you're using.

Secure the top end of the 17" leg to its mounting plate in the swing top. With the shelf and fixed top assembly standing upright, position the swing top over the fixed top and drive the lag bolt up through the fixed top and into the pilot hole in the swing top. Tighten the bolt just enough to secure the swing top while allowing for easy rotation, using a socket wrench.

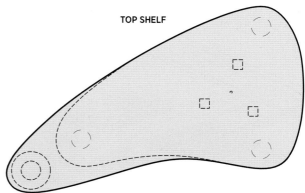

TOP SHELF

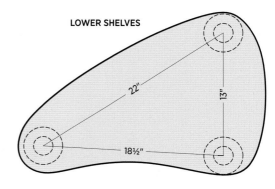

LOWER SHELVES

22"

13"

18½"

Assembly Plan

Cantilever Table

Designed by Brian DuBois

This designer has a flair for blending plywood with metal and, in this case, glass to create striking pieces that are surprisingly easy to build. The Cantilever Table is a case in point. All of its parts (except the glass top) are off-the-shelf materials that are inexpensive and easy to work with. And yet the completed project has an appealing complexity of lines, textures, and shapes that belies its simple construction, clearly elevating these humble materials to a higher purpose.

See page 108 for another work by Brian DuBois.

MATERIALS

- One 5 x 5-foot sheet ¾" Baltic birch plywood
- Finish materials (as desired)
- One 48" length ½" x 4" aluminum plate stock
- One 28⅛" length (at min.) ¼" x 1" aluminum bar stock
- Two 37" lengths (at min.) ⅛" x 1" x 2" aluminum angle
- One 48" length ⅝" all-thread rod
- Thirty-six ⅝" nuts and washers
- Four ¼" x 5½" (from center of eye to end) #20 eyebolts with ⅝" opening
- Four ¼" x 3" (from center of eye to end) #20 eyebolts with ⅝" opening
- Ten ¼" x 1" machine bolts
- Twenty-four ¼" nuts
- Ten ¼" rubber grommets
- One 14¾" x 33" piece ½"-thick tempered glass

TOOLS

- Drill with:
  - ⅝" straight bit
  - 1" straight bit
  - 1" spade bit (optional)
- Drill press with Forstner bit (if not using spade bit)
- Circular saw with straightedge guide
- Sandpaper (including 150 grit)
- Jigsaw with bimetal blade
- Chop saw, reciprocating saw, or hacksaw (if not using jigsaw)
- Socket or open-end wrenches

Note: This project calls for a 14¾" x 33" piece of glass with finished edges. The glass must be tempered for safety, so you have to order it from a glass fabricator (any glass shop can handle it). Tempered glass can't be cut — it's tempered after sizing — so this isn't a DIY option. Discuss your project with the glass dealer to be sure to get the right product for the application.

1. Cut and drill the center leg.
Complete the layout for the center leg on the plywood stock, as shown in the cutting diagram. Drill the 1" hole at the corner of the cutout area, using a portable drill and spade bit or a drill press and Forstner bit (clamp the piece to a sacrificial work surface or backerboard to prevent tearout). Then drill the six ⅝" holes for the table hardware. Cut along the outlines of the piece, using a circular saw and straightedge guide to ensure clean, straight cuts. Sand and/or file the edges as needed so they are smooth and straight.

2. Prepare the outer legs.
Using the center leg as a template, mark, cut, and drill the two outer legs. The outer legs have the same two ⅝" holes along the top and the 1" hole at the corner of the cutout, but they do not get the four ⅝" holes in the body of the piece. Remember to drill the 1" holes before making the cutouts.

3. Finish the legs.
Sand the leg pieces smooth, lightly sanding the edges to prevent splintering while maintaining crisp edges for the proper aesthetic. Stain and finish the pieces as desired. As shown here, the legs were finished with Minwax Polyshades (a combination of stain and polyurethane finish) in walnut.

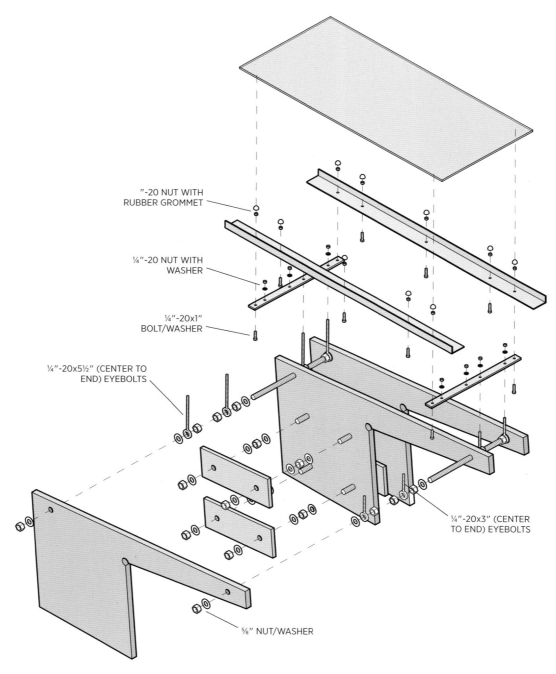

"-20 NUT WITH
RUBBER GROMMET

¼"-20 NUT WITH
WASHER

¼"-20x1"
BOLT/WASHER

¼"-20x5½" (CENTER TO
END) EYEBOLTS

¼"-20x3" (CENTER
TO END) EYEBOLTS

⅝" NUT/WASHER

Exploded View

4. Cut and drill the aluminum parts.

Cut four pieces of ½" x 4" aluminum plate stock to length at 11", using a jigsaw with a bimetal blade or a chop saw (see Cutting and Drilling Metal, page 111). Drill the two ⅝" holes in each piece, as shown in the cutting diagram. You can gang the matching pieces together for accuracy, but give your drill bit a rest between layers to prevent overheating.

Next, cut two 14" lengths of ¼" x 1" bar stock, and drill ¼" holes in each piece, as shown in the cutting diagram.

Finally, cut two pieces of aluminum angle to length at 37", and drill the ¼" holes as shown (you can gang these parts only if you arrange them back-to-back).

Sand the pieces with 150-grit sandpaper for a "raw" look (if desired) and to remove any burrs and rough or sharp edges.

5. Cut the all-thread pieces.

Use a jigsaw, chop saw, reciprocating saw, or hacksaw to cut four lengths of all-thread rod at 4½" and two lengths at 14".

6. Assemble the table.

Assemble all the parts as shown in the exploded-view drawing. For the parts you can't see, simply match everything that you can see; the assembly is perfectly symmetrical. Tighten the nuts with socket or open-end wrenches. Set the glass top on the rubber grommets so it's centered front-to-back on the aluminum angles.

Shop Tip

Working with All-Thread

All-thread (also called threaded rod) is available at home centers and most building materials retailers. The rod is easiest to cut with a reciprocating saw and a fine-tooth, metal-cutting blade, but you can always use a hacksaw and a good deal of elbow grease. To ensure a straight cut, wrap masking tape around the rod at your cut mark to serve as a guide. Carefully align the edges of the tape as you wrap to create a straight line all the way around the rod.

Cutting all-thread often creates burrs that can make it tough to thread nuts. To help alleviate this problem, install a nut on each side of the cut line before making the cut. After the cut is made, unthread the nuts off the cut ends so that the nuts realign any distorted threads.

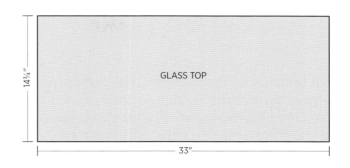

GLASS TOP

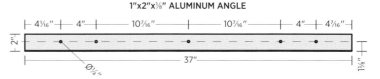

1"x2"x⅛" ALUMINUM ANGLE

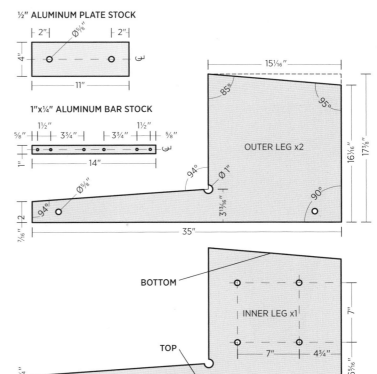

½" ALUMINUM PLATE STOCK

1"x¼" ALUMINUM BAR STOCK

OUTER LEG x2

BOTTOM

INNER LEG x1

TOP

Cutting Diagram

Eclipse Coffee Table

Designed by Steffanie Dotson

Custom-designed for the midcentury decor of a *chocolat café*, this table reprises some of the best characteristics of that era's furnishings. It's pared-down, practical, and elegant, providing the essence of what a table should be and looking great doing it. To suit its home in a retail space, the piece is sturdy and lightweight. It's also surprisingly easy to build. As shown, the table was created with plywood that has walnut veneer on the top (outside) faces and maple on the back (inside) faces. Solid-wood edging in matching species covers the plywood edges for a nicely finished midcentury look.

MATERIALS

- ☐ One 5 x 5-foot or 4 x 8-foot sheet ¾" hardwood plywood
- ☐ Wood glue
- ☐ 20 (or more) coarse-thread pocket screws (see step 2)
- ☐ One 62" length ¾" x ¾" solid-wood stock
- ☐ One 70" length ¼" x ¾" solid-wood stock
- ☐ 1¼" #8 wood screws
- ☐ Wood plugs (optional; see step 4)
- ☐ Three 48" lengths ½" x ¾" solid-wood stock
- ☐ Finish materials (as desired)

TOOLS

- ☐ Circular saw with straightedge guide
- ☐ Pocket screw jig (if available)
- ☐ Clamps
- ☐ Miter saw or miter box and backsaw
- ☐ Masking tape
- ☐ Card scraper
- ☐ Sandpaper (up to 220 grit)
- ☐ Flush-cutting handsaw
- ☐ Drill with #8 combination pilot-countersink bit
- ☐ Router with ¼" roundover bit

Note: This construction works best if the ¾" face of the solid-wood stock is slightly larger than the thickness of plywood

1. Cut the legs, ends, and apron parts.

Following the plan drawings, cut the legs, ends, and apron pieces from ¾" plywood, using a circular saw with a straightedge guide to ensure clean, straight cuts.

Cut the four legs at 15¼" tall, tapering the width from 7" at the top to 3" at the bottom. The grain of the face veneers should run vertically (top to bottom). When laying out the cuts, be mindful of the orientation each leg will have when installed.

Cut two end panels at 15¼" tall and 17" wide, with the grain running vertically.

Cut two long apron sides at 3" wide and 32½" long and two short apron sides at 3" wide and 17" long. The apron is more or less hidden by the table's top, legs, and ends, so it's best to use the panel's factory edges for the other parts.

2. Assemble the apron.

The best way to join the four apron pieces is with glue and pocket screws. If you don't have a setup for pocket screws, you can simply glue and nail or screw the pieces together; these joints won't show, so they don't have to look pretty. However, the frame must be square and flat, so clamp and fasten carefully, making sure the assembly lies flat before letting the glue set.

Assemble the long and short apron sides as shown in the plan on page 86. The outside dimensions of the frame should measure 17" x 38½".

3. Add the solid-wood edging.

The two end panels get ¾" x ¾" solid-wood strips on both side edges. The four legs get a ¼" x ¾" strip along the inside (angled) edge of each piece. Cut the strips for the end panels to length at 15¼", using a miter saw or a miter box and backsaw. Cut the strips for the legs at 17" long.

As noted at the beginning of this project, it's best if the edging strips are slightly wider than the plywood's thickness. This allows you to apply the edging so it overhangs the faces of the plywood on both sides; you can then scrape or sand the edging flush to the faces.

Glue the edging to the sides of the end panels, and clamp the edging in place, making sure it is centered on the panel edges. Glue the thin strips to the legs, using masking tape to secure it while the glue sets. The ends of the strips should extend beyond the top and bottom edges of the legs by about ⅛".

After the glue has dried, remove the clamps and tape and use a card scraper to shave the wood edging flush with the plywood faces. Alternatively, you can sand them flush, but be very careful not to sand through the face veneer of the plywood. On the legs, trim the ends of the edging flush with the top and bottom edges of the plywood, using a flush-cutting handsaw.

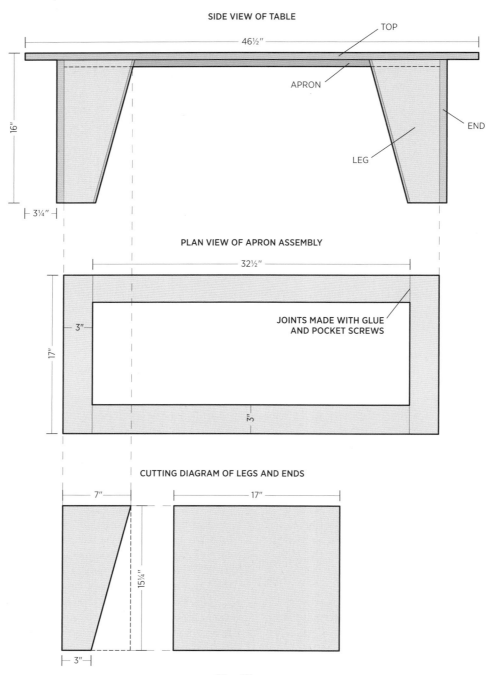

SIDE VIEW OF TABLE

TOP

46½"

APRON

16"

END

LEG

3¼"

PLAN VIEW OF APRON ASSEMBLY

32½"

JOINTS MADE WITH GLUE
AND POCKET SCREWS

3"

17"

3"

CUTTING DIAGRAM OF LEGS AND ENDS

7"

17"

15¼"

3"

Plan Views

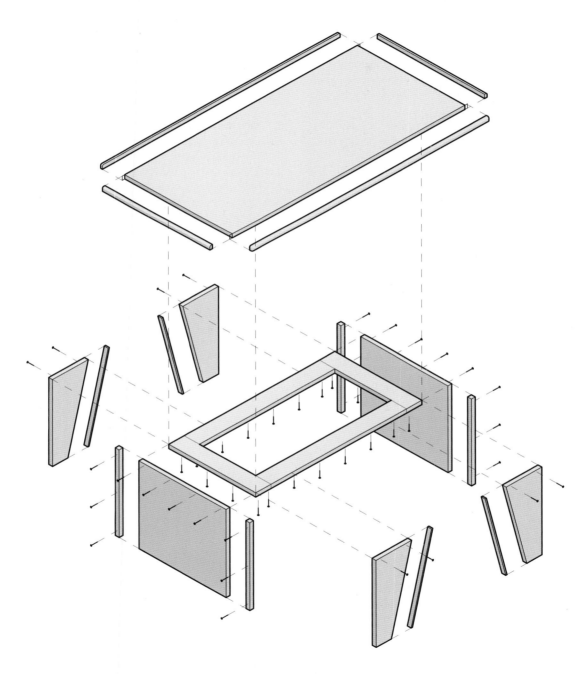

Exploded View

4. Join the legs and end panels.

Fit each end panel over the back edges of a leg pair and clamp the parts so their top edges are flush and the end panel's side edges are flush with the outside faces of the legs. Drill counter-bored pilot holes for screws (these will go through the end panel and into the back edges of the legs). Join the pieces with glue and wood screws, and let the glue dry.

To hide the screw heads, fill the holes with matching wood plugs, glued into place. After the glue dries, saw and/or sand the plugs flush to the surface.

Note: If you're so equipped, you can use biscuits for these joints instead of screws, for completely hidden fasteners.

5. Complete the base assembly.

The leg-end assemblies fit over the ends of the apron frame so the end panels are perpendicular to the apron and all parts are flush at the top. Test-fit the parts and clamp the assembly, making sure the base is square and the top face of the apron frame is level when the base is standing upright. Drill pilot holes for pocket screws on the insides of the base, or drill holes for wood screws that will be driven through the outsides of the legs and ends and into the apron pieces; counterbore these holes for wood plugs, as before.

Assemble the base with glue and screws, and let the glue dry. If you're using conventional screws, fill the screw holes with matching wood plugs, glued into place. After the glue dries, saw and/or sand the plugs flush to the surface.

6. Cut and prepare the tabletop.

Cut the tabletop to size at 21" x 45", with the face grain running parallel to the short dimension, using a circular saw and straightedge guide.

Cut two ½" x ¾" solid-wood strips to length at 21". Glue and clamp these edge strips to the short edges of the tabletop, as before. After the glue dries, scrape or sand the edging flush.

Cut two more strips to span the long sides of the tabletop and cover the ends of the short-side strips (they should be about 46½" long). Glue these in place, then scrape or sand the edging flush.

7. Install the tabletop.

Center the tabletop over the base. Clamp the tabletop in place and drill countersunk pilot holes for eight wood screws, drilling through the apron and into the top; drill two holes on each end, and two on each side of the apron. Fasten the apron to the table-top with 1¼" wood screws, being careful not to penetrate the top face of the tabletop.

Round over the top edge corners of the tabletop, using a router and ¼" roundover bit; test the bit depth on some scrap first.

8. Finish the table.

Lightly sand all parts of the table with 220-grit sandpaper, sanding with the grain. On solid wood areas, where machine marks are visible, sand with progressively finer papers, starting with 80 grit and working up to 220 grit. Be careful not to sand the plywood face veneers with coarse papers.

After sanding, wipe the table down with a clean rag. Wipe once again with a clean, white rag dampened with plain white vinegar. Let the surfaces dry. Apply the finish of your choice. The table shown here was clear-coated with shellac.

Shop Tip

Glue Joints

For the best glue joints, be sure that the mating edges of your plywood and solid stock are perfectly flat. Hold a straightedge along the edges and look for areas where light shines through underneath it. If you see daylight, true up the edge by taking off thin shavings with a hand plane or block plane. Repeat as needed until there's no daylight visible under the straightedge.

Bowlegged Plant Stand

Designed by Spike Carlsen

When he's not building clever projects for loaning out to other authors, the designer of this piece writes his own books about wood, DIY woodworking projects, and other things generally wood-related. So if you like this design, you'll be glad to know there are a lot more where it came from. This uniquely shaped and nicely proportioned stand is great for plants or display pieces and works just as well as a side table or accent table. It uses less than a half sheet of plywood, and while it may not look like it, it's actually a knockdown piece (after a few screws are removed), fitting together somewhat like a brain-teaser puzzle.

MATERIALS

- [ ] One 4 x 4-foot piece ¾" hardwood plywood (AB or better grade)
- [ ] Yardstick (or similar flexible wood strip)
- [ ] Wood glue
- [ ] Twenty 1¼" coarse-thread drywall screws
- [ ] Finish materials (as desired)

TOOLS

- [ ] Circular saw with straightedge guide
- [ ] Compass (standard)
- [ ] Framing square
- [ ] Homemade compass (page 17)
- [ ] Jigsaw
- [ ] Belt sander or random orbital sander
- [ ] Drill with ⅜" straight bit
- [ ] Sandpaper (up to 220 grit)

1. Lay out the parts.

Each of the two bowed legs — A and B — is cut from an 18" x 30" panel of ¾" plywood. The legs are identical except for the orientation of the top and bottom notches on each piece; see the leg diagram. You will lay out and cut leg A first, then use it as a template for laying out leg B.

Cut the two panels to size at 18" x 30", using a circular saw and a straightedge guide. Make sure the 18" end cuts are square and straight, as these will become the top and bottom edges of the finished legs.

To lay out the curved sides of leg A, make three tick marks for each side on one of the blank panels, as shown in the leg diagram: Make the top marks 3" in from each side of the panel, and the bottom marks 1½" from the sides. Make middle marks 10" up from the bottom on each side edge.

Using a wood yardstick (or any flexible slat), bend the strip so it touches all three tick marks, forming a smooth curve. It helps to have a helper, but if you're working alone, you can drive a temporary nail just behind each tick mark, for backing up the stick. Trace along the stick to mark the outside profile of the leg. Repeat the process to draw the other side profile.

Set a compass at a span of 2". Carefully run the point along each leg curve while drawing a matching line 2" to the inside; this marks the inner side of the bowed leg. Use the compass and a framing square to mark out the other lines, notches, and curves of the leg, following the leg diagrams.

Finally, use a homemade compass to lay out the 16"-diameter tabletop and 13¾"-diameter shelf, as shown in the tabletop and shelf diagram. Also mark the four shallow notches on the shelf; the width of the notches should match the thickness of the plywood stock.

2. Cut the main parts.

Use a jigsaw with a fine wood blade to cut out leg A, but do not cut the notches yet. For accuracy with the outer curves, cut just to the outside of the lines, then use a belt sander or random orbital sander to smooth the curves. To make the interior cutout, drill a ⅜" starter hole inside the cutout area, and insert the blade of the jigsaw into the hole to begin the cut.

Trace the finished profile of leg A onto the other plywood blank for leg B. Cut out leg B. Lay out the top and bottom notches on the legs, following the leg diagram. Leg A's notches face up, and leg B's face down. The width of the notches should match

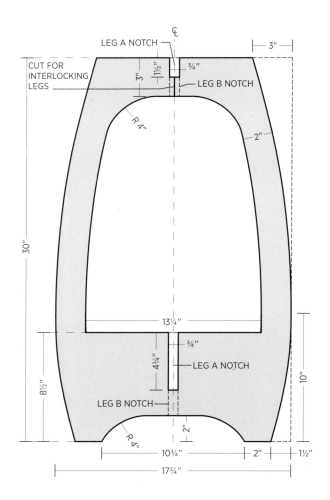

Leg Cutting Diagram

TABLETOP

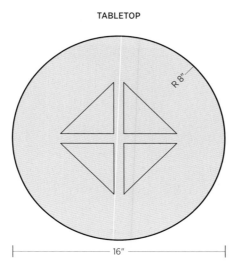

R 8"

|———— 16" ————|

SHELF

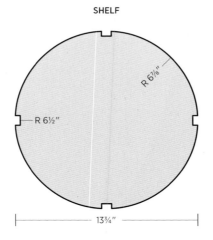

R 6⅞"

R 6½"

|———— 13¾" ————|

Cutting Diagram

the thickness of the plywood stock. Cut out the notches with the jigsaw. Then cut a slit down through the base of the top notch in leg A; this allows you to fit the legs together for the assembly.

Cut out the tabletop and shelf, using the jigsaw. Also cut out the four notches on the shelf.

3. Preassemble the stand.

Assemble the legs (without the shelf) by sliding leg B down through the slot at the top of leg A and then interlocking the notches. Check to see if the four legs sit flat. If not, slightly deepen the notches.

Disassemble the legs. Position the shelf so two of the small notches fit around the sides of leg B. Then fit the legs back together, interlocking the leg and shelf notches. You have to rotate and slant the shelf and leg units to make the parts fit together, but it will work. If the fit is too tight, slightly deepen and widen the notches in the shelf.

Center the tabletop on top of the leg assembly, and trace along the top edges of the legs to mark their positions against the bottom face of the tabletop. Cut four triangular blocks from waste plywood; see the tabletop diagram. Install the blocks on the underside of the tabletop, following your traced lines, using glue and 1¼" drywall screws. Test-fit the top on the leg assembly; the spacing between the blocks should provide a snug fit. Disassemble the stand for finishing.

4. Finish the pieces.

Finish-sand all exposed surfaces of each piece, working up to 220-grit or finer sandpaper. Be careful not to round over the edges of the notches to ensure tight-fitting joints.

Finish the pieces as desired, then reassemble the table. Secure the tabletop to the leg assembly with a few drywall screws.

Note: You can use glue for a permanent final assembly, if you don't care about having the flexibility of knocking down the table for storage or moving. In most cases, it's best to glue and assemble the stand before applying a finish.

Tea Table

Designed by Jin Kim

The gracefully curved top and sweeping legs of this piece are made possible with lamination — face-gluing identical plywood pieces together so that the primary exposed surface is edge grain. One of several laminated designs in this book, the Tea Table is perhaps the best to start with because of its simple construction (the same designer also created the book's most ambitious laminated work, the Chaise Lounge, on page 100). Depending on the plywood you use, the table's top can have a highly variegated patterning, almost like animal stripes, created with standard 5-ply material (not counting the face and back veneers), while premium hardwood plywood, such as 13-ply Baltic birch, will yield a much more orderly, linear effect.

MATERIALS

- ☐ One 2 x 2-foot piece ¼" MDF
- ☐ One 4 x 4-foot sheet ¾" plywood
- ☐ Wood glue
- ☐ 4 x 4 or 2 x 4 lumber (for clamping; see step 4)
- ☐ One 9" length ½"-diam. hardwood dowel
- ☐ Finish materials (see step 9)

TOOLS

- ☐ Jigsaw
- ☐ Sandpaper (up to 220 grit)
- ☐ Router with flush-trimming bit (preferably top-bearing)
- ☐ Bar clamps
- ☐ Belt sander or palm sander (if available)
- ☐ Straightedge
- ☐ Square
- ☐ Drill press (if available)
- ☐ Drill with ½" straight bit (if not using a drill press)
- ☐ Level

1. Create the templates.

Following the template drawings on page 94, draw the profile of the top and leg pieces on ¼" MDF. Carefully cut out the templates with a jigsaw, making sure not to cut inside the marked lines; it's better to cut the pieces a little large and sand the cuts down to the lines than to cut too much.

Sand the edges of the templates so the curves are smooth and the edges are flat, without saw marks or irregularities. Any flaws in the templates will be transferred to each workpiece, so take the time to shape the templates just right.

2. Rough out the plywood parts.

Using the two templates, trace the profiles of all of the parts on the ¾" plywood stock. You need 19 top pieces and eight leg pieces total. Loosely "nest" the pieces in the layout to save material, but be sure to leave about ¼" between them to allow plenty of room for cutting.

Cut out each piece with a jigsaw, staying about ¹⁄₁₆" to ⅛" outside the cutting lines. These cuts don't have to be precise because you will clean up the pieces with a router in the next step.

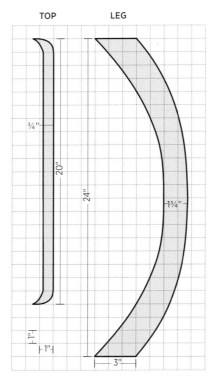

TOP   LEG

¾"

20"

24"

1¾"

1"
1"

3"

Template Drawings

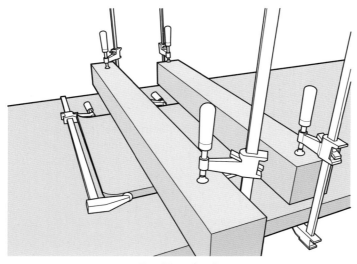

Top Clamping Setup

3. Rout the parts.

Cut a ⅝"-wide, 17"-long spacer strip from scrap plywood. Temporarily screw this to your work surface, near an accessible edge, to serve as a base for supporting the tabletop workpieces during routing.

To rout the top pieces, set each rough-cut workpiece on top of the spacer so the workpiece overhangs the spacer on all sides. Place the top template over the workpiece so it fits inside the workpiece's edges. Clamp the template and workpiece to the work surface with two clamps.

Using a router and top-bearing flush-trimming bit, rout the edges of each workpiece to match the template (see Template Routing, page 19). (If you happen to have only a bottom-bearing bit, simply place the template below the workpiece.)

Repeat the same process with the leg template to clean up the edges of the eight leg pieces, using one or more thin scraps for a spacer.

Note: You'll have to move the clamps to complete the routing of each piece. If you do this carefully, without moving the template, you shouldn't have to hot-glue or otherwise secure the template to each workpiece.

4. Glue up the parts.

Arrange the top pieces into three groups of roughly equal numbers (you'll need three clamps for each group). Apply wood glue to the inside face of each piece and press it against the next piece in the group, making sure all edges are flush. Repeat to glue up all of the pieces in the group, then clamp them all together with three evenly spaced bar clamps. Leave the clamps in place for at least the minimum time recommended by the glue manufacturer. Glue up the remaining two groups in turn.

After all three groups of top pieces have dried overnight, glue the groups together and clamp them laterally (as before) with three clamps. Also clamp them vertically, using a pair of straight 4 x 4s (or 2 x 4s on edge), as shown in the illustration at the left. Make sure the top surfaces of the groups are all flush. Let the glue dry overnight.

Glue the leg pieces together in pairs to create four 1½"-thick legs. Clamp the pairs with three or more clamps; you can also clamp two pairs at a time. Let the leg assemblies dry overnight.

5. Sand the top and legs.

Secure the top faceup on your work surface, and use a belt sander to smooth its top surface. Be careful not to remove too much material, misshape the curved ends, or dull the pointed edges of the top. If you don't have a belt sander, you can use a palm sander or a simple hand-sanding block. As you work, check the top surface with a straightedge to make sure it is perfectly flat.

Flip the top over and set it onto some scrap material so the pointed edges are above the work surface. Sand the bottom surface smooth and flat. Finish by hand-sanding the edges and curves of the top.

Gang the four legs together with clamps so all edges are aligned. Sand the surfaces so they are flush with one another and smooth to the touch.

6. Drill the dowel holes.

With the legs still ganged together, measure and mark the center of one leg along its length, on the back edge of the leg. The center will be at the apex of the curve. Use a square to draw a light pencil line through this mark, transferring the center mark to all the legs.

On two of the legs, make a second mark 5/16" *up* from the centerline. On the other two legs, make a mark 5/16" *down* from the line. Separate the legs, and mark the center along the thickness of each leg, intersecting the second marks. These intersections represent the center of each dowel hole.

The dowel holes must be drilled perfectly straight, so the best tool for this is a drill press. If you don't have access to one, you can use a portable drill, but be careful to hold the drill perfectly plumb as you make the holes. Drill the holes at the marked locations, using a ½" bit, making each hole 1" deep.

7. Test-assemble the table.

Cut two lengths of ½" dowel at 4¼". Round over the cut edges slightly with sandpaper so they'll fit into the leg holes. Stand the legs upright on a level surface, and using the dowels, fit the legs together in two opposing pairs. The dowels will cross in the center of the assembly with a ⅛" gap between them. Position each pair of opposing legs so they are 2½" apart at the apex of the curves.

Center the tabletop on top of the legs. Check the top with a level. Make any adjustments needed so that the legs stand squarely on the work surface and the tabletop is level and sits flush on top of each leg. Mark the legs' positions on the bottom surface of the tabletop, then disassemble the table.

8. Assemble the table.

Coat the first ¾" of each dowel end with wood glue. Reassemble the legs, as before. Each dowel end should penetrate about ⅞" into each leg. Flip the legs upside down so their top ends are resting flat on the work surface, and let the glue dry overnight.

Set the tabletop upside down on the work surface, using scrap spacers to keep the pointed edges elevated. Apply glue to the top ends of the legs, then flip the legs over and set the glued ends on the top, following the reference marks made in step 7. Set two 4 x 4s (or 2 x 4s on edge) across two adjacent legs, and clamp the setup to the work surface, as shown in the illustration below. Let the glue dry overnight.

9. Finish the table.

Finish-sand the table with 220-grit paper. Apply a clear protective finish, such as polyurethane or a furniture-grade oil or wax. If you'd like to stain the wood for coloring, be sure to test the stain on several pieces of scrap plywood. The alternating grain of plywood edges accepts stain much less consistently than the face veneers.

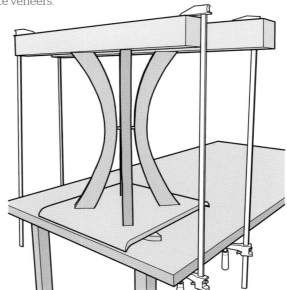

Leg Clamping Setup

Reluctance Sofa Table

Designed by Philip Schmidt

The sofa table exists primarily because no one wants to look at the back of a couch. And granted, it's a handy place for reading lamps and perhaps some photos or display-worthy books. But the problem, for some of us at least, is that a sofa table feels a little too traditional and grown-up, sort of like joining a country club or driving an automatic. Thus the reluctance. This design is one humble attempt at having a sofa table that does its primary job of hiding the sofa without crossing any major style barriers. It even has a drawer for holding things like comics and music magazines — because you're still cool even though you've learned how to decorate.

MATERIALS

- ☐ One 36" x 48" (or larger) piece ¾" hardwood plywood
- ☐ Wood glue
- ☐ One 24" x 48" piece (or larger) ½" MDF or plywood
- ☐ 4d (1½") finish nails
- ☐ Finish materials (see step 7)
- ☐ ⅞" wood screws
- ☐ Four hairpin table legs with mounting screws

TOOLS

- ☐ Circular saw with straightedge guide
- ☐ Table saw and miter saw (if not using circular saw)
- ☐ Router with ½" or larger straight bit
- ☐ Clamps
- ☐ Square
- ☐ Jigsaw with very-fine-tooth wood blade
- ☐ Drill with pilot bits
- ☐ Hammer
- ☐ Nail set
- ☐ Sandpaper (up to 220 grit)

1. Cut the case parts.

The case is the rectangular box that serves as both the tabletop surface and the drawer cabinet. Cut the case parts from ¾" plywood, using a circular saw and a straightedge guide (or a table saw and miter saw, if available). Cut the top and bottom pieces at 12" x 48" each, and cut the two sides at 4¼" x 12" each; see the case plan drawing on page 98.

The case also has a ¾" plywood back panel, at approximately 3½" x 46½". You will cut this to fit the rear opening of the case after it's assembled.

2. Mill the rabbets.

The case is assembled with glued rabbet joints, which are stronger than butt joints and add a nice visible construction detail. Mill the rabbets with a router and a ½" or larger straight bit. Set up a straightedge guide to control the router, and mill a ⅜"-deep, ¾"-wide rabbet into the inside face of the top and bottom panels, as shown in the case plan drawing.

Test-fit the rabbets with the side pieces, and make any necessary adjustments for clean, tight joints.

Note: The width of the rabbets should match the actual thickness of the plywood stock; adjust the width as needed to fit your material.

3. Glue up the case.

Apply wood glue to the mating edges of the rabbet joints, assemble the case, and clamp it securely. Check the assembly carefully with a square to make sure all the pieces are at 90 degrees. Let the glue dry overnight.

4. Cut and install the case back.

Measure the opening at the back of the case, and cut the back panel to fit. Test-fit the panel in the case, and make any necessary adjustments.

In the table shown here, the back panel is set in from the rear edges of the case, creating a slight reveal. This adds some visual interest and gives the assembly a more finished look. It also helps hide any imperfections in the joints along the edges of the back panel. To create a reveal, mark the inside faces of the case with light pencil lines, ³⁄₁₆" in from the rear edges (or as desired). Make another set of pencil lines ¾" in from the first. Apply glue to the case parts, staying in between the two sets of lines. Slip the back panel into place until its rear face is on the reveal lines. Let the glue dry overnight.

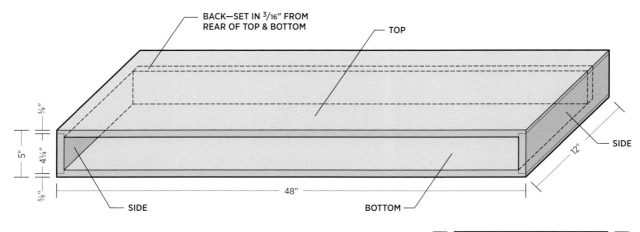

BACK—SET IN $3/16''$ FROM REAR OF TOP & BOTTOM

TOP

SIDE

$3/8''$

$5''$ $4\frac{1}{4}''$

$3/8''$

SIDE

48"

12"

BOTTOM

Case Plan

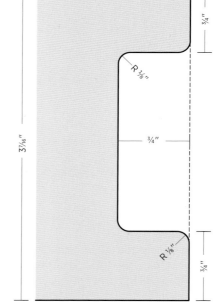

$3\frac{7}{16}''$

$3/4''$

$R\frac{1}{8}''$

$3/4''$

$3/4''$

$R\frac{1}{8}''$

$3/4''$

Drawer Front Detail

5. Cut the drawer front.

Like the back panel, the drawer front is cut to fit the dimensions of the case, minus a little bit for clearance. Measure the front opening of the case. Cut the drawer front from ¾" plywood so that its width is $\frac{1}{16}$" smaller than the height of the opening and its length is ⅛" shorter than the width of the opening.

Side cutouts on each end of the drawer front serve as pulls for grasping the drawer; see the illustration at lower right. If desired, you can leave the ends square and install prefab pulls instead. To make the cutouts, draw the profiles on the ends of the drawer front, following the drawer front detail drawing. Cut out the profiles with a jigsaw and a very-fine-tooth blade.

6. Build the drawer box.

The drawer box is made with ½" MDF or plywood. Cut the box parts as follows:

- Front and back: $2^{11}/_{16}$" x 42⅞"
- Sides: $2^{11}/_{16}$" x 10⅛"
- Bottom: 10⅛" x 42⅞"

Note: In use, the drawer will contact the back panel of the case when pushed in all the way. The dimensions for the sides and bottom of the drawer box shown here provide for a ³⁄₁₆" reveal at the front of the case when the drawer is pushed in. You can adjust the depth of the drawer box as desired for a different reveal or none at all.

Following the drawer plan drawing below, assemble the drawer box with glue, and clamp it securely. Drill pilot holes and fasten all the joints with 4d finish nails, setting the nail heads slightly below the wood surface with a nail set. Let the glue dry overnight.

7. Finish the case and drawer front.

Finish-sand the case and drawer front, working up to 220-grit or finer sandpaper. Finish the pieces as desired. For a decorative touch, stain the drawer front to contrast with the case, or vice versa, before adding a protective topcoat. Because the table will likely hold drinks and plates, it's a good idea to use a moisture- and stain-resistant finish like polyurethane. Let the finish dry completely.

8. Mount the drawer front.

Clamp the drawer front to the drawer box so it overhangs the front of the box equally on both ends and sits about $1/32$" up from the box bottom. The bottom offset centers the front within the case opening. Drill two pilot holes through the drawer box and into the back of the drawer front, and tack the front on with two $7/8$" screws.

Test-fit the drawer in the case, checking for even reveals around the drawer front. Adjust the front's position, if necessary, then secure the front to the box with four more screws driven through pilot holes.

9. Install the legs.

Position the legs on the bottom of the case so they are spaced evenly on all sides. For stability, the legs should be as close as practical to the front and rear of the case. Mark the hole locations, drill pilot holes, and mount the legs with wood screws (make sure the screws won't protrude through the bottom of the case).

Note: You can buy vintage hairpin legs (like those used here) in custom sizes and a few different styles (see Resources).

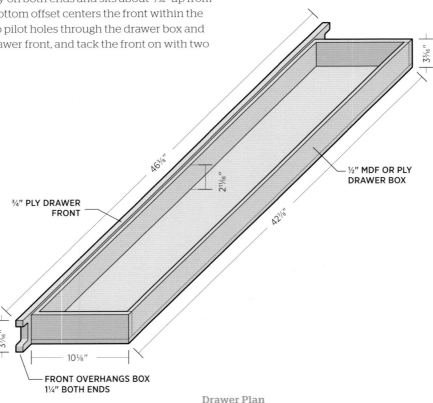

3³⁄₁₆"

½" MDF OR PLY
DRAWER BOX

46³⁄₈"

2¹¹⁄₁₆"

42⁷⁄₈"

¾" PLY DRAWER
FRONT

3⁷⁄₁₆"

10⅛"

FRONT OVERHANGS BOX
1¼" BOTH ENDS

Drawer Plan

Plywood as . . .
A showcase of inspired pieces and
the stories behind them

. . . redefined icon

Chaise

by Lauren Von Dehsen

When I started this project, I was inspired by furniture that merges historical forms with modern materials, techniques, and adaptations. At the time I was obsessed (and still am) with the Cinderella Table (designed by Jeroen Verhoeven), which takes two orthographic outlines of classic table profiles set on adjacent sides of a rectangular prism. The outlines were lofted together in a CAD environment, and the resulting table was milled hollow with a CNC machine. To me, this represents a perfect marriage between historical form and modern techniques and simplicity.

I spent a long time looking at iconic pieces from furniture movements throughout history, as well as modern design blogs, to survey what exists. Through that process I kept gravitating back to the chaise lounge, whether it be Victorian, Egyptian, or something else. The curves and asymmetric form felt like a unique starting point.

My self-assigned task was to create the illusion of the chaise lounge using only wood. I could not use upholstery, and I did not want to focus on ornate details. Rather, I wanted to capture the essence of the chaise through its overall curves and form. Plywood was ideal because it would be strong enough to withstand the curved shapes. Since plywood has grain running in both directions, I had the freedom to cut almost any shape without sacrificing strength.

My first focus was capturing the defining curves of the piece. I developed the profile of the piece through hand drawings and Adobe Illustrator drawings (vector images). I also made many doll-sized models with rough part shapes to get a sense of the overall form and to refine my design-informed decisions.

To create the finished piece, I cut the refined shapes from acrylic, using a laser cutter. I used these as router templates to do the initial shaping on all of the final parts, ensuring the pieces were identical to one another. Next, I established the curved piece by which the parts are suspended and made the secondary cuts to the seat panel parts to accommodate that same curve. At the same time, I formed the connector pieces and made the notches for all joints so that the pieces interlock like a balsa-wood model.

Once all of the parts were cut, I devoted considerable time to fitting each joint (every joint was a custom match). After dry-fitting each component, I gave it a final sanding and sealed it with wipe-on polyurethane.

Eventually, I think this chaise will need cushions. I would like to add two simple but large bolster pillows to either end. I would like to avoid adding a long rectangular pad across the seat, so as not to cover up important details.

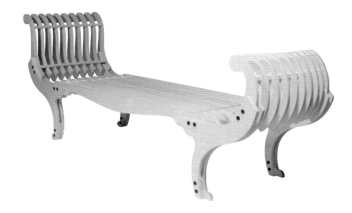

Seating

———

Sit. Perch. Recline. Pose. Take a load off.
Twelve pieces that prove seating can be equal parts practical and sculptural.

Incurvated

Designed by Marcus Papay

Bending plywood has long been an important part of modernist furniture making, but the process of bent lamination — gluing together thin plywood layers around a rigid form — is beyond the scope of this book. Faced with this limitation, the designer of this piece devised a way to bend full-thickness plywood without lamination. By making a regular series of saw cuts, or *kerfs,* on the underside of the seat panel, he was able to reduce the rigidity of the plywood, allowing the seat to flex slightly. The elegantly curved seat, combined with the judicious and artistic use of metals, makes this a truly special piece, something you will fully appreciate not just in the finished product itself but also in the process of creating it.

See page 280 for another work by Marcus Papay.

MATERIALS

- ☐ One 2 x 3-foot piece ½" Baltic birch or similar hardwood plywood
- ☐ One 2" x 10" piece ⅛" aluminum plate
- ☐ One 18" length ½" aluminum rod
- ☐ One 3" length 8-32 all-thread rod
- ☐ Eight 1" #10 square-drive, flat-head wood screws
- ☐ Wood glue
- ☐ Finish materials

TOOLS

- ☐ Circular saw with straightedge guide or table saw
- ☐ Router with ½" straight bit (must equal plywood thickness) or table saw with dado blade
- ☐ Straightedge or right-angle jig (for router)
- ☐ Jigsaw or band saw
- ☐ Sandpaper (up to 400 grit)
- ☐ Drill with:
  - ☐ ¼" straight bit (for metal)
  - ☐ Countersink bit (for metal)
  - ☐ #29 drill bit (for tap hole in metal)
  - ☐ 8-32 tap bit
  - ☐ ½" Forstner bit
- ☐ Die grinder polish system (if available)
- ☐ Hacksaw
- ☐ Metal file
- ☐ Clamps

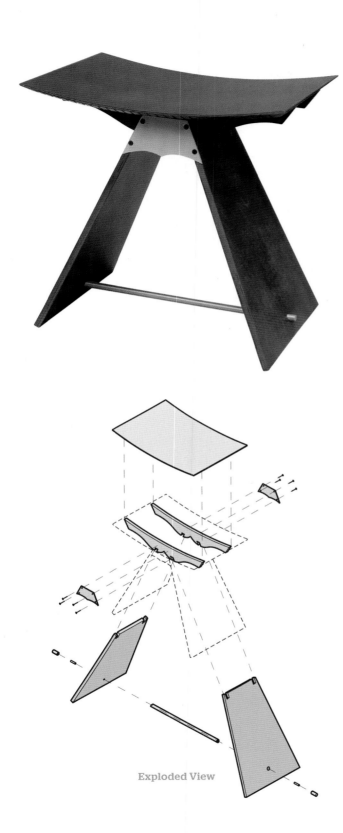

Exploded View

1. Cut the plywood parts.

Cut the plywood pieces to their overall dimensions, following the cutting diagram on page 104. These include:

- 1 top (seat) at 12" x 18¼"

- 2 legs at 12" x 17½" overall, with the sides tapered at 8 degrees toward the top

- 2 aprons at 3" x 17½" overall

Do not cut the apron contours at this time; leave them as rectangular pieces. Use a circular saw and straightedge guide or a table saw to ensure clean, straight cuts.

When laying out the top, it's critical that the grain of the face veneers runs parallel to the short sides (front to back, on the seat); this allows the plywood to bend properly.

2. Prepare the top.

The top gets a 15-degree chamfer on all of its bottom-face edges, followed by the kerf cuts for bending the piece. It also gets two ½"-wide, ⅛"-deep dadoes to receive the aprons.

Cut the chamfers with a circular saw and straightedge guide or (preferably) a table saw. The chamfers should stop ⅛" from the top face of the panel. This leaves you with a ⅛"-thick band of square-cut edge at the top, and the rest of the edge's thickness is beveled at 15 degrees.

To make the kerfs, first lay out the cuts on the bottom face of the top. Draw a line from front to back (parallel to the short edges) at the precise center of the piece. To each side of the centerline, draw 14 parallel lines spaced $^9/_{16}$" on center. You should have 29 lines total, with the outside lines about 1" from the ends of the piece. Set the circular saw depth at ⅜", and cut down the center of each line, using a square or straightedge to ensure straight cuts. You can also make the kerfs with a table saw (see Making Kerf Cuts with a Table Saw, page 105).

To mill the dadoes for the aprons, mark the center of the top piece across its short dimension. Then make a mark 2¾" to each side of the center. Draw lines down the length of the piece at the outer marks; these represent the inside edges of the dadoes, and they should be 5½" apart. Set up a straightedge guide, and mill the dadoes with a router and a ½" straight bit (or use a table saw and dado blade). The dadoes run the full length of the piece.

Note: For the dadoes, the router bit must be equal to or slightly smaller than the plywood's thickness. If your stock measures less than ½", use a smaller bit for a snug fit (you might have to sand the aprons a bit).

3. Cut the half-lap notches.

The aprons and legs fit together with half-lap joints created with two ½"-wide, ⅞"-deep notches in each leg and apron piece, as shown in the cutting diagram. You can cut these notches with a router and straight bit or a table saw and dado blade.

Mark the notches on the faces of the pieces, following the diagram. To use a router, clamp each leg vertically to the edge of a bench, using a sacrificial backerboard between the bench and workpiece to prevent tearout. Then use a straightedge or right-angle jig to guide the router.

Rout the notches on the aprons using the same technique, but clamp the workpiece at a 65-degree angle.

4. Cut the apron profiles.

Lay out the apron profile on one of the apron pieces following the template in the cutting diagram. Clamp the two aprons together and cut out the profile on both pieces at once with a jigsaw or band saw. Sand the edges to smooth the curves and remove any saw marks.

5. Cut the upper braces.

Lay out the profile of the upper braces on ⅛" aluminum stock, following the template in the cutting diagram. Cut the profiles with a jigsaw or band saw.

Drill a hole for a wood screw at each corner of the upper braces, using a ¼" bit and a portable drill or a drill press; the holes should be ¼" from the edges of the braces. Countersink the holes to fit the taper depth of the wood screws' heads, so the flat heads will sit flush with the surface. Sand the braces, working up to 400-grit sandpaper for a polished look. (You can also use a die grinder polish system, if available.)

Note: Be sure to turn off your dust collector when cutting metal with a band saw; hot metal mixing with saw dust is a potential fire hazard.

6. Assemble the legs and braces.

Using a ¼" straight bit, drill a hole through each leg for the all-thread pieces of the lower brace, as shown in the cutting diagram and the lower brace detail drawing. These holes are centered, 2½" up from the bottom edge of the leg, and driven at a 65-degree angle so they will be level when the legs are installed.

Using a ½" Forstner bit, counterbore the hole on the outside of each leg for the ½"-diameter connector nut to sit in (see A Forstner Drilling Jig, page 30, for advice on how to create a simple jig for drilling with a Forstner bit).

Cut 1" off each end of the ½" aluminum rod for the connector nut pieces, using a hacksaw. Then cut the same rod to length at 14¾" to create the lower brace, mitering the ends at 65 degrees, as shown in the lower brace detail drawing. The mitered ends should fit flush against the insides of the legs; you may need to file the cuts for a good fit.

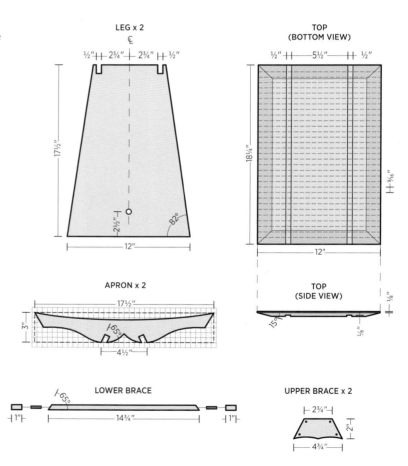

Cutting Diagram

Secure each connector nut in a bench vise or drill press base. Drill a ⅜"-deep tap hole with a #29 bit, then thread the inside of the hole with an 8-32 tap. Do the same with each end of the lower brace rod. (If you also drill a ⅛"-diameter hole into the side of each connecting nut, perpendicular to its length, when you assemble the table, you can tighten the nuts with a ⅛" steel rod or punch.) Use the hacksaw to cut two 1" lengths of 8-32 all-thread rod for joining the lower brace to the connector nuts at each end.

Assemble the legs, aprons, and upper braces by fitting the aprons and legs together at the half-lap joints and mounting the upper braces with screws. As an optional step that's definitely worth doing, you can cut ⅛"-deep mortises into the legs to receive the upper braces, using a jigsaw or band saw and a sharp chisel. This allows the braces to be flush with the legs' edges.

Install the lower brace and connector nuts as shown in the drawing at left.

7. Glue the top.
Finish-sand the aprons and top, making sure the aprons fit snugly into the top's dadoes. With the aprons and legs assembled, apply glue to the dadoes on the bottom of the top piece and clamp the top to the aprons, making sure the top is centered on the aprons. First clamp at the center of the top so the aprons bottom out in the dadoes, then add more clamps as needed, working from the center out toward the ends. Let the glue dry completely.

8. Finish the wood parts.
Disassemble the legs from the upper braces. Finish-sand the legs, and apply the finish of your choice to the legs, aprons, and top. In the project shown here, the wood was finished with Deft green-tinted lacquer applied with an HVLP (high volume, low pressure) spray gun. Reassemble all parts after the finish has cured.

LOWER BRACE

THREADED ROD

CONNECTOR NUT COUNTERSUNK INTO LEG PANEL

Lower Brace Detail

Shop Tip

Making Kerf Cuts with a Table Saw

To cut the kerfs in Incurvated's top with a table saw and sled, you'll want to make a jig:

Cut a rectangular piece of MDF to equal the width of the sled. Make a ⅛" cut in the MDF. Then cut a strip of ⅛"-thick wood to length at 1½" to sit in the kerf of the MDF. Offset this stop at 9⁄16" (distance between kerf cuts) from the blade and clamp the jig to the sled. Once you make the first kerf in the top piece, fit the kerf over the wood strip to set the spacing for the next cut, and so on.

Flat Pack Stool

Designed by Alexis Liu

Flat Pack Stool is furniture design at an inspired, elemental level. The stool consists of three flat plywood parts that slot together in two easy steps. Yet the simplicity of the design still leaves ample room for creativity. As shown here, the designer used paint to create a trompe l'oeil image of a rustic wooden stool, and she encourages builders to experiment with other media, such as photographs or etching, for different effects. Knocked down, a complete four-piece set of these stools can be stashed in a kitchen drawer, under a couch, or on a bookshelf. Simply inspired.

MATERIALS

☐ One 3 x 3-foot piece ½" plywood

☐ Finish materials (see step 4)

TOOLS

☐ Circular saw with straightedge guide or table saw

☐ Jigsaw

☐ Router with homemade trammel (page 18) and straight bit (if available)

☐ Flat wood file

☐ Sandpaper (up to 220 grit)

1. Cut the parts.

Using a circular saw with a straightedge guide or a table saw, cut the two leg pieces to size at 13" x 18".

The top piece is a 13"-diameter disk. It's best to cut this with a jigsaw, followed by a router and trammel (see Two Easy Ways to Cut a Circle, page 18). If you don't have a router, you can make the final cut with a jigsaw and sand the cut edges to smooth the curve and remove any saw marks.

2. Make the cutouts and slots.

As shown in the cutting diagram, the legs get a ½"-deep, 10"-long cutout in their bottom edges, to create "feet." The top edges of the legs get ½"-deep, 7"-long cutouts that accept the solid center of the stool's top and create the tabs for joining with the top. Each leg also gets a ½"-wide, 8½"-long slot for joining with the other leg. Note that one leg's slot is made from the top down, and the other's is made from the bottom up. All the slots and cutouts are centered side-to-side on the legs. The disk gets four evenly spaced slots that are each ½" wide and 3" long.

With the exception of the feet cutouts, all the slots and cutouts must match the exact thickness of your plywood stock, which is likely to be slightly less than the ½" shown in the diagrams. Measure your stock in several places to determine the proper width/depth for your slots and cutouts.

Mark the slots and cutouts on the legs and top, and make the cuts with a jigsaw. Just to be safe, cut on the inside of the cut lines ("leave the line") to ensure a snug fit. At the bottoms of the slots, turn the saw blade as needed to remove most of the waste material, then clean up the corners with a flat (square-edged) file.

3. Test-assemble the stool.

Test-fit the parts by slotting the legs together and then fitting the top over the leg tabs. The pieces should fit together snugly but easily. File and/or sand any slots or cutouts as needed for a proper fit. The tops of the leg tabs should be flush with the top surface of the top piece.

4. Finish the stool.

Finish-sand the parts, working up to 220-grit or finer sandpaper. Sand a slight roundover on the outer edges of the top, for comfort.

Finish the parts as desired. For a decorative painted finish, lightly sketch the design with a pencil first, then add the paint. Whether you paint, stain, or leave the wood natural, it's a good idea to add a protective clear topcoat to make the surface washable and durable.

Let all finishes dry thoroughly before assembling the stool.

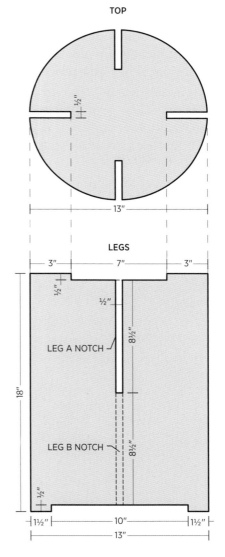

Cutting Diagrams

TAB-1 Chair

Designed by Brian DuBois

The TAB-1 Chair is one of several pieces in this book that feature "laminated" plywood construction — meaning, in this context, that the broadest wood surfaces are made up of plywood pieces set on edge and glued face-to-face. If you do this with solid wood, you almost invariably end up with butcher block; with plywood, however, the result is far more decorative and distinctive. Lamination is a key element of this chair design both aesthetically and practically, allowing you to create a truly high-end look through very simple, repeatable processes.

See page 80 for another work by Brian DuBois.

MATERIALS

- ☐ ¾" Baltic birch plywood (one full 5 x 5-foot sheet is more than enough for three chairs)
- ☐ Three 48" lengths ½"-diam. round birch dowels
- ☐ Four ¼" (inside diam.) #20 threaded inserts
- ☐ Two-part epoxy
- ☐ Wood glue
- ☐ Finish materials (see step 10)
- ☐ One 2 x 2-foot sheet ¼" aluminum plate
- ☐ Eight ¼" x 2½" #20 socket-head bolts with washers and nuts, in black oxide finish
- ☐ Four ¼" x 1½" #20 socket-head bolts with washers, in black oxide finish

TOOLS

- ☐ Table saw or circular saw with straightedge guide
- ☐ Miter saw or miter box and backsaw (optional)
- ☐ Drill or drill press with:
    - ☐ ¼" straight bit
    - ☐ ½" straight bit
- ☐ Jigsaw with:
    - ☐ Wood blade
    - ☐ Bimetal blade
- ☐ Rubber mallet
- ☐ Clamps
- ☐ Japanese flush-cutting saw or similar saw
- ☐ Belt sander or other portable sander
- ☐ Sandpaper (including 150 grit)
- ☐ Metal file
- ☐ Allen wrench (for socket-head bolts)

TAB-1 Chair   109

1. Rip the seat strips.

The plywood seat is made up of 23 strips of plywood that are 1½" wide. Start by ripping eight full-length, 1½"-wide pieces from a 5 x 5-foot sheet of Baltic birch. Use a table saw or a circular saw with a straightedge guide to ensure clean, straight cuts.

2. Cut the seat strips to length.

The best way to cut the seat strips to length is to use a power miter saw set up with a stop block for quick and accurate production cuts. If you don't have a miter saw, you can simply mark each piece for length and make the cuts with a hand miter box and back saw or a circular saw. Cut the 1½" strips into 21 pieces at 17" long and two pieces at 10 $^{11}\!/_{16}$" long; see the cutting diagram on page 110.

3. Drill the seat slat holes.

Select two 17" pieces with a factory edge. These will become your templates for drilling the remaining long seat pieces. Following the cutting diagram, carefully lay out the holes for seat strip B, orienting the factory edge at the top. Mark the piece with a "B," and mark the top edge. Drill the holes as shown, keeping the drill as plumb as possible (you can also use a portable drill stand or a drill press to ensure straight holes). Repeat the process with the other 17" piece to create a template for side strip A. Use these templates to drill a total of six B pieces and 13 A pieces. Before drilling each piece, mark the better long edge as the top, then lay the template over the undrilled piece, with their top edges and ends aligned, and clamp the two pieces together.

Finally, drill the holes in the two C pieces and two D pieces, as shown in the cutting diagram.

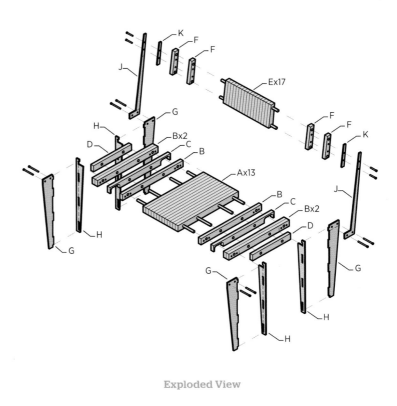

Exploded View

4. Make the cutouts in the C pieces.

Lay out and cut the two matching cutouts near the ends of each C piece, using a jigsaw to make the cuts (see How to Mark & Cut Curves, page 16). These cutouts create access holes for tightening the leg hardware.

5. Cut and drill the backrest pieces.

There are 21 backrest strips: 17 are E pieces and four are F pieces. All have the same dimensions, and each gets two ½" holes for dowels. The F pieces also get two ¼" holes for hardware. Because of their angled ends and front edges, these pieces must be cut individually. You can do this in a couple of ways:

• Rip a long piece of plywood stock at about 6" wide. Use a miter saw to crosscut the front and back edges of each piece, then go back and make the end cuts (these are at the same angle, so you can just turn the piece around for the second cut).

• Lay out each piece using a factory (or straight-cut) edge of stock as the straight back edge of the pieces. Make the angled front cut with a circular saw, then cut the ends with the circular saw or a miter box and back saw.

With all of the pieces cut to size, use the template technique outlined in step 3 to drill the holes in these E and F pieces.

6. Prepare the dowels.

Arrange all the pieces of the seat (A, B, C, and D) as they will be installed; see the exploded-view drawing on page 109. Gang them together tightly and measure across the assembly (from side to side). Cut four ½"-diameter dowels to this dimension plus about 2". Repeat the same process to cut two dowels to size for the backrest. Sand the dowels as needed so they fit snugly but easily into the ½" holes in the plywood pieces.

Cutting Diagram for Seat and Backrest Pieces

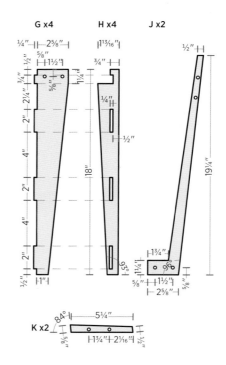

Cutting Diagram for Aluminum Parts

TAB-1 Chair   111

7. Install the threaded inserts.

The backrest is secured with socket-head bolts and threaded inserts. The inserts are epoxied into two of the F pieces; they will be set second in from each end of the backrest assembly. Measure the outside diameter of the threaded inserts, and redrill the ¼" holes in two of the F pieces to match the inserts. Install the inserts in the holes using two-part epoxy.

8. Complete the glue-up.

Arrange the parts for the seat in order of installation. Starting at one side of the seat, insert the dowels into the first 17" A piece. Apply glue to the inside face of this piece, then slip the next A piece down over the dowels and onto the first piece (you can use a rubber mallet for assistance). Work quickly in this manner to glue up the remaining long pieces, then add the two shorter D pieces at the ends. Clamp the assembly and let the glue dry. Follow the same process to glue up the backrest.

9. Sand the seat and backrest.

Carefully trim the dowel ends flush to the outside pieces of the seat and backrest assemblies, using a Japanese flush-cutting saw or other handsaw without "set" teeth (teeth that angle out to the side). Sand the assemblies so they are smooth across the lamination, using a belt sander (on the plywood edges only, not the veneer faces) or another type of power sander. Finish with hand sanding.

Shop Tip

Cutting and Drilling Metal

When cutting and drilling metal, heat is a primary concern. Overheating can melt the metal you're working with and quickly ruin a drill bit or muddle a clean cut. To minimize heat buildup, run your tool at slow speeds, and apply even pressure while letting the blade or bit do the work. You'll know things are getting too hot when you see smoke; it's time to hold off for a moment, then start again at a slower speed. You can also add a few drops of lubricant (such as 3-IN-ONE oil) to the bit's point or the cutting line (when using a jigsaw), and this is fine to do while the tool is going. Also, set your jigsaw for zero orbit, so the blade moves straight up and down.

10. Stain and finish the seat and backrest.

Apply stain and/or surface finish to all wood surfaces, as desired. The project shown here was stained with Minwax stain in ebony. After the stain dried overnight, the pieces were sanded again with 220-grit sandpaper to remove some areas of stain. Then the pieces were finished with furniture wax.

11. Cut the aluminum parts.

Following the cutting diagram, cut pieces G (four total), H (four total), and J (two total) from ¼"-thick aluminum, using a jigsaw with a bimetal blade. Cut the two K pieces from any of the cut-off material from the other pieces. Leave the tabs on the G pieces a little long so you can file them down for a tight fit in the next step.

Note: If desired, you can have the aluminum parts cut at a local metal shop. This is an especially attractive option if you're making a whole set of four or six chairs.

12. Drill and fit the aluminum parts.

Drill the holes in the G, J, and K parts, as shown in the cutting diagram, making sure they line up with the corresponding holes in the chair seat and backrest. Select mating pairs of G and H parts for the legs. Working with one pair at a time, file the tabs on the G piece to fit tightly into the slots on the H piece. You will press the parts together mechanically, so the joints should be a little too tight to close by hand.

13. Assemble and finish the aluminum parts.

Use a bench vise (with blocking to prevent damage to the metal) to press each of the leg pairs together. To create the "raw" look as shown in this project, sand all the metal parts with 150-grit sandpaper, as desired. Be sure to remove any sharp edges and burrs, and soften the edges of the leg ends to prevent them from scratching the floor.

14. Assemble the chair.

Secure the legs and back uprights (J pieces) to the seat with 2½" socket-head screws, using washers and nuts tightened from underneath the seat. Secure the backrest to the uprights with 1½" socket-head bolts driven into the threaded inserts, placing the washers against the bolt heads. Tighten the bolts with an Allen wrench.

Sto#2

Designed by Sean Kelly

Sto was inspired by a tree — not as a building material but as the perfect place to recline with a book. Sto also has places for stowing books, including a shelf and an open storage area inside the bench frame. And it has a quilted pad that rolls down over the backrest and onto the floor. With the pad rolled up, Sto's top makes a great bench-style seat. The Sto shown here is dubbed #2 because it's a home-shop version of the original Sto, whose parts were cut on a CNC machine. Like a handheld router, a CNC uses round cutting bits that can't make square inside corners, necessitating slight overcuts for many joints and, in some cases, adding an interesting design element to the finished piece. This effect is mimicked in Sto#2, for both practical and aesthetic reasons.

MATERIALS

- ☐ One 4 x 8-foot sheet ½" Baltic birch or other hardwood plywood
- ☐ One 4 x 8-foot sheet ½" standard plywood (for sacrificial work surface)
- ☐ One 24" length 1¼"-diam. hardwood dowel
- ☐ One 40" length ⅝"-diam. hardwood dowel (or two 24" lengths)
- ☐ One 36" length 1"-diam. hardwood dowel
- ☐ Glue (optional)
- ☐ Finish materials (see step 10)
- ☐ 3 yards duck cloth (in color of choice)
- ☐ Zipper
- ☐ Quilt batting

TOOLS

- ☐ Circular saw
- ☐ Straightedge guide for saws
- ☐ Square
- ☐ Clamps
- ☐ Drill with:
    - ☐ ½" Forstner or self-feeding spade bit
    - ☐ 1" Forstner or self-feeding spade bit
    - ☐ 1¼" Forstner or self-feeding spade bit
    - ☐ 2" Forstner or self-feeding spade bit
- ☐ Jigsaw
- ☐ Compass
- ☐ Handsaw
- ☐ Router with ⅛" roundover bit (if available)
- ☐ Sandpaper (up to 220 grit)
- ☐ Pins or clips (for sewing pad)
- ☐ Sewing machine
- ☐ Clothes iron

1. Cut the plywood workpieces.

Using a circular saw and a straightedge guide, cut one piece of ½" birch plywood at 31⅝" x 48", using the factory edge for the 48" side. Cut this into two pieces at 22" x 31⅝". Label these pieces A and B.

Cut two more pieces from the panel at 17" x 48", and label these C and D.

2. Mark the holes.

You will mark and drill all the holes (for slat joints, dowels, and slots) in the workpieces before making the saw cuts.

Lay out the holes on the A, B, and C pieces, as shown in the drilling template at right. Use a straightedge to draw the long lines (parallel to the adjacent edges), and use a combination square or other right-angle square with a lipped flange to mark the crosshairs on the long lines and to mark the centers of the holes. Note the four hole sizes specified in the drawings: ¼, ½, 1¼, and 2". To prevent mistakes, it's a good idea to label each hole (or series of holes) with the specified diameter (¼, ½, and so on).

3. Drill the holes.

Use the sacrificial plywood panel as a backerboard for drilling all the holes and for making the saw cuts, as applicable. This helps support the pieces throughout the work and helps prevent tearout on the bottommost veneer. Clamp the workpieces to the sacrificial panel, close to the holes being drilled, to minimize tearout. Drill all holes with self-feeding spade bits or (if you have a drill press or Forstner drilling jig for portable drills) with Forstner bits.

Position piece A on top of B so all edges and corners are aligned, and clamp them both down to the work surface. Using a ½" bit, drill the eight pairs of joint holes along each side edge, starting with those 1" from the end. Start the drill slowly, and keep the tool steady as you drill straight down through both pieces.

Separate the two pieces. Drill the remaining pair of joint holes along each side edge of piece A. Then drill the four ½" holes forming a square in the center of A; these are for the handle cutouts. Drill the four ½" holes in the upper center of piece B; these are for cutouts that provide access for gripping the pad.

Position piece C on top of piece D, align all edges, and clamp them to the work surface. Drill the ¼" holes along the top, bottom, and left edges of the pieces. Then drill the four ½" holes in the upper right corner of the piece. Next drill the 1¼" holes near the top of the piece. (To drill the semicircle on the top edge, clamp a plywood scrap against the top edge of the workpiece, and center the hole on the seam between the pieces.) Finally, drill the six 2" holes; these will become the radiused corners of the large center cutouts (see step 6).

4. Cut the joint slots (A and B).

Use a jigsaw to cut straight lines between all of the joint hole pairs in pieces A and B; see the cutting template on page 116.

Working on one piece at a time, set up a straightedge guide parallel to one long (side) edge of the piece; this is to guide the jigsaw so you can quickly move from cut to cut. (Though if you prefer, you can simply freehand the cuts.) Make the cuts with a jigsaw and a fine-tooth blade (20 teeth per inch is good for minimizing tearout). Cut all the joint slots (holes along the side edges). You will complete the handle and access slot cutouts after cutting the slats.

5. Cut the slats and shelf pieces.

Clamp piece A on top of B so all edges are aligned, as before. Set up a straightedge guide to cut the first slat from the bottom of the pieces, as shown in the cutting template. The slat should be 3" wide after it's cut. Be sure to account for the saw's kerf — the material removed by the blade. The slats in the drawings are laid out for a ⅛" kerf, which is typical for circular saw blades.

Cut the first slat with a circular saw and a fine-tooth blade, cutting through both A and B pieces at once. Repeat this process to make seven more slat cuts, for a total of eight slats. Separate the pieces, then cut one more 3" slat from piece A. You should have 17 slats total, plus a 3½"-wide piece left over from A and a 6⅝"-wide piece from B.

On the 6⅝" piece left over from B, use the circular saw and straightedge guide to cut a saw blade's thickness from the long top edge (the one without the holes). Then use the jigsaw to cut a 1¾" x 1½" notch from each of the four corners, as shown in the cutting template. This is the completed front shelf piece. On the leftover A piece, cut a ¼" x 1½" notch from each corner. This is the completed rear shelf piece.

PIECE A

PIECE B

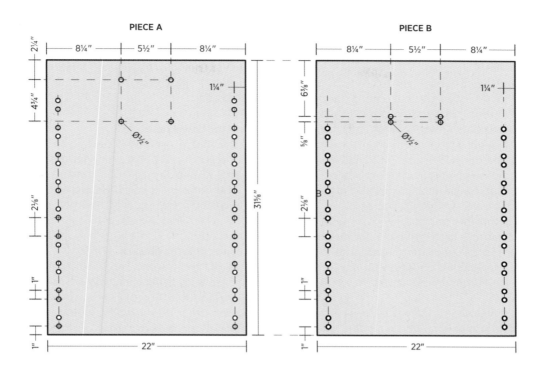

PIECE C

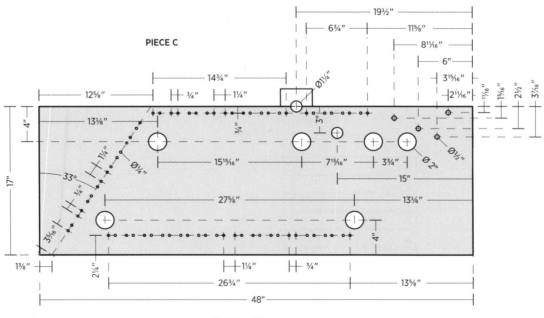

Drilling Diagrams

6. Cut the sides (C and D).

Position piece C on top of D, with all edges aligned, and clamp them down. Measure in ½" from the lower left corner of C and make a mark. Do the same at the upper right corner. From the lower left mark, draw a diagonal line up at a 57-degree angle to the top edge of C. Draw a parallel line (at the same angle) between the upper right mark and the bottom edge of the piece. Cut along the outside of each line, using the circular saw and straightedge guide.

Draw a 1" radius for rounding over the four corners of the cut side pieces, using a compass. Make the cuts with a jigsaw.

Using the jigsaw and straightedge, cut from the top edge to the edges of the ¼" holes. Then measure ½" from the top edge, and draw a line across all the joints. Cut off the ½" of material between the holes, again using a straightedge and jigsaw, leaving platforms for the slats to rest on. Repeat this process on the left (diagonal) edge of the side pieces.

Use the jigsaw and straightedge to cut out the area between all the 2" holes, paying close attention to the area below where the pad will be. To shape the tab between the two central 2" holes, use the compass to draw a 2"-diameter circle ⅛" in (toward the opposing hole) from each hole; at each corner of the tab, cut between the hole and circle, over one and under the other.

Repeat the process described above to complete the cuts for the slat platforms along the line of ¼" holes at the bottom of the interior cutout. Finally, cut between the two ½" hole pairs in the upper right corner of the sides to create the slots for the shelf pieces.

7. Drill the dowel holes.

Separate the pieces C and D and lay them down with their inside faces up. Measuring from each end of the bottom (interior) row of slat joints, make a mark at 1" below and 2" to the outside of the row. Drill a 1"-diameter hole ¼" deep at each mark, being careful not to drill through the piece. These holes will receive the ends of the 1" dowels for the assembly.

8. Cut and drill the dowels.

Secure a 1¼" dowel with scrap wood and clamps or a vise, and cut it to length at 24", using a handsaw. Next, cut a ⅝" dowel into two 8" lengths and one 20" length. Then cut two 19½" lengths of 1" dowel.

Secure the 24" dowel. Make a mark 2" in from each end. Drill a ⅝" hole through the dowel at each mark. These holes will receive the two 8"-long dowels to create the handles for rolling up the pad (see step 13).

9. Preassemble the bench.

Assemble the bench by standing up the sides and placing some slats across the tops and the bottoms for structure. Then insert

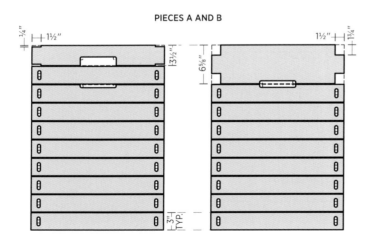

PIECES A AND B

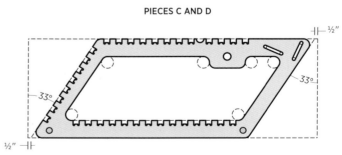

PIECES C AND D

the 1"-diameter dowels into the ¼"-deep holes in the side pieces, and add the shelf pieces by slipping their tabbed ends into the slots in the side pieces. Add the remaining slats. Fine-tune the fit of any joints as needed, sanding the mating edges of the pieces if the fit is too tight. The bench is designed for final assembly without glue, but gluing is an option. If you'd like to glue any joints, do so before adding the finish.

10. Finish the parts.

Disassemble the bench. Mill a slight roundover on all edges that will be exposed in the finished piece, using a router and ⅛" roundover bit (if available) or coarse sandpaper and a sanding block.

Finish-sand all the parts, working up to 220-grit or finer sandpaper. Finish the pieces as desired. The project shown here has a natural wax finish. Allow the finish to dry completely, and assemble the bench again.

11. Prepare the pad attachments.

As shown here, the finished pad is 18" wide and 6 feet long. Yours can be as long as you like. When cutting the cloth for your pad, add at least 2" of extra cloth on all sides for seaming; the pad cover will be turned inside out.

Cut two pieces of duck cloth to size at 22" x 76". Secure the pieces together with pins or clips, and set them aside. Cut two more pieces of cloth at 22" x 8"; these will become the looped ends for securing the pad to the dowels.

To create the first looped end, make a 2"-deep fold on each end of one 8" x 22" piece so that the fabric is 18" wide. Secure the folds with pins or clips, or just use your hands. Use a sewing machine to sew along each fold, staying as close to the edge as you feel comfortable. Fold the fabric over the 20"-long ⅝" dowel so the fabric ends are flush. Pinch the fabric together tightly over the dowel so the fold holds the dowel securely. Use pins or clips to secure the fabric, then slide the dowel out from the loop (you can also mark the fabric where the fold should be sewn). Sew the fabric sides together to complete the loop. When inserted into the loop, the dowel should protrude 1" from either side.

The second loop is similar to the first, but it uses a zipper instead of a sewn seam to secure the loop over the 24"-long 1¼" dowel. Fold and sew the 2" hems on the remaining 8" x 22" fabric piece, as before. Then fold the piece tightly over the dowel and mark it for the zipper location. The zipper pull should be facing

up. You may need to trim the excess fabric at the folds so it doesn't interfere with the dowel. The fabric should just cover the edge of the zipper without covering the teeth. Secure the zipper with pins or clips, and sew it in place, sewing through your pinch mark, the folds, and the zipper. The dowel should fit tightly into the resulting loop.

12. Complete the pad.

Using the cut pieces of fabric for the pad, measure in 2" on each long side and sew the pieces together, creating a 76"-long, 18"-wide piece with an opening at each end. Insert the first attachment loop (for the ⅝" dowel) about 2" into one open end of the pad. Make sure the two pieces are aligned. Sew the pieces together, securing the loop end and closing the end of the pad. If possible, sew along the existing seam for the dowel, for a cleaner look to the looped end.

Turn the pad inside out so that all of the stitching is on the pad's interior. Cut two pieces of quilt batting to fit precisely inside the pad, leaving about 1" of extra fabric at the opening. Double up the batting pieces and work them into the pad so they lie flush and fill each corner. Iron the entire pad with a clothes iron so the batting fuses to the inside of the fabric.

Fold the edges of the open end of the pad in on themselves. Insert the zippered loop end into the folds so that only the metal part of the zipper is showing. Sew through the folds and the edge of the zipper to complete the pad.

13. Attach the pad.

Insert the 1¼" dowel into its hole on one of the bench sides, then wrap the zippered fabric loop over the dowel, making sure the zipper pull will be facing up. Center the loop on the dowel, and fit the leading dowel end into the other bench side. Insert the 8"-long ⅝" dowels into each hole on each end of the dowel.

Lay out the pad over the bench so the zipper halves meet with the zipper pull facing up. Close the zipper all the way, then begin rolling the pad. Before reaching the end, insert the long ⅝" dowel into the sewn loop. Roll the pad up until the dowel rests in the catches on the bench sides. (If you're experienced with sewing, you might want to create a handle for the pad.)

Bug Stool

Designed by Chris Heichel

It shouldn't surprise anyone to learn that this piece has an interesting design story. For a school project the designer was asked (in his own words) "to explore the word *perch* and design a stool based on my interpretation of the word. While outside that day, I noticed a large bug that was perched above the grass as though it were looking for its next meal, or maybe just enjoying the view" . . . and the Bug Stool concept was born. In addition to its leggy physique, the Bug Stool is strong and stable and makes a nice stepstool or a seat for kids or even a perch for a potted plant in the garden.

MATERIALS

- One 4 x 4-foot piece ¾" Baltic birch or similar hardwood plywood
- Paper (for templates; see steps 2 and 4)
- Wood glue
- Finish materials (as desired)

TOOLS

- Homemade compass (page 17)
- Jigsaw
- Router with homemade trammel (page 18) and:
    - ½" or ¾" straight bit
    - ¼" roundover bit (bearing-guided)
    - ¼" cove bit (bearing-guided)
- Table saw or circular saw with straightedge guide
- Miter saw (recommended)
- Band saw (optional)
- Pencil
- Sandpaper
- Double-sided tape
- Clamps

1. Cut the body disks.

The "body" of the bug stool is made up of two 14"-diameter disks. These are sandwiched over four rib pieces and three legs on each side of the body. You'll cut the disks from ¾" plywood, using a jigsaw and a router.

Mark the two disks using a homemade compass set with a 7" radius. Rough-cut the disks with a jigsaw, staying about ⅛" outside the marked line. Using a trammel and a ½" or ¾" straight bit, rout the edge of each disk to create a perfect circle with square edges (see Two Easy Ways to Cut a Circle, page 18, for more on this technique).

Round over the top edge of the top disk, using a ¼" roundover bit. Sand both disks smooth.

2. Cut and shape the ribs.

It's important that the ribs are all the same height. This ensures equal weight distribution over the stool's top. Each rib is 2½" tall and 2" wide, and there are eight ribs total. Using a table saw or circular saw, cut a strip of plywood that is 2½" wide and at least 2 feet long. This provides some extra material in case of error. Cut the strip into eight 2"-long pieces, using a miter saw with a stop block (recommended for accuracy) or a circular saw.

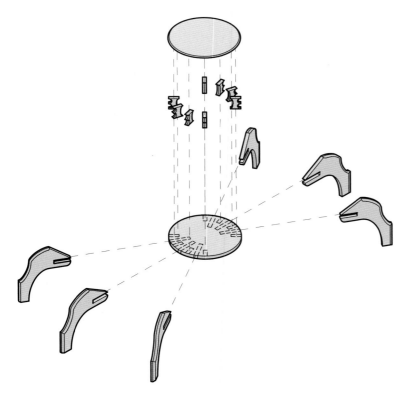

Exploded view

Create a paper template with two half-circles on one side and one large half-ellipse on the other side, as shown in the rib detail drawing below. Use the template and a pencil to transfer the profile to each rib piece, then cut out the profiles with a jigsaw or band saw.

3. Mill the ribs.
Each rib is milled with a cove bit on both sides of its front edge (half-circles) and back edge (ellipse). The top and bottom edges are not milled and should be very flat and smooth. The best tool for milling these small pieces is a router table. If you prefer to use a handheld router, you have to secure each piece to the work surface with something like hot glue or a good vacuum system.

Sand the front and back edges of the ribs so they will mill cleanly, without bumps and dips. Set up the router table with a ¼" cove bit, and set the depth so it cuts a little less than half the thickness of the plywood. This leaves about ⅛" in the middle. For safety, secure each rib to a block, using double-sided tape, and hold the block for making the cut, as shown in the illustration at right. (Holding the rib itself would put your fingers dangerously

close to the bit.) Carefully mill all the ribs in this manner. Sand the milled edges smooth and remove any burn marks from the routing.

4. Cut the legs.
The legs are really what give the stool the fun "bug" look. They are six identical pieces and are made much like the ribs. Start by creating a paper template, following the leg template drawing. Trace the profile onto a 12"-wide (or wider) piece of plywood, as shown in the cutting diagram. On the leg template, note the dotted line directly above the base of the outside notch: it is critical that the legs measure 2½" at this point, so that the top disk rests evenly on the ribs and legs.

Carefully cut out the legs with a jigsaw or band saw, but do not cut the slots yet. Clamp or tape three of the legs together and use a band saw to cut out the slots so they are all alike. If you don't have a band saw, you can cut the slots individually, but take care to mark and cut them accurately. Test-fit the slots on the bottom disk to confirm a snug fit; it's better to be too tight than too loose. Once all the legs are completely cut, gang the cut legs together and sand their edges as needed so the pieces are identical and the edges are smooth.

5. Mill the legs.
Mill the top and bottom edges of the legs with the cove bit, as you did with the ribs, but here, stop the cove cuts at the top of

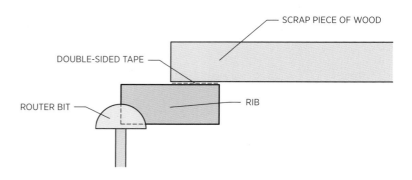

Rib Detail Drawing   **Router Table Setup for Milling Rib Edges**

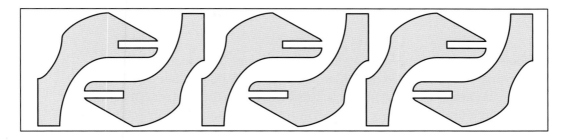

Legs Cutting Diagram

the curve on both top and bottom (inside/outside) edges, and leave a little more material in the center than before (see the leg template). You also won't need the extension block for safety, since these pieces are large enough to handle directly. After routing, sand the legs smooth and remove any burn marks.

6. Assemble the stool.
Lay out the leg and rib locations on the top face of the bottom disk, as shown in the illustration of the leg and rib layout. You have a little bit of design flexibility here: the legs and ribs should be evenly spaced on each side, and each piece should line up with its counterpart on the opposing side of the disk, but the precise spacing is not critical. Experiment with different leg spacing to find the look you like best — and make sure the stool will be stable. Mark the leg positions, then space the ribs evenly in between and outside the legs.

Glue each rib onto the bottom disk, clamp it, and let the glue dry. Then glue up the legs. Finally, apply glue to the top edges of the ribs, center the top disk in place, and clamp it down until dry.

Finish the stool as desired. If the stool will be exposed to moisture, be sure to use a good exterior paint or outdoor-rated varnish (such as UV-protected polyurethane).

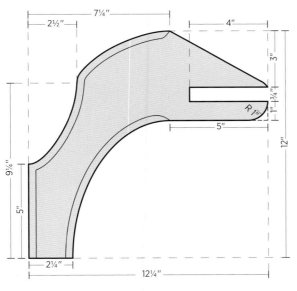

Leg Cutting Diagram

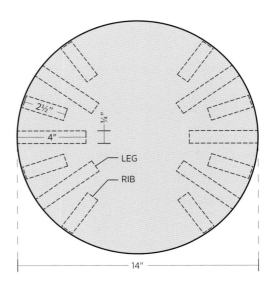

Leg and Rib Layout on Bottom Disk

Symbiosis Chair

Designed by Greg Bugel

This enigmatic piece is a bit of a puzzle in both form and concept. True to its name, it's an assembly of two distinctly different profiles that cannot stand on their own. One profile forms the backrest, seat, and rear legs; the other forms the seat and front legs. The parts are layered like alternating ribs, yet this is not laminated construction (as with the TAB-1 chair, for example; see page 108). In fact, only one piece is glued. To get the gentle curves on the legs and backrest, each piece has a slightly different shape than its neighbor in the layering. In all, there are 12 distinct shapes, and all but two have a twin. So now you can see how their symbiosis is also synergistic. It's symple, really.

MATERIALS

- Two 4 x 8-foot sheets ¾" hardwood plywood
- One 72" length ½"-diam. hardwood dowel (or two 36" lengths)
- 1¼" coarse-thread drywall or wood screws
- Wood glue
- Finish materials (as desired)

TOOLS

- Compass
- Circular saw with straightedge guide
- Jigsaw
- Sandpaper (up to 220 grit) and sanding block
- Clamps
- Drill with ½" straight bit
- Mallet
- Flush-cutting saw (optional)

1. Create the two templates.

Here's how the chair works: There are two main profiles — the back (backrest, seat, and rear legs) and the front (seat and front legs). There are 11 back pieces and 11 front pieces. Moving from the outsides to the center of each profile set, there are five matching pairs of pieces and one unique center piece. The backrest and legs of the profiles get narrower as you move toward the center, and the center pieces have the narrowest legs and backrest. The seat sections (and all of the dowel holes) remain the same throughout.

All the parts for the chair are traced from two templates — one for the back profile and one for the front. The templates begin with the widest leg and backrest dimensions, and you will trace them to lay out the two sets of outside pieces. To lay out the next pieces in toward the center, you will trim off a portion of the backrest and legs from the templates and trace again. After repeating this process three more times, you will trim (or sand) the templates a final time and use the templates as the center pieces of each profile set.

Lay out the front and back templates on ¾" plywood stock, following the template drawings. The cutting diagram shows you how to fit all the parts onto the two panels. The rounded corners at both ends of the seat have a 1" radius. Mark the locations of the four dowel holes on one of the templates.

Carefully cut out the templates, using a circular saw and straightedge guide for the straight cuts and a jigsaw for the curves and inside corners. Sand the cut edges smooth and flat with coarse sandpaper and a sanding block.

Sandwich the two templates together so their seat tops and ends are perfectly flush and the dowel-hole markings are on top. Clamp the parts together. Check to make sure the legs will stand squarely on the floor. Carefully drill the dowel holes through both pieces at once, using a ½" bit. Keep the drill bit perfectly vertical (plumb) as you work so the holes are perpendicular to the faces of the templates.

2. Cut the chair parts.

Set each template on the plywood stock and trace around it to mark the cutting lines for the two sets of outside pieces; you will trace out two pieces for each of the back and front profiles. Cut out the four pieces with a circular saw and jigsaw, as before, and sand any rough edges flat and smooth.

Sandwich the two mating pieces together with their matching template on the outside, aligning all edges, and clamp them securely. Drill the dowel holes through the two new pieces, using the holes in the template as a guide. Repeat with the other pair and template.

Mark and trim the legs (and backrest) of the templates, following the template drawings. This requires one straight cut for each leg/backrest member. Make the cuts with the circular saw and straightedge guide. Sand the cuts smooth, if necessary, but do not round over the edges. Complete the same process of tracing around the templates and cutting and drilling the two pairs for the next front and back pieces, as before.

Repeat the entire process to create the five pairs of front and back pieces. Then trim the templates a final time so they can be used as the center pieces. (The difference in leg/backrest width between the center pieces and their neighboring pieces is only about ⅛". If desired, you can simply sand the legs and backrests to size rather than cutting them.)

3. Assemble the chair.

Cut the ½" dowel into four lengths of 18" each. Sand the ends of the dowels a little so they'll fit easily into the holes of the chair pieces. To assemble the chair, lay down one outside back piece and insert the four dowels into the holes in the back piece. Fit one of the outside front pieces onto the opposite ends of the dowels and carefully work it down, tapping gently with a mallet as needed, until it rests against the inside face of the back piece. Keep the piece as horizontal as possible as you work; striking it while it's at an angle can cause splintering around the dowel holes.

Align the two pieces along the tops and ends of the seats, and fasten through the inside face of the front piece and into the back piece with two or three 1¼" screws — just enough to keep the assembly tight. Repeat with the remaining pieces, alternating backs and fronts. The final piece on the opposite end will be a front; do not screw through this piece, as the screw heads would show. Secure it with wood glue, clamping it to the assembly until the glue dries.

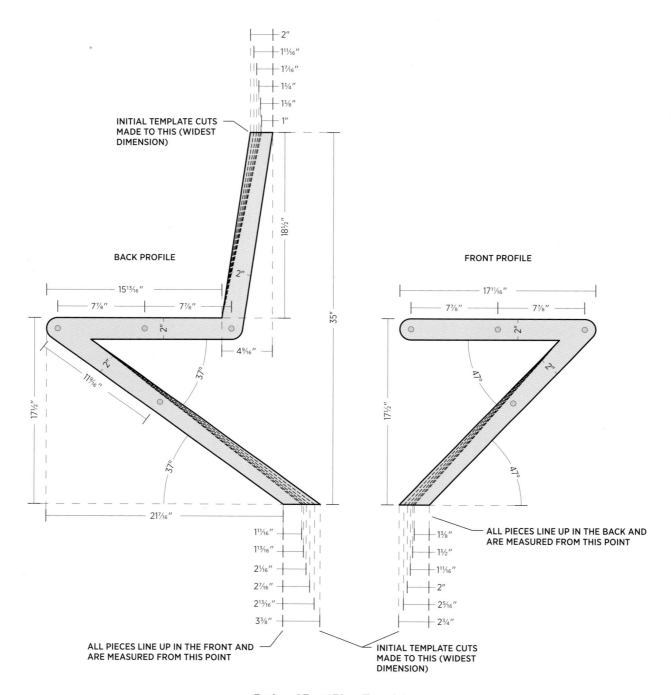

2"
1¹¹⁄₁₆"
1⁷⁄₁₆"
1¼"
1⅛"
1"

INITIAL TEMPLATE CUTS
MADE TO THIS (WIDEST
DIMENSION)

18½"

BACK PROFILE

15¹³⁄₁₆"

7⅞"   7⅞"

2"

2"

35"

37°

37°

2"

4⁹⁄₁₆"

17½"

11⁹⁄₁₆"

2"

21⁷⁄₁₆"

FRONT PROFILE

17¹¹⁄₁₆"

7⅞"   7⅞"

2"

47°

2"

47°

17½"

ALL PIECES LINE UP IN THE BACK AND
ARE MEASURED FROM THIS POINT

1¹¹⁄₁₆"
1¹³⁄₁₆"
2¹⁄₁₆"
2⁷⁄₁₆"
2¹³⁄₁₆"
3⅜"

1⅜"
1½"
1¹¹⁄₁₆"
2"
2⁵⁄₁₆"
2¾"

ALL PIECES LINE UP IN THE FRONT AND
ARE MEASURED FROM THIS POINT

INITIAL TEMPLATE CUTS
MADE TO THIS (WIDEST
DIMENSION)

Back and Front Piece Templates

4. Finish the chair.

Trim the dowels flush to the chair's sides, using a jigsaw or flush-cutting saw. Since the dowels aren't secured, you can mark a cutting line flush with the chair side, tap the dowel out a little and cut it off at the line, then tap it back in so it's flush. This prevents any marring of the plywood face with the saw blade.

Sand the seat surface, as needed, so it is smooth and flat, using a sanding block and various grits of sandpaper. If the chair wobbles at all, sand across the bottoms of the legs so they sit flat on the floor.

Finish-sand all exposed surfaces, working up to 220-grit paper. Finish the chair as desired. Be sure to test any stain or finish on some scrap material to see how it is absorbed by the edge grain of the plywood.

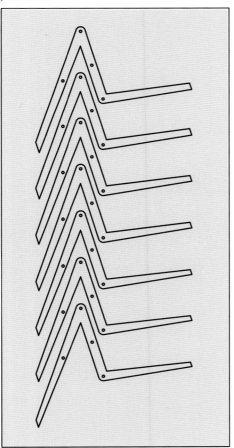
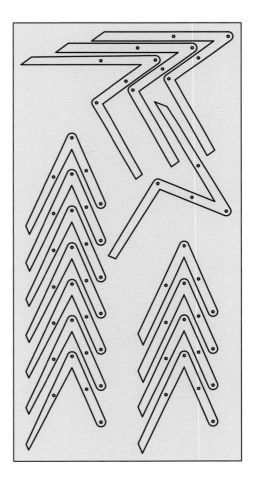

Cutting Diagram

Chalk Back

Designed by Dieter Amick

If you asked a class of early-elementary students to design their own chairs and then incorporated their best ideas into a single creation, you'd probably have something very similar to the Chalk Back chair. In other words, you have to think like a kid to come up with something this cool. It's a kid-size chair that flips onto its front to become a chalkboard and drawing table. It even has a secret art-supply drawer that's revealed only when the chair is in *artiste* mode. The drawer is optional, but it's definitely worth doing because . . . well, because it's a secret drawer. Duh.

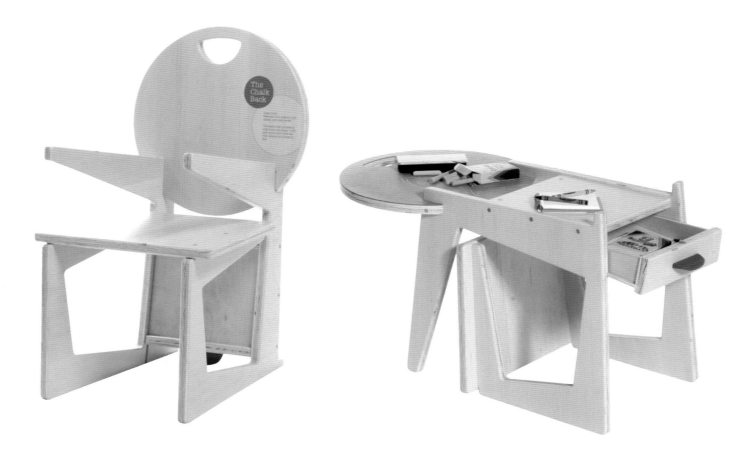

MATERIALS

- One 3 x 4-foot piece ¾" hardwood plywood
- Chalkboard paint and compatible primer
- Wood glue
- Twenty (or more) 6d (2") finish nails
- One 72" length ¼"-diam. wood dowel (or two 36" lengths)
- Finish materials (as desired)

TOOLS

- Homemade compass (page 17)
- Jigsaw
- Router with homemade trammel (page 18) and:
  - ¾" straight bit
  - ⅛" roundover bit
- Hammer
- ½" chisel
- Drill with:
  - ¹⁄₁₆" straight bit
  - ¼" straight bit
  - ½" straight bit
- Sandpaper (including 150 and 220 grit)
- Circular saw with straightedge guide
- Protractor or Speed Square
- Straightedge
- File (optional)
- Nail set
- Handsaw

ADDITIONAL SUPPLIES FOR OPTIONAL DRAWER

- One 2 x 2-foot piece ¼" plywood
- Router bits:
  - ¼" straight bit
  - ⁵⁄₁₆" straight bit
- One drawer handle/pull of choice
- Two ½"-diam. disk magnets
- General-purpose two-part epoxy

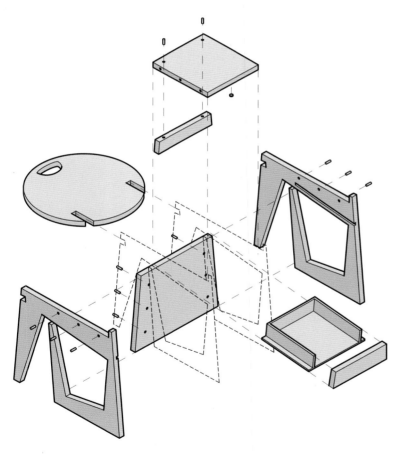

Exploded View

1. Lay out and cut the chair parts.

All the chair parts are cut from a 3 x 4-foot sheet of ¾" plywood. The dimensions and profiles for each part are detailed in the cutting diagram. The following walks you through the process of laying out the more complex parts.

Chair back

The back piece starts with a 14½"-diameter circle. Mark the circle using a homemade compass set with a 7¼" radius. Rough-cut the piece with a jigsaw, staying about ⅛" outside the marked line. Using a trammel and router with a ¾" straight bit, rout along the line to create a perfect circle (see Two Easy Ways to Cut a Circle, page 18, for more on this technique).

Cut two ⅝"-wide, 3"-deep slots, 8½" apart, into the back, as shown in the cutting diagram. A hammer and chisel are handy for cleaning up the corners at the base of these thin slots. (This slot is ⅝" rather than ¾" — the plywood's width — to allow for some fine-tuning during the assembly.)

The outer edge of the chair back's handle is a 3½"-long arch set 1" in from the edge of the back and concentric with the back's edge. Another arch with a radius of 1¾" completes the bottom edge of this handle. Mark the cutout with a compass, then drill a starter hole inside the marked cutout, and cut out the handle with a jigsaw. Sand all the cut edges smooth with 150-grit sandpaper.

Seat panel

The seat is a simple trapezoid shape measuring 14" in the front, 12" in the back, and 11" along both sides. Cut this with a circular saw and straightedge guide. Sand the edges smooth with 150-grit sandpaper.

Arm supports

These two pieces have a fairly complicated profile, but the layout is straightforward if you follow the steps given here and reference the cutting diagram as you go. Use a protractor or Speed Square (rafter square) and a straightedge to lay out the angled lines. Lay out and cut one support (arm support 1 in the cutting diagram), then use it as a template to mark the second support.

Begin by drawing the bottom horizontal edge of the support, which measures 15½". Starting from the right end of this first line, draw an 11"-long line at an 85-degree angle to the left; this represents the front outer edge. Continue this line roughly 8" longer, to mark the end cut for the armrest.

At the 11" mark on the line you just drew, draw an 11½"-long horizontal line to the left; this will become the seat panel mounting point (this cut should be as straight as possible).

Moving to the left end of the very first bottom horizontal line, lay out a small protruding foot (this is to prevent the chair from tipping backward). Draw the foot with a ¾" vertical line and a 1" line at 10 degrees to the right. Continue this line for about 12" to assist with a future 8" cut you will need to make. At the termination of the 1" line, mark a 15"-long line at an 85-degree angle, making sure it is parallel with the right most (front) cut of the profile.

At the end of the left most (rear) line that you just drew, draw a line at a 10-degree angle to the right that intersects with the front 85-degree angle line; this marks the top edge of the armrest. Starting 1" in from the left end of the top edge of the armrest, draw a ⅞" x ¾" slot at an 85-degree angle; this slot will receive the chair back and is parallel to the back edges of the arm support.

At this point, the remaining five lines that complete the inner profile are easy to make using the cutting diagram. Cut out the arm-support profile, using a jigsaw and a straightedge guide, as appropriate. Sand the cuts smooth with 150-grit sandpaper, then use the cut piece as a template to trace the same profile for the second support. Cut the second support, and sand the edges smooth.

Lower back support

This piece spans the two rear verticals of the arm supports and further strengthens the chair (it's also the top of the drawer compartment when the chair is in the forward position). Mark the panel at 8⁹⁄₁₆" x 9¼", as shown in the cutting diagram. Cut the 9¼" (side) edges at a 5-degree outward angle, using a circular saw. This angle will match that of the arm supports, which will be toed outward so that they are wider apart at the front of the chair than at the back. Cut the shorter edges square. Sand the edges smooth with 150-grit sandpaper.

2. Begin the drawer (optional).

To add the drawer to the design, cut a 10"-long, ¼"-deep slot on the inside of both arm supports, using a ⁵⁄₁₆" straight router bit; see the cutting diagram. Set up a straightedge or straight piece of scrap as a template to guide the router base. The slot is parallel to and (along most of its length) ½" from the inside edge of the arm support.

CHAIR BACK

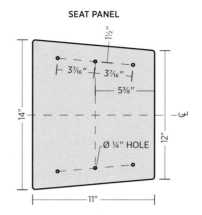

3½"

Ø 14½"

¾" 8½" ¾"

3"

¼" HOLE

SEAT PANEL

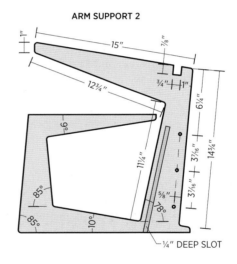

1½"

3⁷⁄₁₆" 3⁷⁄₁₆"

5⅜"

14" 12"

11"

Ø ¼" HOLE

ARM SUPPORT 1

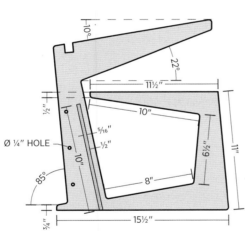

10°

22°

11½"

10"

½"

5⁄₁₆"

½"

Ø ¼" HOLE

10"

85°

8"

6½"

11"

¾"

15½"

ARM SUPPORT 2

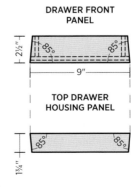

1" 15" ⅞"

12¾" ¾" 1"

6¼"

9"

11¼"

3⁷⁄₁₆" 14¾"

85° 3⁷⁄₁₆"

85° 10° ⅝"

78°

¼" DEEP SLOT

LOWER BACK SUPPORT

1" 1"

¾" WIDE x 5⁄₁₆"
DEEP DADO ½"
DOWN

Ø ¼" HOLE

⅞"

5°
BEVEL

9¼"

5°
BEVEL

8⁹⁄₁₆"

DRAWER FRONT PANEL

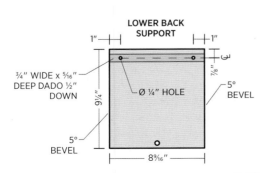

2½"

85° 85°

9"

TOP DRAWER HOUSING PANEL

85° 85°

1¾"

Cutting Diagrams

The next step is to cut the top drawer housing panel, which will slot into the lower back support. This piece is a trapezoid at 9" on the wider end, 8¹¹⁄₁₆" on the smaller end, and 1¾" deep.

Create a shallow slot across the face of the lower back support panel, as shown in the diagram. Use a ¾" router bit to make a ⁵⁄₁₆"-deep slot ½" down from the top edge of the lower back support panel. The top drawer housing panel will be glued and nailed into this slot during the assembly stage.

Mark and cut the drawer front panel: this panel has basically the same shape as the top drawer housing panel, except it is 2½" deep, with the same measurements of 9" on the wider end and 8⅝" on the smaller end.

3. Paint the chalkboard.
The chalkboard surface is the backside of the round chair back. Prepare the surface by sanding the face smooth with 220-grit sandpaper. Wipe down the surface with a wet rag or sponge, and let it dry. Apply two coats of primer (check the chalkboard paint manufacturer's directions for product recommendations), then apply chalkboard paint as directed.

4. Round over the edges.
Use a router (with or without a router table) and a ⅛" roundover bit to mill the edges of all parts, except the following areas:

- All slots and grooves
- Chalkboard side of the chair back
- Edges of the arm supports that will join with the seat panel
- Attachment points of the lower back support and top drawer housing

5. Assemble the chair.

Chair back and arm supports
The first step of the assembly process is to fit the round chair back onto the two arm supports. The supports should fit at a slight angle so that they angle out to match the sides of the seat panel. Using a file, sandpaper, and/or a hammer and chisel, carefully widen the slots in the chair back as needed create a tight fit.

Drill a ¼"-diameter hole to a depth of ⁵⁄₁₆" at the side of each slot of the chair back, as shown in the cutting diagram. Apply a small

amount of glue to the mating parts, and fit the chair back and arm supports together. Drive a finish nail into the center of each ¼" hole, then set it with a nail set (the ¼" bores will be filled with dowel plugs).

Lower back support
If you are making the optional drawer, attach the top drawer housing panel by gluing its 8¹¹⁄₁₆" edge into the slot in the lower back support panel. Drill two ¼"-diameter, ⁵⁄₁₆"-deep bores in the reverse side of the slot and nail the two panels together, as you did for the chair back and arm supports.

To install the lower back support, drill three ¼" bores on the outside rear edge of each arm support, as shown in the cutting diagram. These holes should be centered over the edges of the lower back support. Secure the lower back support with glue and finish nails, driving the nails into the centers of the ¼" bores.

Seat panel
Set the seat panel on top of the arm supports with the wider end facing front. Make sure the front edge of the seat panel doesn't extend past the arm supports (this is important so that the chair sits flat in the forward position). Hold the seat in place, and mark the position of the outer edges of the arm supports on the bottom face of the seat panel.

Remove the seat panel from the arm supports and flip it over so you can see the lines you just made. Make three evenly spaced marks on the bottom face of the seat on each side, ⅜" inside the traced lines. Use a ¹⁄₁₆" drill bit to drill all the way through the seat at each mark. Flip the seat over and drill six ¼"-diameter, ⁵⁄₁₆"-deep bores, centered on the holes you just drilled. Reposition the seat and fasten it to the arm supports with finish nails; set the nails. If the two rear most holes are too hard to reach, you can drive the nails through the underside.

6. Complete the drawer (if applicable).
Set the drawer front panel against the lower back support (between the arm supports) in the precise position where it will be installed (allow for a small amount of clearance for opening and closing the drawer). Holding the panel in place, transfer the locations of the two slots on the supports onto the back face of the drawer panel. Use a router and ¼" straight bit to mill slots at the marks, matching the slots on the arm supports; these slots will receive the drawer's bottom panel.

Drill the screw holes for the drawer handle/pull. You will install the pull at the end of the project.

The drawer bottom is cut from ¼" plywood, and it slides along the slots of the arm supports. Measure the distance between the bottoms of the slots to find the width of the drawer bottom (it's approximately 9"); take a little bit off the measurement to allow for smooth sliding. Next, find the desired length of the drawer bottom by holding the drawer front in its installed position and measuring the space within. Cut the drawer bottom to size.

Mill the slots for the drawer sides: Make two ¼"-wide, ⅛"-deep slots in the top face of the drawer bottom, locating them ½" in from and parallel to each side. Fit the drawer bottom into the slot on the drawer front panel and mark where the new slots intersect with the drawer front. At these points, continue the slots upward across the drawer front, as shown in the cutting diagram.

Cut the two drawer sides from ¼" plywood: they measure 2" tall at the front and 1¼" at the back and are the same length as the drawer bottom. Assemble the drawer front, bottom, and sides with wood glue.

Disk magnets keep the drawer from opening when the chair is upright. To install the magnets, drill a shallow hole of the same diameter and depth as the magnets into the center of the top edge of the drawer front. Drill a corresponding hole for another magnet on the inside face of the lower back support; the magnets should line up and touch when the drawer is closed. Glue the magnets in place with a small amount of epoxy.

7. Finish the chair.

Cut the ¼" dowel into ¼"-long pieces to create plugs to fill the nail-hole bores, using a handsaw. Before cutting each piece, taper the end of the dowel with sandpaper to allow the plug to fit into the bore easily. Leave the butt end of the plug unsanded.

Apply a thin layer of glue around each plug and press into a hole. Using a hammer and scrap wood or a mallet, drive down the plug to get it as flush with the surface as possible. Let the glue dry, then use 220-grit sandpaper to sand the plug flush. Fill all the nail-hole bores in this manner.

Finish-sand the entire piece with 220-grit paper, making sure to smooth all exposed edges. (Wetting the wood a little with a rag during this final sanding will help get the surfaces even smoother.)

Finish the piece with three or more coats of polyurethane or other desired finish so all surfaces are durable and stain-resistant. The chair shown here was finished with Daly's CrystalFin clear polyurethane in satin.

Install the drawer handle/pull after the finish has fully dried.

Three's Company

Designed by Patrick McAffrey

The Three's Company chair, coincidentally, has a lot in common with the TV show of the same name. The design of the chair is very clever (like Janet), while its construction is exceptionally simple (like Chrissy). The chair has three legs, two of which are matching and one of which has a shape that might seem a bit queer (like Jack). Fortunately, Three's Company the chair is likely to age much better than the show, and it does something really far out: the third leg isn't fastened, so the chair can be disassembled into two lightweight parts. This makes it portable enough to take with you for extra seating at the Regal Beagle or wherever you like to hang out and cruise foxes.

MATERIALS

- ☐ One 4 x 4-foot sheet ½" hardwood plywood
- ☐ Wood glue
- ☐ Two 2" Allen-drive, flat-head wood screws
- ☐ Six 1½" Allen-drive, flat-head wood screws
- ☐ Finish materials (as desired)

TOOLS

- ☐ Homemade compass (page 17)
- ☐ Jigsaw or band saw
- ☐ Sandpaper
- ☐ Clamps
- ☐ Drill with bits:
    - ☐ ⅛" or smaller straight bit (for pilot holes; see step 1)
    - ☐ ¼" straight bit
    - ☐ ⅜" straight bit
- ☐ Larger bit for countersinking screw heads (optional)
- ☐ Standard compass
- ☐ Circular saw with straightedge guide
- ☐ Square-edged file
- ☐ Allen wrench

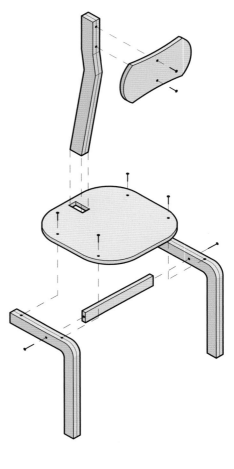

Exploded View

1. Build the legs.

Each of the legs is constructed with two matching plywood pieces glued together to create a 1"-thick member.

Lay out one of the front leg parts on the plywood stock, following the cutting diagram. Note that the radius at the inside of the bend is 1", and the outer radius is 2" (see How to Mark & Cut Curves, page 16). Cut the leg with a jigsaw or band saw. Sand the cut edges so they are as smooth and straight as possible, with no saw marks or rough spots.

Use the cut leg as a template for marking the remaining three front leg pieces. Cut these pieces, then gang the four parts together and sand them as needed so they are perfectly flush along all edges. Glue pairs of the parts together with their edges flush, clamping them securely with flat pieces of scrap wood for blocking to provide even pressure. Clean up any glue squeeze-out, and let the glue dry.

Drill a ¼" hole through the face of each front-leg assembly, as shown in the cutting diagram. This hole is 4" from the edge of the leg's vertical portion and is centered top-to-bottom on the horizontal portion. Drill two more holes into the top edge (horizontal portion) of each leg, as shown in the diagram, using a pilot bit sized for 1½" screws.

Follow the same process to build the rear leg. This leg gets no holes at this time.

2. Create the seat.

Draw the seat shape on the plywood stock, following the cutting diagram. The corners are rounded with a 6" radius. Mark the 1" x 3" slot for the rear leg so it is centered side-to-side on the seat and 1" from its back edge.

Cut the seat outline with a jigsaw or band saw. Drill a ⅜" starter hole inside the leg slot, then complete the cutout with a jigsaw. It's a good idea to cut this slot a little small, so you can fine-tune the fit later with a file.

Sand the seat to smooth the cut edges, but do not sand the leg slot. Drill four ¼" holes through the seat at the locations noted on the cutting diagram.

3. Cut the backrest and cross rail.

Lay out the backrest as shown in the cutting diagram; you can use a standard compass to draw the 4½" radius on the sides, but you'll need a homemade compass to make the 35" radius on the

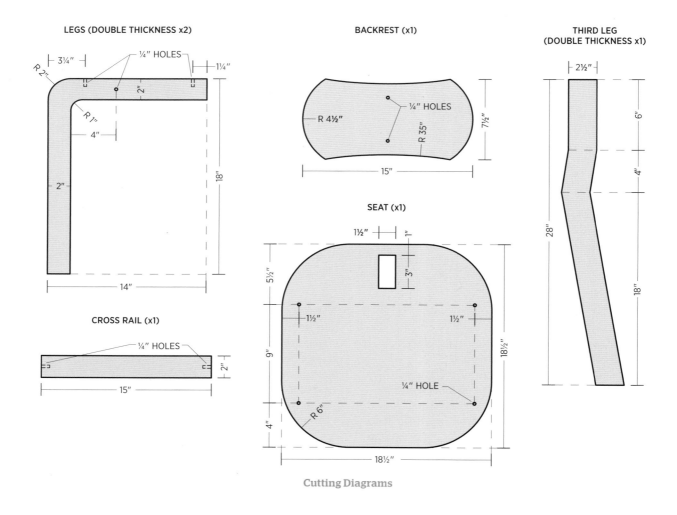

Cutting Diagrams

top and bottom edges. Cut the backrest with a jigsaw or band saw, and sand the cut edges smooth. Drill two ¼" holes through the backrest as shown in the cutting diagram; these are centered side-to-side and 1½" from the top and bottom edges.

The cross rail is a simple rectangle measuring 2" x 15". Cut this with a circular saw and straightedge guide, making sure the end cuts are square (you can also make the crosscuts with a miter saw, if available). Mark the precise center on both end edges of the cross rail, and drill a pilot hole (for 2" screws) at each mark. These holes are parallel to the length of the rail.

4. Test-fit the parts.

Because the chair's parts will be finished individually, it's a good idea to test-fit the assembly and make any necessary adjustments before applying the finish. For this step, it's best not to tighten the screws all the way, allowing for the strongest connections with the final assembly.

Assemble the chair by screwing the cross rail between the front legs, using two 2" screws driven through the pilot holes. Make sure the cross rail is flush with the top edges of the legs. Attach the seat to the legs with four 1½" screws.

Insert the rear leg into the slot on the seat; it should slide in easily with no side-to-side play. File the slot's sides as needed for a good fit. Position the leg so that the lower angle (or "kink") is just below the seat and the chair sits squarely on all three legs; the long bottom section of the rear leg should angle toward the rear.

Position the backrest against the front edge of the rear leg so its top edge is flush with or slightly above the top end of the leg and it's centered from side to side. Mark and drill pilot holes into the leg, using the predrilled holes in the backrest. Fasten the backrest to the leg with two 1½" screws.

Note: For comfort, it's best to countersink the screw heads on the seat and backrest so they are just flush with the wood surface. Drill these countersink holes with a bit that's slightly larger than the screw head diameter, but be very careful to avoid tearout on the faces of the plywood.

5. Finish the parts and complete the final assembly.

Disassemble the chair. Finish-sand all the parts as needed for a smooth finish. Also sand a slight roundover at all outer edges of the pieces. Apply the finish of your choice and let it cure completely.

Assemble the chair as before, tightening the screws with an Allen wrench. Be careful not to overtighten the screws; they can strip fairly easily in the plywood edges.

Children's Chair

Designed by Steven De Lannoy

Comfortable for reading, daydreaming, or holding court (which one does *your* kid do best?), this chair is simple, sturdy, and storage-savvy. All kids will love the private place to stash stuff, and those with a discriminating eye will of course appreciate the originality of the chair's basic form, as well as its clean, modern styling. As shown, the chair is designed for an average-size six-year-old, but you can easily shorten the side panels to accommodate a smaller child or heighten them to suit a larger kid or simply to create a more magisterial perch.

MATERIALS

- ☐ One 2 x 4-foot piece ⅝" hardwood plywood
- ☐ One 3 x 3-foot piece ½" hardwood plywood
- ☐ 1¼" drywall or wood screws
- ☐ Wood glue
- ☐ 1" brads
- ☐ Three 14" (or longer) lengths 2 x 4 scrap lumber
- ☐ Finish materials (as desired)
- ☐ Pipe insulation (optional; see step 6)

TOOLS

- ☐ Circular saw with straightedge guide or table saw
- ☐ Homemade compass (page 17)
- ☐ Jigsaw
- ☐ Drill with small pilot bit (for brads)
- ☐ Long bar clamp
- ☐ Sandpaper

1. Cut the panels.

The chair is constructed of five plywood panels:

- Two side panels at 19¹¹⁄₁₆" x 19¹¹⁄₁₆", cut from ⅝" plywood
- One back panel at 13¹³⁄₁₆" x 25⅝", cut from ½" plywood
- One seat panel at 13¹³⁄₁₆" x 13¹³⁄₁₆", cut from ½" plywood
- One shelf panel at 13¹³⁄₁₆" x 12⅝", cut from ½" plywood

Cut the five panels to size, using a circular saw and straightedge guide or a table saw to ensure clean, straight cuts (straight, square edges are especially important for strong glue joints). Also cut six "beams" from ½" plywood:

- 2 long beams ("E") at ½" x 13¹³⁄₁₆"
- 2 medium beams ("D") at ½" x 12¹³⁄₁₆"
- 2 short beams ("F") at ½" x 8¹¹⁄₁₆"

2. Shape the side panels.

Following the side panel template on page 138, draw line A (running from corner IV to corner I), line B (from corner I to corner II), and line C (from corner III to corner II). Make these lines on what will be the inside face of the side panel.

Place the second side panel underneath the first and screw the panels together at the locations indicated in the plan. Make sure that the panels are neatly aligned and that the screws are close to the corners, as shown. Cut along the marked lines with the circular saw to trim both panels at once.

For now you will round off only corner II. You'll shape the other corners later. Using a homemade compass or an 8½"-diameter dinner plate, mark a 4¼" radius between lines B and C on the top side panel. With the two panels still screwed together, cut along the curve with a jigsaw. Separate the panels.

3. Install the beams.

Following the beam layout illustration on page 138, measure down 8¹¹⁄₁₆" from line B and draw line D parallel to line B. Next, draw line E perpendicular to D and 14⁵⁄₁₆" from the front edge of the panel. Then draw line F parallel to D, running from the very end of line E to the front edge of the panel.

Fasten one long beam (E) along line E on the panel, using wood glue and three 1" brads driven through pilot holes.

Fasten one medium beam (D) along line D. Note that there is a gap between beam D and beam F — this should be just large enough to accommodate the back panel, which will slide in between. A snug fit here is important, as it adds strength to the chair.

Finally, glue a short beam (F) along line F. Note that beam D and beam F do not extend to the front of the side panel. This is to hide the beams from view from the front. Install the three remaining beams on the other side panel to match the first panel.

4. Glue up the chair.

With a helper, dry-fit the entire assembly so it stands upright on a flat, level work surface. The back panel installs against the E beams and is flush with the bottoms of the side panels (it touches the floor). The seat installs on top of the D beams and butts against the back panel. The shelf installs on top of the F beams and butts against the back panel. The front edges of the seat and shelf should be flush with the front edges of the side panels. Make any necessary adjustments for a good fit.

Cut three lengths of 2 x 4 at 13¹¹⁄₁₆". You'll use these in lieu of clamps to draw the side panels together during the glue-up. Set a 2 x 4 between the side panels at each of corners I, III, and IV, and screw through the existing holes in the side panels and into the ends of the 2 x 4s, without tightenening the screws all the way.

Apply glue to the front edges of the E beams, and set the back panel in place. Glue the top edges of the F beams, and set the shelf in place, then glue the seat into place on the D beams. When all panels fit properly, tighten the screws into the 2 x 4s to pull the sides together. Add a bar clamp across the side panels, just below the points where the back meets the tops of the side panels (corner II). Weight down the seat and shelf with heavy objects positioned over the beams. Let the glue dry overnight.

5. Shape the remaining corners.

Remove the screws and 2 x 4s. On each side panel, mark corners III and IV with a 4¼" radius, and cut the curves with a jigsaw, as you did with corner II.

Mark corner I with a 1½" radius, using a compass or a 3"-diameter coffee cup (the size of this curve is not critical). Draw the same radius on each top corner of the back panel. Round off these corners with a jigsaw.

6. Finish the chair.

Finish-sand all surfaces smooth, and slightly round over all edges to prevent splintering. Apply a clear protective finish, such as polyurethane or other varnish, for a durable, washable surface.

If desired, add pieces of pipe insulation to the top edges of the side and back panels, to serve as cushions for the arms and head. Cut the insulation to match the straight portions of each panel, then slit the pieces lengthwise so you can fit them over the plywood edges.

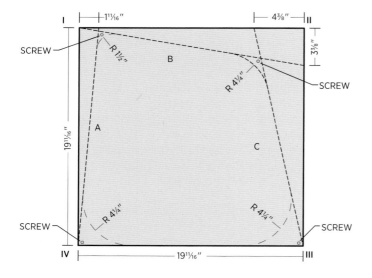

Side Panel Template

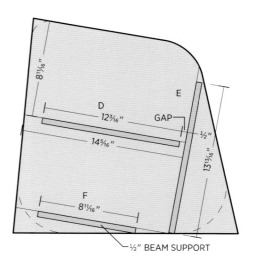

Beam Layout

Rubber Hose Chair

Designed by Will Holman

This piece comes from an architect and designer who makes a lot of great stuff with junk — things like chairs fashioned from road signs, lighting using traffic cones, and tables constructed with cardboard tubes and greenhouse glazing. All are perfectly functional, human-scaled pieces, but none seems more inviting than the Rubber Hose Chair. "It's like sitting on a bed of rubber bands," says its creator. Like many of his other works, this chair can be made primarily with found or reclaimed materials. Just hit up any carpenter, mechanic, or tool hound you know for an old air hose (see Air Hoses, page 142), and you're halfway there.

MATERIALS

- ☐ One 2 x 2-foot piece ¾" plywood
- ☐ Wood glue
- ☐ Sixteen 1¼" coarse-thread drywall screws or deck screws
- ☐ Polyurethane
- ☐ Four 24" lengths ¾" zinc-plated all-thread rod
- ☐ Sixteen ¾" zinc washers
- ☐ Sixteen ¾" zinc nuts
- ☐ One 40-foot (or longer) length ¾" (outside diam.) rubber air hose
- ☐ Two #10 zinc washers
- ☐ Two 1" coarse-thread drywall screws or deck screws

Note: Use only exterior-rated materials if the chair will reside outdoors.

TOOLS

- ☐ Circular saw
- ☐ Straightedge
- ☐ Jigsaw or handsaw
- ☐ Level
- ☐ Drill with:
  - ☐ ¾" spade bit
  - ☐ ⅞" spade bit
  - ☐ 1½" spade bit
- ☐ Sandpaper (up to 220 grit) with sanding block
- ☐ Router with ¼" or ⅜" roundover bit
- ☐ Socket and adjustable wrenches
- ☐ Utility knife

1. Lay out the plywood parts.

The chair's four legs and two L-shaped side supports are cut from a 2 x 2-foot piece of plywood. Because virtually every cut affects more than one piece, it's important to cut with accuracy and avoid overcutting all interior cuts.

Lay out the parts on your 2 x 2 panel, following the cutting diagram: Start by drawing two straight lines that run diagonally between opposing corners. Mark one of these diagonal lines 3" in from each opposing corner. Mark the other diagonal line 7" in from its opposing corners. Connect these four points to create a parallelogram on the interior of the panel; the four legs will be cut from this section.

Across the top of the parallelogram, mark off the leg ends alternately at 3½" and 5". Do the same at the bottom of the parallelogram, starting with 5". Mark a 3" right triangle at the two panel corners corresponding to the 7" marks. Finally, erase or cross out the original diagonal lines from the 7" marks to the panel corners; you will not make cuts here.

2. Cut the plywood parts.

Using a circular saw with a straightedge guide, cut out the parallelogram from the panel. This requires a plunge cut to get the blade started inside the panel. Cut just to the marked corners of the parallelogram (do not overcut), then finish the cuts with a jigsaw or handsaw. Remove the parallelogram piece, and cut along its marked lines to create the four legs.

Next, cut along the 3" diagonal lines to separate the two side supports, then make the 3" triangular cutoffs at the bottom of each L-shaped side support.

3. Customize the chair geometry.

This step sounds more complicated than it is. All you're doing is setting two of the legs over one of the side supports and experimenting with different positions to find the ideal reclining angle and seat height for your comfort; see the side view drawing.

In the chair shown here, the front legs are at a 61-degree angle from the ground, and the back legs are at a 50-degree angle. The lowest point of the seating surface is about 12" above the ground.

Once you find the geometry you like, have a helper hold the legs in place while you place a straightedge between the front bottom corner of the front leg and the rear bottom corner of the back leg, and draw a line along the straightedge to mark a bottom-end cut for each leg. Also mark the legs' positions on the side support, and trace along the front edge of the front leg onto the side support; trim off the side support at this line, to match the angle of the leg.

4. Cut and install the legs.
Cut off the two leg bottoms at the newly marked angle lines. Test-fit the legs on the side support and make any necessary adjustments.

Place each cut leg over its corresponding uncut leg and trace the end cut (and trim cut, if applicable; see the note below) to the uncut leg. Cut the other two legs to match the originals. Fasten the legs to the side supports with wood glue and 1¼" screws driven through the insides of the legs and into the side supports.

Stand each side assembly upright and use a level to mark a level line along the top end of the side support. Trim at this line so the top end of the support is level with the ground.

5. Drill holes for the hose.
Mark the holes for the hose on the outside face of each side support; see the side view. On each side support, the first hole is centered 1" from the top and front edges of the support; the remaining nine are spaced 1½" on center, in a line parallel to the seat.

Mark the bottom most backrest hole so it's aligned with the crook of the side support (between the seat surface and backrest surface), then mark 10 more holes going up the backrest portion of the side support, again with 1½" on-center spacing.

Drill the holes with a ⅞" spade bit. To prevent tearout on the inside faces of the side supports, drill about halfway through from the outside face, then flip the side support over and complete the hole from the inside face.

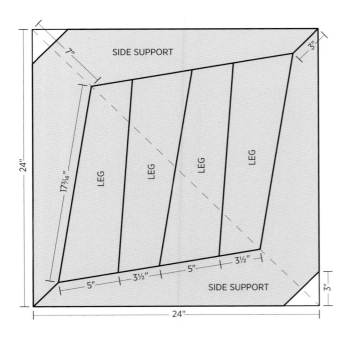

Cutting Diagram

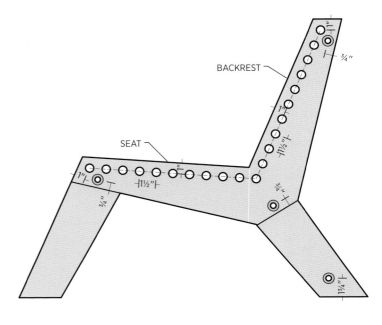

Side View

Smooth the edges of the holes with sandpaper, creating a slight roundover for a finished look.

6. Drill holes for the all-thread.

Lay out the four holes in each side assembly for the all-thread rods, following the side view drawing. The holes near the top of the legs are centered over the width of the legs.

At each hole location, drill a counterbore for the washer and nut, using a 1½" spade bit (the bit must be slightly larger than the outside diameter of the washers). Check the depth of each hole as you work, drilling until the washer and nut will be flush or nearly flush with the plywood surface, but don't drill any deeper than about ½". Then drill through the piece(s) at the center of each counterbore with the ¾" spade bit.

Sand the edges of the counterbores and through holes, as before.

7. Rout the side assemblies.

Mill a roundover on all the edge corners of each side assembly, using a router and ¼" or ⅜" roundover bit. A partial roundover is sufficient for a finished look and a comfortable edge. Test the bit depth on some scrap plywood to find the roundover depth you like best. If you don't have a router, you can simply hand-sand the edges with 60-grit sandpaper and a sanding block, then work up to finer grits until the edges are smooth.

8. Finish the side assemblies.

Finish-sand all the plywood surfaces, working up to 220-grit paper. Finish the assemblies with three coats of polyurethane (use an exterior-grade product if the chair will be used outdoors), as directed by the manufacturer.

9. Assemble the chair structure.

Assemble the chair structure with the four all-thread rods and 16 washers and nuts; each rod gets a washer and nut on each side of the side assemblies. Use a socket wrench and an adjustable wrench to tighten the nuts and rigidify the chair. The outer nuts should be flush with the ends of the rods.

Note: To keep the nuts from working loose over time, apply a touch of thread-lock, polyurethane glue, or similar adhesive to the all-thread ends or nuts before installing the nuts.

10. Thread the hose.

Cut the metal fittings off the ends of the hose with a utility knife. Feed one end of the hose through the inside of one of the front-most seat holes (in the side support), and secure the end to the outside of the side support with a #10 washer and 1" screw (place the washer on the outside of the hose, and drive the screw through the center of the hose and into the wood).

Thread the hose through the seat holes, looping it on the outsides of the side supports. Stretch the hose tightly as you lace up the seat; it's even okay if the side supports flex inward a little bit.

Continue lacing up the hose to complete the backrest, then secure the end to the side support with another screw and #10 washer — this will be on the opposite side support from the first screw. Trim the hose end about ¾" from the washer.

Note: Rubber air hose is very strong and elastic, and the tighter you stretch it, the more comfortable and long-lasting the chair will be. However, if the hose begins to loosen or sag over time, simply remove the screw at one end and rethread the hose, stretching it tight again.

Shop Tip

Air Hoses

Air hoses are commonly used for pneumatic shop tools and are typically ¼ to ¾" in diameter, with a wall thickness of up to ⅛". They are made of tough, flexible rubber. Once a hose develops hairline cracks or pinhole leaks, it has lost its usefulness for pneumatic tool applications, but it's still plenty strong enough to make a comfortable lounge chair. New air hoses can be quite expensive, so look for discarded hoses at places like cabinetry shops and construction sites (including Dumpsters), or you might post a wanted ad on Craigslist to ask for decent used hoses. To clean an old hose, start with a damp soapy rag, and use denatured alcohol to remove varnish, paint, and old stains.

Telephone Book Chair

Designed by Christy Oates

When you see the range of materials in this designer's portfolio — from recycled film reels to cast aluminum to electroluminescent wire — you're not entirely surprised to find a chair made with blocks cut straight from a phone book (but you're no less delighted). The "fragile" labels on the chair are for real, too; the plywood sides are recycled from an old shipping crate. So now you know what to *do* with all those unwanted directories that migrate to your doorstep.

MATERIALS

- ☐ One 4 x 4-foot piece ¾" plywood (or two 2 x 3-foot pieces)
- ☐ Finish materials (see step 3)
- ☐ 10 to 12 phone books (depending on size and thickness)
- ☐ Two 72" lengths ⅜" all-thread rod (or three 48" lengths)
- ☐ Twelve ⅜" acorn-style cap nuts
- ☐ Thread-locking adhesive (such as Loctite)
- ☐ ⅜" washer (see step 6)
- ☐ ⅜" short, standard nut (see step 6)
- ☐ One 48" length metal tubing with ⅜" inside diameter (or two 24" lengths)

TOOLS

- ☐ Jigsaw or circular saw
- ☐ Straightedge
- ☐ Handsaw (if not using jigsaw)
- ☐ Drill press or portable drill with drill guide and ⅜" straight bit
- ☐ Sandpaper (up to 220 grit)
- ☐ Tools for cutting phone books (see step 4)
- ☐ Four (or more) bar clamps
- ☐ Wrenches
- ☐ Hacksaw or grinder with cutting wheel
- ☐ Pipe cutter (optional)
- ☐ Metal file

3. Finish the chair sides.

Finish-sand the two plywood sides, working up to 220-grit sandpaper. Also sand a slight roundover on all of the edges, for comfort and to prevent splintering.

Finish the pieces with a durable, clear finish, such as polyurethane, applied as directed by the manufacturer. Let the final coat cure completely before assembling the chair.

4. Cut the phone book pieces.

Now comes the fun part: cutting the phone books into pieces. The pieces should be roughly equal to the thickness of the seat and backrest portions of the chair sides. Cut enough pieces so that the chair will be at least 14" wide (with the book pieces tightly compressed). If you have books of different thicknesses, be sure to match up cut pieces on both the seat and backrest so the overall width of each will remain the same.

1. Cut the chair sides.

Following the side template at right, draw the profile of the chair side on ¾" plywood stock. Rough-cut the profile with a jigsaw or circular saw, staying well outside the lines.

Place the cut piece on top of the remaining plywood stock and clamp the pieces together. Cut through both pieces with a jigsaw and a straightedge guide (or use a circular saw and guide, then finish the inside corner cuts with a jigsaw or handsaw), cutting to the lines. To make the interior cutout, drill a starter hole inside the cutout, using a ⅜" straight bit. Insert the jigsaw blade into the hole to begin the cut.

With the two cut pieces clamped together, sand the edges so they are flat and smooth and the pieces are identical.

2. Drill the side holes.

Keeping the chair sides clamped together with their edges precisely aligned, mark the six holes for the all-thread rod on the top side piece, as shown in the side template. Drill the holes with a ⅜" bit and a drill press or a portable drill set up with a drill guide to ensure the the holes are perfectly straight. If necessary, use a backerboard to prevent tearout on the bottom piece.

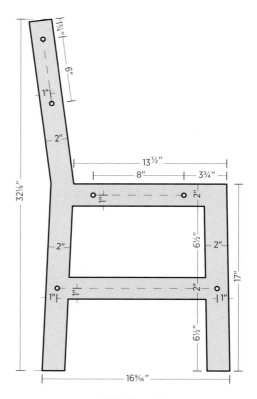

SideTemplate

You can cut a phone book with a variety of tools, including a table saw, a circular saw, and even a utility knife. To use a table saw, you'll need to create a custom sled/jig that supports the back of the book and allows for clamping on a top support to hold the pages together. You'll know your saw and technique best, so a description isn't provided here.

To use a circular saw, mark the cut line on the book, and set the phone book on a sacrificial work surface. Set a piece of scrap plywood or other material that's several inches longer than the book on top, and clamp the assembly together; clamp on one side of the cut line only. Make the cut by cutting through the plywood and slightly into the work surface below, stopping just after the phone book is cut through along its length, and leaving a portion of the plywood uncut, as shown in the cutting jig illustration below right. Align the saw kerf with the cutting line for the next cut.

To cut with a utility knife, mark the cut line on the book, then clamp a straightedge or straight scrap material along the cut line. Cut along the straightedge repeatedly until you're all the way through the book, being careful to keep the blade perpendicular to the book throughout the cut. If the blade is too short to cut through from one side, clamp the book between two pieces of scrap so the scrap edges are aligned, and make the cut from both sides of the book.

5. Drill the book pieces.
Using scrap plywood, create two drilling templates that match the backrest and seat portions of the chair sides, including the two holes in each piece.

Referencing the same edge of each template, clamp each book piece under the template so it is flush with the template's reference edge, and drill the two holes through the book piece with a ⅜" bit, using a drill press or portable drill and drill guide.

6. Assemble the sides and book pieces.
Cut four lengths of ⅜" all-thread about 2" longer than the assembled width of your chair (both chair sides, plus all the seat/backrest book pieces); see Working with All-Thread, page 88, for advice on cutting all-thread. Insert one end of each rod through the inside of the seat and backrest holes on one chair side, then add a cap nut to the end, using a small amount of Loctite (thread-locking adhesive) to keep the nut from loosening over time.

Begin sliding the book pieces onto the rods, alternating between the seat and backrest to maintain matching widths. When all book pieces are in place, fit the other chair side onto the rods, and clamp the entire assembly together, using a bar clamp placed near each of the four rods. Align the book pieces as you clamp so they create a flat surface across the top and front of the seat and backrest. Tighten the clamps firmly and evenly, and measure to make sure the overall width of the chair is consistent over the entire backrest and seat areas.

Add a washer and short standard nut to the loose end of one of the rods (the nut and washer together should be shorter than the threaded depth of the cap nut), and tighten the nut snug. Cut off the excess from each rod so the rod end is flush with the standard nut, using a hacksaw or a grinder with a cutting wheel. Remove the nut and washer and replace them with a cap nut (with Loctite). Repeat this process with the three remaining rods, then remove the bar clamps.

7. Install the lower rods.
The two all-thread rods on the chair legs are concealed inside hollow metal tubes, which also act as spacers to help rigidify the chair. Measure the overall length of the installed rods (on the seat or backrest), and cut two more rods to this length. Then measure the distance between the inside faces of the chair sides — measuring in the seat or backrest area — and cut two lengths of tubing to this length, using a pipe cutter or hacksaw.

File and/or sand the cut ends of the tubing to remove any burrs or correct unevenness. Install the rods with Loctite, as before, threading them through the tubes between the chair sides.

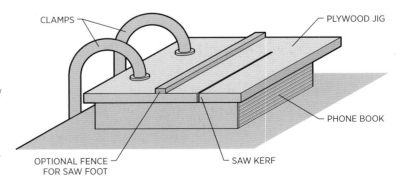

CLAMPS   PLYWOOD JIG   PHONE BOOK   OPTIONAL FENCE FOR SAW FOOT   SAW KERF

Cutting Jig

Ribbed Bench

Designed by Justin Orton

For inspiration, the designer of the Ribbed Bench looked to Gothic cathedrals of early twelfth-century Europe, which had the express design goal of letting in plentiful light. The bench achieves the same with its slatted construction, allowing light to travel through the top and legs and giving the whole piece an airy feel. And with their alternating curves, the legs have a distinctive architectural look reminiscent of the ribbed vaults of classic Gothic structures.

MATERIALS

- One 4 x 8-foot sheet ¾" hardwood plywood or 5 x 5-foot sheet Baltic birch (42" x 54" min.)
- One 2 x 2-foot piece ½" MDF (2" x 18" min.)
- Finish materials (as desired)
- Nine linear feet ⅜" all-thread rod (one 6-foot length and one 3-foot length)
- One 36" length ½"-diam. plain metal tube, with 1⁄16"-thick walls
- Twelve ⅜" zinc washers (⅞" outside diameter)
- Twelve ⅜" dome-style zinc cap nuts

TOOLS

- Circular saw with straightedge guide or table saw
- Miter saw (optional)
- Jigsaw
- Sandpaper (up to 220 grit)
- Double-sided tape
- Clamps
- Router with:
  - ¼" or ⅜" roundover bit
  - Flush-trimming bit
- Drill with:
  - ⅜" straight bit
  - ⅞" Forstner or spade bit (must be slightly larger than outside diameter of the ⅜" washers)
- Reciprocating saw with metal blade or hacksaw
- Metal file
- Bench vise (if available)
- Wrenches

1. Cut the top pieces.

Cut the 12 top pieces to size at 2" x 42", using a circular saw with a straightedge guide or a table saw to ensure straight, accurate cuts. The layout in the cutting diagram below shows you how to make the most of your plywood panel. If you have a miter saw, use it with a stop-block setup to cut the pieces to length. Otherwise, measure and cut each piece carefully so all are the same length.

2. Create the leg template.

There are 22 leg pieces total. All are rough-cut from the plywood panel with a jigsaw and then cleaned up with a router and an MDF template (see Template Routing, page 19).

Create the template by drawing the leg profile on the MDF stock, following the leg template. Carefully cut out the template with a jigsaw, making sure not to cut inside the marked lines; it's better to cut the piece a little large and sand down to the line than to cut too much.

Sand the edges of the template so the curves are smooth and the edges are flat, without saw marks or irregularities. Any flaws in the template will be transferred to each workpiece, so take the time now to shape the template just right.

3. Cut and rout the legs.

Use the leg template on page 148 to trace the 22 pieces on the plywood stock, as shown in the cutting diagram; be sure to leave enough space between pieces for making the cuts. Rough-cut the legs with a jigsaw, staying ⅟₁₆" to ⅛" outside the cutting lines.

Using a small amount of double-sided tape to prevent slipping, place a plywood workpiece on top of the template (for a bottom-bearing router bit) so the plywood overhangs the template along all of its edges. Clamp the parts to your work surface. Rout along the perimeter of the template to create an exact duplicate in the plywood, using a router and flush-trimming bit.

Note: If you have a top-bearing bit, the template goes on top of the workpiece, and you'll need some spacers to raise the work for each cut.

4. Round over the edges.

Using the router and a ¼" or ⅜" roundover bit, shape the edges of all of the top and leg pieces at the desired depth. Be sure to test the bit depth on scrap material first, and round over less than half the plywood's thickness (see Finishing Plywood and MDF, page 20).

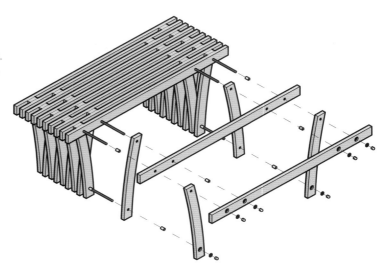

Exploded View

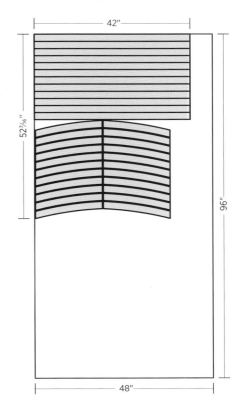

Cutting Diagram

Leg Template

5. Drill the holes for the all-thread rod.

Each leg gets two ⅜" holes, and each top piece gets four ⅜" holes, as shown in the front-view drawing on page 149. The holes will receive the ⅜" all-thread rods that bolt the bench together. In addition, the two outside top pieces and four outside legs receive a ¼"-deep counterbore to partially recess the washers and cap nuts. Select these pieces now and set them aside; you will drill the counterbores and holes for them in step 6.

Mark the locations of the leg holes on the MDF template: The top hole is 1" from the top edge and centered side-to-side on the width of the piece. The bottom hole is 2" from the bottom end and centered side-to-side. Carefully drill the holes with a ⅜" bit. Use the template to drill the holes into the leg pieces. To save time, you can clamp the template and two leg pieces to your work surface, using a sacrificial backerboard to prevent tearout, and drill both legs at once.

Mark the locations for the four holes on a top piece: The two outer holes are 4" from each end, and the two inner holes are 4⅞" from the outer holes; all holes are centered (top-to-bottom) on the width of the piece. Drill the holes, then use the piece as a template to drill the remaining top pieces, as with the legs.

6. Drill the counterbores.

Mark the hole locations on the four outside legs and two outside top pieces, as with the others. Drill the counterbores using a ⅞" spade bit or Forstner bit to a depth of ¼"; the bit must be slightly larger than the outside diameter of the ⅜" washers. (If you're using a Forstner bit in a portable drill, set up a homemade jig to keep the bit in place (see A Forstner Drilling Jig, page 30, for advice). If desired, you can countersink the nut completely, provided the washer and nut have a combined height of about ½" or less.

Once all the counterbores are complete, drill a ⅜" hole through the center of each counterbore, going completely through the piece (this hole comes after the counterbore because spade bits can't be started in holes larger than their guide points).

7. Finish the plywood parts.

Using 220-grit sandpaper, lightly sand the faces and edges of all the legs and top pieces. Finish the pieces as desired. Because refinishing or touching up the pieces requires disassembly, it's a good idea to use a durable varnish such as polyurethane. In the project shown, the parts were finished with clear, wipe-on polyurethane in satin. This typically yields a somewhat more hand-rubbed look and feel, while standard brush-on poly is thicker and will coat over surface imperfections better, for a smoother finish than you get with wipe-on formulations.

8. Cut the all-thread and spacer tubes.

Cut four lengths of ⅜" all-thread at 17⅜", using a reciprocating saw or a hacksaw. Cut two lengths of rod at 15¹³⁄₁₆". File away any edges or burrs created by the cut, being careful to not damage the threads (see Working with All-Thread, page 88, for tips on cutting all-thread).

Use the same saw to cut the metal tubing into 42 pieces at ¾" each. A bench vise (if available) is the best tool for holding the tubing during the cut. For a finished look, file away any burrs or rough edges left from the cuts.

9. Assemble the bench.

Assemble the parts in sequence from one outer top piece to the other, with the bench on its side as you work. Place a washer and a cap nut (also called an "acorn nut") on one end of each piece of all-thread. The four 17⅜" rods join the tops of the legs and the top pieces, and the two 15¹³⁄₁₆" rods join the bottom ends of the legs.

Fit one outside top piece over the four upper rods with the counterbores facing the washers and nuts. Next, fit one outside leg onto each of the outside upper rods and the lower rods, with the legs curving out, as shown in the front-view drawing. Fit a ¾-inch spacer tube onto each upper rod, sliding it up against the top piece, as shown in the top-view illustration. Add a spacer to both lower rods, against the legs. Fit an interior top piece onto the upper rods, followed by two interior legs (with curves facing in), then add two spacers on the outside upper rods.

Repeat this alternating pattern to complete the assembly, and finish with washers and nuts on the outside faces of the remaining outside top and leg pieces. Tighten the nuts to secure the assembly.

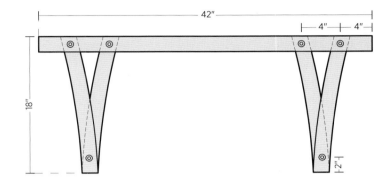

Front View

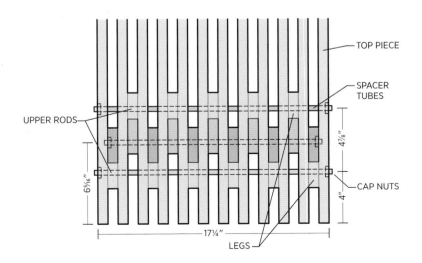

Top View

Bespoke Chair

by Kristin Hare

I designed this chair as an industrial design studio project. The assignment was to design and build a custom-fit studio stool for another person, and I made the chair for my studio partner, Derek, to specifically fit his body and needs. He liked the height of his original studio stool, but it was uncomfortable after long periods because he couldn't rest his back. To remedy this, I decided to upholster the seat of his new chair and included a backrest. To allow for a full range of movement, I installed a lazy Susan below the seat, so the seat and backrest can turn in a full circle.

This is the first piece of furniture I've ever built, and the biggest challenge was forming the backrest. To make it conform to the curves of Derek's back, I laminated thin layers of bendy plywood, using a comfortable preexisting chair as the mold. I laminated seven layers of the plywood, one at a time, clamping them to the chair. After lots of wood glue and many hours, the backrest was sturdy and formed the complex curves I wanted. I covered the backrest with a cherry veneer for an elegant look.

The rest of the chair is a half sheet of ¾" white oak plywood. I simply cut one curved form five times for the chair legs. The five legs are splayed outward for radial symmetry, and the footrest holds them together. I finished the plywood with a cherry stain for a uniform appearance.

5 Places for Everything

Ask Frank Gehry for a museum . . . don't expect the Met.
Ask some designers for storage pieces . . . don't expect pegboard and spice racks.

Revue Magazine Table

Designed by Beth Blair

Combining clean lines, a sculptural form, and a clever hidden storage compartment, this elegant table has the makings of a modernist classic. Its designer clearly wanted to keep things simple as well as sustainable: the case is made with a half sheet of FSC plywood and uses no hardware. Aside from glue and finishes, the only other material is a flexible panel of recyclable polyurethane. For a striking decorative touch that adds depth and contrast, you can color the interior of the case — a bright blue stain was used for this model — and keep the exterior natural with a clear finish.

MATERIALS

- One 4 x 4-foot sheet ¾" hardwood plywood
- Finish materials (as desired)
- Wood glue
- Four cabinet door bumpers (clear, self-adhesive)
- One 34½" x 14½" panel ⅛" polyurethane

Note: All the plywood parts making up the case are joined with glued miter joints. This means that you cut all the pieces with a 45-degree bevel, except for the two top edges at either side of the curved cutout. It's difficult (though possible) to make clean bevels with a circular saw and straightedge, so it's recommended that you use a table saw for the initial parts cuts. As shown in the cutting diagram, you can cut all the plywood parts from a 4 x 4-foot sheet, but you might prefer to have the margin of error afforded by a 5 x 5-foot sheet of Baltic birch or a full 4 x 8 sheet of other plywood.

TOOLS

- Table saw (recommended) or circular saw with straightedge guide
- Jigsaw
- Wood file
- Sandpaper
- Router with:
  - Flush-trimming bit
  - ⅛" rabbeting bit
  - ¼" straight bit
- Ratcheting band clamps
- Machinist's square
- Utility knife
- Quarter or similar coin (as template for finger tab)

1. Cut the plywood parts.
Lay out and cut the case parts as shown in the cutting diagram. As noted above, the inner 15¼" side of each top piece gets a straight edge; make all other cuts with a 45-degree bevel, with the long points on the outside (exposed) faces of every piece.

2. Make the side cutouts.
Draw or trace the side cutout on the inside face of one of the side panels, following the cutting diagram and side cutout template. Use a jigsaw to cut out the bulk of the waste inside the cutout, staying about ¼" inside the cut line. Then make a second pass, cutting precisely to the line. Use a wood file and sandpaper to smooth the cut edge and perfect the curve, as needed. (Any bumps or dips in the edge will be transferred to the other side cutout, so you want the edge to be as smooth as possible.)

Use the first side piece as a template to trace the cutout on the remaining side piece. Remove the bulk of the waste from the second cutout, again using a jigsaw and staying about ¼" inside the line. Clamp the two sides together and use a router and flush-trimming bit to complete the second cutout (the bit's bearing follows the first cutout to make an identical cut in the second piece).

3. Mill the access panel side grooves.
Using the router and a ⅛" rabbeting bit, mill a ⅛"-wide, ⅛"-deep groove along the inside edge of each side cutout. A rabbeting bit is a bearing-guided bit that cuts at a set side-to-side depth, while the vertical depth is adjustable and is determined by the router's depth setting. In this operation, the bit's bearing rides along the edge of the cutout (not the panel's surface).

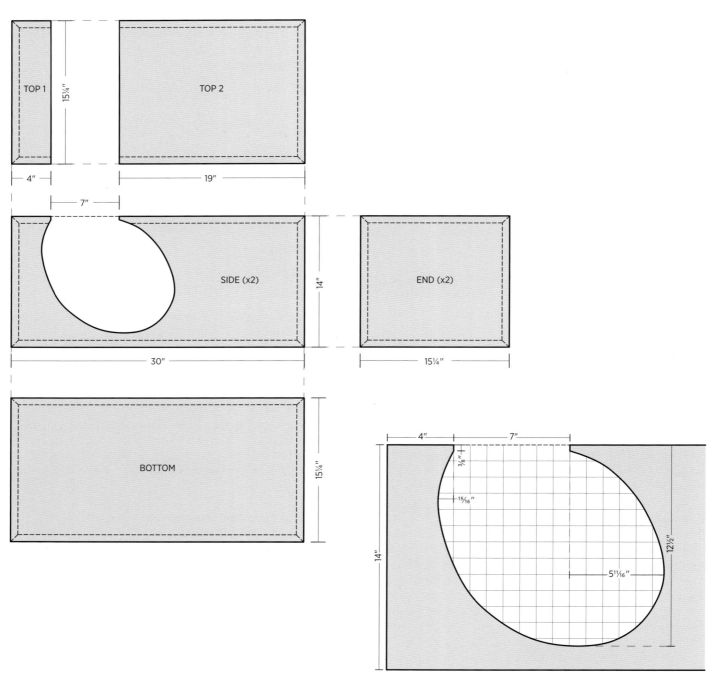

Cutting Diagram   **Side Cutout Template**

4. Mill the access panel end grooves.

Each top piece gets a ⅛"-deep straight groove underneath and just behind its square edge, to accommodate the ends of the polyurethane panel. Mill this groove with a ¼" straight router bit. Set up the router with a guide fence (parallel to the square edge of the top) so the inside edge of the groove is ¼" away from the straight edge of the top piece. The groove will not be visible on the finished piece and can be adjusted before gluing to ensure a proper fit for the polyurethane panel.

5. Prepare the case interior.

Lay out all of the case pieces, interior side up, as in an exploded view, with the bottom piece in the center. Use sandpaper to smooth any imperfections on the interior surfaces. Apply wood stain or other finish, if desired. As shown, the case interior is stained with Daly's Semi-Transparent Exterior Stain, which comes in 30 colors and requires only one coat. It soaks into the wood, allowing the beauty of the grain to remain visible while providing bright, vibrant color. To ensure a strong glue bond, do not apply stain to the beveled edges of the panels.

6. Complete the glue-up.

To ensure that all the miter joints fit well, you have to glue up the entire case in one go. This step is fast and furious, and you'll definitely want at least one helper. Starting with the bottom and one end panel, apply glue to both mating edges, and set the end panel in place. Follow with the side pieces, the other end panel, and the two top pieces, one at a time. Clamp the entire assembly with several ratcheting band clamps running in both directions. As you clamp, check to make sure the miters are closed and the panel edges are flush, and use a machinist's square to ensure the case is square on all sides. Finally, wipe off excess glue from the exterior and interior surfaces with damp paper towels. Let the glue dry.

7. Prepare the access panel.

Cut a rounded finger tab at the center of each end of the polyurethane panel using a sharp utility knife and a quarter or similar coin as a template.
Note: You can use other types of ⅛"-thick material for the panel, but they must be flexible enough for the application.

8. Finish the case.

Sand and finish the case exterior, as desired (see Sanding for a Superior Finish, below). The finish used here is Daly's CrystalFin Acrylic Polyurethane in satin. This water-based, low-toxicity, quick-drying formula provides a beautiful finish. When the finish has dried, apply cabinet door bumpers at each corner of the bottom panel. Insert the polyurethane panel into its grooves.

Shop Tip

Sanding for a Superior Finish

For superior finishes on wood pieces, sanding is key. Once the wood is smooth and flat, you can start moving up the grit scale (the higher the number, the finer the grit). A good starting point for a high-quality finish is in the 300- to 400-grit range. Always sand in the same linear direction, following the grain of the wood. Move incrementally from lower grits to higher grits until you have a surface finish that is smooth to the lightest touch. The more time spent sanding, the better the surface will look in the end.

Stacked Box

Designed by Rachel Gant

As its name implies, this pretty little box is made with a layering, or lamination, of plywood. Its diminutive size makes the box all the more satisfying to create. Each layer of the box has a square window cut out of its center, so that the piece resembles a miniature picture frame. When the frames are stacked, the cutouts create the vessel's interior space, while the solid top and bottom layers provide secure enclosure. Stacked Box happens to be the smallest piece in this book, and yet it's one of the best examples of, in the designer's own words, "celebrating the layers within the plywood and using them to aesthetic advantage." And that, in a nutshell, is why we're here.

See page 180 for another work by Rachel Gant.

MATERIALS

☐ One 12" x 12" piece ¼" plywood (or 2" x 20" min.)

☐ Wood glue

☐ Finish materials (as desired)

TOOLS

☐ Circular saw with straightedge guide or table saw

☐ Miter saw or miter box and backsaw

☐ Drill with ⅜" straight bit

☐ Jigsaw and fine wood blade

☐ Sandpaper (up to 220 or 300 grit)

☐ Clamps

☐ Square-edged file (optional)

☐ Measuring calipers (if available) or measuring tape

☐ Portable power sander (if available) or sanding block

Note: The project shown here is made with eight layers of ¼" plywood, resulting in a 2" cube. To create a box with different dimensions, you can use thicker or thinner plywood, change the number of layers, and/or modify the shape as desired. The following instructions are for the box as shown.

1. Cut the blank layers.

Rip a 2"-wide strip from the factory edge of a piece of ¼" plywood. One 20"-long strip is enough for the whole box; otherwise, rip more than one strip. Use a circular saw with a straightedge guide or a table saw to ensure a very straight, clean cut.

Crosscut the strip into eight 2" squares. The best tool for this is a miter saw set up with a stop block (to cut at 2" each time). If you're making several boxes and you don't have a miter saw, it's worth borrowing or renting one for a couple of hours. Otherwise, you can make the crosscuts with a miter box and backsaw (also set up with a stop block), a jigsaw, or even a circular saw. Make the cuts as straight as possible.

2. Cut the frames.

On one face of one of the blanks (the 2" squares), draw a ¼" margin along the piece's perimeter, as shown in the plan drawing. Drill a ⅜" starter hole for a jigsaw blade just inside the marked margin. Then carefully cut along the lines with a jigsaw. Sand the inside edges of the cutout flat and smooth.

Use the cut frame as a template to mark the window cutout on one of the uncut blanks. Clamp five uncut blanks together, with the marked one on top, so all of their edges are perfectly flush. Drill a starter hole through all five clamped blanks, being careful to stay well within the cutout area. Make the cutouts with the jigsaw. The remaining two uncut blanks will remain solid for use as the top and bottom of the box.

Sand any loose fibers from the inside edges of the frames. If necessary, use a square-edged file to clean up any of the inside corners of the cutouts.

3. Glue up the box.

Apply a very thin layer of glue to the bottom edges of each frame. Stack the frames, one on top of the other, and add the bottom (solid blank) to the bottom of the assembly. Carefully align each layer, making sure the box is square (90 degrees) to a flat work surface. Clamp the assembly with clamps or a heavy, flat weight, and let the glue dry overnight. Lightly sand the interior of the box so all surfaces are flat and smooth.

4. Fit the lid.

Measure the dimensions of your top frame cutout using calipers (if available) or a measuring tape. Transfer the dimensions to a leftover piece of plywood stock, marking a square that will fit inside the top frame. Cut the square with a miter (or other) saw, cutting it just a hair large in both directions.

Test-fit the square in the box, and sand the edges of the square as needed for a snug fit — the slightest bit of resistance is nice so that the lid feels attached. Glue and clamp the square to the underside of the lid blank so it is precisely centered in both directions. Let the glue dry.

5. Sand the box.

Using a power sander or a flat sanding block (made from scrap wood), sand the exterior faces of the box (including the lid, which you should hold in place by hand or with clamps) until they are perfectly smooth. To flatten a face, it helps to sand diagonally across the layers. Start with medium-grit paper and work up to fine-grit (at least 220 or 300 grit).

6. Finish the box.

You can finish your box with any appropriate product. Just keep in mind that a thick finish may affect the fit of the lid. Here's how to create the aged effect of the box shown: Carefully apply very thin layers of dark wood stain, using a small brush. Be careful not to get stain on the top or bottom of the box, unless desired. Apply two or three layers, and let them dry overnight. Once dry, roughly sand the stained surfaces by hand, without a block, using 220-grit sandpaper. This results in a mottled look, as some of the light-blonde layers are exposed among the darker stained layers.

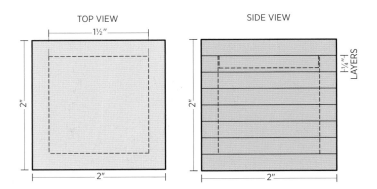

Plan Drawings

Capsa

Designed by Bryce Moulton

Capsa is a modular, wall-mounted, fully enclosed bookcase/storage unit made with ¾" plywood and clear plastic. Its dynamic shape isn't only for looks — it also keeps books or magazines from tipping over. When the lid is closed, the stored contents are protected from dust and moisture by a cork lining, while the shatterproof and scratch-resistant Lexan window provides a full view of the case interior. All of these features make Capsa a fitting piece for any room in the house, including the garage and outdoor areas. And, as you can see here, Capsa also looks great in pairs.

MATERIALS

- ☐ One 2 x 4-foot piece ¾" hardwood plywood
- ☐ Wood glue
- ☐ One 2 x 2-foot piece ⅛" Lexan (or Plexiglas or glass)
- ☐ One 2 x 4-foot piece ³⁄₁₆" lauan paneling (optional)
- ☐ Two 1½" x 2" butt hinges (each leaf measures ¾" wide)
- ☐ One roll ³⁄₁₆"-thick cork (available at hardware and auto parts stores)
- ☐ Finish materials (as desired)
- ☐ Four neodymium magnets
- ☐ Two-part epoxy
- ☐ Screws for mounting
- ☐ Heavy-duty hollow-wall anchors (as needed)

TOOLS

- ☐ Table saw
- ☐ Router or router table with:
  - ☐ ¼" straight bit
  - ☐ ¾" straight bit
- ☐ Jigsaw with straightedge guide
- ☐ Ratcheting band clamps
- ☐ Drill with:
  - ☐ ⅜" spade bit (must be slightly larger than magnet diameter)
  - ☐ Combination pilot-countersink bit
- ☐ Sandpaper (up to 600 grit)

1. Cut the full panels.

Lay out the cuts for all the full panels on a 2 x 4-foot piece of hardwood plywood, as shown in the cutting diagram on page 161. The dimensions are as follows:

- Top = 12" x 14"
- Right = 12" x 11½"
- Left = 12" x 15½"
- Bottom = 12" x 13"

Cut the panels on a table saw, with the blade at 90 degrees (or 0 angle). Later, you will bevel some of these edges and cut the top, right, left, and bottom panels into two pieces (for creating the case and the lid). Remember to mark and cut from what will be the inside face of the piece when installed (to minimize any visible tearout), and be mindful of the grain patterns for best appearance.

2. Cut the miter-joint bevels.

Bevel all the 12"-long edges of the panels, following the cutting diagram and miter detail drawing. For the 45-degree bevels, tilt the table saw blade to 45 degrees, and run the panels through on the flat. For the 53-degree bevels, tilt the blade to 37 degrees and run the panels on the flat. To make the 37-degree bevels, keep the blade at 37 degrees, but run each panel through vertically, on its edge. For safety and improved stability, clamp some scrap material around the workpiece for the vertical cuts.

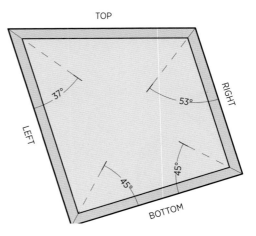

Miter Detail

3. Rout the sides.

As insets for the back panel, cut a ¼"-wide, ¾"-deep rabbet into the rear inside edges (not beveled) of the top, side, and bottom panels (note that here the width is measured across the panel edge; depth is measured along the panel face). You can use a handheld router or a router table for this operation.

4. Cut the grooves for the window.

The inside faces of the side, top, and bottom panels receive a ⅛"-wide (the width of the saw cut, or kerf) groove to accept the Lexan window (the window goes into what will become the lid). These grooves are directly opposite the rabbeted edges. Set up the table saw with the fence ¼" from the blade, set the blade to cut ¼" deep, and cut each groove with a single pass.

5. Divide the panels into case and lid pieces.

Following the cutting diagram, mark the lines as shown to divide each side panel. Make these cuts with a jigsaw in a single pass

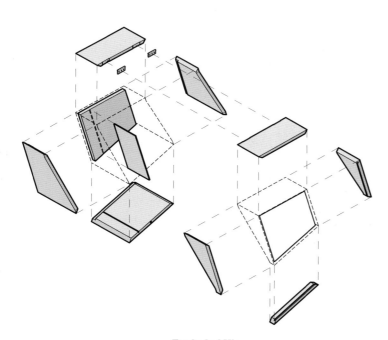

Exploded View

per piece – this means that the turns will be slightly rounded, but that is desirable. Mark the straight cuts for the top and bottom panels, and make these cuts on the table saw.

Note: With all panels, cut to the same side of your marked lines, so that the corresponding widths of the different pieces will match.

6. Cut grooves for the dividers (optional).

The grooves for the dividers are cut into the case pieces only. Do not tilt (angle) the blade for the grooves on the bottom piece, but tilt it at 12 degrees for the top piece. The paneling going into these slots is ³⁄₁₆" thick, so two overlapping passes is just the right width. You'll have to experiment with blade depths for the top-piece grooves, and they should be no deeper than ¼".

The number and locations of the dividers are optional, and you can opt to omit them altogether. In any case, it's best to configure the dividers based on the items you want to store. Using your items as a guide, dry-assemble the case, and measure from a side panel to mark layout lines for the grooves. Measuring from the same side panel ensures the grooves will line up from top to bottom.

7. Rout the hinge mortises.

On the rear edge of the top piece of the lid, use a router and straight bit to cut mortises (recesses) for the two hinges. Mark each mortise so its center is about 3½" in from the long point (toe) of each mitered end of the top piece (make sure the hinges don't interfere with the divider grooves). Cut the mortises to match the length and thickness of the hinge leaves.

8. Glue up the case and lid.

Apply glue to the beveled edges of the case pieces, fit the pieces together so the miters are closed and the front and back edges of the pieces are aligned, then clamp around the entire assembly with ratcheting band clamps.

With the lid pieces, apply glue to only the left, top, and right pieces. Assemble all of these, along with the bottom piece (without glue), and clamp the assembly with a band clamp. You're leaving the bottom piece loose so that you can add the window later.

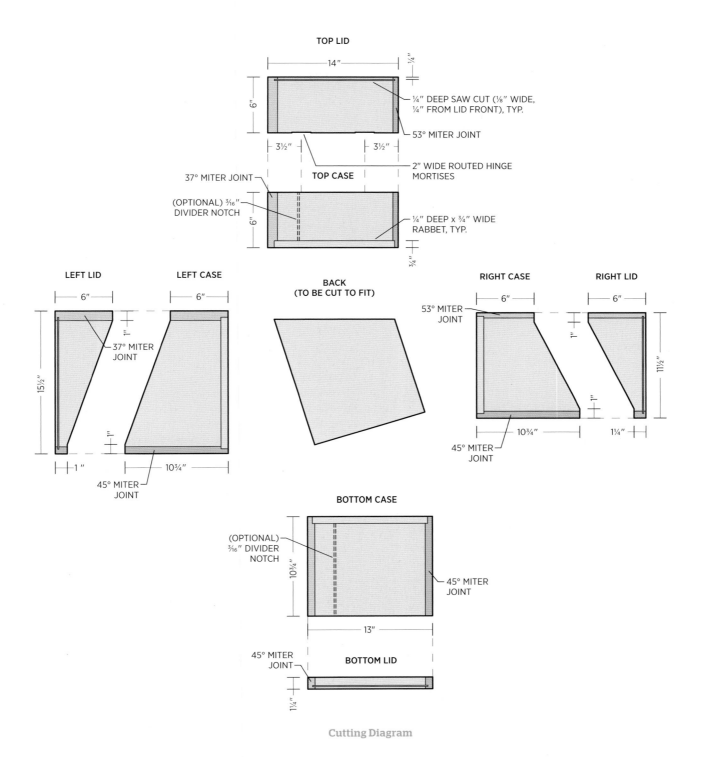

TOP LID

14"

¼"

6"

¼" DEEP SAW CUT (⅛" WIDE, ¼" FROM LID FRONT), TYP.

53° MITER JOINT

3½"   3½"

37° MITER JOINT

TOP CASE

2" WIDE ROUTED HINGE MORTISES

(OPTIONAL) ³⁄₁₆" DIVIDER NOTCH

6"

¼" DEEP x ¾" WIDE RABBET, TYP.

¾"

LEFT LID   **LEFT CASE**

6"   6"

1"

37° MITER JOINT

15½"

1"

1"

10¾"

45° MITER JOINT

**BACK
(TO BE CUT TO FIT)**

RIGHT CASE   **RIGHT LID**

53° MITER JOINT

6"   6"

1"

11½"

1"

10¾"   1¼"

45° MITER JOINT

BOTTOM CASE

(OPTIONAL) ³⁄₁₆" DIVIDER NOTCH

10¾"

45° MITER JOINT

13"

45° MITER JOINT

BOTTOM LID

1¼"

Cutting Diagram

9. Cut and install the back panel.

Position the assembled case over a leftover piece of ¾" plywood. Trace along the inside faces of the sides, top, and bottom of the case to transfer the precise shape to the plywood. Use a straightedge to mark cutting lines ³⁄₁₆" outside each traced line. Cut the back piece along the cutting lines. Test-fit the back panel to make sure it fits well into the rabbets, and then install the back with glue.

10. Cut the window.

Measure the inside dimensions (width and height) of the lid assembly. Add ⁷⁄₁₆" to each of these dimensions, and cut the Lexan sheet to this size, using a jigsaw with a fine-tooth blade and a straightedge guide.

Note: If you're using Plexiglas or glass instead of Lexan, cut by scoring and breaking the material.

11. Cut the dividers (optional).

Measure between each set of slots for your dividers, and cut a strip of lauan paneling to fit. Where horizontal "shelves" meet vertical dividers, support the shelf ends with lauan strips or pieces of small molding glued to the vertical divider.

12. Adjust the case and lid.

Install the hinges into their mortises in the lid, using the provided screws driven into pilot holes. Align the lid and case, and screw the loose hinge leaves to the edge of the top case piece (no mortises here). Slide in the window and temporarily fit the bottom lid piece into place. Close the lid: It won't fit properly yet because the curved section on the case will not quite match the curve of the lid, due to the hinge-leaf thickness. Now you must sand (or use a hand planer, if available) the case edges to create a consistent ⅛" gap all the way around, using a piece of cork as a spacer. Test your progress by placing the cork on the bottom edge of the case and closing the lid, and continue sanding as needed.

13. Finish the wood.

Remove the hinges and window. Sand all the wood parts (moving from lower grits of paper up to 600 grit is recommended). Finish the wood as desired. The units shown here are finished with spar urethane. Do not finish the mating edges for the bottom lid piece.

14. Complete the lid.

Remove any protective covering on the Lexan window and slide the Lexan into the lid assembly. Glue on the bottom lid piece, clamp it, and let the glue dry.

15. Install the magnets and lid.

Drill ⅜" holes in corresponding locations on the bottom edges of the lid and case (or size the holes based on the diameter and thickness of your magnets). Glue the magnets in place with general-purpose two-part epoxy. Reattach the hinges and lid.

16. Add the cork.

Cut the cork roll into ¾"-wide strips, then cut the strips to length, using one full strip for each edge of the lid. You can miter the ends of the strips at the corners, if desired. Depending on the thickness of the cork, you may need to run it just up to the edges of the hinge leaves. Secure the cork to the lid edges with wood glue.

17. Install the unit.

To install the unit, drill three mounting holes in a straight, level line along the back panel. Countersink the holes so the screw heads will be flush to the back panel. Mount the unit with screws driven into wall studs, as applicable, or heavy-duty hollow-wall anchors.

Dyed MDF Storage Cabinet

Designed by Camden Whitehead

This piece, shown here in a pair as part of a wall unit, comes from an architect who clearly has a Midas touch with off-the-shelf materials (his other design in the book transforms AC-grade plywood into beautiful wall panels). Here, MDF, conventionally labeled as merely paint worthy, is completely made over with a fabulous dye job and a few select pieces of builder's bling: custom pulls made with PVC pipe, a rocker-shaped hardwood foot, and (what else?) croquet balls. Now you have a use for that old set with the three broken mallets.

See page 222 for another work by Camden Whitehead.

MATERIALS

- ☐ Three 4 x 8-foot sheets ½" MDF or AC-grade plywood
- ☐ Wood dye (in desired color)
- ☐ Water-based polyurethane
- ☐ #10 biscuits (for joinery; optional)
- ☐ Glue (suitable for prefinished panels)
- ☐ 1⅝" coarse-thread drywall screws (if not using biscuits)
- ☐ Wood putty or homemade filler (sawdust and white glue)
- ☐ Four to six cabinet hinges (depending on load rating)
- ☐ One pair drawer slides
- ☐ ⅞" coarse-thread drywall screws
- ☐ One 4" x 8" (or larger) piece ⅛"-thick sheet PVC
- ☐ One 6" (or longer) length 3"-diameter PVC pipe
- ☐ PVC solvent welding cement
- ☐ ½" #8 pan-head screws
- ☐ One 4" x 32" (or larger) piece 1½"-thick rock maple or other hardwood
- ☐ Two 4"-diam. croquet balls or wood spheres and fasteners (see step 8)

TOOLS

- ☐ Medium-nap paint roller
- ☐ Sandpaper (up to 220 grit)
- ☐ Table saw, panel saw, or circular saw with straightedge guide
- ☐ Biscuit joiner (optional)
- ☐ Bar clamps
- ☐ Square
- ☐ Drill with:
  - ☐ Combination pilot-countersink bit
  - ☐ ¾" bit (for PVC)
  - ☐ 3½" hole saw
- ☐ Router with:
  - ☐ Flush-trimming (laminate) bit
  - ☐ ½" straight bit
- ☐ Double-sided tape
- ☐ Jigsaw or band saw

1. Prefinish the panels.

If you're using MDF, coat both faces of each panel with wood dye, using a paint roller. If you're using AC-grade plywood, first sand the good ("A") face of each panel with 120-grit sandpaper. Experiment with different dilutions of the wood dye, testing each sample on scrap material, to find the desired coloring. Then use a roller to apply the dye to the sanded surfaces of the panel.

After the surface is dry, apply a generous coat of polyurethane, again using a roller. Sand with 220-grit paper after the first coat is dry. Apply two or more coats of poly, sanding between coats but not after the last coat.

Note: The project as designed calls for prefinishing the pieces before cutting them, but you could opt to finish the entire cabinet after assembly. Prefinishing leaves you with unfinished edges that express the parts and construction of the cabinet, while finishing after assembly results in a more monolithic piece whose parts are subordinate to the whole.

2. Cut the cabinet parts.

Using a table saw, panel saw, or circular saw (with a straightedge guide), cut the parts as shown in the cutting diagram. Note that the layouts shown in the diagram are designed for standard 4 x 8 MDF panels, which have actual dimensions of 49" x 97".

3. Prepare the joints.

You can assemble the cabinet with biscuit joints or 1⅝" drywall screws. Biscuits will be hidden from view, of course. With screws, you can either fill the countersink holes with putty or a homemade filler (sawdust and white glue), or leave the screw heads exposed as part of the "construction" aesthetic.

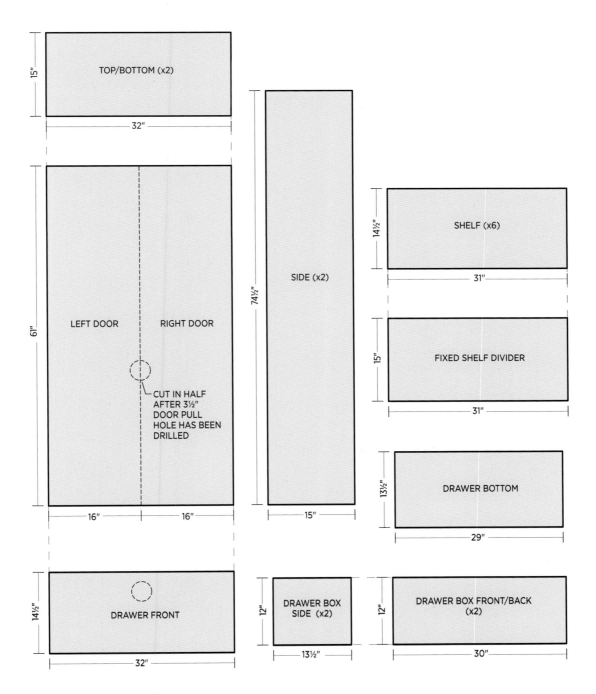

TOP/BOTTOM (x2)

15"

32"

SIDE (x2)

74½"

15"

SHELF (x6)

14½"

31"

FIXED SHELF DIVIDER

15"

31"

61"

LEFT DOOR   RIGHT DOOR

CUT IN HALF
AFTER 3½"
DOOR PULL
HOLE HAS BEEN
DRILLED

16"   16"

DRAWER BOTTOM

13½"

29"

DRAWER FRONT

14½"

32"

DRAWER BOX
SIDE (x2)

12"

13½"

DRAWER BOX FRONT/BACK
(x2)

12"

30"

Cutting Diagrams

Arrange the cabinet parts roughly in the form in which they will be assembled — with the back panel in the center and the sides, top, and bottom positioned around the back accordingly; see the section drawing below. Note that the back panel covers the rear edges of the sides, top, and bottom.

If you're using biscuits, mark the adjoining edges every 3" for the biscuit joints. Cut the biscuit slots for #10 biscuits. If you're using drywall screws, simply mark the joints.

4. Assemble the cabinet case.

Using a minimal amount of glue and your preferred fastener (biscuits or screws), assemble the sides, back, and top in one operation. First glue the sides to the back, then glue the top and bottom to the sides and back. Use bar clamps to secure the assembly. Check the case for square (if the panels are cut and fastened properly, the parts should true themselves to square). Adjust for square, as needed, and let the glue dry overnight.

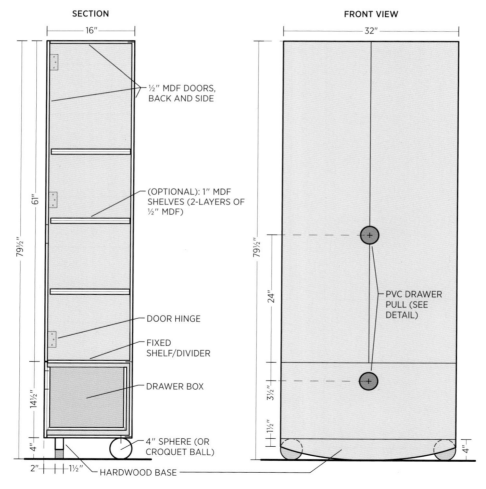

SECTION

FRONT VIEW

16"

32"

½" MDF DOORS, BACK AND SIDE

(OPTIONAL): 1" MDF SHELVES (2-LAYERS OF ½" MDF)

DOOR HINGE

FIXED SHELF/DIVIDER

DRAWER BOX

PVC DRAWER PULL (SEE DETAIL)

4" SPHERE (OR CROQUET BALL)

HARDWOOD BASE

61"

79½"

14½"

4"

2"   1½"

79½"

24"

3½"

1½"

4"

Assembly Plan

5. Complete the doors.

Mark a centerline down the length of the door panel, then mark the location for the door-pull cutout, as shown in the front view of the plan. Use a hole saw to cut a 3½"-diameter hole through the door panel. Rip the panel down the centerline to create the two identical doors. Hang the doors with the cabinet hinges of your choice.

6. Build the drawer.

The drawer box is constructed in a similar way to the cabinet box, but the bottom panel is set into ½" dadoes in the front, back, and sides of the box.

Cut the dadoes with a router and ½" bit so the bottoms of the grooves are ¼" from the bottom edges of the panels. Assemble the box with glue and biscuits or screws, as with the cabinet case.

The outside width of the drawer box is 1" narrower than the inside width of the cabinet case, allowing for the drawer slides. Install the drawer slides as directed by the manufacturer. Slide the drawer box into the cabinet. Set the cabinet on its back and align the drawer front, attaching the front to the drawer box temporarily with double-sided tape (or as desired). Remove the drawer, and fasten the front to the box with ⅞" screws driven through the box and into the back side of the front. Locate and drill the 3½" hole for the drawer pull on the drawer front, as with the door.

7. Create the pulls for the doors and drawer.

Though you could install standard manufactured pulls, these custom pulls are easy to make; see the pull detail drawings. Start by cutting two 4"-square pieces of ⅛" sheet PVC (available at plastics supply houses), using a jigsaw or band saw; these are the mounting plates that will secure the pulls to the back sides of the cabinet doors and drawer box. Then cut one ½" length of 3" PVC pipe for the door and one 1" length for the drawer.

Glue each pipe to the center of a mounting plate with PVC solvent welding cement. Drill a ¾" starter hole through the plate material, inside the pipes. Use a router and a flush-trimming bit to cut out the plate material inside the pipes, leaving two open tubes with a square flange glued to their rear edge. Drill a countersunk pilot hole at each corner of the mounting plates, as shown in the detail drawing; the countersink is on the back side of the plates.

Fit the drawer pull through the back side of the hole in the drawer, and center it in the hole. Fasten the plate to the drawer box front with ½" #8 pan-head screws.

For the doors, cut the pull in half on a table saw (preferably) or a band saw, running the flat edge of the mounting plate along the saw fence. Mount the two halves to the back sides of the door panels so the pull pieces are perfectly aligned when the doors are closed.

8. Add the feet.

The project shown here was installed as a built-in that's supported at the back by the wall and at the front by a curved foot of rock maple. To make the cabinet freestanding, cut, finish, and install the maple foot at the front of the cabinet, as shown in the plan drawing, and add two 4"-diameter spheres or cubes at the back. (Wooden or polyethylene croquet balls work well for the spheres.) Fasten the feet to the cabinet bottom with screws driven through the inside of the cabinet case.

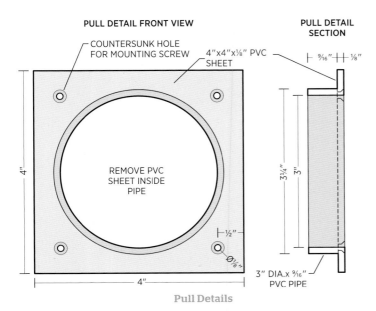

PULL DETAIL FRONT VIEW

COUNTERSUNK HOLE
FOR MOUNTING SCREW

4"x4"x⅛" PVC
SHEET

REMOVE PVC
SHEET INSIDE
PIPE

4"

½"

⅛"

4"

PULL DETAIL SECTION

⁹⁄₁₆"   ⅛"

3¼"   3"

3" DIA.x ⁹⁄₁₆"
PVC PIPE

Pull Details

Pinstriped Console

Designed by Chad Kelly

Always impeccably dressed, the Pinstriped Console mixes well in any company. In other words, it's versatile. As its designer suggests, the piece works equally well as an occasional table, entryway console, side table, and nightstand. The cabinet between the two table surfaces helps keep the look neat and clean, even if the inside happens to be crammed with mail, books, or a mess of remote controls.

See page 68 for another work by Chad Kelly.

MATERIALS

- [ ] One 2 x 4-foot piece ¼" MDF
- [ ] One 5 x 5-foot sheet ¾" Baltic birch plywood (24" x 60" min.)
- [ ] One 9" x 40" piece walnut veneer
- [ ] One 2" x 40" piece maple veneer
- [ ] Distilled water in spray bottle
- [ ] Wood glue
- [ ] Polyurethane finish
- [ ] Two full-overlay cabinet hinges (see step 5)
- [ ] Thirteen 1⅝" coarse-thread drywall screws
- [ ] #10 biscuits (for joinery; see step 6)
- [ ] Door pull
- [ ] Four 14" wrought iron hairpin table legs
- [ ] ⅝" wood screws (for table legs)

TOOLS

- [ ] Carpenter's square
- [ ] Compass
- [ ] Jigsaw
- [ ] Sandpaper (up to 440 grit)
- [ ] Circular saw
- [ ] Straightedge
- [ ] Router with flush-trimming bit (top-bearing)
- [ ] Utility knife
- [ ] Trim roller
- [ ] Clothes iron
- [ ] Masking tape
- [ ] Biscuit joiner
- [ ] Corner clamps
- [ ] Drill with #8 combination pilot-countersink bit
- [ ] Small foam brush
- [ ] Bar clamps

Note: You can glue veneer to a plywood surface in a variety of ways. If the process described here seems too labor-intensive, try using contact cement. You could also use preglued veneer that can be ironed on or pressure-sensitive veneer that is simply pressed on with a veneer-smoothing blade.

1. Create the tabletop template.

Draw the shape of the tabletop on ¼" MDF stock, following the tabletop template on page 170. Use two of the factory edges for one right-angle corner, and use a carpenter's square to lay out the adjacent right-angle corner. The outside corner on the 14"-wide end is rounded with a 2¾" radius; the outside corner on the 11¼" side gets a 1½" radius.

Carefully cut out the template with a jigsaw, then sand the edges, working up to 220-grit sandpaper, so they are smooth and flat.

2. Cut the tabletops and cabinet pieces.

On the bottom face of the ¾" plywood stock, mark a cut line 14¼" from one factory edge, along the length of the stock. Make this cut with a circular saw and a straightedge guide. On the opposite factory edge of the panel, mark a cut line 9½" wide along the length of the stock, and make the cut.

On the 14¼" strip, place the tabletop template in the corner of one end, lining up the factory edges of the template with those of the plywood. Trace around the template. Flip the template, and repeat the process in the other factory corner of the strip. Rough-cut both pieces with the jigsaw, cutting ⅛" outside the lines.

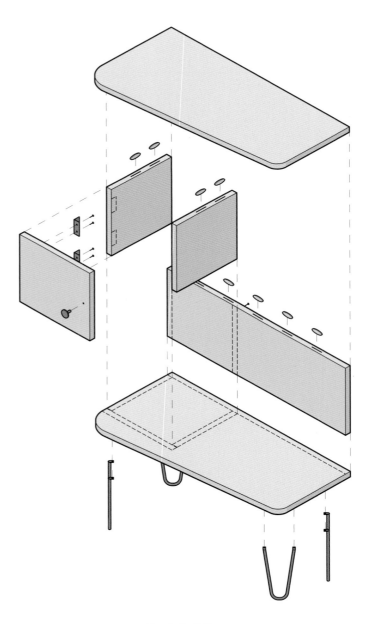

Exploded View

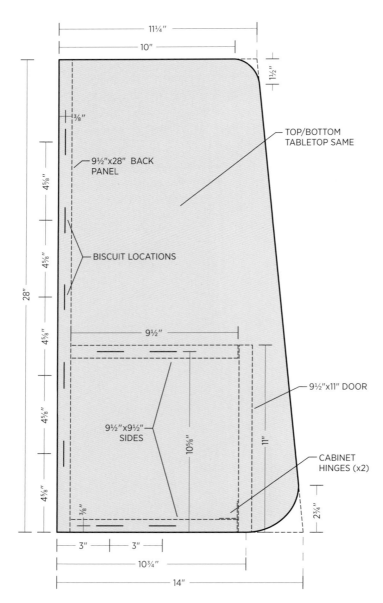

11¼"

10"

1½"

TOP/BOTTOM
TABLETOP SAME

⅜"

9½"x28" BACK
PANEL

4⅝"

BISCUIT LOCATIONS

4⅝"

28"

4⅝"

9½"

9½"x11" DOOR

4⅝"

9½"x9½"
SIDES

10⅝"

11"

CABINET
HINGES (x2)

4⅝"

⅜"

2¾"

3"   3"

10¾"

14"

Tabletop Diagram

Position the template over one of the rough-cut tops so their factory edges are aligned, and clamp both pieces down. Using a router and a top-bearing, flush-trimming bit, clean up the edges of the tabletop to match the template. Do the same with the other tabletop piece.

On the 9½" plywood strip, mark a line 39" from one end. From the opposite end, mark a line at 9½" and another at 19". Crosscut the strip at the center of all three lines, using the circular saw and straightedge guide. These pieces will become the back panel and the cabinet sides and door.

3. Veneer the cabinet pieces.

Cut one piece of walnut veneer to size at 8½" wide and 39" long, using a sharp utility knife and a straightedge. (Tip: Putting painter's tape on all cut lines can help keep the fibers of the veneer intact and the lines straight as you cut.) Mark a line 5⅜" from the top of the piece along its entire length, then cut along this line. Finally, cut one piece of maple veneer to size at 1" wide and 39" long.

On the 39" piece of plywood, mark a straight line 5⅜" from the top edge, along the length of the piece. Make another line 1" below and parallel to the first line.

Spritz the faces of the three pieces of veneer with distilled water; this helps prevent the veneer from rolling up when the glue is applied to the back side. Using a small trim roller (small paint roller), spread wood glue over the face of the plywood and the back side of the three pieces of veneer, and let the glue dry completely.

Align each piece of veneer along the marked lines on the plywood. With a clothes iron set to medium heat, apply firm pressure on the exposed (unglued) faces of the veneers, causing the glue to melt and bonding the veneers to the plywood. Let the piece sit for a couple of hours until the glue has cooled.

Mark a crosscut line 11" from one end of the piece, and make the cut with a circular saw. The resulting 11" piece is for the cabinet door. In order for the door to open freely, use a straightedge and the router and flush-trimming bit to shorten the piece lengthwise by ⅛".

4. Finish the wood parts.

Finishing the wood before assembling the table is much easier than doing it afterward. Mask off all mating edges and faces of the plywood pieces; you don't want to finish the glue-joint areas.

Apply three coats of clear polyurethane (Minwax Polycrylic in satin was used for the console shown) to both sides of each piece of wood. After the first coat, lightly sand all sides with 220-grit sandpaper, and wipe them down with a tack cloth. After the second coat, repeat with 440-grit paper. Do not sand after the final coat.

5. Preinstall the door hinges.
Lay the door and one of the 9½" cabinet sides facedown beside each other, and center the door along the side. Install the two cabinet hinges on both pieces, following the manufacturer's directions. When closed, the door should cover the front edge of the cabinet side (full-overlay configuration). Remove the hinges in preparation for the next two steps.

Note: You can use standard European "cup" hinges or surface-mount hinges, which are much easier to install.

6. Cut the biscuit slots.
You'll join the upper tabletop, the back panel, and the cabinet side pieces with biscuit slots. (The lower tabletop will be attached with screws in the next step.) To begin, align the back panel with the underside of the upper tabletop, marking both pieces five times, every 4⅝", as shown in the tabletop template. Cut the biscuit slots in the top edge of the back panel and the bottom face of the tabletop using a biscuit joiner.

With the bottom face of the lower tabletop faceup, set the back panel on top of the tabletop, with the biscuit slots aligned and the back side of the back panel flush with the edge of the tabletop. Mark the front edge of the back panel down the length of the tabletop. Starting at the wider edge of the tabletop, make a tick mark on this line at ⅜" and again at 10⅝". Using a carpenter's square, and beginning at the line marking the edge of the back panel, draw a line perpendicular to the back-panel line at each tick mark location. Make a mark at 3" and again at 6" along each perpendicular line, and cut a biscuit slot at these locations; see the tabletop template.

Starting from the edge that will butt against the back panel, mark a spot in the top edge of both cabinet sides at 3" and 6", and cut these four slots in the middle of each piece.

Note: In the table shown, the cabinet pieces and top tabletop are assembled with biscuit joints, so that no fasteners are visible. If

you're not equipped for biscuits, you can use glued dowels for the joints. To use dowels, dry-assemble the parts, and clamp them securely. Mark the dowel locations with 3- to 4" spacing, and drill through the tabletops and into the edges of the cabinet sides and back. Glue up the pieces (as in step 7), then drive glued dowel pieces into the holes. After the glue dries, sand the dowels flush to the plywood surfaces.

7. Glue up the cabinet and tabletops.
Apply glue along the bottom edge of the back panel, and use two corner clamps to hold the lower tabletop and back panel together. Using a pilot-countersink bit, drill five holes 4⅝" apart through the underside of the lower tabletop and into the back panel. Secure the two pieces with 1⅝" drywall screws.

Make a tick mark 10⅝" from the wide edge on the face of the lower tabletop, along the back edge. Apply glue to the bottom and rear edges of the cabinet sides. Clamp the hinged side piece to the outside edge of the bottom tabletop. Drill two holes through the bottom face of the lower tabletop and into the cabinet side, at 3" and 6" from the rear edge, and screw the two pieces together.

Line up the center of the remaining cabinet side with the tick mark at 10⅝", clamp it, and drill and screw the pieces together in the same fashion. Drill pilot holes through the back panel and into both cabinet sides at 3" and 6" from the top of each side, and attach them with screws.

Apply glue to nine biscuits and their slots, using a small foam brush. Place the biscuits in the top of the back panel and the tops of both cabinet sides, and position the top tabletop in place, aligning the slots and biscuits. Use bar clamps to clamp the top down until the glue dries.

8. Complete the assembly.
Reinstall the door hinges, and fine-tune the hinge adjustments as directed by the manufacturer. Install the door pull following the manufacturer's directions, positioning it approximately 1" above the maple veneer and 1¼" from the edge of the door.

Turn the table upside down, and arrange the table legs ¾" away from each corner. Mark the mounting holes, drill pilot holes, and fasten the legs with ⅝" wood screws.

Note: You can order authentic reproductions of 1950s-style hairpin table legs in custom lengths from Hairpinlegs.com (see Resources).

Angle Shelf

Designed by Gavin Engel

Angle Shelf is a perfectly useful set of bookshelves with an uncommon architectural design. In the words of the designer, "The rectangularity of the common bookshelf is not essential to its function. By giving this shelf pronounced angular geometry it has an aesthetic purpose as well as a functional purpose. The angular and cantilevered shelves define a more open, dynamic space, while still providing plenty of storage area. The black pipe, in its simplicity, complements the energy of the angular form and busy texture of the wood grain." Indeed, why have a bookshelf when you can have Angle Shelf?

MATERIALS

- One 4 x 4-foot sheet ½" plywood
- Twenty-seven 1" #10 brass wood screws
- Finish materials (as desired)
- One 32" length steel pipe with 2" outside diam.
- Spray paint (black, or as desired)
- Clear spray-on enamel

TOOLS

- Circular saw with thin blade and straightedge guide
- Drill with:
  - ⅛" straight bit
  - 1⅞" hole saw
- Clamps
- Sandpaper
- 2-foot level
- Hacksaw or reciprocating saw
- Metal file

1. Cut the wood parts.

Lay out pieces A through H on a 4 x 4-foot sheet of ½" plywood, as shown in the cutting diagram. For best appearance, the long dimensions of the parts should parallel the grain direction of the panel faces.

Cut the parts with a circular saw and straightedge guide to ensure straight cuts. Because the layout is a tight fit, use a thin ("panel" or "plywood") blade, and cut along the center of your cut lines to remove the same amount of material from all neighboring parts.

2. Drill the pipe hole.

On piece A, measure and mark a centerpoint for the pipe hole, 2" up from the front right corner and 1¾" in from the right side edge; see the cutting diagram. Drill the hole down through the top face of the panel, using a 1⅞" hole saw.

3. Assemble the wood parts.

Make the connections listed below as shown in the assembly diagram. You'll use two 1" #10 brass wood screws for each joint (unless otherwise noted). Clamp the boards together at right angles and drill ⅛"-diameter pilot holes, locating the holes ¼" from the side edges and 2" from the front and back edges of the boards. Join the parts in the following order:

- A to E, C to F, and C to D (drive the screws through the faces of the longer boards and into the edges of the shorter boards)
- B to E
- G to back of A
- G to back of B (use 3 screws; make sure top surface of B is 12" from bottom surface of A)
- H to back of A, B, and E (use 2 screws each)
- B to D
- G to D
- H to back of C (make sure top surface of C is 12" from bottom surface of B)
- G to back of C (use 3 screws)
- H to back of F

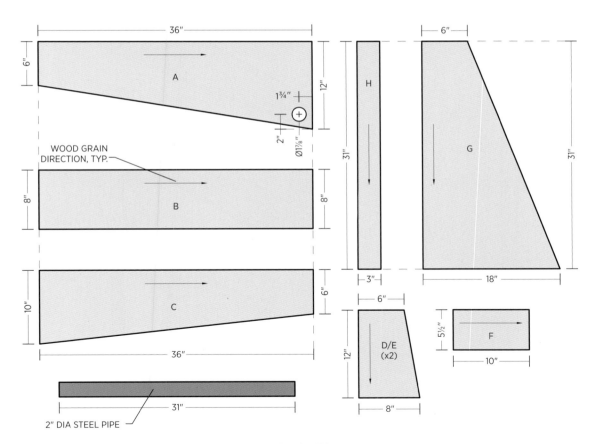

Cutting Diagram

4. Finish the shelves.

Finish-sand the shelf assembly and apply the finish of your choice. As shown, the project was finished with clear polyurethane in satin.

5. Prepare and install the pipe.

Stand the shelf assembly upright on a level surface. Place a 2-foot level on top of shelf A. With a helper, hold shelf A so it is level, then measure up from the floor to the top surface of shelf A. Add about ¼" to this dimension to find the length for the steel pipe.

Cut the pipe to length, using a hacksaw or reciprocating saw, being very careful to make a straight cut. File the cut end to remove any burrs or rough spots. If necessary, sand the outside of the pipe with 220-grit sandpaper so the surface is smooth.

Paint the pipe with black spray paint (the project as shown used a Rust-Oleum paint in matte black), then apply a clear protective enamel, as directed by the manufacturer. Let the finish dry thoroughly.

Carefully twist the top end of the pipe into the hole in shelf A until the shelf is level. This is a very tight fit, so no fasteners are required; however, you may have to sand the inside of the hole a bit to fit the pipe.

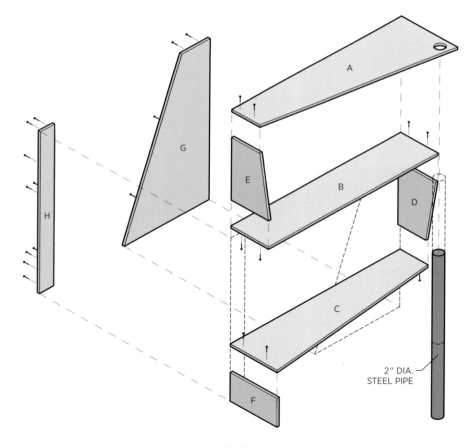

2" DIA.
STEEL PIPE

Assembly Diagram

Paint Chip Modular Bookshelf

Designed by Matt Kennedy of port rhombus design

The familiar paint chip is more than just a clever idea for the finish of this piece; it's the central design concept. For just as the colors on a chip are complementary to one another, like the shelves of a bookcase, they are also individual and distinct — in a sense, modular. Each color, or shelf, in this assembly is a self-contained unit that can be lifted from the stack and transported with all of its contents. The modularity also allows you to build as many units as you need and to mix things up with different shelf arrangements or color schemes. By building multiples of the top unit, which has a top panel, you can arrange pieces side by side under a window or cap a grouping of shelves to create a work surface with storage below. And perhaps best of all, you never have to settle on just one color.

MATERIALS

- ☐ One 4 x 4-foot piece ½" hardwood plywood (for top unit)
- ☐ One 4 x 8-foot sheet ½" hardwood plywood (for three side/bottom units)
- ☐ Card stock or thin cardboard
- ☐ Wood putty or auto-body filler (as needed)
- ☐ Finish materials (see step 5)
- ☐ Wood glue
- ☐ Wood veneer edge tape (optional; see step 7)
- ☐ ¼" x 1½" wood dowel pins

TOOLS

- ☐ Circular saw with straightedge guide or table saw
- ☐ Drill with ¼" straight bit
- ☐ Self-centering doweling jig (see the shop tip below)
- ☐ Router with straightedge and:
  - ☐ ½" straight bit
  - ☐ Flush-trimming bit
- ☐ Scissors
- ☐ Jigsaw or band saw
- ☐ Sandpaper
- ☐ Masking tape
- ☐ Small paint roller
- ☐ Stenciling tools (see step 5)
- ☐ Square
- ☐ Mallet
- ☐ Clamps
- ☐ Utility knife, razor blade, or veneer trimmer (if using veneer edge tape)
- ☐ Clothes iron (if using veneer edge tape)

1. Cut the panels.

Following the cutting diagram, cut the plywood panels for each unit, using a circular saw with a straightedge guide or a table saw to ensure clean, straight cuts. Because this bookshelf is modular, consistency and accuracy in the pieces are essential for proper alignment.

For each standard unit you'll need:

- 2 side panels at 14" x 12"
- 1 bottom panel at 11¼" x 27"
- 1 back panel at 14" x 27"

For each top unit you'll need:

- 2 side panels at 14" x 12"
- 1 bottom panel at 11¼" x 27"
- 1 back panel at 13¾" x 27"
- 1 top panel at 12" x 27"

Also cut one extra side panel to use as a routing template.

2. Drill the dowel holes.

When stacked, the units are aligned and secured with dowel pins (precut dowels) set into holes in the top and bottom edges of the side panels. On the top unit, only the bottom edges of the side panels get dowel holes. It is imperative that these holes are placed accurately and drilled straight, so measure, mark, and drill with care, and use a self-centering doweling jig (see the shop tip on page 179) to keep the holes straight and aligned between units.

Using a doweling jig and a drill with a ¼" bit, make two ⅞"-deep holes in the top and bottom edges of each side panel. All the holes are 1½" from the corners and centered on the edge of the stock. Use a drill stop or a piece of masking tape to mark the bit at the proper depth, taking into account the jig thickness. Remember, for all top units, drill holes only in the bottom edges of the side panels.

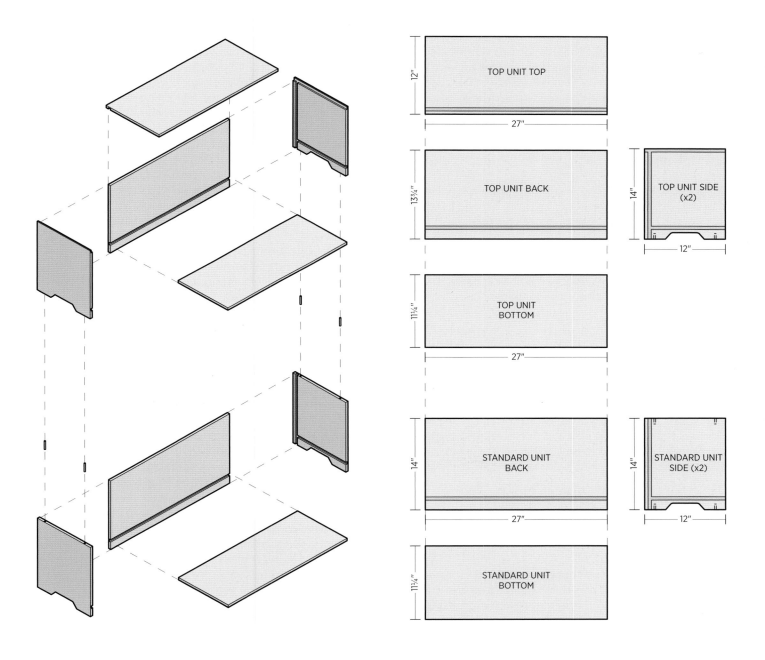

TOP UNIT TOP

12"

27"

TOP UNIT BACK

13¾"

TOP UNIT SIDE (x2)

14"

12"

TOP UNIT BOTTOM

11¼"

27"

STANDARD UNIT BACK

14"

STANDARD UNIT SIDE (x2)

14"

27"

12"

STANDARD UNIT BOTTOM

11¼"

Exploded View

Cutting Diagram

3. Rout the dadoes.

The panels of each unit are held together with glued dado joints. All of the dadoes (continuous grooves) are ½" wide and ¼" deep. Following the cutting diagram, mill the dadoes with a router and ½" straight bit, using a straightedge or an edge guide on the router to guide the cut. Before you start, make a test cut in scrap material and test the fit of the plywood in the dado. It should fit snugly; if it's loose at all, use a smaller bit (you may have to sand the mating panels slightly for a good fit).

For each standard unit:

- Mill the back-panel dado at 1½" from one of the long edges.
- Mill two dadoes in each side panel: one at ½" from the long (rear) edge of the panel and one at 1½" from the bottom edge.

For each top unit, do the same as above, plus:

- Mill one dado flush with the top edge of each side panel (technically, this is a rabbet — a continuous notch at the edge of a piece).
- Mill one dado on the inside of the top panel, ½" from the rear edge.

4. Make the handle cutouts.

Draw the handle profile on a piece of card stock or thin cardboard, following the handle detail drawing, and cut out the shape with scissors. Place this cardboard template on the extra side panel you cut in step 1, with the handle centered along the bottom edge. Trace the profile onto the panel. Cut out the profile with a jigsaw or band saw, then sand the cut edge so it is smooth and free of saw marks.

Position the side-panel template on a side panel so all edges are flush and the cutout in the template is underneath the bottom dado in the side panel. Trace the cutout onto the side panel. Rough-cut the handle with a jigsaw, staying about ⅛" away from the line.

Clamp the side panel over the plywood template so all edges are aligned. Use the router and a flush-trimming bit to clean up the handle cut. The bearing on the bit follows the template for a perfectly matching cutout.

Repeat the tracing, cutting, and routing for all the side panels.

5. Paint the panels.

To create a natural-looking gradient of paint colors, it's best to use the colors from an actual paint chip. Instead of buying a quart of paint in each color, see if you can find 2.5- or 3-ounce samples, which should cost about $3 each. Just make sure the paint sheen is gloss (preferably) or semigloss; eggshell, satin, and flat sheens just aren't slick or durable enough for furniture.

You can paint the plywood edges (first fill any voids with wood putty or auto-body filler), or you can apply veneer edge tape, which doesn't go on until the project is assembled (step 7).

Finish-sand the panels, being careful not to round over any of the dado edges. Remove all dust from the panels. Tape over the dadoes with masking tape; you don't want paint in them. Also tape any edges that will get veneer tape, if you're using it.

Coat all surfaces with a primer, using a small paint roller. Add two or three coats of paint in the desired base colors.

To add the names of the colors (as shown in the project here), you can use a vinyl cutter to make transfer stickers (preferred method), or you can create your own stencils with a computer: Choose a font style and size in a graphics or word processing application, and print out the names on your own printer or at a local printing service. (Adding crop marks in the lower right- and left-hand corners is a great way to register your text to the lower corners of the board so that all the text will be at the same height.)

Simply cut out the printed letters to make your stencil. You can choose to attach floating items with bridges, such as the center of a P, or secure it in place to be painted over. Paint the lettering onto the back panels of each unit, as desired, being careful to keep the paint from bleeding under the stencils.

If desired, you can add a protective finish of polyurethane or poly-acrylic over the paint. This is especially advisable for the insides of the units.

6. Glue up the units.

When gluing and clamping, always check that the mating pieces are square (90 degrees) before letting the glue set.

Arrange all the pieces for each unit. It's a good idea to check that all pieces fit and align well before gluing.

Start by laying one side piece down on a perfectly flat surface. Apply glue to the side panel's dadoes. Insert the back panel into its dado, making sure the edges are flush and the dadoes are perfectly aligned. Tap softly with a mallet (use a scrap block to protect the panel's edge, if necessary). Glue the bottom panel into its dadoes in the side and back panels. Instead of hammering, use clamps to pull these pieces together. Protect all edges with scrap blocks when clamping, and check for square as you work.

Add the other side piece and tap it into place, keeping all the dadoes aligned. Once this assembly is complete, set the unit upright, and add clamps to bring the sides in toward each other. Three to five clamps should be sufficient. It may help to use a scrap board to span over the open side of the unit, to keep everything square.

When gluing up the top unit, assemble and clamp all but the top panel, and let the glue set. Then add the top panel and clamp it in place.

Let the glue dry for 24 hours.

7. Apply edge veneer tape (optional).
If desired, apply veneer tape to the front edges of each unit: Starting with the side panels, cut pieces of the tape ½" longer than each edge. Hold the tape flush to the inside face so it overhangs on the outside face of the panel. Apply a hot iron to the exposed side of the tape to activate the adhesive, as directed by the manufacturer. After the tape cools, trim the excess with a utility knife, razor blade, or veneer trimmer.

To cover the units' longer edges, cut the tape a little long. Iron down one end, then move toward the opposite end, stopping just a few inches from the other side edge. Lay the tape flat (without ironing), and make a small cut with a utility knife on each side of the tape at the exact point it needs to terminate. Then carefully cut between those notches with scissors. The remaining portion can now be ironed down and should be perfectly flush.

8. Assemble the shelves.
Stack the units by placing a dowel pin in each hole on top of the bottom unit. Carefully set the next unit on top so that each dowel is aligned with its bottom hole. Repeat this process to stack the rest of your shelf.

Note: Because the units are not permanently fastened, never try to move your shelf without disassembling it first.

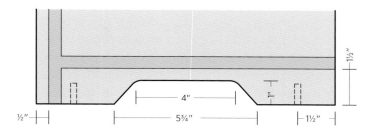

Handle Detail

Shop Tip

Self-Centering Doweling Jigs
Doweling jigs (or dowel jigs) come in a range of prices and capabilities. For a one-off project or occasional use, you can probably get by with a simple plastic self-centering jig. These start at about $12. Better-constructed metal jigs start at about $30 and go up from there.

To use a self-centering jig, outfit the jig with the appropriate size of bushing for your drill bit (as applicable; some jigs have only a few different hole sizes bored into the jig itself). The bushing helps guide the bit for a clean, straight hole. Next, align the jig with your marked line, and clamp the jig to the workpiece. As its name indicates, a self-centering jig automatically centers the hole/bushing over the stock. Then all you have to do is drill the hole.

Jigs that aren't self-centering simply have a flange that registers against one side/face of the workpiece, and the jig's holes set the spacing, which will be roughly centered if you're using standard stock. The key to accuracy with these is to mark all of the sides/faces you will register the jig against before drilling, so even if the holes aren't precisely centered they will all be the same distance from the marked points.

Laptop Stand

Designed by Rachel Gant

The poor ergonomics of a flat laptop keyboard make a stand essential equipment for anyone who does a lot of typing on a laptop, particularly when sitting at a desk. Laptop stands are commercially available in countless iterations, but for those who value beauty and good design in everyday objects, cheap plastic and institutional forms just won't do — not if they have an alternative like this design. It's simple, it's elegant, and it knocks down into four slender pieces that easily slip into a case alongside the laptop itself. (Looking for a good designer, Apple?)

See page 156 for another work by Rachel Gant.

MATERIALS

☐ One 12" x 12" piece ⅛" plywood

☐ Finish materials (see step 4)

TOOLS

☐ Jigsaw (with fine wood blade) or band saw

☐ Double-sided tape or hot glue gun

☐ Sandpaper (up to 300 grit)

☐ Rotary tool with cylindrical sanding attachments (optional)

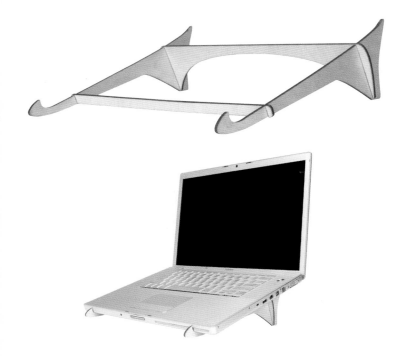

Note: This project is sized for 13" laptops, but it can accommodate some larger sizes, or can be scaled for a custom fit.

1. Lay out the parts.

Draw the four parts on the plywood stock, following the cutting templates. The critical elements of the layouts are the overall dimensions, the slots, and the slot spacing. For the curves, you can follow the plans precisely or create your own design (a French curve tool helps for marking smooth curves in almost any shape).

There are four pieces total: one each of A and B, and two C pieces; however, draw only one C piece now, and leave enough space for a second C piece in the layout. Be sure to allow for plenty of space between all pieces in the layout, to provide access for a saw.

2. Cut the parts.

Using a jigsaw or band saw, cut out the profile of each piece, staying on the outside edges of your cutting lines. Do not cut the slots at this time. To cut the C pieces, rough-cut the marked C piece, staying well outside the lines. Then stick the cut piece over the reserved area of the stock for the second C piece, using double-sided tape or small dabs of hot glue. Cut out both C pieces at once so they are identical, and leave the pieces joined.

Measure the precise thickness of your plywood, then cut the slots so they are just a hair narrower than the plywood. Make the cuts with a jigsaw or band saw, first cutting at each side of the slot, then making additional passes in between to remove any waste material, if necessary.

3. Sand the parts.

Test-fit the slot joints by fitting the pieces together (see the photo of the finished piece as reference). If necessary, carefully sand the sides of the slots for a good, snug fit.

Sand the edges of the pieces to smooth the curves and remove any saw marks. Keep the C pieces stuck together for this step. You can also use a rotary tool (such as a Dremel) with cylindrical sanding attachments for the curves.

Sand the faces smooth with fine sandpaper, and sand a very slight roundover on the edge corners to prevent splintering.

4. Finish and/or assemble the stand.

Since a laptop is more vulnerable to moisture damage than plywood, it's probably safe to leave your stand unfinished. However, a protective topcoat will prevent discoloration from fingerprints and will make the surfaces washable. A good finish to use here is something thin, like a penetrating-type oil or wipe-on polyurethane. For a nice detail, carefully stain just the edges of the pieces with dark stain, then clear-coat everything with a thin protective finish (like wipe-on poly).

Note: If you would like to glue the stand together permanently, add a small amount of glue to the edges of the slots, assemble the stand and make sure it's square, then weight it down and let the glue dry. Do this before applying a protective finish.

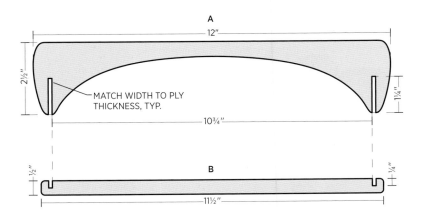

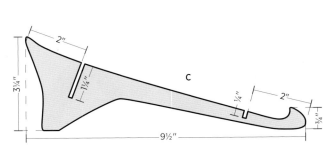

Cutting Templates

Drunken Monkey

Designed by Paolo Korre

The Drunken Monkey speaks for itself, if perhaps with some slurring. But rest assured, this monkey knows how to take care of wine. It will hold your bottle securely whether it's hanging from a rod or resting on a flat surface. And it always keeps the neck pointing down to prevent the cork from drying out. The Monkey works well as a solo novelty piece and is even better as a group. After all, monkeys, like (most) humans, prefer not to drink alone.

MATERIALS

- ☐ One 15" x 24" (or larger) piece ¾" hardwood plywood
- ☐ Wood glue
- ☐ Two 1" flat-head wood screws
- ☐ Wood filler (optional)
- ☐ Finish materials (as desired)

TOOLS

- ☐ Jigsaw
- ☐ File
- ☐ Sandpaper
- ☐ Clamps
- ☐ Drill with combination pilot-countersink bit

1. Cut the parts.

Using the cutting templates, lay out the profiles of the main body and two leg parts on the plywood stock. Cut out the parts with a jigsaw. It's a good idea to cut just outside the lines for the notches, then file the sides as needed for a tight fit.

2. Assemble the monkey.

Finish-sand the parts, being careful not to round over the edges of the notches. Apply glue to the notches of the main body, covering all three sides. Fit the legs into the notches, and gently clamp the parts together. Let the glue dry.

Drill a single countersunk pilot hole through the center of each notch joint, from underneath, and reinforce the joint with a wood screw. Drive the screws to just below the surface of the wood.

3. Finish the monkey.

If desired, cover the screw heads with color-matched wood putty, let it dry, and sand it flush. Finish the monkey as desired.

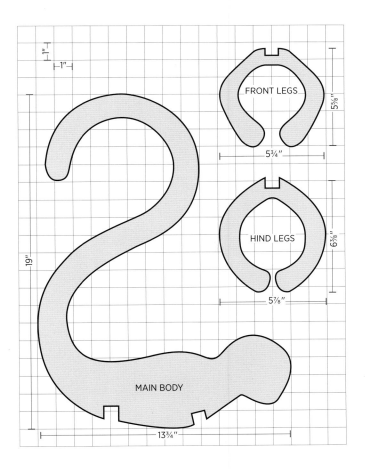

FRONT LEGS

5⅝"

5¾"

HIND LEGS

6⅜"

5⅞"

MAIN BODY

19"

1"

1"

13¾"

Cutting Templates

Toolboxes

Designed by Paul Steiner

These projects were designed by a high school instructor for the purpose of offering students a choice (novel idea). The kids decide which version to build based on their personal interests and storage needs. The large box is a traditional builder's design, perfect for carpentry and woodworking tools. The small box is a handy little tote for art supplies or specific tool accessories. Whichever one you choose, you'll have a classic workshop sidekick and the best kind of heirloom piece — the heavily patinated kind. Sure beats the heck out of a shop-class cutting board or wooden bookends.

See page 277 for another work by Paul Steiner.

MATERIALS

- ☐ 24" x 24" (or larger) piece ½" or ¾" plywood
- ☐ Wood glue
- ☐ Fasteners (2" finish nails, 1½" coarse-thread drywall or wood screws, or wood dowels; see Choosing Fasteners on page 186)
- ☐ Finish materials (optional)

TOOLS

- ☐ Circular saw with straightedge guide
- ☐ Framing square
- ☐ Jigsaw (optional)
- ☐ Handsaw (optional)
- ☐ Sandpaper (80 to 150 grit)
- ☐ Clamps
- ☐ Combination square
- ☐ Drill with pilot bits
- ☐ Miter saw or miter box and backsaw
- ☐ Router with ¼" roundover bit (optional)

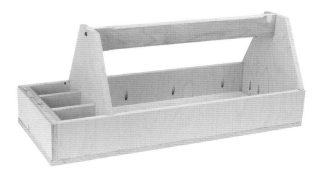

Note: For either toolbox, you can easily modify the length of the main compartment by lengthening or shortening the sides, bottom, and handle pieces by the same amount.

To Build the Small Toolbox

1. Cut the sides and bottom.

Lay out and cut the two sides and bottom from ½" plywood, using a circular saw and a straightedge guide for clean, straight cuts. The sides are 3" x 14", and the bottom is 8" x 14".

2. Cut the ends.

Draw the shape of the end piece on ½" plywood stock, following the small toolbox plan. Use a framing square to make the perpendicular lines and as a straightedge. The ½" x 3" side cutouts are to accept the ends of the side pieces.

Cut out the overall shape with a circular saw, then make the side cutouts with a jigsaw, circular saw, or handsaw. Sand the cut edges smooth and free of saw marks. Then use the cut piece as a template to trace the shape for the second end piece. Cut out and sand the second end piece.

3. Glue up the box frame.

Dry-assemble and clamp the sides and ends to make sure everything fits properly. Use a combination square to check the inside corners of the frame for squareness. Make any necessary adjustments. Drill pilot holes for the fasteners you're using (see Choosing Fasteners, page 186).

Apply glue to the edges of the cutouts in the end pieces, and assemble and clamp the frame. Add fasteners to the joints. Let the glue dry overnight.

4. Create the handle.

Cut two 1"-wide strips of ½" plywood to length at about 14". Glue and clamp the strips together face-to-face, with their edges and ends aligned. Let the glue dry overnight.

Measure between the inside faces of the box ends and cut the handle to length for a snug fit in between the ends; use a miter saw or a miter box and backsaw for a straight cut. Sand the corners and edges of the handle for a comfortable feel, as desired. You can also round over the corners with a router and ¼" roundover bit, if available. Don't sand or round over the ends of the handle.

5. Install the handle and bottom.

Dry-fit and clamp the handle and bottom to the frame assembly. The top edge of the handle should be flush with the top edges of the end pieces, and the bottom should be flush with the frame on all sides. Drill pilot holes through the bottom and into the sides and ends. Also drill pilot holes through the end pieces and into the ends of the handle.

Disassemble the parts. Apply glue to the ends of the handle, and clamp and fasten it in place. Glue the bottom edges of the sides and end pieces, and clamp and fasten the bottom panel in place. Let the glue dry overnight.

6. Sand and finish the piece.

Sand all surfaces of the box, working up to 150-grit or finer sandpaper. Slightly round over all edge corners to prevent splintering. If desired, apply a finish of your choice. Finishes such as penetrating oils and paste wax retain the natural look and feel of the wood and can be refreshed when they get worn.

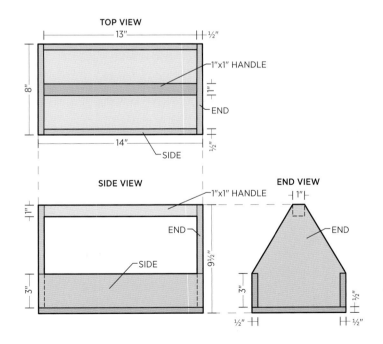

Small Toolbox Plan

To Build the Large Toolbox
1. Cut the box parts.
All the parts are cut from ½" plywood. For a heavy-duty box, substitute ¾" plywood and adjust the dimensions accordingly.

Using a circular saw and a straightedge guide for clean, straight cuts, cut the following pieces:

- 2 sides at 3" x 17½" each
- 1 bottom at 10" x 18"
- 1 inner short end at 3" x 9"
- 1 outer short end at 3" x 10"
- 2 dividers at 3" x 3" each

Shop Tip

Choosing Fasteners
You can use almost any fastener to reinforce the glued joints of your toolbox, including finish nails or screws driven in the standard fashion or through pocket holes (which would require a pocket-hole jig and bits).

Another option, which adds a nice decorative effect, is to use glued wood dowels as fasteners: With the joint dry-assembled and clamped together, drill holes along the centerline of the joint, going through the first piece and into the mating piece. Cut a short length of dowel for each hole. Glue up the project, then add a thin layer of glue to the dowels and drive them into the holes until they are flush with or just above the surface. When the glue dries, sand the dowel ends flush with the surface. For ½" plywood, drill ¼"-diameter holes a total of 1⅛" deep and fill them with ¼"-diameter, 1"-long dowels; for ¾" plywood, drill ⅜"-diameter holes 1⅝" deep and fill them with ⅜", 1½"-long dowels.

Instead of dowels alone, you can also use screws driven through counterbored pilot holes (made with a combination pilot-countersink bit), then hide the screw heads with precut dowel plugs glued into the counterbores and sanded flush.

You'll also need to cut the two tall ends. Lay out the shape of one piece on your stock, following the large toolbox plans. Use a framing square to make the perpendicular lines and as a straightedge. The ½" x 3" side cutouts are to accept the ends of the side pieces. If desired, mark a rectangular cutout for storing a level across the two tall ends, as shown in the end-view drawing; base the dimensions on your own level.

Cut out the overall shape of the tall end piece with a circular saw, then make the side cutouts with a jigsaw, circular saw, or handsaw. If you want a cutout for a level, make it with a jigsaw. Sand the cut edges smooth and free of saw marks. Then use the cut piece as a template to trace the shape for the second tall end piece. Cut out and sand the second tall end piece.

2. Mark the divider locations.
On the outside face of one tall end piece, measure in 2½" from the vertical edge of the side cutout, and mark a line perpendicular to the bottom edge of the end piece. Draw a matching line on the opposite side of the same tall end piece. Next, draw lines on the inside face of the inner short end piece, 2½" from each end. All these lines represent the outside faces of the divider pieces (see the top view in the plan).

3. Drill pilot holes for the frame.
Dry-assemble and clamp the parts of the box frame: sides, tall ends, short ends, and dividers. Make sure that everything fits properly and the assembly sits flat. Use a combination square to check the inside corners of the frame for squareness. Make any necessary adjustments.

Drill pilot holes for the fasteners you're using, starting with the side tall-end joints and outer short-end joints. To drill holes for the dividers, remove the outer short end piece and drill through the inner short end and into the dividers. Drill pilot holes in the opposite divider ends through the adjacent tall end piece.

4. Glue up the frame.
Apply glue to the edges of the cutouts in the tall end pieces, and fit and clamp the sides in place. Add fasteners to the joints.

Glue and fasten the dividers between the inner short end and tall end pieces; also glue and fasten the inner short end to the sides. Cover the inside face of the outer short end piece with glue and fasten it to the sides. Clamp the entire assembly, making sure all corners are square. Also clamp the two short end pieces together. Let the glue dry overnight.

5. Create the handle.

Cut two 1"-wide strips of ½" plywood to length at about 14". Glue and clamp the strips together face-to-face, with their edges and ends aligned. Let the glue dry overnight.

Measure between the inside faces of the tall ends and cut the handle to length for a snug fit in between; use a miter saw or a miter box and backsaw for a straight cut. Sand the corners and edges of the handle for a comfortable feel, as desired. You can also round over the corners with a router and ¼" roundover bit, if available. Don't sand or round over the ends of the handle.

6. Install the handle and bottom.

Dry-fit and clamp the handle and bottom to the frame assembly. The top edge of the handle should be flush with the top edges of the tall end pieces and centered side-to-side. The bottom should be flush with the outside of the frame on all sides. Drill pilot holes through the bottom and into the sides, tall ends, and outer short end. Also drill pilot holes through the tall end pieces and into the ends of the handle.

Disassemble the parts. Apply glue to the ends of the handle, and clamp and fasten it in place. Glue the bottom edges of the sides and all end pieces, and clamp and fasten the bottom panel in place. Let the glue dry overnight.

7. Sand and finish the piece.

If desired, drill a series of vertical holes into the top edges of the short end pieces (or along the joint between the two); they are handy for storing drill bits, marking tools, and so on, and they keep valuable accessories like router bits out of the common bin area, where they can easily become chipped and damaged.

Sand all surfaces of the box, working up to 150-grit or finer sandpaper. Slightly round over all edge corners to prevent splintering. If desired, apply a finish of your choice. Finishes such as penetrating oils and paste wax retain the natural look and feel of the wood and can be refreshed when they get worn.

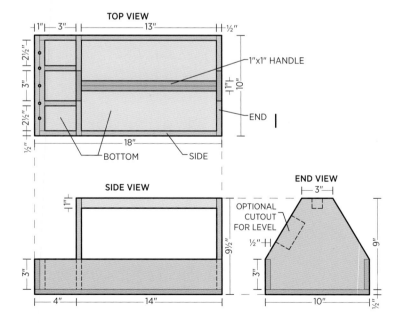

Large Toolbox Plan

Super Shelves

Designed by James Scheifla

You're probably wondering what makes the Super Shelves so super. Well, apart from their super cool look, made possible with their super unusual laminated construction, take a look at the shelf span: it's over 6 feet. To put that into perspective, most references will tell you that plain plywood shelves should not exceed 3 feet without some kind of (often unsightly) support. How do these shelves seem to be stronger than steel? Because they are steel, at least partially. Each shelf plank is reinforced with 1" square steel tubing recessed into its bottom face. And the planks themselves are cut from 1"-thick Russian birch. That's good, thick plywood. Super good.

MATERIALS

☐ One 4 x 8-foot sheet 1" Russian birch plywood

☐ Wood glue

☐ Three 72" (or longer) lengths 1" square steel tubing

☐ Construction adhesive

☐ One 30" x 74" (or larger) piece ¼" plywood

☐ 1" wood screws

☐ Finish materials (see step 12)

TOOLS

☐ Circular saw with straightedge guide or table saw (with miter gauge)

☐ Sliding miter saw or radial arm saw

☐ Bar clamps

☐ Belt sander, other portable sander, or stationary sander

☐ Router with:

    ☐ ⅜" rabbeting bit (bearing-guided)

    ☐ ½" or larger straight bit (1" min. cutting depth)

☐ Hacksaw or reciprocating saw

☐ Caulking gun (for adhesive)

☐ C-clamps (at least 4)

☐ Mineral spirits

☐ Square

☐ Low-angle block plane (if available) or sanding block

☐ Wood chisel

☐ Drill with combination pilot-countersink bit

☐ Sandpaper (up to 220 grit)

1. Cut the sidewall pieces.

Using a circular saw and straightedge guide or a table saw, cut two 10¾" x 48" pieces from one end of the full plywood panel, with the length of the pieces perpendicular to the face grain. Set the remainder of the sheet aside.

    Set up a stop block on a sliding miter saw or a radial arm saw for cutting the ripped plywood pieces into 1⅛"-wide, 10¾"-long pieces for the sidewalls. Make sure the block is parallel to the saw blade so the pieces are perfect rectangles. Cut at least 60 sidewall pieces from the two plywood planks (and it never hurts to cut a few extras while the jig is set up). In later steps, you'll sand and trim these pieces to their finished size of 1" x 10½"; see the plan.

2. Glue up the sidewalls.

Arrange the sidewall pieces into six groups of ten. Apply a liberal amount of wood glue to the face of each mating piece and clamp the entire group, being careful not to let the pieces slip out of square. The corners of the pieces should be perfectly aligned. Excess glue should drip from the joints; wipe off as much as possible with a wet rag. Keep the clamps on each group for the amount of time recommended by the manufacturer, then remove the clamps and glue up the next group. Let the assemblies dry overnight.

3. Sand the sidewalls.

Use a belt sander (or better yet, a large stationary sander, if available) to sand the front and back of each sidewall group so the surfaces are flat and parallel to each other and the finished piece measures 1" thick (down from the original 1⅛"). This requires a good deal of sanding. If you don't have a belt sander, you can use another type of portable sander, working up from 80-grit paper.

4. Trim the sidewall pieces.

It's likely that the glued-up sidewalls are no longer perfectly square, which is why the pieces are cut ¼" longer than the finished size. Square them up using a miter saw and a stop block or a table saw and a miter gauge. First trim off about ⅛" from one end of each piece. Then set up the stop block or table saw fence for a 10½" cut and cut the pieces to size by trimming off the uncut ends.

5. Cut the shelves.

If you used a table saw for the sidewall cuts, you can leave the fence in place for the shelves. Otherwise, use a circular saw and a straightedge guide to rip the remaining plywood stock into four pieces at 10½" wide. Cut the pieces to length at 74¼", using the miter saw. (The long waste piece left from the rip cuts – provided it has a factory edge – makes a handy straightedge for routing the shelf grooves.)

6. Mill rabbets for the back panel.

The sidewall pieces and the top and bottom shelves get a ⅜"-wide, ¼"-deep rabbet to accept the ¼" plywood back panel. The two middle shelves get a ¼"-deep "through rabbet" (continuous notch) cut into their back edges.

Use a router and a ⅜" rabbeting (bearing-guided) bit to mill the sidewall pieces. Make the rabbets just a hair deeper than ¼". These rabbets run along the entire length of each sidewall piece on one inside rear corner.

To rabbet the top and bottom shelves, make a mark ⅝" in from each end of each piece; this is where you will start/stop the rabbets. Mill the shelves as you did the sidewall pieces.

If you're using a rabbeting bit, switch to a straight bit with at least 1" of cutting depth. Mark each end of the two middle shelves at ⅝", as before. Cut the notches a hair deeper than ¼", as before,

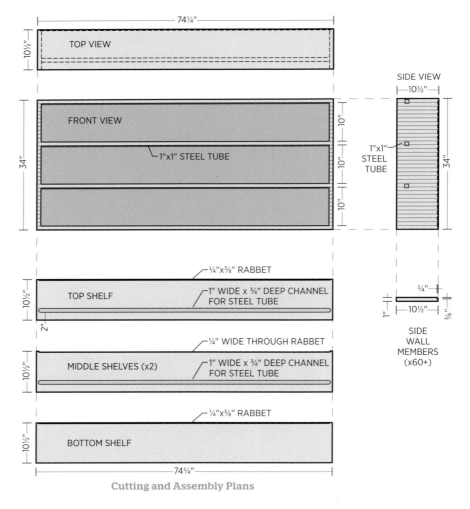

Cutting and Assembly Plans

stopping at the marks on each end. Again, these notches run through the full thickness of the shelf material.

7. Mill the tubing grooves.
The top and two middle shelves each get a ¾"-deep groove to accept a steel tubing stiffener. (The tubing will extend about ¼" below the underside of each plank.) The bottom shelf does not require a stiffener because it rests directly on the floor. To mill each groove, set up a long straightedge to mark the groove's front edge, 2" from the front edge of the shelf. Mark the shelf ½" in from each end; this is where you will start/stop the groove.

If you have a 1"-diameter router bit, you can mill each groove without moving the straightedge. Otherwise, cut one side of the groove, then move the setup to cut the other side, for a finished width of 1". Mill the groove with multiple passes (about ⅛" deep for each is recommended), stopping at the ½" marks at either end. Complete the groove in all three planks.

8. Cut and install the tubing.
If necessary, cut the three pieces of tubing to length at 72", using a hacksaw or reciprocating saw. Make sure the tubes will fit into the grooves of the shelves.

Working with one shelf at a time, lay the shelf bottom face up, and apply a generous bead of construction adhesive along the entire length of both sides of the groove. Set the tube into the groove so it is centered on the shelf's length; the tube should stop about 1⅛" from each end of the shelf.

Clamp the tube in place with four C-clamps, placing one at each end, with the two others spaced evenly in between. Carefully clean up any squeeze-out of adhesive, using mineral spirits and a rag; any adhesive residue left on the surface will likely be there permanently. Let the adhesive dry for 24 hours (or as directed by the manufacturer), then repeat the process with the remaining two planks.

9. Glue up the shelves and sidewalls.
This glue-up involves two stages. First you will glue two planks and two sidewalls at a time to create two rectangular assemblies. Then you glue the rectangles together with the remaining two sidewalls.

Apply glue to the top and bottom edges of two sidewall pieces, and fit them between the bottom shelf and one of the middle shelves so the ends of the shelves overhang the outside faces of the sidewalls by ¹⁄₁₆" and all pieces are flush at the front. Clamp the assembly and make sure it is square. Keep the clamps on for at least the amount of time recommended by the glue manufacturer. Repeat the process to glue up the top and remaining middle shelf with two more sidewalls.

Complete the glue-up by gluing the remaining two sidewalls between the middle shelves, making sure the entire unit is perfectly square after clamping. Let the assembly dry overnight.

Note: If desired, you can reinforce the joints with wood screws driven through the bottom and middle shelves and into the sidewalls (use countersunk pilot holes to recess the screw heads).

10. Clean up the shelf ends.
The best way to bring the overhanging shelf ends flush with the sidewalls is with a low-angle block plane. If you don't have a plane, you can simply sand the shelves with coarse sandpaper and a flat sanding block (any scrap piece of wood will do).

Set the plane's cutting height extremely low, so that it shaves only a small sliver at a time. Plane the shelf ends flush with the sidewalls, working from the front and back edges of each shelf toward its middle, to prevent tearout at either edge corner.

11. Cut and install the back panel.
Use a sharp chisel to square off the ends of the ¼" rabbets in the top and bottom shelves and in the notches of the middle shelves (these will have been left rounded by the router bit).

Measure between the rabbets in the sidewalls and between the top and bottom shelves to find the dimensions for the back panel. Cut the back panel from ¼" plywood to fit snugly within the rabbets. Set the panel in place, and confirm that the unit is square. Drill pilot holes with slight countersinks, and fasten the back panel to the shelves and sidewalls with 1" wood screws.

12. Finish the unit.
Finish-sand all the surfaces with 150-grit sandpaper, creating a slight roundover on any sharp or splintered edges. Work up to 220-grit or finer paper for the final preparation. Finish the piece as desired. Since you'll want to emphasize the laminated edges of the sidewalls (and the thick plywood shelf edges), it's best to use a semitransparent colorant (if desired) and a clear protective finish. Be sure to test any stains on some scrap wood to see how the edges absorb the finish.

Hardwareless Shelf

Designed by Norman Stuby

Of all the easy-assembly designs in this book, this shelf is one of the few knock-down pieces that uses no (you guessed it) hardware — at least not hardware in the conventional sense. Its "fasteners" are twelve interchangeable plywood tongues that fit into slotted tenons on the shelf ends, while the back and sides are held together with interlocking hooks cut into the panels. Combining the crisp lines of plywood with ancient forms of joinery, the look is both modern and medieval, resulting in an uncommonly decorative solution to storing notoriously undecorative digital media.

MATERIALS

- ☐ One 4 x 8-foot sheet ⁷⁄₁₆" hardwood plywood
- ☐ ⅞" brads
- ☐ Finish materials (as desired)

TOOLS

- ☐ Circular saw with straightedge guide or table saw
- ☐ Drill with ⁷⁄₁₆" straight bit
- ☐ Double-sided tape
- ☐ Router with ⅜" flush-trimming bit (with min. 1"-long cutter)
- ☐ Jigsaw
- ☐ Band saw (optional)
- ☐ Square-edged file
- ☐ Sandpaper
- ☐ Hammer
- ☐ Hot glue gun (optional)

1. Create the side template.

Cut the full sheet of plywood roughly in half, using a circular saw and a straightedge guide. This is to make handling easier, since all the parts are under 4 feet long. From one half sheet, rip three pieces at 7" wide. Two of these will become the sides of the unit; the third is for the side template.

Lay out all the cuts for the template on one of the cut pieces, following the side template drawing at right. For the ½" radii on the top corners and the hooks, you can use a quarter to make the curves.

Drill a ⁷⁄₁₆" hole inside the cutting lines of the four shelf slots, to accept the ⅜" flush-trimming router bit. To mill these slots with a router, use double-sided tape to secure four scrap pieces of MDF or other material along the marked cutting lines, as shown in the shelf-slot guides drawing below. Cut the first slot with the router and flush-trimming bit (the bit's bearing rides along the MDF pieces). Test-fit the slot with a scrap of the plywood stock; it should be snug but not so tight as to hinder assembly. Rout the remaining shelf slots.

Set up a straightedge guide and make the straight cuts along the back edge of the template, using a circular saw or a jigsaw. Then rough-cut the profiles of the hooks and bottom "foot" cutout, using a jigsaw or a band saw. Fine-tune these curves by carefully freehanding with the router, or you can simply cut them close with a saw and then file and sand them smooth. Test-fit the inside (throat) of the hooks with scrap plywood, filing and sanding as needed for a snug fit.

Sand the template's edges to smooth out all the curves and remove any saw marks. Confirm that the slots and hooks will accept the plywood's thickness, as now is the time to make any adjustments.

2. Shape the side pieces.
Place the two side pieces face-to-face with their edges aligned, and nail them together with a couple of brads. Position the side template over the side pieces so their front edges and bottom ends are aligned, and tack the template to the sides with brads.

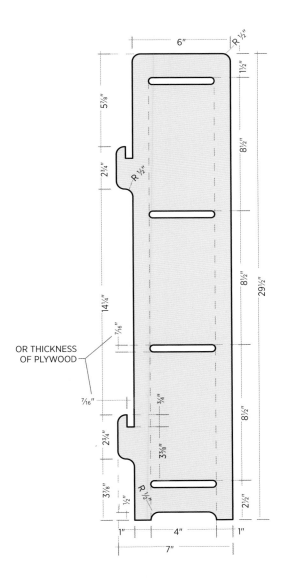

Side Diagram

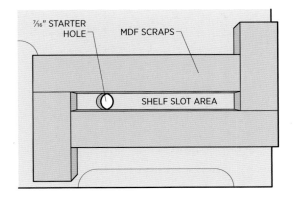

Shelf-slot Guides

Drill ⁷⁄₁₆" starter holes in the shelf slots for the flush-trimming bit, as before. Use a jigsaw to rough-cut the shelf slots and the profiles of the back and bottom edges, following the template. Do not cut along the rounded top end of the template at this time. Use the router and flush-trimming bit to clean up the slots and edges of the side pieces.

Separate the template from the side pieces and move it up, aligning the bottom two shelf slots on the template with the top two slots on the sides (use pieces of scrap plywood to align the slots perfectly). Nail the template to the side with brads, then repeat the process of sawing and routing to cut the top third of the side pieces. You will have a total of six shelf slots and three hooks per side piece. Now you can cut the rounded top end of the side pieces, following the template.

Remove the template, and sand the edges of the sides, as needed. Separate the side pieces.

3. Create the shelf template and cut the shelves.
Create the shelf template from a 6" x 6" piece of plywood stock, as shown in the shelf template drawing below. Follow the same process as before to mark, cut, and rout the template, and sand the cut edges smooth.

Using the leftover material from the side pieces, rip three pieces at 6" wide. Cut these to length at 23⅜" so you have six pieces total; these are for the shelves. You can make your shelves shorter or longer, as desired — just make sure that all the shelves are precisely the same length. Also keep in mind that the longer they are, the less rigidity they have.

Secure the shelf template to one end of one of the shelf pieces, and shape the shelf end as before, using the jigsaw for a rough cut and the router and flush-trimming bit for cleaning up the edges. Move the template to the other end and repeat. Now you can use the cut shelf as a template to shape the remaining shelves or continue to use the original shelf template. Use a square-edged file to clean up the inside corners at the base of each shelf tongue.

4. Create the tongues.
Rip a 4"-wide piece from one of your 4-foot-long leftovers. Crosscut 13 pieces from the strip at 2⅞" each. Follow the tongue template below to draw the profile of the tongue on one of the cut pieces. Cut the template with a jigsaw or band saw and smooth the edges with sandpaper. Test-fit the template on the shelves, and adjust as needed. (To make fitting easier, you can "cheat in" the side edges of the 2½" section by tapering the sides slightly toward the bottom end; just check the measurement on your shelf pieces.)

Use the template to make a total of 12 tongues. For routing, secure the template to the workpieces with brads, double-sided tape, or hot glue, as desired. Again, use the square-edged file to square the inside corners so the tongues will seat nicely.

5. Cut and shape the back.
Assemble the shelves and sides, using the tongues to secure the shelf ends. Place the unit facedown, and make sure the assembly is square. Measure the length between the sides to find the width

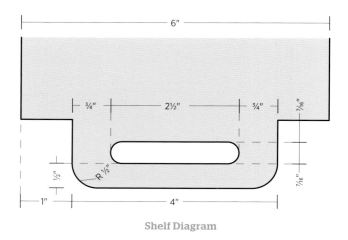

Shelf Diagram

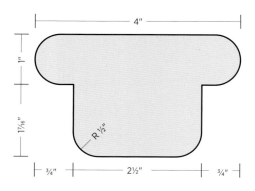

Tongue Diagram

of the main part of the back panel. Add 2" to this dimension to find the overall width of the back.

Disassemble the shelves and sides. You will use the side pieces as templates for the edge details of the back panel: On each long edge of the back panel, make a mark 4" up from the bottom. Set a side piece upside-down on the back panel. Align the bottom of the throat of the top hook with the mark you just made, keeping the outside edges of the hooks flush with the long edge of the back (see the hook layout on the back panel template). The top of the side piece will hang over the bottom edge of the back. Nail the side down carefully, using brads, making sure the hooks stay flush with the back's edge.

Rough-cut the side's profile into the back with a jigsaw, then use the router to clean up the profiles, as you did with the other parts. Do not cut across the top edge of the back panel (around the feet of the side piece); you will trim the back panel to length later. Repeat the process to shape the other side edge of the back panel.

6. Complete the final fitting.
Assemble the shelves and sides, as before, then test-fit the back panel. Getting a good fit here requires squaring the inside corners of all the hook throats, using the square-edged file. Use a piece of scrap plywood to check the fit as you work. The scrap should slip in easily; if it's tight, remove material from the outer wall of the hook throat rather than the edge of the side or back panel.

When all 12 hooks fit properly, replace the back on the assembly. When fully seated, the top and bottom edges of the back should be parallel to (but not flush with) the shelves. The bottom is the easiest to check — the back should overhang the bottom shelf by about ⅛". Wiggle the unit from side to side while applying downward pressure to the back until you're sure it's fully seated. Mark the back panel along the top face of the top shelf and the bottom face of the bottom shelf. Remove the back, and trim the ends of the back panel along your marked lines.

7. Finish the piece.
Disassemble the entire unit, finish-sand all parts as needed, and apply the finish of your choice. To prevent fitting problems, a relatively thin but durable finish material is recommended, such as a penetrating-type oil finish, wax, or wipe-on polyurethane.

Tips for a Growing Collection
If your DVD collection grows off the shelves, you can expand your shelf unit by making new, taller sides and a few new shelves and tongues, using the original templates. Expand the back with a filler piece rather than a whole new panel, and hide the seam behind a shelf edge. To store items taller than the shelves can accommodate, simply take the unit apart and remove a shelf or two.

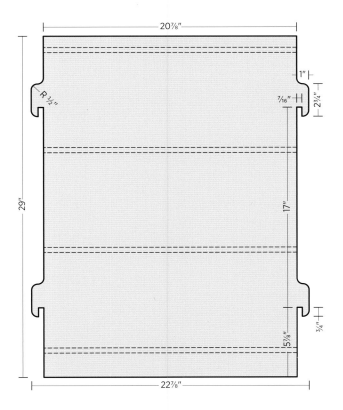

Back Panel Template

Gather

Designed by Ryan Mahan

Gather is a functional piece of art in the form of a mailbox. It's also an exceptional example of plywood construction: its body is made with lamination — face-gluing multiple pieces together to create a form that's primarily edge grain — while its door is a broad, flat panel that displays the natural beauty of face grain, creating the perfect contrast with the distinctive lines of the lamination. The manageable size and nice woodworking details, such as simple mortises and closure magnets hidden within the wood, make Gather a great project for practicing template routing and lamination techniques.

MATERIALS

- ☐ One 2 x 4-foot piece ³⁄₁₆" hardboard
- ☐ One 4 x 4-foot sheet ¾" hardwood plywood
- ☐ One 84" length (or longer) ⅜" hardwood dowel
- ☐ Two ⅜"-thick, ½"-wide, ¾"-tall neodymium bar magnets
- ☐ One 2" length ¼" x 1" solid pine board
- ☐ One 5" length ¼" x 3" solid maple board
- ☐ 10-24 brass or stainless steel knife-thread insert
- ☐ General-purpose two-part epoxy
- ☐ 10-24 ½" stainless steel pan-head bolt
- ☐ Wood glue
- ☐ Two ⅜" stainless steel or brass washers
- ☐ Two ⁹⁄₁₆"-wide, 3"-long, heavy-duty double keyhole hangers with screws
- ☐ Clear hardwood floor filler (optional)
- ☐ Finish materials (see step 12)

TOOLS

- ☐ Jigsaw
- ☐ Band saw (optional)
- ☐ Drill with:
  - ☐ ⅛" straight bit
  - ☐ ⅜" straight bit
- ☐ Sandpaper
- ☐ Hammer
- ☐ Clamps
- ☐ Double-sided tape (optional)
- ☐ Router with:
  - ☐ Flush-trimming bit
  - ☐ ⅜" straight bit
  - ☐ ½" roundover bit
- ☐ Straightedge
- ☐ Circular saw or table saw (optional)
- ☐ Doweling jig (optional)
- ☐ Wood chisel
- ☐ Coping saw (optional)
- ☐ Glue brush (optional)
- ☐ Three bar clamps (36" min.)

1. Create the body template

The main body of this project consists of two end caps, a door stop, and 19 identical body pieces. All the parts are assembled with glue and two dowels running through each body piece and the door stop and into the inside faces of the end caps. You will use a hardboard template to drill dowel holes and cut the profiles of the body pieces.

Draw the shape of the body on hardboard stock, following the cutting diagram. Also mark the centers for the two dowel holes. Cut out the profile with a jigsaw or a band saw, then drill the dowel holes with a drill and ⅜" bit.

Sand the edges of the template so they are smooth and free of saw marks. It is critical that the template have the proper shape and clean edges, as it will determine the quality of every plywood body piece.

2. Cut the body pieces.

Clamp the template over the plywood stock. Carefully drill a ⅜" hole through the stock, using the predrilled holes in the template as guides. Cut two lengths of dowel at ¾". Insert each dowel piece into one of the dowel holes, securing the template to the stock. Tap the dowels with a hammer so they're flush with the hardboard surface.

Use a jigsaw to rough-cut around the template profile, staying about ⅛" from the edges. Keeping the template in place, secure the pieces to your work surface with clamps or double-sided tape. Use a router and flush-trimming bit to clean up the edges of the plywood workpiece, creating an exact copy of the template. Remove the dowels and template, then repeat the same process to cut the 18 remaining body pieces.

3. Cut the door stop.

In its outside dimensions and shape, the door stop is identical to the body pieces, so you can use the body template to drill the dowel holes and create most of the door stop's profile. With the template in place on the workpiece, draw the unique interior profile of the door stop, as shown in the cutting diagram. Cut and rout all the edges common to the template, then remove the template and cut the remainder of the profile with the jigsaw.

4. Cut the end caps.

The right and left end caps are virtually identical in shape to the body pieces, but they have no cutout for the cavity; see the cutting diagram. Using the body-piece template as before, drill the two dowel holes into one of the end cap workpieces, making them only ⅜" deep (be especially careful to drill no deeper than ⅜" with the top hole on the right end cap, lest the hole become exposed by the flag mortise; see step 8). With the template in place on the workpiece, use a straightedge to draw the line that marks the front of the end cap. Rough-cut the workpieces with a jigsaw, then rout the matching edges with the template in place. Remove the template and complete the front edge of the end cap with a jigsaw. Repeat the process with the other end cap.

5. Cut the door panel.

Detailed dimensions for the door are given in the cutting diagram. However, because plywood can vary slightly in thickness, it's a good idea to preassemble the body – including all body pieces, door stop, and end caps – and clamp the parts together. Then measure the width of the door opening to find the precise width for your door panel. The door should be about ⅛" narrower than the opening, to allow for 1/16" of clearance on each side.

Lay out the door profile on the plywood stock, and make the cuts with a jigsaw (you might prefer to use a circular saw and straightedge guide or a table saw for the straight cuts).

Round over the inside and outside edges along the bottom of the door, using a router and ½" roundover bit. Do not rout too deeply on the first cut; the bearing needs a flat surface to ride along for the second cut.

Note: The project shown was constructed with furniture-grade maple plywood for its door panel.

6. Drill the door-hinge holes.

The door hinges on ¾" lengths of dowel glued into the door's edges and captured by the end caps. With the body still clamped together, test-fit the door in the opening and make any necessary adjustments for a proper fit. Hold the door in the closed position, and make matching marks on the door face (near each side edge) and the corresponding end cap; these should be about 7/16" up from the bottom edge of the door.

Using a doweling jig (or just measure and mark very carefully), drill a ½"-deep dowel hole into the door's side edges, using a ⅜" bit; these should be centered on the reference marks and on the thickness of the door's edges. Drill corresponding holes halfway into the end caps.

7. Create the door-magnet cavities.

The door and door stop each get a ⅜"-thick, ½"-wide, ¾"-tall bar magnet. The magnets are embedded in the plywood and are invisible in the finished piece. On the door stop, the magnet is covered by the right end cap. On the door, the magnet is covered by a plug cut from a piece of solid pine and glued into place.

Mark the magnet cavity on the right face of the door stop so it is ¼" from the lower front edge of the piece; see the exploded-view drawing. The cavity is ¾" tall, ⅜" wide, and ½" deep. Remove most of the waste in the cavity with a drill and ⅜" bit (you can also use a plunge router and ⅜" straight bit to cut the cavity). Clean up the sides of the cavity with a sharp chisel. Test-fit the magnet and make any necessary adjustments.

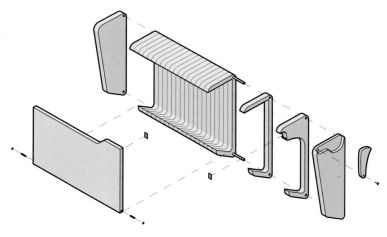

Exploded View

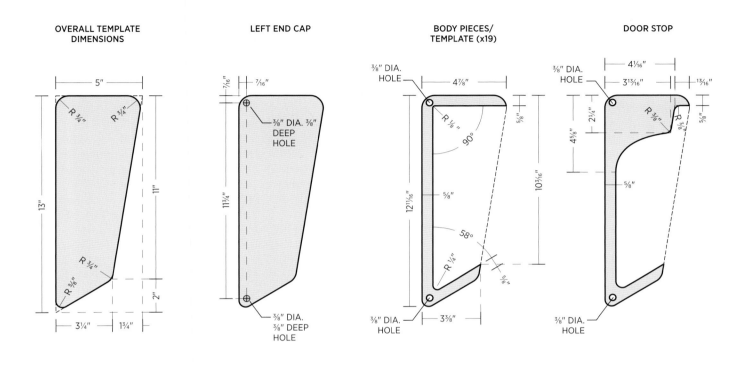

OVERALL TEMPLATE DIMENSIONS

LEFT END CAP

BODY PIECES/ TEMPLATE (x19)

DOOR STOP

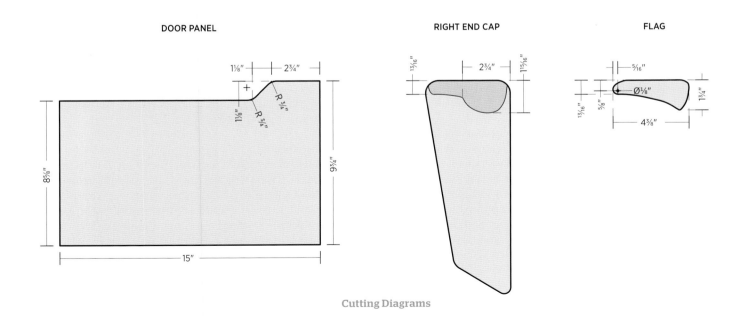

DOOR PANEL

RIGHT END CAP

FLAG

Cutting Diagrams

Mark the door cavity on the door's right edge so it will be aligned with the door-stop cavity and centered on the edge of the door. Drill and chisel the cavity as before, using a doweling jig if available. Make this cavity about ⅝" deep to provide space for the pine plug. Cut a piece of ¼"-thick pine to fit snugly into the cavity. Set a magnet into the cavity, then glue the pine plug into the hole, about ⅛" deep, and let the glue dry. Sand the plug flush to the plywood edge.

You will install the door-stop magnet during the final assembly.

8. Create the flag mortise and flag.

The flag fits into a ¼"-deep mortise milled into the outside face of the right end cap. Draw the outline of the mortise on the end cap, as shown in the cutting diagram. Cut the mortise with the router and a straight bit. Freehanding with the router works fine. It's best to remove most of the waste with two passes, staying a little inside the marked line. Then make a single, full-depth pass, cutting to the line.

Cut the flag from ¼"-thick maple (or other) stock, following the cutting diagram. A coping saw or band saw works well for this cut (or you can use a jigsaw). Sand the edges smooth and test-fit the flag in its mortise.

Mark a mounting hole on the flag, as indicated on the template. Drill the hole through the flag with a ⅛" bit. Position the flag into its mortise, and use the mounting hole to mark the location for a threaded insert in the end cap. Drill a ⅜" hole at ½" deep for the insert. Glue the insert into the hole with epoxy. Once the epoxy sets, mount the flag with a ½" bolt, and check the flag motion — it should be able to stand completely upright; if it doesn't, sand the flag as needed for a proper fit.

9. Glue up the main body.

Cut two lengths of dowel at ¾" each for the door hinges, and set them aside. Cut the remaining dowel piece in half. Slide all the body pieces and the door stop onto the two dowels, leaving plenty of space in between for applying glue. Position the door stop about an inch from the dowel ends. Have your clamps and all other supplies ready for the glue-up, because you have to work quickly. You might want to use a glue brush for easy glue application.

Apply glue to the outside face of the first body piece, and press it against the door stop. Glue the inside face of the first body piece, then slide the next body piece down against the first. Repeat this process to glue all the body pieces, then clamp the entire assembly with bar clamps. Quickly clean up as much glue

squeeze-out as possible, using damp paper towels. You can leave the dowels long for now. Let the glue dry overnight.

Trim the dowel ends so they extend ⁵/₁₆" beyond the outer left body piece and the door stop. Sand the interior of the body so it is smooth and flat.

10. Add the door and end caps.

Glue the remaining bar magnet into the door-stop cavity with epoxy and let it set. Glue the ¾" hinge dowels into the door, using wood glue, so they extend ⅜" beyond the door's edges. Let the glue set.

Test-fit the door by placing a thin washer on each hinge dowel and then fitting the end caps over the hinge dowels and the dowel stubs on the body. Check the door operation, making sure the side clearances are adequate, the gaps (reveals) along the door's edges are even, and the magnets hold the door securely closed. You may have to sand or file the washers so they aren't visible in the final assembly.

When all looks good, apply glue to the outer left body piece and door stop, and complete the assembly. Clamp the end caps in place, applying pressure on the body, not the door. Check the door operation, and loosen or tighten the clamp pressure accordingly. Wipe off excess glue with a damp paper towel. Let the glue dry overnight.

11. Mortise for the keyhole hangers.

Mark the locations for two keyhole hangers on the back of the unit, near the upper ends of the body. Space the hangers evenly, making sure they are the same distance from the top of the body. Trace around the outer edge of the hangers to mark the mortises.

Mill the mortises with the router and a straight bit to a depth equal to the hangers' thickness. Drill shallow pilot holes for the hanger screws.

12. Finish the piece.

Finish-sand the entire project, including the flag. If the exposed plywood edges have any voids, you can fill them with clear hardwood-floor filler, as directed by the manufacturer, and sand the filler flush. Stain or paint the flag, then finish the body, door, and flag with a clear protective finish. In the project shown, the flag was colored with bright-red stain, and everything was finished with spar varnish.

Install the keyhole hangers with short screws. Attach the flag with the bolt. Hang the finished piece under a roof eave or other location where it will stay dry.

Mudroom Organizer

Designed by Sascha Ayad

Imagine, if you will, the unutterable bliss of having every little shoe, every backpack, every hat and glove, and every ball not strewn about the floor or piled in a corner, but neatly displayed in an attractive, wonderfully rational storage unit designed by a cabinetmaker and fellow parent (he feels your pain). This state of serenity can be yours with two simple steps: 1) build this project, and 2) nag your kids approximately 1,200 times to use the darned thing. This organizer measures just 3' x 4' x 1' feet and contains 20 cubbies ranging in size from about 7" to over 11" square. If you need a different configuration or overall size to fit your space or storage items, you can easily modify the given plan and stick with same basic construction. Serenity now!

MATERIALS

- ☐ One 4 x 8-foot sheet ¾" plywood
- ☐ One 4 x 4-foot sheet ½" plywood
- ☐ Scrap materials for dowel jig (see steps 1 and 5)
- ☐ Wood glue
- ☐ 1½"-long, ⅜"-diam. wood dowel pins
- ☐ 1⅝" #8 coarse-thread drywall screws
- ☐ 6d (2") finish nails (for optional base)
- ☐ Wood veneer edge tape (optional)
- ☐ Finish materials (see step 9)

TOOLS

- ☐ Drill with:
  - ☐ ⅜" straight bit
  - ☐ #8 combination pilot-countersink bit
- ☐ Circular saw with straightedge guide
- ☐ Table saw (if available)
- ☐ Framing square
- ☐ Bit stop (or masking tape)
- ☐ Clamps
- ☐ Hammer and nail set (for finish nails in optional base)
- ☐ Utility knife (if using veneer edge tape)
- ☐ Clothes iron (if using veneer edge tape)
- ☐ Sandpaper (up to 220 grit)

1. Build the dowel jig.

All the parts of the organizer (except the back) are joined with glued dowel pins (precut dowels). A homemade dowel jig will help ensure that the dowel holes line up between mating parts. You use the same jig for all the parts. To account for the ¼" setback between the vertical dividers and the horizontal shelves, you will simply add a ¼"-thick spacer to the jig before drilling the holes in the vertical pieces.

Create a jig with two pieces of scrap plywood, as shown in the illustration of the jig for face dowel holes, joining the jig base to the ledger with screws to form a right angle. Draw a centerline perpendicular to the ledger, then mark the centerline at 2" and 8" from the inner edge of the ledger. Drill a ⅜"-diameter hole at each mark; these are the guide holes for drilling the dowel holes in step 4.

2. Cut the parts.

Cut the vertical dividers, shelves, sides, bottom, and top from ¾" plywood, as listed at right. Arrange the parts so that the length of the pieces parallels the grain of the plywood's face veneers. Cut the back panel from ½" plywood.

Cut all the parts with a circular saw and a straightedge guide to ensure clean, straight cuts. If available, a table saw is preferable for ripping the ¾" plywood pieces.

CUTTING LIST

Part	Quantity	Width	Length
Small vertical dividers	13	10¾"	7"
Large vertical dividers	3	10¾"	11¼"
Shelves	3	11"	46½"
Bottom	1	11"	46½"
Top	1	11½"	46½"
Sides	11	11½"	36½"

3. Mark reference lines for dowel holes.

The divider and shelf locations are shown on the plan drawing. On the bottom face of the lowest shelf (not the bottom piece), make a mark 11 ⁷⁄₁₆" from each end of the shelf. Use a framing square to draw a line at each mark perpendicular to the front edge of the shelf. Next, draw a line at the precise center of the shelf's length, again perpendicular to the front edge. Transfer these line locations to the top face of the bottom piece.

On the top face of the lowest shelf, mark lines at ⁹⁄₁₆" from each shelf end, then mark two more lines at 9 ⁷⁄₁₆" from the first marks. Transfer these lines to both faces of the next shelf up and to the bottom face of the top shelf.

On the top face of the top shelf, mark lines at 7½" from each end, then three more lines at 7⅞" in between. Transfer these lines to the bottom face of the top piece.

Finally, mark lines on the inside face of one of the side panels (perpendicular to the front edge). The first line is ⅜" from the bottom. From that line, make a line at 12", then make three more lines spaced at 7¾". The topmost line should be ⅜" from the top of the side piece. Transfer these lines to the other side piece.

4. Drill the face dowel holes.

Position the dowel jig at the *front* edge of one of the workpieces and align the jig's centerline with each marked line on the workpiece face; see the drawing of the jig for face dowel holes. Clamp or securely hold the jig in place, and drill a ⅜"-diameter hole straight down through each guide hole in the jig, going halfway (⅜") into the workpiece. Mark the drill bit with tape or a bit stop at the proper depth, to prevent drilling all the way through the material. In this way, drill the two holes at each line on the faces of the top, bottom, shelves, and sides.

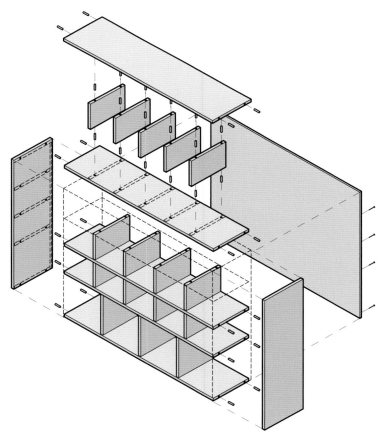

Exploded View

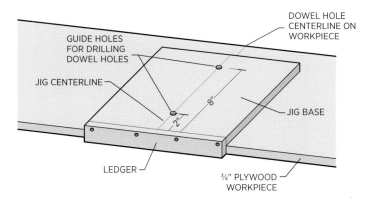

Jig for Face Dowel Holes

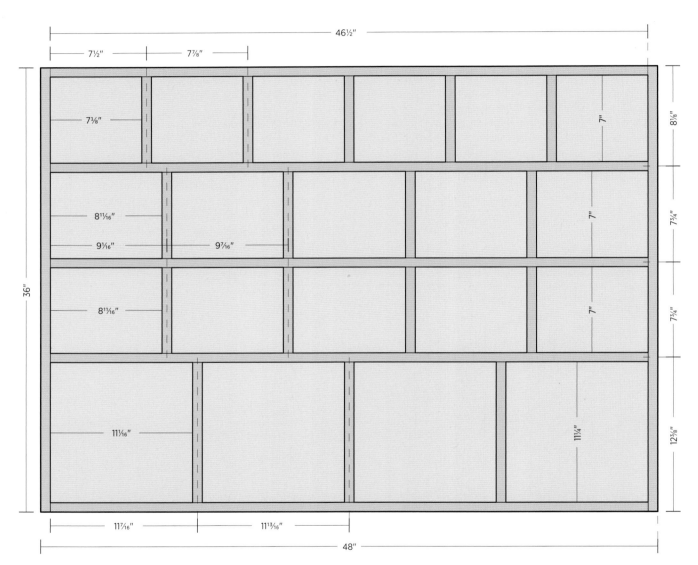

OPTIONAL BASE NOT SHOWN

Assembly Plan

5. Drill the edge dowel holes.

Now you will use the dowel jig to drill holes on the edges at the ends of the dividers, top piece, and bottom piece (the holes will be parallel to the front and back edges of the pieces). But first you have to modify the jig so that the holes will be 1¾" and 7¾" from the front edge of each piece (instead of 2 and 8") and centered on the ¾"-thick edge of the material.

Modify the jig by gluing a ¼"-thick strip of wood to the inside face of the ledger, so it is centered on the jig's centerline. Then screw a second ledger cut from a straight piece of scrap to the underside of the jig base so it is perpendicular to the front ledger and its inside face is ⅜" away from the centers of the holes; see the drawing of the jig for edge dowel holes.

Set the tape or stop on the ⅜" drill bit for a depth that's ¼" shorter than the length of your dowel pins (or 1¼" for 1½"-long pins). Drill the dowel holes on both ends of the dividers and top and bottom pieces, making sure to register the ledger of the jig against the *front* edge of each piece.

6. Dry-assemble the organizer.

Glue dowel pins into both holes in all of the top and bottom edges of the dividers, and let the glue dry.

Dry-fit the organizer to make sure everything fits before the final glue-up. Start at the bottom and work up, fitting together all the shelves and dividers, then adding the top piece and finally

the sides. Remember that the dividers will sit ¼" back from the front edges of the shelves, top, and bottom. Make sure the assembly is square, and fit the back panel into the recess created by the sides, top, and bottom. Make any necessary adjustments.

7. Complete the final assembly.

With clamps at the ready, begin the final glue-up, again working from bottom to top, then adding the sides. Apply glue not only to the dowels but also to the edges of the mating pieces. To save on clamps, you can add screws to any joints where the screw heads won't be visible, such as under the bottom piece, under the lowest shelf, and (if the organizer will abut a wall when installed) on either side. Drive the screws through pilot holes to prevent splitting an edge. Clamp the assembly securely, making sure it is square, and let the glue dry overnight.

Install the back by drilling countersunk pilot holes and screwing through the back and into the rear edges of the dividers, shelves, and bottom piece.

8. Add a base (optional).

A base adds a finished look and makes it easier to level the unit on an out-of-level floor. To create a base, rip 3"-wide strips of ¾" plywood. From these strips, cut the front and back of the base to length at 44", and cut the sides at 7½". (If you prefer to miter the base's corners rather than butt them, miter the ends of the strips at 45 degrees, and cut the sides to length at 9".)

Glue and finish-nail the base frame together so the front and back cover the ends of the sides. Glue the base to the bottom face of the bottom piece so the front and sides of the base are 2" from the front and sides of the unit.

9. Finish the unit.

If desired, cover the front edges of the pieces with veneer edge tape, following the manufacturer's directions (use self-adhesive, iron-on tape for easy application). Otherwise, sand the bare plywood edges smooth with sandpaper, rounding over the corners slightly to prevent splintering. Finish-sand the entire piece, working up to 220-grit or finer sandpaper.

Finish the piece with three coats of wipe-on polyurethane or other desired finish. Because the unit is assembled, wipe-on poly and other rag-applied finishes are easier to work with than brushed-on materials.

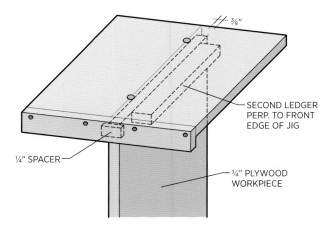

⅜"

SECOND LEDGER
PERP. TO FRONT
EDGE OF JIG

¼" SPACER

¾" PLYWOOD
WORKPIECE

Jig for Edge Dowel Holes

Sliding Mirror Shelves

Designed by Shawn Calvin

This clever storage system is bound to prompt the old question, "How come no one's ever thought of *that* before?" The simple box shelves are perfect for holding everyday bedroom items, like jewelry and perfume bottles, and the mirror performs more than its standard function — it also glides from side to side to conceal stored items while maintaining easy access to the entire shelf. The piece shown here was made largely with salvaged materials, including the mirror frame, which used to house a picture (another good idea suggested by the designer).

MATERIALS

- ☐ One 2 x 3-foot piece ¾" plywood
- ☐ Staples (for staple gun)
- ☐ Four recessed mounting brackets with screws
- ☐ Mirror (cut to fit frame) or picture insert
- ☐ Picture frame
- ☐ Flat clips or metal strips and screws (for securing mirror)
- ☐ One set sliding closet hardware
- ☐ Heavy-duty hollow-wall anchors (as needed)

TOOLS

- ☐ Circular saw with straightedge guide
- ☐ Square
- ☐ Staple gun
- ☐ Wood chisel
- ☐ Drill with standard bit set
- ☐ Hacksaw
- ☐ Level

1. Cut the box parts.

Following the plan drawings below, cut the eight box parts to size with a circular saw and straightedge guide. These include:

- 4 side pieces at 5½" x 12"
- 1 top and 1 bottom for the long box at 5½" x 30"
- 1 top and 1 bottom for the short box at 5½" x 12"

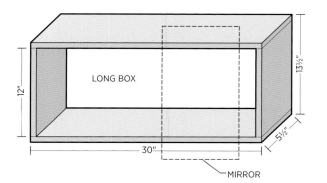

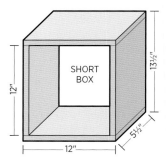

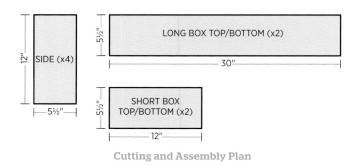

Cutting and Assembly Plan

2. Assemble the boxes.

Assemble each box by placing the top and bottom pieces over the ends of the side pieces, with their edges flush at the front. Use a small square (such as a Speed Square or combination square) to make sure the box parts are square, then fasten them together by stapling through the top and bottom pieces and into the sides' edges with a staple gun.

Note: If you don't have a staple gun or prefer a less-visible fastener, you can assemble the boxes with wood glue and 6d (2") finish nails.

3. Install the mounting brackets.

Cut mortises to recess the mounting brackets into the back edges of the box sides, using a sharp wood chisel. Also drill holes, as needed, to provide clearance for the wall-mounting screw heads (step 6). The brackets should be flush with the box edges. Install the brackets with the provided screws.

4. Assemble the mirror.

Have the mirror cut to size at the hardware store or home center, so it fits snugly inside the picture frame. Set the mirror in the frame and secure it at the back with flat clips or metal straps. Alternatively, you can fill the frame with artwork, a photograph, or other decorative materials, as desired.

5. Add the closet hardware.

Cut the sliding closet track to fit snugly inside the top of the long box, using a hacksaw. Position the track against the box top so it is flush with the front of the box, and install the track with the provided screws.

Fasten the sliding closet brackets to the backside of the mirror frame, in the desired location.

6. Install the shelves.

Position each box on the wall, and use a level to make sure each one is level across the top and level with the other box. Mark along the box top and sides with light pencil marks.

Drive mounting screws into the wall following your reference marks. Drive the screws into wall studs whenever possible; otherwise, use heavy-duty hollow-wall anchors to secure the screws (don't use the cheap plastic friction-type sleeves). Hang the boxes on the screws.

Hang the mirror by fitting the sliding brackets into the closet track.

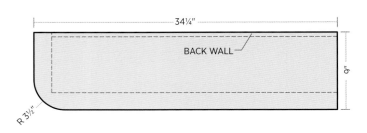

Cantilevered Shelves

Designed by Larry Finn

These elegant shelves were designed to accompany the Peninsula Workstation (page 48), and they feature some of the same clever construction details — namely, the triple-layer built-up edge. With the shelves, however, the layered construction is not only decorative, it also creates a cavity for concealing the mounting hardware, the secret bit of engineering behind all cantilever shelves. The design technique can be used for shelves of any length and up to about 9" deep.

See page 48 for another work by Larry Finn.

MATERIALS

☐ One 4 x 4-foot sheet ¾" hardwood plywood

☐ One 64" (or longer) length ½" x ½" galvanized metal angle (with holes)

☐ ¾" coarse-thread wood screws with washers (for mounting angle to shelf)

☐ Wood glue

☐ Heavy-duty hollow-wall anchors (as needed)

☐ 2" coarse-thread wood screws with washers (for mounting angle to wall)

☐ Four (or more) 1½" finish nails or brads

☐ Finish materials (see step 5)

☐ Caulk (optional)

Note: The materials listed here will yield two matching shelves.

TOOLS

☐ Compass

☐ Circular saw with straightedge guide

☐ Jigsaw

☐ Sandpaper (up to 220 grit) and sanding block

☐ Hacksaw or reciprocating saw

☐ Drill with pilot bits

☐ Clamps

☐ 4-foot level

☐ Stud finder (wall scanner)

☐ Hammer and nail set (if using finish nails)

☐ Brad nailer (if using brads)

☐ Masking tape

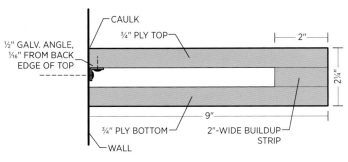

Cutaway Side View

Top View

1. Cut the plywood pieces.

Each shelf is made up of a full-size top and bottom panel and a 2"-wide buildup strip running along the front and exposed side edge of the shelf. All parts should be cut from the same sheet of ¾" plywood. The shelves shown here measure 34¼" long and 9" deep. Your shelves can be any length; just make sure that long shelves won't end up overloaded with stuff, especially books. These shelves are pretty sturdy, but excessive weight will likely crush the drywall, causing the shelves to tip downward.

Lay out the cuts for the top and bottom panels for each shelf on ¾" plywood stock. Use a compass to draw the 3½" radius at the outside corners, as shown in the top-view drawing. Cut the pieces with a circular saw and a straightedge guide, cutting the outside corners square. Lay out and cut the 2"-wide buildup strip for each shelf, forming an L that matches the outside dimensions of the tops and bottoms.

Stack the three pieces for each shelf with their edges flush, and clamp them to a work surface so the corner to be rounded is fully accessible. Cut the radius with a jigsaw and a very-fine-tooth wood blade (to minimize splintering), cutting through all three pieces at once. Sand the rounded edges with coarse sandpaper and a sanding block, as needed, to smooth the curve and remove any rough or flat spots.

2. Prepare the angle.

Cut two pieces of ½" x ½" metal angle at 32" each (or 2¼" less than the shelf length), using a hacksaw or reciprocating saw. Position a piece of angle near the rear edge of the bottom face of each top panel, with one end of the angle just inside the square end of the top. Carefully adjust the angle so its back flange is ¹⁄₁₆" in from the rear edge of the top, as shown in the cutaway side-view drawing, and clamp the angle in place. Drill pilot holes, and fasten the angle to the shelf with ¾" wood screws and washers. The ¹⁄₁₆" inset will help hold the shelf tightly to the back wall.

3. Add the buildup strips.

For each shelf, apply wood glue to both faces of the buildup strip. Position the strip on the bottom face of the top panel. Clamp the pieces, making sure all exposed edges are flush and there are no visible gaps between the layers. Let the glue dry overnight.

4. Hang the top panels.

Determine the hanging height of each shelf. Using a 4-foot level, draw a level line on the back wall (where the shelf will mount) to represent the shelf's top surface. Locate the wall studs within the shelf area along the back wall, using a stud finder (wall scanner) or your preferred manual technique. Ideally, you'll be able to anchor into the corner stud (where the back wall meets the adjacent side wall) and the nearest two studs from the corner, along the back wall. If you can't find three studs, you'll have to install one or more heavy-duty hollow-wall anchors (such as toggle bolts) to anchor the angle.

Set each shelf top into position against the wall, with its top face on the level line, and screw through the angle and into each stud with a 2" wood screw and washer. The ¹⁄₁₆" offset will cause the shelf to tip downward slightly; this will be corrected in the next step.

Note: Instead of installing the top panel (with strip) now, you can attach the bottom panel to the top panel (using finish nails, as described in step 5), sand and finish the completed shelf, and then remove the bottom to install the shelf.

5. Complete the shelves.

With clamps at the ready, position each bottom panel in place against the buildup strip, push up slightly until the shelf is level and the bottom panel is flush with the edges of the strip, then clamp the pieces tightly together. Drill pilot holes for four or more 1½" finish nails (or use a brad nailer) and fasten the bottom panel to the strip. This will hold the entire shelf tightly against the wall. Remove the clamps.

Finish-sand the exposed surfaces of the shelves, working up to 220-grit or finer sandpaper. Tape off the walls around the shelves, and apply the finish of your choice. Finishing the bottom panel requires working upside down, so it's a good idea to use a wipe-on finish rather than a brush-on formulation. Furniture oils (Danish, tung, linseed, et cetera) and paste wax are good options if the shelves don't need to be moisture-resistant. If they do, wipe-on polyurethane is a good choice. Let the finish cure fully before using the shelf.

If desired, caulk the joints where the shelves meet the walls, using a fine bead of caulk that matches the wall color.

Built-In Hutch

Designed by Anton Willis & Kate Lydon of Civil Twilight

This may just be the easiest and most elegant built-in storage solution ever devised. The designers are two architects who love their historic residence and its quaint appointments, such as the cabinets for pies and irons. But the fact is, they just don't bake pies. Nor could they make the most of a nicely sized but empty alcove in their entryway. So they installed four simple bracket-hung shelves, two of which support sliding acrylic doors to create a "floating" cabinet. Shoes go below the cabinet, mail and keys go on top, and anything else can be stashed inside. The frosted acrylic lightens the piece and, in the words of the designers, "makes objects inside look more abstract than messy." Simple design magic.

MATERIALS

- ¾" Finnish birch or other hardwood plywood (quantity as needed)
- Wood glue
- Finish materials (see step 4)
- ¼" aluminum sliding door track
- Four ¾" metal L brackets with screw holes (per shelf)
- Hollow-wall anchors (as needed)
- 1½" or 2" coarse-thread drywall screws or wood screws
- ½" wood screws
- ¼"-thick frosted acrylic panels

TOOLS

- Circular saw with straightedge guide or table saw
- Clamps
- Sandpaper (up to 220 grit)
- Hacksaw
- Drill with:
  - Pilot bits
  - 1½" hole saw (see step 7)
- Level
- Cutting tools for acrylic panel (optional; see step 7)

1. Plan your built-in.

The project shown here consists of two 8"-deep shelves for books and display items and two deeper shelves that form the top and bottom of the cabinet. The alcove is 20" deep, and the cabinet shelves are 18" deep, so they look nicely tucked in. The cabinet hangs 12" above the floor; its top is at a comfortable height of 36". The shallower shelves are spaced at 10" intervals above the cabinet, as shown in the plan drawings.

All the construction details, including the size and number of shelves and the configuration of the pieces, can be modified to suit your space, design preferences, and storage needs. Once you've determined the size and layout of all the elements, draw level lines on both side walls of the alcove to mark the shelf locations. These will help you take accurate measurements and install the shelves.

As for additional decorating ideas, the designers offer a few suggestions: Add more shelves, or build multiple cabinets. Paint the back of the alcove or line it with wallpaper. Use painted hardboard or pegboard, instead of acrylic, for the doors. And if you want to get fancy, mount stick-on, battery-operated lights under the shelves as mini-spotlights for special displays.

2. Cut the shelves.

Measure the width and depth of the alcove at each shelf location. When checking for width, take a few measurements for each shelf — at the front, middle, and back of the shelf location; this will account for any variation in the wall planes (a common reality in older homes). If the measurements vary significantly, you'll have to size the shelf to the smallest dimension or cut one or both ends at an angle to follow the wall(s). Also keep in mind that one or both walls might be out of whack.

To find the cutting width for the shelves, subtract ¼" from the alcove dimensions. Cut the shelves to size from ¾" plywood, using a circular saw with a straightedge guide or a table saw. Also cut two ½" strips of plywood and trim them to length to match the width of the cabinet shelves; these will be used to build up the edges of the cabinet shelves and to hide the door tracks.

3. Attach the cabinet strips.

Apply wood glue to one ½" face of one of the ½" x ¾" strips, and clamp it to the bottom face of the top cabinet shelf so the front edges of both pieces are perfectly flush. The layered edge of the plywood strip should face forward, just as it does on the shelf edge. Let the glue set, as directed by the manufacturer, before removing the clamps. Repeat the same process to glue the other strip to the top face of the bottom cabinet shelf.

4. Finish the shelves.

Finish-sand all four shelves, working up to 220-grit or finer sandpaper. Finish all surfaces of each shelf as desired. The shelves in the hutch shown here were given two coats of Danish furniture oil.

5. Install the door tracks.

Cut two pieces of aluminum door track to match the width of the cabinet shelves, using a hacksaw. Position the top track (which should be deeper than the bottom track) against the top cabinet shelf so it's flush against the plywood strip. Drill pilot holes, and fasten the track with the provided screws. Be careful not to drill or screw through the top face of the shelf. Repeat the process to install the bottom track on the bottom cabinet shelf.

6. Install the shelves.

Each shelf is supported by four small metal angle brackets. Be sure to use brackets that have a hole in each of their two flanges, for driving screws. It's best to drive the screws into wall studs, whenever possible. Therefore, check for wall studs at each shelf location, using a stud finder (wall scanner) or the old-fashioned method of tapping with a hammer and probing with a finish nail. The brackets should go near the back corners of the shelves and about 1" back from each front corner. Make sure the two front brackets for the top cabinet shelf will be clear of the door track.

There should be studs in the rear corners of any alcove or closet. If you can't find studs elsewhere, you'll have to use hollow-wall anchors, such as toggle bolts. Don't use cheap plastic cone anchors, which have very little holding strength.

Mark the bracket locations, following your reference lines from step 1. Drill pilot holes, as needed, and install the brackets with 1½" or 2" coarse-thread drywall or wood screws. Place each upper (shallow) shelf in position on its brackets, drill a small pilot hole for each bracket, and fasten the brackets to the shelf with ½" wood screws.

Set the cabinet shelves on their brackets. Use a level to make sure the front edges of the shelves are perfectly aligned — the level should read plumb when set against both front edges of the shelves. Secure the shelves with ½" screws.

7. Add the doors.

You can cut the acrylic (a.k.a. Plexiglas) doors to size yourself or have them cut by a plastics retailer (online or at a store), usually for a small fee. If you're having them professionally cut, also have the finger-pull holes drilled, as both operations come with the risk of damage when you do them yourself.

The width of each door should be 1" more than half of the alcove width. For example, if the alcove is 30" wide, each door should be 16" wide. The door height should be ½" less than the interior face-to-face distance between the cabinet top and bottom; be sure to confirm this dimension with your own door tracks.

You can cut the acrylic sheet with a jigsaw, circular saw, band saw, or (preferably) a table saw. For a circular saw or table saw, use a blade with a carbide-tipped, triple-chip tooth design. For a jigsaw, use a new blade with 10 teeth per inch. Lay the acrylic sheet on a sacrificial piece of Styrofoam insulation board, to provide support (there's no need for the board with a table saw), and cut through the sheet and board at the same time.

Create the 1½" finger holes (see the plan) using a sharp, coarse-tooth 1½" hole saw. As with sawing, use a Styrofoam board to support the acrylic, and be careful not to apply too much pressure and risk cracking the plastic. Drill halfway through the plastic from one face, then flip the sheet over and complete the hole from the other face. To prevent the acrylic from melting, lubricate and cool the cutting area as you work with water and a small amount of colorless liquid soap (such as Ivory).

Remove the protective plastic layer from each door face. Install the doors by slipping their top edges all the way into the top door track, then dropping the bottom edges down into the bottom track.

FRONT VIEW

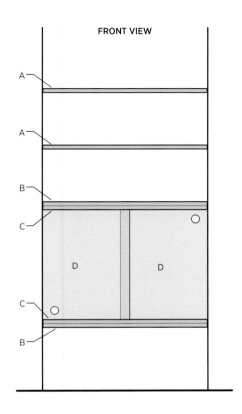

A

A

B

C

C

B

D   D

SIDE VIEW

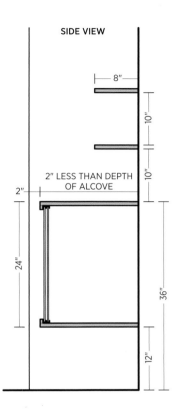

8"

10"

10"

2" LESS THAN DEPTH
OF ALCOVE

2"

24"

36"

12"

¾" PLYWOOD SHELVES

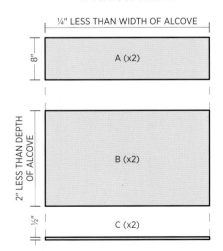

¼" LESS THAN WIDTH OF ALCOVE

8"

A (x2)

2" LESS THAN DEPTH OF ALCOVE

B (x2)

½"

C (x2)

¼" FROSTED ACRYLIC

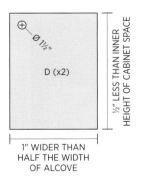

⌀ 1½"

D (x2)

½" LESS THAN INNER
HEIGHT OF CABINET SPACE

1" WIDER THAN
HALF THE WIDTH
OF ALCOVE

Assembly Plan

Plywood as . . .

A showcase of inspired pieces and the stories behind them

. . . inherent potential

Flip Chair

by Igor Zemskov

The Flip chair was designed as a lounge chair formed from a 4 x 8-foot sheet of bendable plywood. The entire piece is first bent into its unique U shape. After bending the plywood, I cut out the center of the U-shaped form to create the seat. My inspiration came mainly from IKEA and the idea of trying to ship the least amount of air. By being cut down the center, the chair's parts can be stacked for shipping.

The biggest challenge was trying to achieve the sharp curves with the material without splitting the plywood. The process I used to bend the wood was vacuum forming. I built a buck (out of MDF board) with the negative of the shape I wanted. By adding one layer of ¼" bendable plywood at a time into the vacuum

bag and using watered-down wood glue, I was able to avoid any cracking in the plywood.

Using a jigsaw to cut out the seat while keeping the walls straight was a great struggle, but sanding helped afterward. After the seat is flipped around, the chair is assembled into an invigorating yet relaxing lounge chair.

To attach the sides together I used lap joints on the feet, and after routing two grooves on each side, I fit the seat between the two sides. The finish on the Flip chair is a Honduran mahogany veneer, with handmade foam cushions for extra padding.

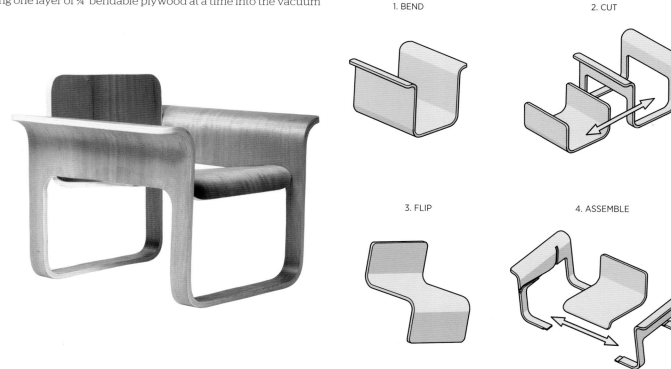

1. BEND

2. CUT

3. FLIP

4. ASSEMBLE

Art & Deco

Decorative things for walls and other areas.
Tip: If it doesn't look like plywood, it didn't turn out right.

Light Within

Designed by Philip Schmidt

Oddly enough, this is the only plywood light fixture in the book, even though the malleability and light weight of very thin plywood make it a pretty darned good material for fixturey things. And since the book has virtually everything else for the house, including a play slide, doghouses, and a boomerang, surely it needs at least one light fixture. This one is surprisingly easy to build and involves no wiring. It also uses no glue or fasteners. And every part besides the electrical stuff comes from a tree. Why does all this matter? It doesn't, really. But it might make for good conversation if anyone asks.

MATERIALS

- [ ] One 17" x 24¼" (or larger) piece ⅛" Baltic birch or other hardwood plywood
- [ ] Materials for router jig (see step 2)
- [ ] One 6" x 12¼" (or larger) piece ¼" Baltic birch or other hardwood plywood
- [ ] One 30" length ³⁄₁₆"-diam. birch dowel
- [ ] Finish materials (optional)
- [ ] One 12" x 13" sheet vellum paper (or two 12" x 12" sheets)
- [ ] Hanging light fixture socket (with cord, in-line switch, and metal cage)
- [ ] Scotch tape or clear glue

TOOLS

- [ ] Circular saw with straightedge guide or table saw
- [ ] Router with ¼" straight or spiral bit
- [ ] Clamps
- [ ] Drill with:
  - [ ] ³⁄₁₆" straight bit
  - [ ] ⅜" straight bit
- [ ] Compass
- [ ] Jigsaw with ultra fine-tooth wood blade
- [ ] Sandpaper (80 to 220 grit)
- [ ] Straightedge
- [ ] Utility knife
- [ ] Wood chisel

1. Cut the side pieces.

Lay out the two side pieces at 12" x 17" on the ⅛" plywood stock, with the grain of the face veneers parallel to the 12" dimension. This is necessary because thin plywood is more flexible *across* (perpendicular to) the grain of its face veneers. Cut the pieces to size with a circular saw and a straightedge guide or a table saw.

2. Mill the side flutes.

The nine flutes (or grooves) in the side pieces are cut with a router and ¼" straight or spiral bit. For accuracy and efficiency, it's best to build a simple jig to guide the router for each cut.

Create the jig with an 8" x 20" piece of hardboard or thin plywood and three lengths of 1 x 2 or other straight scrap lumber. Glue and/or screw a long piece of 1 x 2 parallel to the long edges of the hardboard base, to serve as a side fence; see the fluting jig drawing below. Secure a short 1 x 2 near one end of the base, perpendicular to the long piece; this is the beginning stop block.

Measure the offset between the edge of the router's base and the outside edge of the bit's cutter; multiply this dimension by 2, then add 9½. This sum equals the distance (in inches) between the beginning and ending stop blocks. Install the ending stop block perpendicular to the side fence.

Test the jig on a sacrificial surface, cutting through the jig base with the ¼" bit, and keeping the router base tight against the side fence throughout the cut. The resulting slot in the base should be ¼" wide and 9½" long.

Mark the flute layout on one of the side pieces, as shown in the side view of the plan on page 218. The flutes are laid out over the center of the side and are spaced 1¼" apart. Mark all edges of each flute to prevent confusion during the routing.

Clamp the two sides together on top of a sacrificial surface, with the sides' edges perfectly aligned. Clamp the jig at the first flute location, aligning the slot in the jig with the flute markings. Rout the flute through both pieces in one or more passes. Repeat the process to cut the remaining eight flutes.

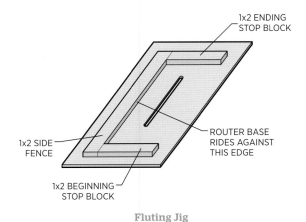

Fluting Jig

3. Drill the dowel holes.
The side pieces get four dowel holes near each side edge. Mark the dowel hole locations on the face of one side piece, following the side view drawing on page 218. Align the two sides and clamp them to the sacrificial surface, as before. Drill the holes through both pieces, using a ³⁄₁₆" bit.

4. Cut the rings.
The top and bottom rings are cut from ¼" plywood, using a jigsaw. If your router base is small enough, you can use the router and a trammel (see page 18) to cut the outer diameters of the rings, if desired.

Mark two 6"-diameter circles on the ¼" plywood stock, using a compass. Pivoting from the centerpoint in each circle, mark a 3½"-diameter circle on the bottom ring and a 1⁷⁄₁₆"-diameter circle on the top ring. The latter is a cutout for the body of the light socket, so confirm this dimension with your own lighting parts.

Drill a ⅜" starter hole inside the inner circle of each ring. Insert the jigsaw blade into each hole and cut out the inner circle. Then cut out the outer circles.

Note: Be sure to use a very fine, or "clean," jigsaw blade to minimize splintering. A narrow blade with 20 tpi (teeth per inch) works well, or you might prefer to use a "scroll" blade.

5. Prepare the dowels.
Cut eight lengths of dowel at 3" each, using the jigsaw. Sand the ends of the dowels slightly for a finished look and to facilitate insertion into the holes in the side pieces.

6. Notch the sides.
Shallow notches in each side piece aid in assembly and help hold the top and bottom rings securely in place. You'll cut the notches with a utility knife and a sharp wood chisel.

On the inside face of each side piece, measure and mark a 1"-long, ¼"-tall notch centered along the width of the side piece and ½" away from the bottom edge. Mark a similar notch along the top edge. Using a straightedge, score along the perimeter of each notch with a utility knife, cutting no more than ¹⁄₁₆" into the wood. Complete the notches by carefully removing the material between the scored lines with a chisel. Test-fit the rings in the notches and make any necessary adjustments for a good fit.

7. Sand and finish the wood parts.
Sand the cut edges of the sides and rings, using coarse sandpaper to shape or smooth any rough spots. Finish-sand all surfaces and edges of the pieces, working up to 220-grit or finer paper, so everything has a finished look and is smooth to the touch.

At this stage, you have the option of adding a wood finish. However, a protective finish most likely isn't necessary unless you want to protect the wood from fingerprints. The fixture as shown was given two light coats of "natural" Danish oil.

8. Create the shade.

The shade is simply a piece of white (or clear) vellum wrapped around the cage of the light socket assembly. The shade eliminates glare from the naked bulb and creates a column of soft light within the fixture's interior. It's also the reason for the cage — keeping the paper vellum from touching the heated light bulb.

The cage for a standard-size socket is likely to be about 4" in diameter. Wrapping around that diameter takes a little more than 12½", plus a bit of overlap for the seam. If you can find a vellum sheet at least 11" x 13", use it. Otherwise, you'll have to graft a strip onto a smaller sheet.

Measure between the inner edges of the notches on each side piece, and trim the vellum sheet to this dimension (it should be close to 10½"). Wrap the vellum around the cage and secure the seam with clear tape or glue, forming a cylinder that fits snugly over the cage.

Assemble the socket, fitting the top ring onto the socket body, followed by the cage, and securing both with the provided screw rings. Install a new light bulb in the socket. Slip the shade over the cage so it touches the top ring, and set the assembly aside.

*Important note: Use only a CFL (compact fluorescent lamp) or LED bulb in this fixture. Do **not** use incandescent, halogen, or other types of bulbs that get very hot, creating a dangerous fire hazard. As with any light fixture containing paper, do not leave the light on while unattended for long periods.*

9. Assemble the fixture.

Place the sides together with their inside (notched) faces against each other. Insert the dowels through the eight holes so they extend beyond both sides about the same distance. Carefully separate the two sides to create an even 1"-wide gap, as shown in top view in the plan. Adjust the dowels as you work so they project equally beyond both side pieces.

Now it's time to flex your fixture: Spread the sides apart at the bottom and fit the bottom ring into place inside its notches. Measure to make sure the ring is centered from side to side. Then spread the sides at the top and fit the socket (with shade and top ring) into place. Adjust the top ring as needed so the shade is plumb and centered over the bottom ring. The shade should just touch the bottom ring all the way around. Make any final adjustments so all looks good, then hang the fixture from the cord as desired.

Note: If you ever need to replace the light bulb, spread the fixture's sides apart slightly at the bottom, remove the bottom ring, reach into the shade to unscrew and replace the bulb, then fit the bottom ring back into place.

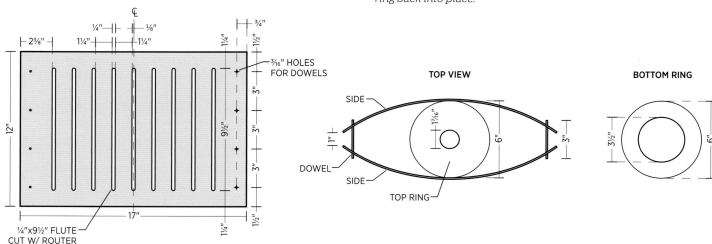

SIDE VIEW (x2)

¾"x9½" FLUTE CUT W/ ROUTER

³⁄₁₆" HOLES FOR DOWELS

TOP VIEW

SIDE

DOWEL

SIDE

TOP RING

BOTTOM RING

Cutting Plan   Assembly Plan

Resin Art Panels

Designed by Andrew Williams

No matter how much you've paid for an artwork or print, the cost of custom framing is exorbitant. And cheap frames in stock sizes are both limiting and, frankly, a little boring. These clever art panels solve both problems. Originally created as a gift, the panels received so many compliments that the designer just kept on making them. They can be custom-sized to fit any artwork or space, so they're ideal for both one-offs or elaborate salon-style arrangements. The crisp plywood edges provide a subtle decorative touch and just the right thickness for a satisfying visual depth.

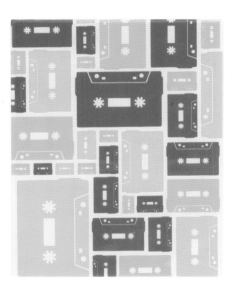

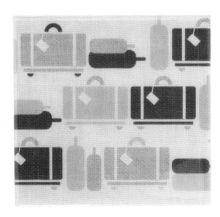

MATERIALS

☐ Artwork or print

☐ ¾" plywood (AC or better grade; quantity as needed)

☐ Contact cement or other adhesive suitable for use with artwork

☐ Two-part resin/bar-top finish

☐ Mineral oil (with rag for applying it)

☐ Picture-mounting brackets

☐ ¼" self-adhesive rubber or felt bumpers or protective pads

TOOLS

☐ Table saw or circular saw with straightedge guide

☐ Fine sandpaper

☐ Tack cloth

☐ X-Acto knife

☐ 1"-wide masking tape

☐ Safety goggles and rubber gloves

☐ Plastic stir stick

☐ Disposable mixing cups

☐ 3" rubber or plastic spreader or mud knife

☐ Razor (optional)

Note: This mounting technique works for many kinds of materials, from images cut from art books to photographs and original works. What's important is having the right material: Printed paper works best. Fabric tends to absorb a lot of resin. If you want to mount a fabric piece or collage of fabrics, you might scan it and print out a color replica on paper. You can choose any size of artwork, but keep in mind that large panels can create an undesirable glare in some settings.

1. Cut the plywood panel.

Measure the artwork, then lay out and cut the plywood panel so it's at least ¼" smaller than the artwork in both height and width. Use a table saw or circular saw with a straightedge guide for clean, straight cuts. Remember that these edges are aesthetically critical, so make sure they are square and free of burn marks.

2. Glue down the artwork.

Sand the face and edges of the panel as needed, then wipe them with a tack cloth to remove all dust. These surfaces must be smooth, clean, and dust-free. Apply adhesive to the panel face and/or the back of the artwork, as directed by the manufacturer. Glue down the artwork, face up, so all its edges overhang the panel by at least ⅛".

Note: Contact cement works well as an adhesive for paper and some other materials. If contact cement isn't right for your artwork material, choose an adhesive that bonds well to both your material and the wood; otherwise, the piece can delaminate.

3. Trim the artwork.

Lay the panel facedown on a cutting mat. Carefully trim the edges of the artwork flush with the plywood, using an X-Acto knife with a new blade.

4. Mask the edges.

Apply masking tape to all four edges of the panel, so that the top edges of the tape rise at least ¼" above the panel face, creating a reservoir for the resin. Use your fingers or fingernails to burnish the tape and create a tight seal along the panel edges; any gaps here will allow the resin to leak out.

5. Pour the resin.

Mix the resin as directed by the manufacturer (see Working with Two-Part Resin, opposite). Wear safety goggles and gloves, and work in a well-ventilated area. The amount of resin you need depends on the size of your panel; mix enough to cover the panel face with a $1/16$"-thick layer. Carefully pour a small puddle of resin on the panel face and spread it around with a spreader. Add a little bit of resin at a time, as needed, and spread until you've achieved the desired thickness. Resin is self-leveling, so once the surface is coated it's time to leave it alone. If necessary,

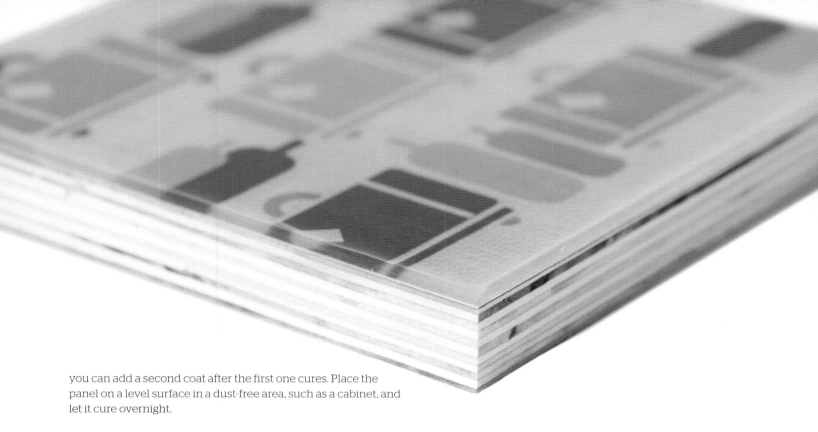

you can add a second coat after the first one cures. Place the panel on a level surface in a dust-free area, such as a cabinet, and let it cure overnight.

Note: The project shown used Parks' Super Glaze Pour-On Finish and Preservative, a high-gloss epoxy resin.

6. Remove the tape and sand the edges.
Peel the tape from the edges of the panel. If any resin seeped under the tape, scrape it off with your fingernails or a razor, and sand the plywood edge smooth. Sometimes the resin pools against the tape, leaving a raised edge that can be sharp. Knock this down with sandpaper, rounding over the edge slightly.

7. Finish the plywood edges.
Seal the edges of the plywood with mineral oil (or other desired finish) applied with a rag. This helps preserve the wood and creates a finished look.

8. Mount the panel.
You can use any standard picture-mounting bracket — the little metal strip with teeth works well and is easy to install. Be sure to install the bracket parallel to the top of the panel. Apply felt or rubber bumper disks to the bottom two corners of the panel's back to ensure that the panel rests level against the wall.

Shop Tip

Working with Two-Part Resin
When working with two-part resin, the most important thing is mixing part A (resin) and part B (activator) in equal amounts. Disposable measuring cups are great for maintaining proper proportions.

When pouring the resin, the main challenge is getting an even coat all the way to the edges. Use a rubber or plastic spreader or mud knife to push the resin in all directions. With an overhead light trained on the panel, move your head from side to side to note the glare along the surface. A dull spot indicates that you need more resin in that area.

Whitewashed Ply Paneling

Designed by Camden Whitehead

If you're into building materials, you undoubtedly love to discover common products used in uncommon applications. You also know that sometimes this works and sometimes it doesn't. Well, here's an idea for the top of the "works" category. It's ½" AC-grade pine plywood, whitewashed and urethaned, and installed with a fine reveal between panels and along the trim and ceiling finish (battens or butt joints just wouldn't do). The treatment works so well that the designer used it as the only wall finish in one of his custom home projects. That's right — no drywall, no plaster; just plywood. (You can see the house on Camden Whitehead's website; see page 315.)

See page 163 for another work by Camden Whitehead.

MATERIALS

- ☐ 4 x 8-foot sheets AC-grade ½" plywood (quantity as needed)
- ☐ Flat white exterior latex paint (or other color, as desired)
- ☐ Water-based polyurethane in satin finish
- ☐ 6d (2") or 8d (2½") finish nails or pneumatic brads (see step 4)
- ☐ White glue

TOOLS

- ☐ Orbital or random orbital sander with 120- and 220-grit sandpaper
- ☐ Medium-nap paint roller
- ☐ Router with ½" rabbeting bit (bearing-guided)
- ☐ Chalk line
- ☐ ⅛"-thick scrap material (for spacers)
- ☐ Hammer and nail set or brad nailer
- ☐ Circular saw with straightedge guide or table saw

Note: The layout and installation of this paneling over an entire wall is straightforward and well within the skill set of a finish carpenter or even an experienced DIYer. If you're not used to working with paneling and trim elements, you might want to contract with a skilled helper for the installation, while you can easily take care of the more time-consuming steps of prefinishing the panels.

1. Prefinish the panels.

It's best to prefinish the plywood panels before installing them. This results in a much cleaner installation with crisper joints and less damage to adjacent finishes. The basic finish for the paneling is a whitewash of diluted latex paint topped with two coats of polyurethane. You can buy whitewash as a premixed product, but it's preferable to mix your own, so you can vary the opacity to your liking by adjusting the paint-to-water ratio. A good mix to start with is three parts water to two parts paint.

To finish the panels, sand the good ("A") face of the plywood with 120-grit sandpaper, using an orbital or random orbital sander (if available). Mix the paint with clean water to the desired consistency, and apply it to each panel face with a medium-nap paint roller. Apply the whitewash generously, taking care to coat the surface as evenly as possible. Let the wash dry completely.

Next, apply a generous coat of water-based polyurethane to the whitewashed surfaces, again using a roller. Let the poly dry completely, then sand the surface with 220-grit sandpaper. Apply a second coat of poly, and let it dry overnight (at least).

2. Plan the installation.

As shown here, the plywood panels are joined with overlapping ½"-wide, ¼"-deep rabbets cut into the edges where panels meet one another and where they meet the baseboard trim; see the paneling detail drawing. The baseboard shown in the detail drawing is custom-milled hardwood stock; this is just one way to finish the bottom edges of the paneling. The drawing also shows an option for continuing the paneling treatment over the ceiling.

At this stage, you need to plan the panel installation to determine which panel edges to rabbet. To facilitate installation, it's recommended that you rabbet one long and one short edge on the front side of each panel, then rabbet the remaining two edges on the back side.

If you're using a baseboard like the one shown in the drawing, plan to install the baseboard first, then work up the wall to the ceiling. The panels can simply be butted together at wall corners (without rabbets). If you're paneling the ceiling and the wall(s), plan to cover the ceiling first.

Note: Before applying plywood paneling directly over wall or ceiling framing, check with the local building department regarding fire ratings. Building codes may require drywall behind any wood paneling, or they may specify that the plywood must be treated for fire resistance.

3. Mill the rabbets.

Cut the rabbets into the panel edges according to your layout, using a router and a ½" bearing-guided rabbeting bit. The depth of the rabbets must be precisely half the thickness of the plywood for the panels to install flush with one another. If desired, you can cut the rabbets during the installation to minimize planning errors.

4. Install the panels.

You should have at least one, but preferably two, helpers for this step. Snap or draw reference lines on the wall to represent the top edges of the bottom course of panels. Install baseboard or other base trim, as applicable. Set the first panel in place, following the reference line. If you're using baseboard like that shown below, set the ⅛" reveal between the panel and trim with ⅛"-thick spacers of scrap hardboard or other flat material.

Tack the panel in place with a few 6d finish nails (use 8d nails if you're going over drywall) or pneumatic brads, driving all nails into the wall framing. The reveal will let you cheat the panels a little to follow your layout, as needed.

Set the next panel and tack it in place, maintaining a ⅛" reveal between the two panels. Repeat the process to complete the first course. Trim panels to size as needed, using a circular saw and straightedge guide or a table saw. Confirm that everything fits well in the first course, then go back and nail the panels fully. Set the nails slightly below the surface, using a nail set for hand-nailing or by adjusting the nailer pressure to countersink the brads.

Follow the same procedure to install the remaining courses of panels, using the spacers to set the reveals at all edges of the panels (except at inside wall corners, where the panels should be butted). If you're paneling up to an existing ceiling finish, you can leave a reveal at the top (with no rabbet on the top edges of the wall panels) or add another trim element.

Mix fine sawdust with white glue and a little pigment so the mixture (when dry) matches the coloring of the panels. Use the mixture to fill the nail holes. Touch up any scratches or other damage to the panels with paint and/or polyurethane, as needed.

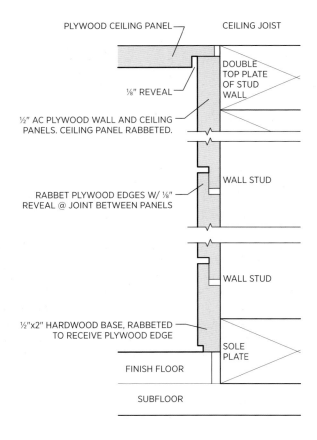

Paneling Detail

Book of Plies

Designed by Carl Harris

In the words of the designer, the goal for this design was "to get back to basics and to understand the qualities of a material and its constraints. As a designer, it is imperative to understand how a material works from the inner threads to overall aesthetics. I chose plywood because it's a versatile and flexible material that can be simply manipulated using low-tech or high-tech processes." Clearly, he also set out to have some fun, and the resulting piece offers both function and folly — the Book of Plies makes a great accent piece but can also be put to work as a magazine holder, a side table, or a stool.

MATERIALS

- ☐ 3 mm (³/₁₆") beech plywood (quantity as needed)
- ☐ Scrap 2x lumber
- ☐ Wood glue
- ☐ Finish materials (as desired)

TOOLS

- ☐ Circular saw with straightedge guide or table saw
- ☐ Sandpaper (220 to 600 grit)
- ☐ Bucket or plastic tub (large enough to submerge one or more cut plywood pieces)
- ☐ Speed Square (rafter square)
- ☐ Clamps
- ☐ Band saw or crosscut handsaw

Note: This project offers numerous opportunities for customization. You can change the size and number of cut plywood sheets ("leaves"). You can make the curves of the individual leaves as subtle or pronounced as you like. And you can arrange the leaves in different ways, keeping them perfectly lined up or slightly tilting some or all of the leaves out to the side in random or ordered patterns. (In step 6, you will cut the glued ends of the leaf assembly to create a flat surface for the base, so any corners and edges sticking out will be trimmed flush with the others.)

Indeed, customization is an important part of this design, so plan to experiment a little, with both the curves and the leaf arrangement. The basic construction process is given here; it's up to you to add creativity and a personal touch.

1. Cut the plywood leaves.

Cut the plywood stock into as many leaves as you desire, using whatever dimensions you desire. In the project shown, the leaves measure 11¹¹/₁₆" x 15⅝". The grain of the plywood's face veneers should parallel the long dimension of the leaves. Cut the leaves with a circular saw and straightedge guide or a table saw to ensure straight, clean cuts.

2. Sand and soak the leaves.

Sand each leaf with 220-grit to 600-grit sandpaper to achieve the desired smoothness. Fully submerge one or more of the leaves in hot water for 1 hour, or until the plywood is flexible enough to bend without cracking.

3. Cut the wedges.

While the leaves soak, you can cut 2x lumber (use scrap material, if available) into wedges for shaping the leaves (see the drawing showing the shaping process). Begin with the wedge for the steepest degree of angle desired. Use a Speed Square (rafter square) to mark the angled line across the face of the lumber, noting the degree of angle for reference. Cut along the angled line with a circular saw. Create two wedges with this angle.

4. Form the leaves.

Each leaf must be clamped and dried for 3 hours, so it takes a while to form all of them. If you have enough clamps and wedges, you can shape more than one leaf at a time.

Remove a leaf from the water and immediately clamp one of the shorter ends to a work table, with a wood block on top of the leaf to prevent the shoe of the clamp from marring the plywood. Slide the angled wedges underneath the opposite end of the leaf, pushing them in as needed to achieve the desired amount of curve. You may have to add clamps and blocks behind the wedges to keep them in place. Let the leaf dry undisturbed for 3 hours, then unclamp and remove the leaf, setting it aside for now.

Repeat the process with the remaining leaves, one at a time, reducing the angle of the wedges as you go. You can reuse the same wedges by shaving them down to a less-acute angle. Decreasing the wedge angle incrementally results in an open-book effect, as shown in the project here.

Keep in mind that the sheets will bend back slightly toward a flatter shape as they dry completely. Also, if you want a symmetrical piece, you can shape two leaves at each level of arch. As you work, lay out the bent leaves in order, moving from the most curved at the outside to the least curved in the center.

Note: If you try for too much curve, you might find some cracking on the veneer; this may be hidden in the finished product.

5. Glue the leaves.

After all the sheets are shaped and completely dry, glue each piece to its neighbors, using wood glue applied along the same edge where the clamp went. Glue as many sheets as you can (or want to) within the working time of the glue, then clamp the pieces together, again using wood blocks to prevent marks.

Start the glue-up with the straighter leaves in the center,

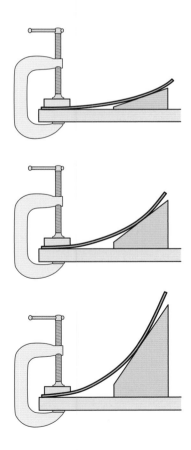

Shaping the Leaves: the steeper the wedge,
the greater the curve on the leaf

working out to the sides with increasingly curved leaves. Let each phase of the glue-up dry for 24 hours, then remove the clamps.

6. Cut the straight edge.

Mark a straight line at the same height across all four edges, near the glued end of the assembly. The best tool for making this cut is a band saw, which can accommodate the entire piece and allow for a single cut. Lay the assembly on one of its flat sides. If the leaves tilt out to the side at all, place some blocking under the flattest portion of the assembly, so that the end to be trimmed is perpendicular to the saw blade. Push the assembly slowly through the saw to make a straight cut.

If you don't have access to a band saw, you can make the straight-edge cut with a good crosscut handsaw. Clamp a straight stick of 1x lumber (preferably hardwood) along the cutting lines on both sides of the assembly; this will help keep the saw straight as you make the cut and will minimize tearout.

7. Finish the piece.

Sand the straight-cut bottom of the assembly so it is flat and smooth. Also sand the outer leaves and all edges as needed until you are happy with the finish. Apply oil or a clear varnish (such as wipe-on polyurethane) to all exposed surfaces to protect the plywood.

Shop Tip

Bending Thin Plywood
Thin beech plywood is available in thicknesses such as 1.5 mm (1/16"), 3 mm (1/8"), and 5 mm (3/16") and in constructions with three, five, and seven plies. In general, the thicker the material, the harder it is to bend. To create more pronounced bends to your leaves, you can glue together two 1.5 mm sheets, forming the curve at the same time. Better-quality plywood has even thickness among the layers. One thing to avoid, for example, is a 5 mm sheet with one thick layer in the middle and two thin layers on the outside; the layers should all be roughly equal in thickness.

Candleholders

Designed by Philipp Herbert

Like most people who craft with wood, the designer of this piece regularly accumulates a surplus of scrap material that's too small to build with and too big to throw away. (If you're a wood person, you know how ridiculously small that can be.) This simple candleholder is just one of his clever solutions for using up the smaller leftovers. Whether you create one or many holders, the process is simple and satisfying, and the result is a decorative display of wood's beauty in its many forms, from stratified plywood edges to solid hardwood to edge-glued panels . . . whatever you can find in your pile.

See page 252 for another work by Philipp Herbert.

MATERIALS

- ☐ Wood pieces in the desired size (see step 1)
- ☐ Wood glue
- ☐ Finish materials (see step 6)

TOOLS

- ☐ Miter saw or other saw
- ☐ Clamps
- ☐ Sandpaper (from 60 to 400 grit) and sanding block
- ☐ Bench vise (if available)
- ☐ Square
- ☐ Drill or drill press with 40 mm Forstner bit (must be slightly larger than candle diameter)
- ☐ Paintbrush

1. Plan the design.

Determine the best size for your candleholders, considering the size of your scrap, the diameter of the candles you will use, and the desired size of the finished piece. The holders shown here are about 3" x 3" and hold 1½" candles. For an appealing look, each holder should include at least two (three or more is better) different types and/or colors of material, and it's best to combine plywood pieces with solid material.

2. Cut the materials.

The best way to cut numerous small squares of stock is with a miter saw set up with a stop block. Otherwise, you can use any saw you're comfortable with and mark the stock with cutting lines in the conventional manner. Carefully cut the first piece to size so all four edges are straight and square, then use the cut piece as a template for marking the remaining pieces. Stack up the pieces for each holder as you work to make sure you have enough pieces for the desired height.

3. Glue up the layers.

To prepare for the glue-up, stack the layers of each holder in the desired arrangement, considering grain, coloring, and other features for the best appearance. For example, it usually looks best to orient the grain of similar woods in the same direction. Also think about the hole depth for the candle and in which layer the hole's bottom will be.

Apply a layer of glue to one face of the mating layers, and fit the pieces together so all outside edges are flush. You should

get a small amount of glue squeeze-out at the edges. Depending on how many layers you have, you can glue up all of them for each holder or split them up into two assemblies, and glue the assemblies together in a second round. Clamp all glued layers, wipe off any squeeze-out, and let the glue dry. If you don't have enough clamps to go around, you can substitute with any heavy, flat weight.

4. Sand the holders.

Using a sanding block (any piece of scrap wood will do) and coarse sandpaper, sand the sides of each holder until all the layers are flush. (It helps to secure the holder in a bench vise, if you have one. Just be sure to protect the sides of the piece with scrap.) Sand diagonally across the side of the holder (this makes it easier to get the surface flat). As you sand, check periodically with a square to make sure the sides are flat and square. Mark any high spots with a pencil for further sanding.

Once the sides are flat and square, move to medium-grit sandpaper and sand some more. This pass should remove the scratches from the coarse paper. After that, move up the grit scale to the finer papers (at least 220 grit), so that the surfaces are smooth to the touch.

5. Drill the candle hole.

Mark the center of the topmost layer by drawing perpendicular lines from corner to corner across the holder's top face (diagonals always cross in the center of a square).

Set up the Forstner bit in a drill press (preferable) or a portable drill, and secure the holder to the drill table or a bench. Bore the candle hole to the desired depth at the center mark. The depth should be at least ¼" to prevent the candle from falling out easily.

If you're using a portable drill, keep the drill plumb throughout the operation, and use a homemade jig to keep the bit from wandering as you start the hole (see A Forstner Drilling Jig, page 30).

Smooth the edge of the hole with fine sandpaper.

6. Finish the holder.

Apply a clear protective finish, such as polyurethane or lacquer, using a paint brush. Let the first coat dry, then sand the surfaces lightly with 400-grit sandpaper, and apply another coat (unless directed otherwise). A clear finish does a nice job of bringing out the different colors of the wood layers.

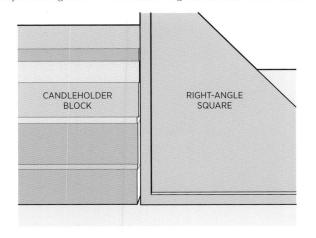

CANDLEHOLDER BLOCK

RIGHT-ANGLE SQUARE

Checking the Holder Side with a Square

Desk Coverlet

Designed by Jorie Ruud

When this designer moved into her first apartment, she loved the built-in desk by the window, but (being an incurable aesthete, no doubt) she couldn't live with the old laminate desktop. So she devised this clever plywood cover that completely hides the old top and, because it's removable, won't jeopardize her damage deposit. The basic design can easily be adapted to cover all sorts of surfaces, from built-in shelves and countertops to freestanding desks and tables. Adding decorative embellishments is also up to you. Here, the whole coverlet receives a whitewashed, wood-grain finish created with a graining tool and ordinary interior paint, and the front apron is bejeweled with a random collection of drawer knobs.

MATERIALS

- ☐ ½" or ¾" plywood (enough to cover desk, plus front apron; see step 1)
- ☐ Wood glue
- ☐ 6d (2") finish nails
- ☐ Finish materials (see step 3)
- ☐ Decorative drawer knobs (quantity as desired)
- ☐ Foam shelf liner (if needed; see step 4)

TOOLS

- ☐ Circular saw with straightedge guide
- ☐ Bar clamps (if available)
- ☐ Drill with:
  - ☐ ⅟₁₆" straight bit
  - ☐ Bit sized for knob mounting bolts
- ☐ Hammer
- ☐ Nail set (if available)
- ☐ Sandpaper (see step 3)
- ☐ Wide paintbrush
- ☐ Wood-graining rocker tool (optional)

1. Cut the plywood top and apron.

The top panel is simply cut to fit the surface or space you're covering, so start by taking careful measurements of the area. Measure in several places to account for variances created by out-of-square corners and adjoining walls or other surfaces.

One decision you have to make is whether to cover the apron with the top or vice versa. In the project as shown, the apron fits over the front edge of the top panel, creating an uninterrupted front face. To do this, plan to cut the top flush with the front edge of the existing surface. To have the top panel cover the top edge of the apron, measure to the edge of the surface, then add the thickness of your plywood stock.

The apron can be any height you desire; just be sure to add or subtract the plywood's thickness depending on the arrangement of the two pieces.

Cut the top and apron with a circular saw and straightedge guide to ensure clean, straight cuts. Whenever possible, use the panel's factory edges for the front edge of the top (or whichever is the most important exposed edge) and the top edge of the apron.

2. Assemble the coverlet.

Position the top and apron together according to your plan. Make sure the outside surfaces of both pieces are perfectly flush. If you have a couple of bar clamps, clamp the pieces together; otherwise, have a helper hold them in place. Drill $1/16$" pilot holes about 4" apart, drilling through the apron or top (whichever is the overlapping piece) and into the edge of the mating piece.

Apply glue to the mating surfaces, and fasten the pieces together with 6d finish nails driven into the pilot holes. If desired, you can drive the nail heads slightly below the surface with a small nail set; otherwise, set them flush with the hammer. Let the glue dry overnight.

3. Finish the coverlet.

Finish-sand the top surfaces of the entire cover with 150-grit sandpaper (for a painted surface) or 220-grit paper (for a clear finish). Carefully sand the joint between the apron and top so the two are perfectly flush.

Apply the finish of your choice. To create the wood-grain effect shown here, apply a thick coat of white interior paint in an eggshell finish over the exposed surfaces, using a wide paintbrush. The thicker the coating, the better — but you don't want so much that the paint puddles.

Graining the Surface with a Rocker Tool

While the paint is wet, drag and roll a wood-graining rocker tool through the paint, working in about 3" (or the width of your tool) sections at a time; see the drawing above (and there are loads of videos online demonstrating how to use this tool). The goal is a realistic-looking grain. If the look is too uniform, "grain" a few random areas at the end to add realism. Let the paint dry completely.

4. Add the knobs.

Mark the locations for the decorative knobs (or other features), positioning them as desired. Drill holes through the front of the apron for each mounting bolt. Install the knobs with the bolts inserted through the back of the apron.

Install the cover by simply setting it in place. If sliding or slight rocking (due to warpage of the plywood or the old top) is a concern, you can lay a sheet of grippy foam shelf liner under the coverlet to cushion and grip the plywood top.

Note: Most drawer knobs have bolts sized for ¾" material. If you use ½" plywood, you may need to find shorter bolts — just be sure to bring the knobs with you to the hardware store, because the bolt threads have to match the knobs precisely. Also, you might want to drill a slight counterbore for the bolts so the heads will be flush with the apron surface.

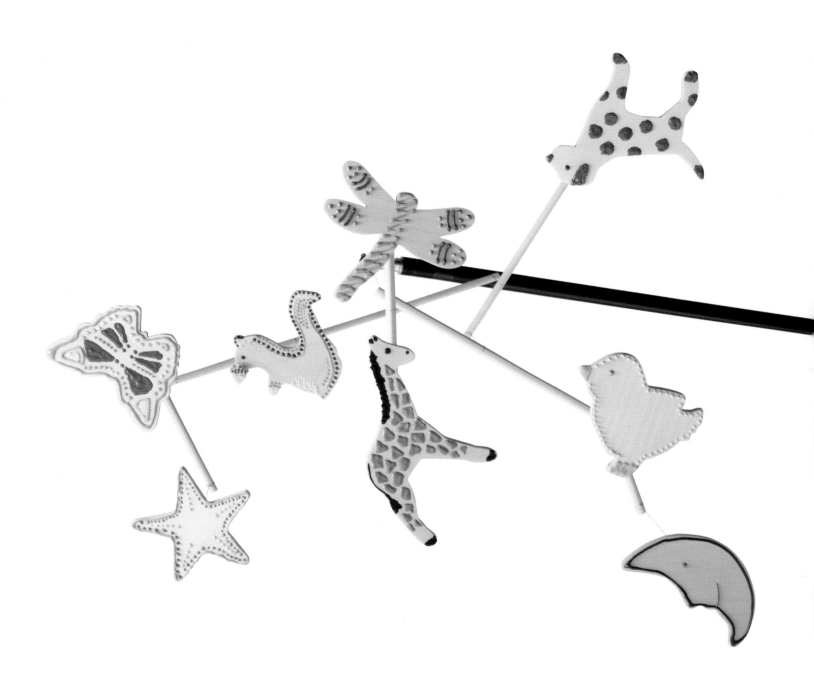

Kidnetic

Designed by Christie Murata, adapted by Kathy and Philip Schmidt

Delighted, fixated, entranced, giddy, zoned out, amused, bewitched . . . any of these enviable states of mind fairly describes a baby caught in the spell of a mobile. And the best kind of mobile is moved by the silent forces of air and gravity (not a wind-up model that spins in one direction while playing off-key snippets of Mozart). The traditional mobile shown here is a simple adaptation of one of the designer's more elaborate originals, pieces that require considerable skill with a scroll saw, not to mention an artist's attention to detail. This version lets you use cookie cutters to draw the mobile figures and a jigsaw to cut them out. But don't worry — a quick Internet search yields thousands of different cookie cutters for sale, so your own mobile will be anything but, you know, cookie-cutter.

MATERIALS

- ☐ Seven (or more) cookie cutters
- ☐ ¼" Baltic birch plywood (quantity as needed; see note below)
- ☐ Finish nail or brad
- ☐ Foam core or scrap wood
- ☐ Craft paint
- ☐ One 40" length ¼"-diam. birch dowel
- ☐ Seven (or more) ½" screw eyes
- ☐ Superglue or white glue (optional)
- ☐ Strong, lightweight string
- ☐ Fishing swivel
- ☐ One small metal washer or ring

TOOLS

- ☐ Mechanical pencil
- ☐ Jigsaw with ultra-fine-tooth wood blade
- ☐ Drill with 1⁄16" straight bit
- ☐ Sandpaper (100 to 220 grit) with sanding block
- ☐ Paintbrushes
- ☐ Pliers
- ☐ Scissors

Note: Thin birch and Baltic birch plywood are commonly available in small pieces at craft stores (in sizes such as 12" x 24") and woodworking retailers (24" x 30" is common). For this project, the material should be relatively flat and have at least one good face (without patches).

As mentioned, cookie cutters are available in a vast range of shapes and sizes. Since they're made for fragile cookies, the shapes and contours tend be simple enough; just keep in mind when choosing cutters, that you will be cutting the shapes out of thin plywood. You can find cool and unusual cookie cutters at specialty kitchen stores or from online retailers. Choose at least seven different characters; you can follow a specific theme or just pick a random collection.

1. Cut out the shapes.

Place each cookie cutter on ¼" plywood stock. Holding it down firmly, trace around the outside of the cutter with a mechanical pencil (which has a very fine point).

Cut out the figure with a jigsaw and a very fine, or "clean," blade. A narrow blade with 20 tpi (teeth per inch) works well with minimal splintering. A "scroll" blade is another option. The finer the blade, the more maneuverable it will be. To cut tight curves and tricky details, make relief cuts as needed. A relief cut is roughly perpendicular to the cutting line, and it allows the waste to fall away, freeing up the blade to approach the cut at a more direct angle; see the drawing of relief cuts at right.

As you cut, try to keep the figure attached to the stock for as long as possible; once you cut it free, a small piece can be difficult to secure by hand and is likely to bring your fingers close to the saw blade. For this same reason, it's best to trace and cut the pieces one at a time. If you try to save material by fitting them closely together (as you might when cutting rolled-out cookie dough), you'll end up having to cut each piece free from the stock prematurely.

2. Find the balance point.

To ensure that the figures will hang level (facedown), you have to install the screw eyes as close as possible to each figure's center — not the center of its area, but the center of its weight. A simple balancing jig will help you find the weight center and mark it for locating the screw eye. Make the jig by pushing a small finish nail or brad up through a piece of foam core or scrap wood so the nail stands plumb with its point up.

To find the weight centers, place each figure with its back side on the nail point, and move the figure around until it balances itself (or nearly so). Then press the figure onto the nail to mark the back side with a small hole.

Drill a shallow (about ⅛") pilot hole at the mark, using a 1/16" bit, being very careful not to drill through to the front face of the figure. Repeat the process with the remaining figures.

3. Sand and paint the figures.

Sand the edges and faces of each figure. Use coarse sandpaper to shape edges, keeping the strokes parallel to the edge to prevent splintering. A flat sanding block helps shape straight edges and gradual convex curves. For detail sanding, wrap the sandpaper around a bit of dowel or a pencil, using it like a file. Use fine paper to smooth the edges and face veneers.

Decorate the figures with paint. The blonde plywood provides a nice background for painted details. The figures shown here were painted with acrylic craft paint in squeezable bottles with decorator tips. Let the paint dry completely.

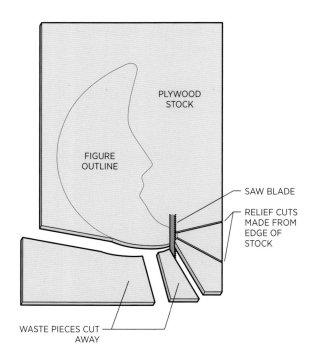

PLYWOOD STOCK

FIGURE OUTLINE

SAW BLADE

RELIEF CUTS MADE FROM EDGE OF STOCK

WASTE PIECES CUT AWAY

Making Relief Cuts

4. Cut the dowels.

Using the jigsaw, cut six pieces of ¼" dowel as follows
(or as desired):

- 1 at 10½"
- 1 at 7½"
- 1 at 7"
- 2 at 5"
- 1 at 4¼"

These pieces are the balancing rods that will suspend the
mobile figures. If you have more than seven figures, cut as many
additional rods as you need. You can also change the length
and configuration of the rods; anything will work, as long as the
pieces are balanced and can move freely.

5. Assemble the mobile.

Assembling a mobile is a study in trial and error. Since every
piece is counterbalanced by another, each tiny adjustment
changes their weight relationship. The two factors that affect the
balance are the relative weights of the pieces and the positions of
the strings on the rods. The lengths of the strings have little effect
on the balance.

First install the screw eyes. Using pliers for a good grip,
carefully drive the threaded end of a screw eye into the pilot hole
in the back of each figure, going in only about ⅛". Push in as you
turn to engage the threads and prevent stripping the hole. If this
does happen, just install the eye with a little glue and let it dry
undisturbed.

Because each mobile is unique, there are no standard
dimensions or layout guidelines for assembly. As an example,
the mobile shown here is detailed in the mobile assembly
drawing.

Start the assembly by cutting a length of string about 3 feet
long and tying a fishing swivel to one end; this allows the
mobile to spin without twisting the string. Tie a small washer
or other type of ring to the free end of the swivel; this is for
hanging the mobile.

Lay out the dowels and figures in the desired configuration,
then start tying them off one by one. You can work from the top
down or from the bottom up, whichever you prefer. First tie off
the figures near the end of their supporting rods; most of the

figures will be in pairs on a short rod. Then find the approximate
balancing point of each rod with figure pairs, and loosely tie a
string at this point. Again, you can adjust the length of any string
throughout the assembly. To hang a single figure from a rod,
counterbalance it with another rod.

As you work, move the strings sideways on the rods as needed
to achieve balance. When all is properly balanced and all of the
elements can rotate freely without touching one another, tie off
the strings with strong knots, and trim the excess. If the string
is slippery and doesn't grip the dowels well, affix it with a small
drop of superglue or white glue.

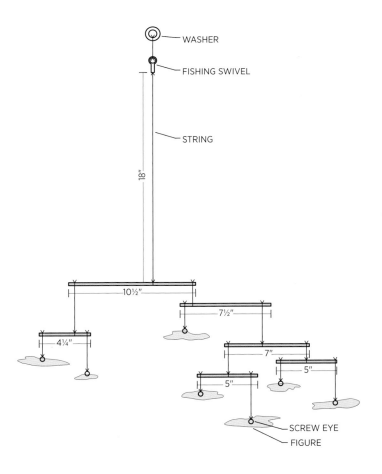

Assembly Plan

Light Headboard

Designed by Katherine Belsey

This custom headboard for nighttime readers is named for its two best features: the built-in lighting, of course, and the light visual quality of the evenly spaced planks; these are hung on the wall and appear to float above the bed, offering a creative alternative to the traditional monolithic headboard. The simplicity of the design also makes it highly customizable. You can use almost any plywood or other sheet good for the planks, and the light fixtures can be assembled with lamp parts in any style, finish, or configuration you like. In fact, the composition shown here was made with mahogany plywood shelf boards and lighting parts salvaged from an old ceiling fan.

See page 54 for another work by Katherine Belsey.

MATERIALS

For a queen-size headboard:

- One 3 x 4-foot piece ¾" plywood or other sheet good (grain of face veneers should parallel 4-foot dimension)
- Wood veneer edge tape (optional)
- Finish materials (as desired)
- Four 10" or 12" two-part aluminum cleat hangers with ¾" screws
- 2" wood screws
- Hollow-wall anchors (as needed)
- Eight rubber bumpers (self-adhesive; sized to match depth of cleat)

For each light fixture:

- One metal cylinder light shade or tin can (see step 7)
- 2"-wide tape roll or larger sheet of pressure-sensitive (peel-and-stick) wood veneer
- Finish materials (as needed)
- ⅛ IP threaded hollow all-thread lamp tubing (length as needed; see step 8)
- General-purpose two-part epoxy
- Two lamp swivels

- Lamp cord
- One 18" length ⅜"-diam. lamp pipe with threaded ends
- One 3" length ⅜"-diam. lamp pipe with threaded ends
- One Edison-base socket with ⅛" rear IPS
- One in-line cord switch

TOOLS

- Circular saw with straightedge guide or table saw
- Clothes iron (if using veneer edge tape)
- Utility knife, razor blade, or veneer trimmer
- Sandpaper
- Square
- Straightedge
- Drill with:
  - ⅜" straight bit
  - ⁷⁄₁₆" straight bit
  - Pilot bits
- 4-foot level
- Hacksaw

Note: Because the light shades are small and are close to your head and combustibles like bedding, don't use standard incandescent bulbs for the light fixtures. Instead, choose LED or CFL (compact fluorescent) bulbs, which will stay relatively cool when running. LED bulbs are ideal because they can provide better directional light and run cooler than CFLs, but they are more expensive. A bulb with light output equivalent to a 40-watt incandescent is sufficient for most reading lights.

1. Cut the planks.

Cut four planks to size at 12" wide x 27" long, with the length running parallel to the grain of the face veneer of the material. To keep the pieces as equal as possible when cutting from a 4-foot-wide sheet, mark the first cut line at 12" from a long factory edge, and make the cut down the center of the line. Mark the next cut line at 12" and cut down the center, and so on. This should give you four equal pieces that are slightly under 12" wide. Use a circular saw and straightedge guide or a table saw to ensure clean, straight cuts.

2. Apply edge tape (optional).

If you prefer that the headboard planks look like solid wood, you can cover the edges with iron-on edge tape in a matching wood species. Apply the tape as directed by the manufacturer. For most types, you simply hold the tape against the panel's edge, making sure it is perfectly aligned along the entire length of the panel and it overhangs both faces of the panel slightly. Then press a hot clothes iron to the exposed side of the tape to activate the adhesive, bonding the tape to the wood. When the tape has cooled, trim off the excess with a sharp utility knife, a razor blade, or a veneer trimmer. Sand the edges of the tape carefully with fine sandpaper to soften the edge slightly and feather it into the panel.

3. Mark the cleat locations.

Draw a horizontal line about 3" down from the top edge of one plank, on its back side. Use a square registered against the side edge to make sure the line is precisely perpendicular to the side edges of the plank.

Arrange all the planks side by side so their side edges are touching and their top ends are flush. Transfer the horizontal line from the marked plank to the other planks, using a straightedge and a square. This helps ensure that all the plank-side cleats will be hung at the same height, so the planks will hang at the same elevation (provided you hang the wall-side cleats all at the same height).

4. Prepare the plank(s) for a light.

On each plank on which you intend to install a light, mark the centerpoint on the top edge. Drill a 2"-deep hole at the centerpoint using a ⅜" bit, being careful to drill straight in so the hole will be perfectly plumb when the plank is installed. This hole will receive a piece of all-thread lamp tubing for mounting the lower lamp swivel, as shown in the rear view illustration.

Drill a second hole through the back face of the plank, intersecting the first hole at its bottom end. For this hole, start drilling straight down, then angle the bit toward the top of the plank to create a hole that slopes down and back from the top edge of the plank. Be careful not to drill through to the plank's front face. This tunneling hole is for threading the lamp cord through the plank.

Test-fit the all-thread tubing by threading one end partially into the top hole. It should thread in snugly. Remove the tubing.

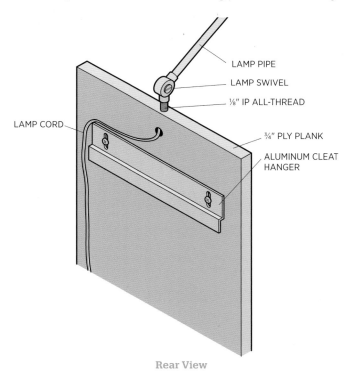

LAMP PIPE

LAMP SWIVEL

⅛" IP ALL-THREAD

LAMP CORD

¾" PLY PLANK

ALUMINUM CLEAT HANGER

Rear View

5. Finish the planks.

Finish-sand the planks and apply the finish of your choice. Because a headboard essentially is furniture, you want a durable, washable finish, like polyurethane or a highly buffed furniture wax. Don't finish inside the holes for the lamp parts.

6. Install the cleats.

Each cleat has two parts: the panel-mounted side, whose slot faces down, and the wall-mounted side, whose slot faces up. Mount the panel-side cleats to the back faces of the planks, centered from side to side, using ¾" screws driven through pilot holes. Make sure the top edges of the cleats are on the reference lines you made in step 3.

Fit one set of the cleat halves together and measure from the bottom edge of the wall-side half to the bottom edge of the plank. Add 6" (or as desired) to this dimension. Using this dimension, measure up from the top of the bed mattress and mark a level line across the wall at the desired plank elevation.

Use a 4-foot level to extend the level line on the wall to the other cleat locations. As shown here, the planks are spaced about 1½" apart, but you can choose any spacing you like. Install the wall-side cleat halves on their lines using 2" wood screws. Screw into wall studs whenever possible, or use heavy-duty hollow-wall anchors (don't use those cheap, plastic plug anchors).

7. Cover the light shades.

The best light shades to use are 1950s-style cylinders that you can often find at thrift stores and the like, or you can look for them at local retailers. Barring that, you can use a tin can with the lid removed. At the closed end, drill a ⁷⁄₁₆" hole through the center of the end; this will accept the lamp pipe or nipple.

Wrap the outside of each light shade with self-adhesive wood veneer in a species that matches or complements the plank material. Cut the veneer a little large so you can trim the edges after applying it to the shades; trim with a sharp utility knife or razor blade. Finish the veneer to match the planks.

8. Complete the lights.

Not all lamp parts are alike, so you'll have to follow the manufacturer's directions for assembling and wiring the lights. But here is the basic process:

Cut a piece of all-thread lamp tubing about 1¾" long, using the hacksaw; cut from a factory end so you have clean threads for the top end. Apply epoxy to the tubing and thread it into the hole in the top edge of the prepared plank, leaving the top end extending about ⅜" above the plank. You can use pliers to help thread the piece, but protect the threads with a scrap of leather or thick rubber. Let the epoxy dry.

Screw the lower swivel onto the exposed tubing end. Feed the cord through the back of each plank and up through the tubing and swivel. Insert the long lamp pipe, followed by the upper swivel and the short lamp pipe, threading the cord through each piece as you go. Wire the cord to the socket, then assemble the socket and shade and mount the socket to the short pipe, using retaining nuts and/or nipples, as appropriate.

9. Mount the planks

Install a rubber bumper on the bottom corner of each plank, on the back side. These keep the planks plumb when installed. Hang the planks on the wall-side cleats and adjust their side-to-side positions for even spacing.

Run the light cord down behind its plank so it is out of view. Find a convenient location for the light switch, and install the switch onto the cord as directed by the manufacturer.

Shop Tip

Lamp Fittings
Lamp parts of all descriptions are sold at hardware stores, home centers, lighting stores, and online retailers. The various fittings, pipes, cords, and other elements are conveniently standardized, so it's easy to mix and match pieces to get just what you want. To find parts for your headboard project, your best bet is to visit a well-stocked hardware store and start fitting pieces together. The bulb socket is the most critical element, so choose that first, then build the hardware set around it. If you can't find the finish or exact size you want at local stores, check online, making sure that any threaded ends and other fittings are the right size for the other parts.

Groovy Headboard

Designed by Kathy and Philip Schmidt

. . . as in lots of grooves, see? It was the express intention of the designers of this piece *not* to have a monolithic hulk of a headboard, so they decorated it with negative space. The grooves also highlight the edge strata of the plywood, adding depth and interest that change with your viewing angle. And if you really want to get groovy, you can install some hidden lighting in the back (letting the glow play through the slats or throwing bars of light onto the ceiling). At 60" wide, a sheet of Baltic birch is perfect for a queen-size bed; larger beds might call for a standard 4 x 8-foot panel running lengthwise. In any case, this is a job for good material with thin, even plies (and minimal voids, of course).

MATERIALS

- ☐ One 5 x 5-foot sheet ¾" Baltic birch plywood (26¼" x 60" min.)
- ☐ Scrap materials for routing jig (see step 4)
- ☐ Finish materials (as desired)
- ☐ One 8-foot length 2 x 4 lumber
- ☐ Coarse-thread drywall screws or wood screws (length as needed)
- ☐ Wood glue
- ☐ 6d (2") finish nails
- ☐ Wood putty or white glue

TOOLS

- ☐ Circular saw with straightedge guide
- ☐ Table saw (optional)
- ☐ Jigsaw
- ☐ Router with ½" straight bit
- ☐ Wood file or sanding block
- ☐ Sandpaper (up to 220 grit)
- ☐ Level
- ☐ Drill with:
    - ☐ Pilot bits
    - ☐ Counterbore bits
- ☐ Nail set

1. Cut the panel to size.

As shown here, the headboard measures 60" wide and 26¼" tall. If you're using a 5 x 5-foot panel with its edges in good shape, you need to make only one cut to size the piece. Make the cut with a circular saw and a straightedge guide (or a table saw) for a clean, straight edge.

For a bed size other than a queen, cut the panel to the desired dimensions. You can also make your headboard as tall as you like. And keep in mind that the groove sizing and layout are almost infinitely customizable.

2. Mark the grooves.

Lay out the grooves on the back face of the headboard panel, following the cutting diagram. The headboard shown here has 1"-wide grooves spaced ¾" apart. Again, you can adjust the dimensions or layout as desired. To prevent mistakes and to make sure the design is right for you, it's a good idea to draw the entire groove pattern on the panel, then fill in each of the grooves with scribbled pencil lines. With repeating linear patterns like this, it's easy to lose your bearings when making cuts. Taking the time to mark everything carefully can save you from a disastrous miscut.

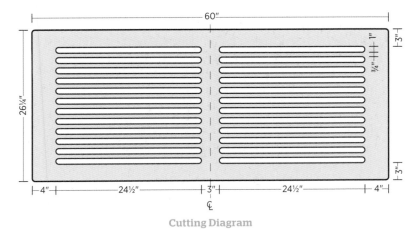

Cutting Diagram

3. Rough-cut the grooves.

Precutting the grooves with a circular saw and jigsaw will save considerable wear on your router bit (and your patience). Working from the back face of the panel, cut the long edges of the grooves with a circular saw, staying about ⅛" inside the cutting lines. Stop each cut about 1" or so from the end of the marked groove.

With both long edges cut on all of the grooves, finish the rough cutouts with a jigsaw. Keep in mind that the router, when making the final cuts, will round over the corners of the grooves with a ¼" radius (if you're using a ½" bit). Therefore, keep the saw cuts about ½" from the groove ends; the router will clean up the rest.

Note: Cutting the grooves with a circular saw requires plunge cuts — lowering the spinning blade into the work by pivoting on the front edge of the saw's foot. If you're not familiar or comfortable with this operation, you can drill a ⅜" starter hole inside each marked groove and insert the jigsaw blade into the hole to initiate the cut. With this method, you will rough-cut the groove entirely with the jigsaw.

When using either saw, be very careful to prevent tearout (splintering) on the faces of the panel, especially the front face. Use sharp blades, and take your time. Even the router can cause splintering if it's not sharp.

4. Build the router jig.

A simple shop-made jig makes the routing process easy and relatively foolproof; see the illustration of the router jig setup. You can cut the jig base from any flat sheet material, preferably something thin, like hardboard or thin MDF, and use straight scraps of plywood, solid stock, or old trim for the guide (fence) pieces.

The jig base is a rectangle that's about 32" long and at least 10" wide. Mark a straight reference line across the base, 3" from (and parallel to) one long edge. Cut two fence pieces to length at about 30". Glue or fasten one of the fence pieces to the base, aligned with the outside of your reference line.

Set up a router with a ½" straight bit. Using the router to guide the spacing, secure the other long fence piece to the jig base so the two fences are perfectly parallel and the router, when floating between them, will cut a 1"-wide groove. Cut two short fence pieces to fit between the long fences. Secure these to the base to serve as end stops for the router so the groove will be 24½" long.

Clamp the jig over a sacrificial surface, then carefully cut through the base with the router and ½" bit, with the fences guiding the router. The finished cutout will match the final grooves cut into the headboard.

5. Rout the grooves.

Prop the headboard panel back side up on scrap material (or you can use a sacrificial backerboard if it will help prevent tearout), and clamp the jig to the board so its cutout edges are aligned with one of the groove's cutting lines. Clean up the groove's edges with the router and ½" bit, making several passes and increasing the bit depth about ⅛" with each pass. Repeat to rout the remaining grooves. Again, watch carefully for tearout as you work.

Note: Once you've cut the first few grooves, you'll need a relatively narrow C-clamp to secure the inside end of the jig, as shown in illustration of the router jig setup. The clamp fits through the adjacent groove to secure the jig.

6. Finish the headboard.

Mark the ¼" roundovers on the corners of the headboard, as shown in the cutting diagram; tracing around a 9 mm or 1¹/₃₂" socket makes this easy. Shape the corners by sanding them with a file and/or coarse sandpaper and a sanding block.

Finish-sand the entire headboard, working up to 220-grit or finer sandpaper. Carefully sand the outside edges of the panel and all the grooves' edges to smooth the sharp corners and prevent any splintering, while maintaining crisp edges with minimal rounding. Finish the headboard as desired. The piece as shown was finished with paste wax. Another good finish option is a penetrating oil, such as Danish oil, that doesn't require sanding between coats. This is not a fun project to sand.

7. Prepare the mounting cleats.

The headboard shown here was mounted to a wall so that it reclines at a 5-degree angle; see the side-view illustration. This slight slope softens the look just a bit, and it makes the headboard more comfortable as a backrest for sitting up in bed. You can slope your headboard as much or as little as you like, or you can position it vertically.

To create mounting cleats for the sloped installation, cut two lengths of 2 x 4 at about 46". Bevel one short edge of one of the pieces at 5 degrees so the longer side is about 3" wide, using a circular saw with the blade (foot) tilted at 5 degrees.

Bevel the other piece of 2 x 4 at 5 degrees so its narrow side is about ½" wide. This is the upper mounting cleat.

8. Install the headboard.

Determine the desired location of the headboard. Mark a level line on the wall to represent the top edge of the upper mounting cleat; the cleat should be roughly centered on the 3" solid space at the top of the headboard. Drill pilot holes, and mount the upper cleat to the wall with drywall or wood screws, driving the screws into wall studs. Alternatively, if you'd like the headboard to be movable (see note at right), glue the cleat to the backside of the headboard instead of fastening it to the wall.

Measure down from the upper cleat location and make reference marks for the lower wall cleat, roughly centering it on the bottom solid portion, as before. Drill pilot holes through the cleat at the wall stud locations, then drill a deep counterbore into each hole so the screws will reach at least 1½" into the wall studs. Fasten the lower cleat to the wall with screws.

With a helper or two, position the headboard over the cleats, making sure it is centered behind the bed and level across the top. Drill pilot holes, and fasten the headboard to the cleats with one 6d finish nail near each corner of the headboard. Set the nails slightly below the surface with a nail set, then fill the holes with color-matched wood putty or a homemade blend of white glue and sawdust. Touch up the putty with finish, if desired.

Note: To make the headboard movable, you can hang its bottom edge from the lower cleat using two homemade metal clips. Cut two strips of any stiff scrap metal (¾" wide, or so) about 3" long. Use pliers to make two bends in one end of each strip to form a square-cornered "J" that hooks onto the headboard's bottom edge. Drill a hole through the upper portion of the strip for a mounting screw. Fasten the clips near the ends of the lower mounting cleat, using 1¼" wood screws or drywall screws. Set the headboard into the clips, resting the upper cleat against the wall. The 5-degree angle keeps the headboard in place.

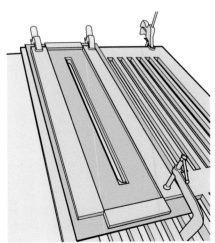

Router Jig Setup

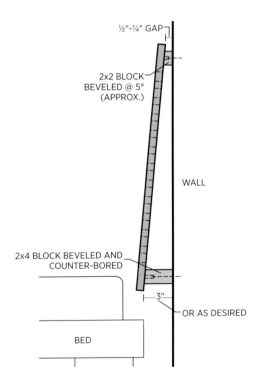

Side View

File Cabinet Cap

Designed by Dan Biller

Few fixtures in the modern home are as necessary and as unattractive as the basic file cabinet. As popular as the two-drawer model is for the home office, you'd think manufacturers would have come up with *something* to make them more livable. But no. Well, here's a custom treatment that works perfectly on a standard low boy cabinet and can be adapted to fit almost anything else that could use a new top. It's a great weekend project for any hobby woodworker who's comfortable with a table saw (or a router table). Hardwood trim keeps the top in place, and a simple inlay gives the plywood slab some furniture-grade detailing.

MATERIALS

- One 17" x 29" (or larger) piece ¾" oak or other hardwood plywood
- One 36" length 1 x 4 solid walnut or other hardwood
- Wood glue
- Finish materials (see step 7)

TOOLS

- Table saw with standard and ¼" dado blades
- Flush-trimming saw
- Sandpaper (up to 220 grit)
- Miter saw
- Bar clamps
- Router with chamfer bit

1. Cut the plywood top.

Mark the layout for the panel on ¾" plywood, sizing the piece to match the cabinet dimensions plus ⅛" in both directions. The panel in the cap shown here is 16⅝" x 28¾". Cut the panel to size on a table saw.

2. Cut the inlay strips.

The inlay strips can be cut from solid stock in any suitable hardwood (walnut is used here). They measure ¼" wide and ³/₁₆" thick. You need two strips slightly longer than the length of the panel and two slightly more than its width. Cut the strips on the table saw.

3. Mill the edge dadoes.

The ¼" x ¼" dadoes centered in the plywood panel's edges will receive the tongue of the hardwood edge trim; see the panel detail drawing. To mill the dadoes, set up the table saw with a

¼" dado blade. Position the fence ¼" from the blade, and set the blade height at ¼" above the table. Run the panel on its edges, with one face against the fence, to create the dadoes around the perimeter of the panel.

4. Install the inlays.

To cut the dadoes into the panel face for the inlay strips, set the fence on the table saw 3" from the dado blade, and set the blade height at ³⁄₁₆". With the plywood panel facedown, run the panel across the saw lengthwise. Turn the panel around, again facedown, and mill a groove on the opposite side of the panel so the two grooves are parallel.

Apply a small bead of glue in the grooves, and lay in the two longer walnut strips so they overhang the panel edges at both ends. Clean any glue residue from the panel face, and let the glue set. Trim the ends of the strips flush to the panel edges, using a flush-trimming saw (or as desired). Sand the inlays flush with the panel face, using 220-grit sandpaper, being careful to not oversand into the plywood's thin face veneer.

Turn the panel widthwise and cut two more dadoes in the face for the crossing inlay strips, creating a grid pattern. Glue the remaining strips into the grooves, then trim and sand them flush, as before.

5. Cut and install the trim.

Using the table saw and standard blade, cut the remaining walnut stock into four strips at ⅝" x ⅞". Set up the saw with the dado blade, and cut ¼" of depth from the top and bottom edges of the strips, creating the ¼" x ¼" tongue, as shown in the frame detail drawing. The tongues should match the edge dadoes in the plywood panel. Note that the bottom shoulder below the tongue is ⅜" wide; this will create a ⅛" lip around the bottom face of the panel to keep the cap from shifting on the cabinet.

Cut the trim to fit around the panel, mitering the corners with a miter saw. When all four pieces are precisely fitted, glue the trim to the panel edges, clamp the assembly, and let the glue set.

6. Chamfer the trim.

The outside corners of the trim get a slight chamfer, about ⅛" or as desired, as shown in the frame detail drawing. Mill the chamfer with router and chamfer bit.

7. Finish the cap.

Finish-sand all surfaces of the cap, working up to 220-grit or finer sandpaper. Apply the finish of your choice. The project shown here was given a medium oak stain, followed by three topcoats of clear polyurethane for a durable, washable surface.

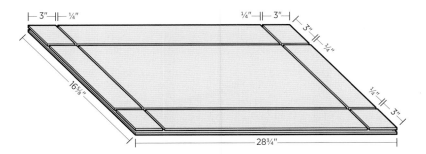

Panel Detail

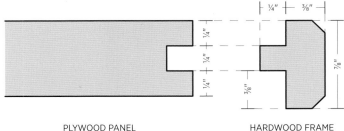

PLYWOOD PANEL   HARDWOOD FRAME

Frame Detail

Repair-a-Chair

Designed by Philip Schmidt

Whether you're a garage-sale junkie, a hopeless sentimental, or just plain cheap, there's a good chance you're holding on to a tired old chair that could use a little love. Why not treat it to a complete plywood makeover? It has to be a good candidate, of course — plywood's not exactly cozy, so easy chairs and anything that needs a lot of give are out. But for many straight-back chairs and even stools and ottomans, a new outfit of sheet material can be the perfect upgrade. This old aluminum-frame workhorse is a case in point. Built by GoodForm for the General Fireproofing Company of Youngstown, Ohio, it has dutifully served insurance offices for decades, and now it's time to retire in style. Since every chair is more or less unique, the following is an overview of some basic techniques you can use to spruce up your seat.

MATERIALS (AS NEEDED)

☐ Hardwood plywood

☐ Heavy paper or poster board (for making a template)

☐ Adhesives (wood glue, epoxy, or polyurethane glue, as applicable)

☐ Fasteners (screws, nails, brackets, or dowel pins, as applicable)

☐ Finish materials (as desired)

TOOLS (AS NEEDED)

☐ Pencil (carpenter's or standard)

☐ Scissors (if making a paper pattern)

☐ Tape, double-sided tape, or hot glue gun

☐ Foam brushes or paintbrushes

☐ Clamps

☐ Bucket or plastic tub (for soaking plywood prior to shaping)

☐ Jigsaw, band saw, or scroll saw

☐ Router with flush-trimming bit

☐ Sandpaper (60 to 220 grit)

1. Plan the makeover.

Spend some time deciding what type and thickness of plywood to use for the various replacement parts. You can use rigid material, such as ⅜" or thicker plywood, for parts that are flat. If a piece needs to bend a little to conform to the chair's frame, you'll need something thinner. Standard ¼" plywood will bend some but not much. For more curve, you can laminate layers of ⅛" or thinner material. "Bendy" plywood is another option. It's a flexible plywood made with all of its plies' grain running parallel (instead of cross-grained). For cosmetic touches in hard-to-reach areas, you can use self-adhesive veneer tape or sheets in a wood species that matches the plywood.

If you've been paying attention, you may have read that bent lamination is too complicated for this book. Well, we lied, but only just a little. The project shown here uses a simple process of laminating two layers of ⅛" plywood into curves, using the chair itself as the form.

2. Remove the bad parts.

Carefully disassemble the chair as needed to remove the seat, backrest, or any other parts you plan to replace. If any pieces can be used as a pattern for marking the plywood substitutes, be careful to keep them completely intact.

Clean up the chair and make any necessary repairs to prepare for the makeover.

Note: For loose joints on old wood chairs, clean up the mating pieces as well as possible, then apply some Gorilla Glue (standard formula) as directed and clamp the parts while the glue cures. Gorilla Glue is a polyurethane adhesive that expands as it dries. It does a nice job of filling gaps in old, worn wood joints.

3. Lay out the parts.

Laying out and cutting the new parts to fit the chair might prove a little tricky and painstaking, but the process usually involves more trial and error than skill. A couple of classic finish carpentry techniques can help.

The first technique is scribing. If, for example, your seat or backrest is accessible enough that you can place a rough-cut workpiece directly on the chair's structural framework, you can simply trace around the frame to lay out the piece, as shown in the illustration on page 248. To create a decorative overhang, use a carpenter's pencil set flat against the frame; the thickness of the pencil will make the traced outline a little bigger than the frame's edges. Otherwise, trace along the frame so the pencil line is flush with the frame.

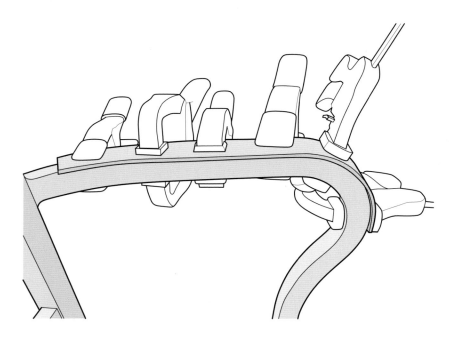

Preshaping Pieces for Tight Curves

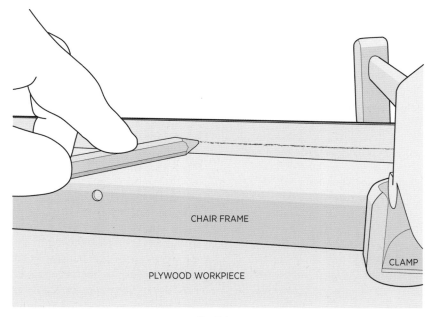

CHAIR FRAME

PLYWOOD WORKPIECE

CLAMP

Scribing

The other layout technique is to make a pattern, using heavy paper or poster board. This is necessary when you can't fit a workpiece into position (because arms or other chair parts are in the way) for accurate scribing. First cut the paper roughly to fit the space. Set it on the chair frame, and scribe to the frame as best you can. Recut the paper, and repeat, as needed. (If it's difficult to scribe and cut the pattern as one piece, use two pieces that overlap roughly in the middle of the area you're fitting to. Once both pieces are scribed and fitted to their respective sides, tape them together to form a single pattern.)

When the paper pattern is complete, lay it over your work-piece (taping it down, if desired) and trace around the edges to mark the piece for cutting.

Note: If you will laminate any parts, oversize the pieces somewhat, then scribe and cut them to fit after the lamination.

4. Laminate the curved parts.

For a simple two-layer lamination, rough-cut the two plywood layers, oversizing them as much as possible so you can scribe and trim the edges after the glue-up. Apply a thin, even layer of wood glue to one face of one piece, spreading it out with a finger or foam brush. Lay the other piece on top and set the assembly into place on the chair.

Starting at the center (or apex) of the curve, clamp the layers tightly to the chair frame. Add clamps every few inches, maintaining even spacing and working out from the center to the side edges. Clamp along the edges carefully to close the seam between the two layers. Let the glue dry overnight.

To form tight curves with relatively small pieces, such as over an armrest, preshape the pieces before laminating them with glue. First soak the pieces in hot water for at least 1 hour (if they're small enough, set them in a baking pan, cover with boiling water, and place the pan in the oven at 200 degrees to keep the water hot). Remove the pieces, quickly pat them dry, then clamp them together onto the chair frame, as shown in the drawing at left. Let the pieces dry overnight, or longer, as needed; if they're not dry, they won't hold their shape. Unclamp and separate the pieces for several more hours of drying. Finally, glue the preshaped pieces together and clamp them to the chair, as described above, to complete the lamination.

5. Cut the parts.

The standard tool for cutting to a scribed line is a jigsaw (or a band saw or scroll saw). Be sure to use a very-fine-tooth blade (such as 20 teeth per inch) to minimize splintering. If desired, you can play it safe by cutting a little outside the marked lines, then sanding down to the line. Another option is to clamp the piece in place on the chair and use a router and flush-trimming bit to mill the edges flush to the chair frame; however, try this only if the router base will remain flat and fully supported, and if the frame can easily be repaired if it gets buzzed by the bit's cutter.

Cut and/or sand the pieces as desired. Test-fit the pieces on the chair, and sand any edges as needed for final shaping and to smooth saw marks and rough spots. Finish-sand the completed parts, working up to 220-grit or finer sandpaper. Slightly round over any exposed or visible edges for comfort and a finished look, and to prevent splinters.

6. Install and finish the parts.

You might have to think like a furniture maker for the parts installation, which may require some creative solutions. Often the main goal is to conceal all fasteners from view, so screws are appropriate if they won't be seen. Metal brackets facilitate fastening in hard-to-reach places. Alternatively, the hardware can become an aesthetic feature. For example, you could use oval-head screws with finish washers driven through the exposed surfaces of the plywood.

As an alternative to fasteners, epoxy and other adhesives are an easy option for joining wood to metal and plastic (or to wood), but keep in mind that the installation is permanent. In the project shown here, all the parts were installed with general-purpose two-part epoxy. At ¼" thick, the plywood was too thin to screw into from behind, and exposed hardware was not desired. In addition to invisibility, adhesives are good for holding bent pieces tightly to the frame with a continuous bond.

Install and finish the wood parts as desired. The plywood parts in the chair shown here were finished with natural Danish oil.

Note: The fastening method will determine whether to finish the parts before installing them or afterward. If you're using adhesive and would like to prefinish, make sure the finish won't prevent a good bond with the wood.

Twinkle Board

Designed by Maya Lee

At the time of this book's writing, this designer's website bore the slogan "Martha and MacGyver's love child," which applies equally well to this clever decoration. The original was made with a found plank of wood, a string of twinkle lights bought on sale, and a borrowed drill. And the whole idea is about getting creative with whatever you have — a scrap of plywood, an old shelf, a salvaged desktop . . . You can choose your own word and typeface (Archer was the designer's choice) and even do something funky with the lights (LEDs, color, pulsing . . .). In case you're wondering, *delight* was inspired by Horace: "The role of art is to inform and delight."

MATERIALS

- ☐ ¾"-thick plywood or other sheet material (size as desired)
- ☐ Finish materials (as desired)
- ☐ Paper and tape (for paper template; see step 2)
- ☐ Twinkle lights (plug-in string; quantity as needed)

TOOLS

- ☐ Circular saw with straightedge guide and/or jigsaw
- ☐ Sandpaper (up to 220 grit) and sanding block
- ☐ Computer and printer
- ☐ Awl or hammer and small finish nail
- ☐ Drill with straight bit sized for light bulbs

1. Cut and finish the board.

Cut the plywood or other material to the desired size, using a circular saw with a straightedge guide to ensure clean, straight cuts. Alternatively, you can shape the board with curves or rounded corners, making the cuts with a jigsaw.

Sand the cut edges smooth and flat, using coarse sandpaper and a sanding block (any flat piece of scrap wood will do). Finish-sand the front face and edges of the board, working up to 220-grit or finer sandpaper. Finish the board as desired.

2. Create the paper template.

Your twinkle message can be anything you like — a word or short phrase, a custom design, or representative shapes or figures, anything you can print out on a computer, copy, or draw by hand.

To create one or more words, choose a typeface (font), preferably one with clean lines and an unfussy look overall. Print out the message at full size, using a word processing (or other) application on your computer. For large letters, print out one letter at a time or even partial letters, if necessary. If you can, print in a light color or gray tone, which makes it easy to mark inside the lines for the light locations (see step 3).

Tape the printed sheets together to form the complete message, making sure the letters are aligned properly and evenly spaced.

3. Mark the light holes.

Position the paper template on the board so the message is centered from top to bottom and side to side. Secure the template in place with tape. Mark the light locations, using the desired spacing (¾" between lights is a good place to start), making little tick marks on the paper and following the contours of the letters.

Mark the hole locations on the board by poking the point of an awl through the template to make a small dent in the wood surface, as shown in the illustration at right. If you don't have an awl, you can use a small finish nail, tapping it lightly with a hammer to make the marks. Follow the tick marks (or eyeball the spacing) carefully to maintain even spacing as you work. Mark the entire message, then remove the template from the board.

4. Drill the holes.

Place the board faceup on top of a piece of sacrificial plywood or other flat material as backerboard, and clamp them both down to your work surface. The sacrificial backerboard helps prevent splintering (tearout) on the back face of the board when the drill bit comes through. Tearout won't affect the finished product, but it's best to keep the holes clean.

Find a drill bit that creates a snug fit for the bulbs of your twinkle lights (¹³⁄₆₄" works well for standard-size lights), using scrap plywood to test the size. If you're using thick board material (1½" or so), you might want to insert the plastic casing of each light into the hole, instead of just the glass bulb, to bring the light closer to the front surface. Be sure to use a sharp bit, to minimize splintering on the front face of the board.

Wrap some masking tape around the bit, 1" from the point (assuming the project board is ¾" thick); this is a depth guide to prevent you from drilling through the backerboard. Drill the holes through the front face of the board, using the awl marks to center the bit.

5. Install the lights.

Plug in the light string(s) to make sure all the lights are working, then unplug. Starting at the end of the string (opposite the plug), insert the light bulbs into the holes, working from one end of the message to the other; see rear-view illustration. If you need more than one string, simply plug a second string into the end of the first and continue filling the holes.

After all the lights are installed, you can tidy up the loose wiring in the back with dabs of hot glue or duct tape. Be sure to leave some slack at the plug end of the string for plugging in the lights.

Due to the tangle of wiring in the back, the light board works best when placed on a table or other surface with its back against the wall or, preferably, a wall corner. If you'd like to mount the board to the wall, position it so that the wiring will be hidden from view.

Note: Twinkle lights are low-wattage, and typically the bulbs do not get very hot. However, because the bulbs are in direct contact with wood (a combustible material), never leave your board plugged in overnight or when you're not at home.

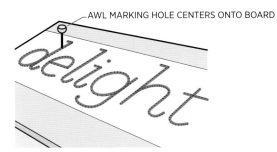

AWL MARKING HOLE CENTERS ONTO BOARD

Marking Holes for the Lights

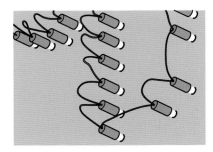

Lights — Rear View

Plywood as . . .
A showcase of inspired pieces and
the stories behind them

. . . sculpture

Propeller Bowl

by Philipp Herbert

This project started with a picture of a vintage wooden airplane propeller made of many layers of wood, which gave it strength and prevented deformation.

So I started thinking about how I could make an object with a similar construction that also reinterprets the typical rotation of a propeller in its form and shape.

After some sketching and a little calculating, I bought the plywood and cut out the 13 layers (like overlapping rings) that make the rough shape of the bowl. After gluing them together, I came to the hardest part: shaping the inner surface. I started with the roughest sandpaper I could buy and attached it to a rounded sanding block. It took me about eight hours to make that inner surface smooth. The outer surface was done in about two hours.

Actually, I consider this bowl more as a prototype, since the layers of the wood are very thin — so thin, in fact, that they almost form a pattern on the surface and aren't really recognizable as layers of wood orthogonal to each other anymore. So maybe one day I will make another one with the perfect number of layers to reach the perfect design.

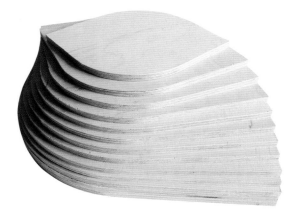

Playthings

Of course sheet goods can be fun.
Diversions for kids, pets, and adults.

Indoor Doghouse

Designed by Adele Cuartelon

In Japan, the *noren* curtain tastefully decorates and obscures the entranceways of shops, homes, and secluded rooms. This piece applies the same colorful touch to an elegant private parlor for your pooch. After all, doesn't every discriminating dog deserve nicely appointed accommodations indoors as well as out?

MATERIALS

☐ One 4 x 8-foot sheet ¾" hardwood plywood

☐ Twelve 36" lengths ¾"-thick square dowels

☐ 1¼" coarse-thread drywall or wood screws

☐ Wood glue

☐ 3d (1¼") finish nails

☐ Finish materials (as desired)

☐ One 15" x 21" piece fabric

☐ Staples (for staple gun)

TOOLS

☐ Table saw or circular saw with straightedge guide

☐ Miter saw or miter box and backsaw

☐ Drill with pilot bits

☐ Clamps

☐ Square

☐ Nail set

☐ Staple gun

1. Cut the house panels and base supports.
Lay out and cut all the panels and base supports on a single sheet of plywood, following the cutting diagram on page 257. The mating edges of the back, right side, left side, and front top are mitered at 45 degrees. On the front bottom piece, the left edge is square and the right edge is mitered. The dimensions shown on the cutting diagram are to the long points of the miters. Use a table saw or a circular saw with a straightedge guide to ensure clean, straight cuts.

2. Cut the supports and window slats.
Measure and cut the following lengths from the square dowel stock, using a miter saw or a miter box and backsaw:
- 5 at 23" (long vertical supports)
- 7 at 18" (1 horizontal support, 6 front slats)
- 2 at 14" (horizontal supports)
- 6 at 11¼" (side slats)
- 1 at 2" (short vertical support)

3. Attach the horizontal supports.
On the inside faces of the left side, back, and front top panels, draw a horizontal line 3" down from the top edge. Using the 1¼" screws driven through pilot holes, fasten horizontal supports to the panels, with their top edges on the lines, as follows: the left side gets a 14" support, centered side-to-side; the back gets an 18" support, centered side-to-side; and the front top gets a 14" support, positioned with one end 1¼" from the short point of the miter, on the left side of the panel (when viewing the inside face of the panel); see the top view of the construction on page 258.

4. Assemble the base.
Assemble the base frame using wood glue and 3d finish nails (driven through pilot holes) at each corner, as shown in the base support plan. Clamp the assembly so all corners are square. Apply wood glue along the top edges of the base supports, and attach the bottom panel so it is aligned flush at the front left corner of the base assembly and overhangs the base by 2" everywhere else.

5. Assemble the wall panels.

Fasten the right and left side panels to the back panel and front top panel, using wood glue and nails driven through pilot holes. Stand the assembly upside down and apply glue along the bottom edges of the side and back panels. Set the base on top (upside down) and nail it to the wall panels. Repeat the process to install the front bottom panel. Make sure the wall-panel joints are square at the top of the house. Let the glue dry.

6. Add the vertical supports.

On the interior of the dog house, nail the five long vertical supports at the corners and sides of the panels, as shown in the top view of the construction. The long supports positioned at the windows should be set just inside the window openings, with their rear edges flush with the side edge of the "cutouts." Position the short support in the left front corner, so its top end is 3" below the tops of the mating panels.

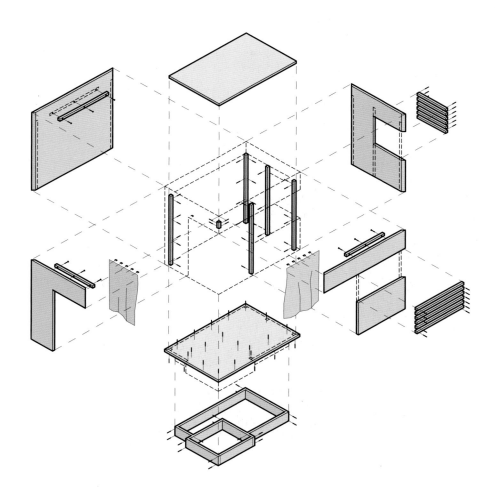

Exploded View

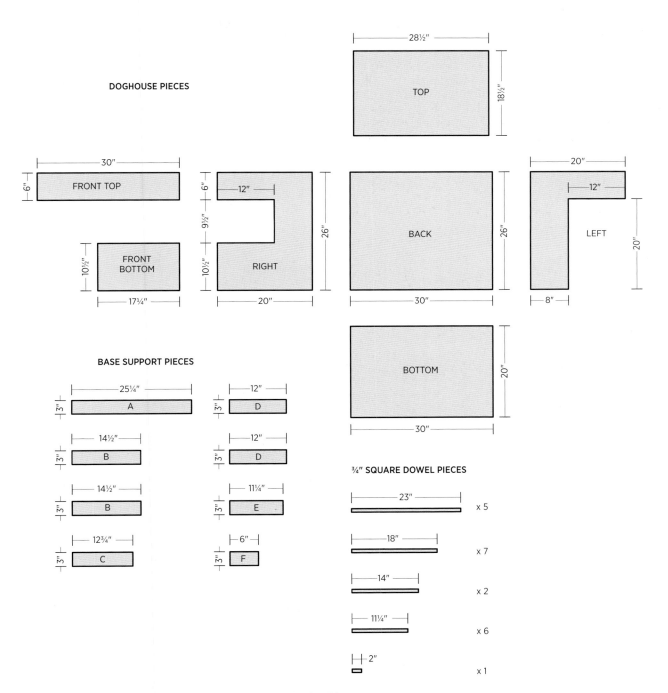

DOGHOUSE PIECES

TOP — 28½" × 18½"

FRONT TOP — 30" × 6"

FRONT BOTTOM — 17¼" × 10½"

RIGHT — 20" × 26", 12", 6", 9½", 10½"

BACK — 30" × 26"

LEFT — 20" × 20", 12", 8"

BOTTOM — 30" × 20"

BASE SUPPORT PIECES

A — 25¼" × 3"

B — 14½" × 3"

B — 14½" × 3"

C — 12¾" × 3"

D — 12" × 3"

D — 12" × 3"

E — 11¼" × 3"

F — 6" × 3"

¾" SQUARE DOWEL PIECES

23" x 5

18" x 7

14" x 2

11¼" x 6

2" x 1

Cutting Diagrams

7. Install the window slats.

Nail the slats to the vertical supports, starting at the bottom of the window opening. Space the bottom slats ¾" from the bottom of the window cutouts, and maintain a ¾" gap between slats as you go up. The front slats cover the ends of the side slats.

8. Finish the house.

Use a nail set to set all the nails slightly below the surface. Clean all surfaces of the house and apply a polyurethane or other durable, washable finish, as desired. (The project shown was finished with polyurethane in a clear matte finish.) Also finish all surfaces of the top panel.

9. Add the curtains.

Cut two 10½" x 15" panels from your desired fabric. Secure the panels so they cover the top portion of the door by stapling their top edges to the back faces of the front and left side panels, using a staple gun.

10. Position the top panel.

Set the top panel on the horizontal supports to complete the project. Leaving the top panel unfastened allows easy access to the house interior.

Note: You can use the top panel for holding lightweight supplies for your pet, such as treats and toys, but it should not be used for heavy objects.

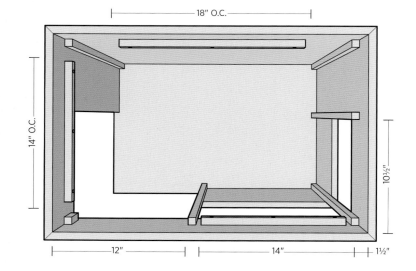

Top View

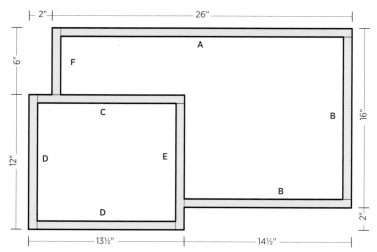

Base Support Plan

Jumbo Eames Cards

Design adapted by Philip Schmidt

Charles Eames's House of Cards is one of the best toys of all time. The cards are simple, beautiful, and really satisfying to build with. Lots of toys claim to be fun *and* intellectually stimulating, but these really pull it off, perhaps more than any other toy. So why adapt such a perfect design? It sort of happened by accident: Two siblings were having a hard time sharing one House of Cards set — a set that was clearly starting to show signs of its popularity. The children's father, a thrifty man who likes to find uses for his ever-growing supply of scrap building materials, decided to make an additional set out of thin plywood.

At the older child's request, the cards were made about 20 percent larger than the originals, and a few were made with holes and cutouts for windows and doors. The new set has the same great function as the original (and is decidedly more durable) but with none of the beautiful and striking images. It's sort of a *builder's* version of the original. So while the plywood set is an imperfect substitute for the real House of Cards, it does make an excellent companion.

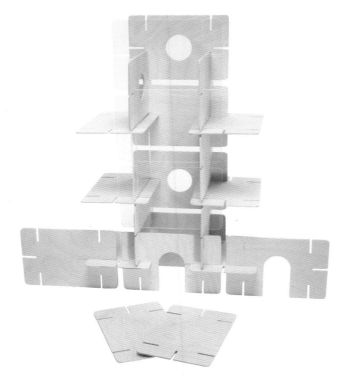

MATERIALS

- ☐ Heavy card stock or poster board
- ☐ Two 24" x 30" pieces ⅛" Baltic birch plywood
- ☐ Finish materials (optional)

TOOLS

- ☐ Straightedge
- ☐ Drafting square or T square
- ☐ Pencil
- ☐ X-Acto knife
- ☐ Circular saw with straightedge guide or table saw
- ☐ Clamps
- ☐ Jigsaw with very-fine-tooth wood blade
- ☐ Utility knife or small wood chisel
- ☐ Sandpaper (80 to 220 grit) and sanding block
- ☐ Drill with 2" hole saw (optional)

Note: In all, House of Cards has been produced in five different sizes at various times. The original version, created in 1952, consisted of two sets of 54 pieces that were the size of playing cards. Today, this is called the "small" size. The most popular version (as a toy) is the "medium" card set, which has cards measuring 4½" x 6¹³⁄₁₆". They're made with dense cardboard and come in a set of 32 cards. The Jumbo Eames Cards project, as described here, yields one set of 24 cards.

1. Create the template.

Following the cutting diagram, use a straightedge, drafting square (or T square), and a sharp pencil to draw the card layout on card stock, poster board, or thin (noncorrugated) cardboard. Mark the slots so they are equal to the measured thickness of your plywood stock (or you can simply use the plywood itself as a marking gauge).

Cut out the template with the straightedge and an X-Acto knife, cutting along the lines as precisely as possible. If the template has inaccuracies, the finished pieces won't be interchangeable, and you might have to do a lot of sanding to get them to fit properly.

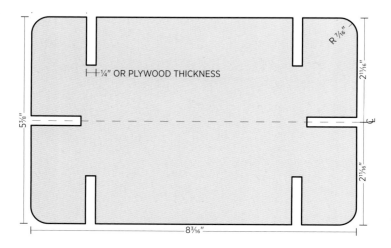

Cutting Diagram

2. Cut out the cards.

Cut 24 pieces of ⅛" plywood to size at 5⅜" x 8³⁄₁₆", using a circular saw with a straightedge guide or a table saw to ensure accurate, straight cuts.

Using the template, trace the entire card layout on one of the plywood blanks. Stack three or four blanks together, with the marked card on top, and clamp them to a work surface. Carefully cut the sides of each of the notches, cutting through all the cards at once, using a jigsaw with a very-fine-tooth wood blade; a 20 tpi (teeth per inch) blade works well for this fragile material. You can experiment to find the ideal number of pieces to cut at once. Don't worry about cutting out the waste of the notches or the corner roundovers with the jigsaw.

When you're done with the notches, separate the pieces, and cut out the notch waste with a sharp utility knife or a wood chisel, if you have one that's small enough. Shape the corners with coarse sandpaper and a sanding block; this goes quickly with one card at a time.

Test-fit the cut cards to see how tightly all the notches interlock. If necessary, sand the sides of the notches for an easier fit, and, if applicable, remember to cut the notches a little wider on the next batch.

Repeat the process to cut all 24 cards.

3. Sand and customize the cards.

Finish-sand the cards, working up to 220-grit sandpaper. Be sure to round over all the edges slightly to prevent splinters. You can apply a wood finish, if desired, but this isn't necessary. Be aware that finishes often are toxic materials, so you probably want to avoid them if babies will play with the cards.

To customize some of the cards, you can drill a hole through the center, using a 2" hole saw, a jigsaw, or a large drill bit. You can cut a simple doorway shape by making a hole, then cutting straight lines up from the bottom edge of the card to meet the sides of the hole.

Note: One way to embellish the set is to give it see-through pieces by making a few cards with ⅛"-thick acrylic sheeting (Plexiglas). Mark the card layout on the protective film of the acrylic, using a fine permanent marker. Lay the acrylic on a sacrificial piece of Styrofoam insulation board, to provide support, and make the cuts with a jigsaw and a new 10 tpi (or finer) blade, cutting through the sheet and insulation at the same time. Sand the cut edges and corners carefully to remove any sharpness.

Plywood as . . .
*A showcase of inspired pieces and
the stories behind them*

. . . model of understanding

Dollhouse

by John Malinoski
The dollhouse design was inspired by our own house, which was designed by Camden Whitehead. The dollhouse was a way for our young daughter to visualize the house, which was under construction during the time the dollhouse was made.

THE MATERIALS:

- ☐ Casters
- ☐ Assorted plywood and lumber scraps
- ☐ Wire brads
- ☐ Assorted hooks, eye screws, knobs, hinges, handles, and hardware
- ☐ Acrylic paint
- ☐ Plastic self-adhesive L-channel
- ☐ Dowels
- ☐ Assorted metal parts

The process:

1. Receive command from your daughter that it is time: "I want a dollhouse."

2. Choose a house that you are enamored with and roughly measure it. Consider contemporary architecture that perhaps will lead the child to think of and experience unconventional structures and modes of living.

3. Draw a rough scaled sketch.

4. Begin (and continue) to evaluate the possibility of using waste and scrap during the building process. (I continually raided the Dumpster of a nearby custom furniture shop.)

5. Think of the child's playing habits and creative intentions and the house's potential for open-ended play.

6. Create a house that has one side offering easy access, while the other side can easily close up to conceal childhood mess. This is where the L-channel comes in — sliding panels allow for access and quick concealment.

7. Do not be afraid of a diverse or unexpected use of materials.

8. Consider the house as a work in progress with the potential for additions and deletions throughout the course of its use.

9. Put the house on wheels so it can easily be moved for cleaning and a new play location.

Design tip:

Consult with the child to determine his or her expectations and desires. Listening to and acting upon a child's request will result in unexpected solutions, new ways of thinking and making, and mutual parent and child satisfaction — an objective that was made as a result of a unique team process.

Doggie Dwelling

Designed by Jennifer Anderson

While the general public remains on the fence about modular housing, it should be more than ready to greet this new home design with a big, wet kiss. Introducing the doghouse of the future: a full-size, knockdown, and truly flat-pack poochie palace that assembles with an Allen wrench. It's strong and attractive enough for taking up permanent residence indoors or out, and it's lightweight enough to tote along for extended slumber parties and camping trips. The finish includes magnetic paint, so you can personalize your pup's house with decorative magnets. And while the house shown here is sized for a small dog, such as a pug, you can easily modify the dimensions to accommodate a larger homeowner (or maybe even yourself, if you're into not only modular housing but also the tiny-house trend).

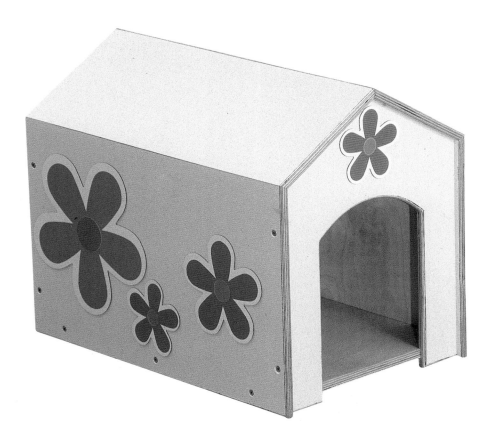

MATERIALS

- ½" Baltic birch, apple, or other hardwood plywood (quantity as needed)
- General-purpose two-part epoxy
- Eighteen ¼" (outside diameter) stainless steel threaded inserts with matching socket-head machine screws (see step 9)
- Spray-on lacquer (or other clear finish of your choice, for house interior)
- Magnetic paint
- Exterior paint (for topcoat over magnetic paint)
- Decorative magnets (as desired)

TOOLS

- Circular saw or table saw
- Straightedge
- Clamps
- Homemade compass (page 17)
- Drill with:
    - #6 combination pilot-countersink bit
    - ³/₁₆" straight bit (must be slightly smaller than threaded inserts)
    - ½" straight bit
- Jigsaw
- Wood file (optional)
- Sandpaper (up to 400 grit)
- Router with:
    - ½" straight bit
    - ¼" roundover bit
- Bar or strap clamps
- Hammer
- Masking tape
- Steel wool (if needed for lacquer)
- Paint roller
- Allen wrench (for socket-head screws)

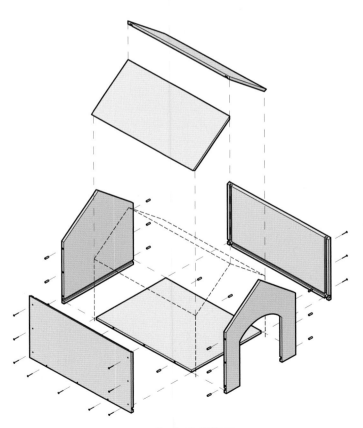

Exploded View

1. Cut the bottom, front, and back panels.

Lay out the cuts for the bottom, front, and back pieces along the factory edges of the ½" plywood, being sure to take into account the saw's kerf (width of the material removed by the blade), as shown in the cutting diagram. Make the cuts with a circular saw and straightedge guide or a table saw to ensure straight cuts. For convenience, you can rip one long piece at 16½", then crosscut the three pieces from there.

2. Cut the roof gables.

On the front panel, lay out the slope of the roof, following the cutting diagram. Mark each side edge 13" up from the bottom, then mark the center of the panel along the top edge. Use a straightedge to draw a line from the side marks to the top centerpoint.

Place the front panel (with the marked face up) on top of the back panel, making sure all edges are flush, and clamp the pieces together. Cut along the slope lines with a circular saw and straightedge guide, cutting through both panels at once.

3. Cut the door.

On the front panel only, draw a vertical line 3¼" in from the lower left corner, then mark the line 9½" up from the bottom edge. Draw a matching line on the right side of the front panel. Then draw a centerline on the panel, and mark it 12" up from the bottom edge. Use a homemade compass to draw a 6"-radius arch that ends at the two side-line marks and intersects the centerline mark.

Drill two ½" starter holes just inside where the vertical lines meet the arc. Be sure to drill in the waste area, where the dog door is being removed, and use a backerboard to prevent tearout on the underside. Use a jigsaw to carefully cut along the waste side of your lines. File and/or sand the cut edges.

4. Cut the sides.

Lay out the cuts for the side panels, following the cutting diagram and detail drawing of the roof and side angles. Again, you can make one long rip cut — this time at 24" — and then come back and make the crosscuts.

The top edges of the sides are cut at 25 degrees to follow the roof slope. Make these bevel cuts with a circular saw or table saw.

Cut one side panel at 13", measuring from the square edge to the long point (toe) of the bevel cut. Then, using the beveled edge on the leftover piece as the top, cut the second side piece at 13", making a square (90-degree) cut to create the bottom edge.

5. Cut the roof pieces.

The two roof panels get a 40-degree bevel at the top and a 25-degree bevel at the bottom. Make the 40-degree cut first to create the top bevels for both pieces, then cut the bottom edges at 25 degrees. The two bevels on each piece should point in opposite directions, with the overall width (from long point to long point) measuring 1¹¹⁄₁₆".

6. Mill the dadoes.

All the house parts fit together with ½"-wide, ¼"-deep dadoes (grooves) routed into the back, front, side, and roof panels, as shown in the cutting diagram.

Using a router and ½" straight bit, make a test cut in a scrap piece of material to confirm that the dadoes will accommodate the thickness of the plywood. The dadoes should be approximately ¹⁄₃₂ to ¹⁄₁₆" wider than the plywood to allow for the added thickness of the paint. All of the dadoes are ½" from the nearest parallel edge and on the interior faces of the panels only.

Set up each cut with a straightedge guide, and mill the dado in multiple passes to prevent undue wear on your bit. Begin by routing on the interior, lower portion of the front, back, and side panels; these dadoes will receive the edges of the bottom panel. Then rout the dadoes near the interior ends of the side and roof panels.

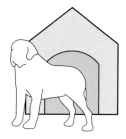

CHIHUAHUA
18"L x 11"W x 16"H

PUG
24"L x 17"W x 20"H

BULLDOG
30"L x 21"W x 24"H

SAINT BERNARD
42"L x 26"W x 30"H

Sizing the Doghouse to Your Dog

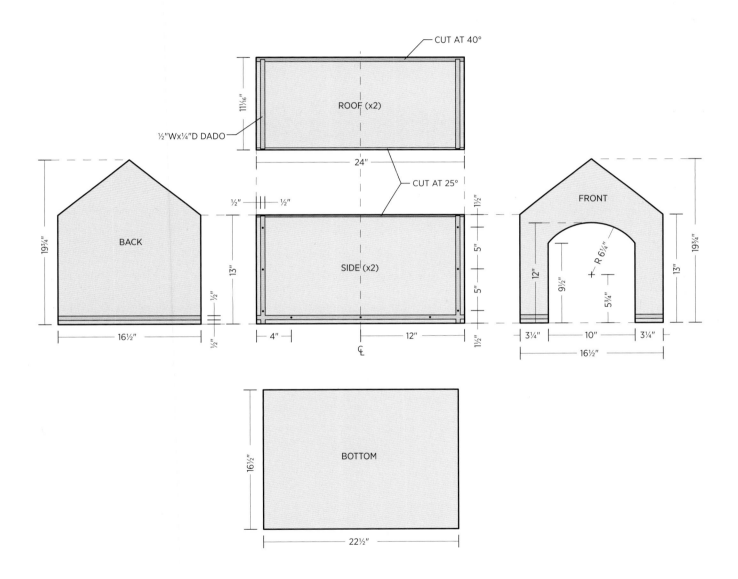

CUT AT 40°

ROOF (x2)

1¹¹⁄₁₆"

½"Wx¼"D DADO

24"

CUT AT 25°

BACK

19¾"

16½"

½"

½"

½"

½"

13"

½"

SIDE (x2)

5"

5"

1½"

5"

1½"

4"

12"

1½"

Cʟ

FRONT

12"

9½"

R 6¼"

5¾"

19¾"

13"

3¼"

10"

3¼"

16½"

BOTTOM

16½"

22½"

Cutting Diagram

7. Test-fit the structure.

Preassemble the house to make sure everything fits properly and to prepare for step 8. First slide the bottom panel into the dadoes of the front and back panels. You may want to give a slight roundover to the mating edges of the bottom, front, and back panels to facilitate assembly, using a file or sandpaper. Next, fit the sides into place, and gently clamp the front, back, and sides together, making sure that the pieces bottom out in the dadoes. Finally, fit the roof pieces into place.

8. Drill the threaded insert bores.

While the house is assembled and clamped, mark the locations for the threaded inserts, as shown in the cutting diagram. Each side of the house has a total of nine inserts. Mark the holes ¾" from the side and bottom edges of the side panels (the holes will be centered on the edges of the front and back panels), spacing them evenly, as shown in the diagram. At each location, drill a countersunk pilot hole through the side panel and into the edge of the mating panel.

9. Install the inserts.

Disassemble the house. At each pilot hole in the front, back, and bottom panels, use the drill and a ³⁄₁₆" bit to bore a hole that's

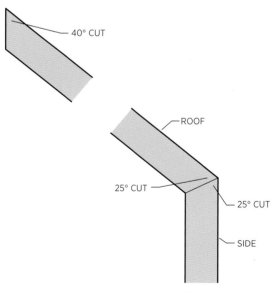

Detail of Roof and Side Angles

40° CUT

ROOF

25° CUT

25° CUT

SIDE

slightly deeper than the exposed end of the machine screw when inserted into the side-panel pilot holes.

Apply a small amount of epoxy to the outside of each threaded insert, and carefully drive it into a ³⁄₁₆" hole with a hammer, making sure it goes in straight. Be careful not to get epoxy on the threads inside the inserts. (It's a good idea to buy an extra insert and test it in a scrap piece of plywood stock first to make sure it fits properly.)

10. Mill the panel edges.

Using a router and ¼" roundover bit, rout all exposed edges of the front, back, and side panels. Do not round over any of the beveled edges or any square edges that will be held in a dado.

11. Sand, finish, and paint.

Lightly sand each piece with 220-grit sandpaper, and remove all dust with a clean, lint-free cloth. In a dust-free environment, lay all the parts down with their interior side facing up. Tape off all the dadoes and any exposed areas that will be painted.

Apply several coats of spray-on lacquer, as directed by the manufacturer, to the interior faces and the panel edges. Allow each coat to dry. You may need to sand between coats with 400-grit sandpaper or steel wool to achieve a smooth finish.

After finishing the interior, flip the panels over, and tape off all areas that won't get paint, including the edges. Apply the first coat of magnetic paint, using a paint roller. Add more layers until you have the desired amount of magnetism. The more coats you apply, the more magnetic the surface will be; however, be sure not to add so many coats that the material will be too thick to fit in the dadoes. Roll on one or two exterior topcoats in the color of your choice. Let the paint dry, and carefully peel off the tape.

12. Assemble the structure.

Assemble the structure as before. Set machine screws into the countersunk holes and tighten them in the threaded inserts, using an Allen wrench. Set the roof panels into place; these are not fastened.

13. Accessorize.

Decorate your doggie dwelling with magnets!

Tot Cart & Cradle

Designed by James A. Dyck

These two projects make a great play set for a pair of young siblings or one *really* lucky tot (of course, you can always build just one). Both pieces were created for the children of the designer's friend, in the 1970s, which means the originals you see here have been thoroughly kid-tested. Obviously, the mother hasn't wanted to part with them and has kept them for the next generation, which officially makes them heirloom pieces. And they're still just as honest and cool as ever.

MATERIALS

For the cart:

- ☐ One 40" length 1 x 8 solid hardwood lumber of choice
- ☐ One 48" length 2 x 2 solid hardwood lumber of choice
- ☐ ⅛" solid-rubber spline (optional; see step 2)
- ☐ One 12" x 36" piece ⅜" hardwood plywood
- ☐ Wood glue
- ☐ One 12" (or longer) length 1"-diam. hardwood dowel (for handle)
- ☐ One 24" length 1 x 6 solid hardwood lumber of choice
- ☐ Finish materials (see step 7)
- ☐ One 30" (or longer) length ½"-diam. hardwood dowel (for axles)
- ☐ Eight ½" washers

For the cradle:

- ☐ One 12" x 36" piece ⅜" hardwood plywood
- ☐ One 36" (or longer) length ½" x 2¾" (or wider) solid hardwood lumber of choice
- ☐ Wood glue
- ☐ Finish materials (see step 5 of cradle instructions)

TOOLS

- ☐ Circular saw with straightedge guide
- ☐ Router with homemade trammel (page 18) and ⅜" straight bit
- ☐ Drill with:
  - ☐ ½" straight bit
  - ☐ ⁹⁄₁₆" straight bit
  - ☐ 1½" hole saw or spade bit (optional)
- ☐ Miter saw
- ☐ Clamps
- ☐ Table saw (optional)
- ☐ Square
- ☐ Sandpaper
- ☐ Compass
- ☐ Jigsaw
- ☐ Hot glue gun

To Build the Cart

1. Cut and mill the sides.

Following the cart side panel diagram, cut the two side panels to shape from 1 x 8 solid lumber stock, using a circular saw and straightedge guide.

Each side gets two dadoes — one parallel to the bottom edge to receive the ⅜" plywood bottom panel, and one at a 70-degree angle between the top and bottom edges to receive the back panel. Both dadoes are ⅜" wide and ¼" deep. Mill the dadoes with a router and ⅜" straight bit.

Both side panels get a 1½"-wide, 1"-tall, ¼"-deep rabbet at each end, to receive the nose and tail pieces. Mill the rabbets with the router and straight bit, as before. These rabbets will join the dadoes for the bottom panels, with no transition between.

Finally, drill the holes for the wheel axles, using a ⁹⁄₁₆" bit, as shown in the cart side panel diagram.

Note: The plywood panels must fit snugly into the dadoes, so make sure the bit you use to rout the dadoes is the same size as (or very slightly smaller than) the ⅜" plywood stock.

2. Cut the nose and tail.

The nose and tail are cut from 2 x 2 solid stock. Both pieces end up at 1⅜" in height, and the nose has a beveled front edge to match the angle of the side panels. Both the nose and tail pieces get a ⅜"-wide, ½"-deep rabbet to receive the bottom panel; see the nose and tail detail drawings.

If you're using a handheld router and/or a circular saw, it probably will be easier to cut the nose bevel and the rabbets before cutting the pieces to length, so you'll have some room for clamping the workpiece. Bevel about 14" of one edge of the 2 x 2 at 20 degrees; run some test cuts first to confirm that this angle matches that of the top edge of the side panels. At the opposite end of the stock, rip about 14" of material to 1⅜" for the tail piece.

Use the router and ⅜" bit to mill a ⅜"-wide, ½"-deep rabbet down the length of the 2 x 2, on the edge opposite the beveled edge of the nose section.

Cut the nose and tail pieces to length at 12" each, using a miter saw. Test-fit the nose and tail between the side pieces, making sure the rabbet joints fit well and the assembly is square at the corners. It's okay if the outside edges aren't precisely aligned; you will sand them all flush after the glue-up. Clamp the pieces together.

Optional: In the cart shown here, the nose and tail pieces have a ⅛"-wide "bumper strip" of solid rubber beading. The strips are pressed into ⅛"-wide slots, or kerfs, made with a table saw blade. The kerfs are ½" up from the bottom edge on the front (narrow) edge of the nose and the rear edge of the tail piece. These are optional elements; if you'd like to include them, cut the kerfs on a table saw (after cutting the pieces to length) or with a circular saw (before cutting to length).

3. Cut the bottom and back panels.

The bottom and back panels are cut from ⅜" plywood. With the side, nose, and tail pieces clamped together, measure the inside dimensions of the assembly, from side to side and front to back. Add ⁷⁄₁₆" to the side-to-side dimension to find the width of the bottom and back panels. Cut both panels to width at this dimension, with the face grain running perpendicular to the width. Cut the bottom panel to length so it fits snugly into the rabbets of the nose and tail pieces. Cut the back piece to length at 16¾".

4. Glue up the sides, nose, tail, and back.

Apply glue to the mating surfaces of the rabbet joints and both dadoes of each side piece, and assemble the parts, leaving a gap of about ⁵⁄₁₆" between the back and bottom panels. Clamp the assembly, making sure it is square. Let the glue dry overnight.

Sand the areas where the sides meet the nose and tail so all exposed surfaces are flush and smooth.

5. Cut and install the handle.

The cart handle is cut from a 1"-diameter dowel and attaches to the top edge of the back panel with a glued dado joint. To mill the dado, secure the dowel on a flat surface, holding it between two flanking pieces of scrap lumber that are slightly thicker than the dowel's diameter. Set up a straightedge or fence parallel to the

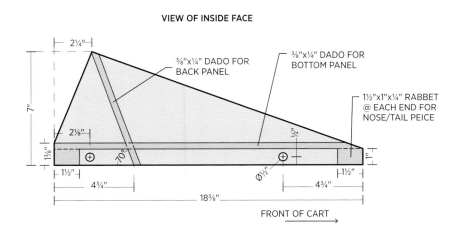

Cart Side Panel

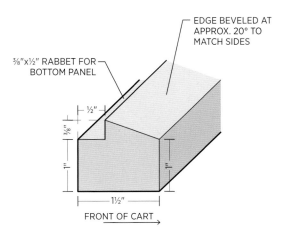

Nose Detail

dowel to guide the router's bit down the center of the dowel. Mill the dado ¼" deep, using the ⅜" bit.

Cut the dowel to length at 12", if necessary. Apply glue to the dado, stopping about ¾" from each end. Fit the handle over the back panel so it overhangs the panel equally on both sides, and clamp it in place. Let the glue dry overnight.

Note: The dado will show at the dowel ends, and this is an intentional aesthetic element. A similar detail shows up at the ends of the cradle's sides.

6. Make the wheels.
The wheels are cut from 1 x 6 solid stock (or from leftover 1 x 8 material). Mark the outline of each disk at 5½" in diameter, using a compass. Rough-cut the wheels with a jigsaw, staying about ⅛" outside the marked line. Secure each rough-cut wheel to a sacrificial work surface with small dabs of hot glue. Using the router with the straight bit and a homemade trammel, clean up the edge of the wheel. Depending on the size of your router base, the pivot nail for the trammel may be very close to the base; if it's too close, you can use a larger-diameter bit to add a little clearance.

Drill a ½"-diameter hole straight through the center of each wheel, using the hole from the trammel's pivot nail as the centerpoint. These are the axle holes, and they must be straight for the wheels to roll properly, so use a drill press or a portable drill with a drill guide to ensure straightness.

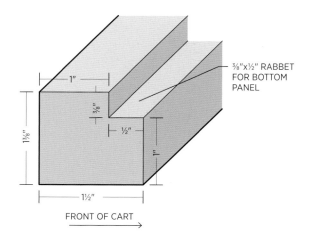

Tail Detail

Sand the wheels smooth, rounding over the edges slightly, but do not sand the edges of the axle holes.

7. Finish the parts.
Sand and finish the cart assembly and wheels as desired. For a clear finish on the plywood panels and the wheels, polyurethane is a good choice for a hard, washable surface. For painted elements, a high-gloss, oil-based (alkyd) lacquer will yield a tough, shiny finish with minimal brush marks.

8. Add the wheels.
Cut two axles to length at 14" from ½"-diameter dowel. Glue one dowel end and insert it into one of the wheels, tapping the dowel in until it's flush with the outside face of the wheel. Repeat with another axle and wheel. Let the glue dry.

Place one or more washers on each axle (total washer thickness should be about ⅛"). Fit the axles through the holes in the cart sides, add more washers over the free ends of the axles, then glue the remaining wheels to the axles. Let the glue dry overnight. Touch up the ends of the axles with the same finish used on the wheels.

To Build the Cradle
1. Cut the headboard and footboard.
Lay out the headboard and footboard pieces on ⅜" plywood, following the cutting diagram. Cut out the pieces with a jigsaw.

To make the interior cutouts, use a drill and 9⁄16"" bit to drill a starter hole for the jigsaw blade, staying just inside the marked cutout. Insert the blade into hole to begin the cut. Alternatively, you can use a 1½" spade bit or hole saw to create the radius of each corner and then complete the cutout with a jigsaw, connecting the holes with straight cuts. To prevent tearout with a spade bit or hole saw, drill only halfway through the panel's thickness, then flip the panel over and complete the hole from the other face.

2. Cut and mill the sides.
Using the circular saw and miter saw, cut the two side pieces to size at 2¾" x 17⅝" from ½"-thick solid stock. Each side gets three ⅜"-wide, ⅛"-deep dadoes to receive the bottom panel and the headboard and footboard. Using a router and ⅜" straight bit set up with a straightedge guide, mill the horizontal dado for the bottom panel so its bottom edge is ⅜" from the bottom edge of the side

piece. Mill the two vertical dadoes so their outside edges are ⅝" from each end of the side piece.

Note: As with the Tot Cart, the plywood panels must fit snugly into the dadoes, so make sure the router bit is the same size as (or very slightly smaller than) the ⅜" plywood stock.

3. Cut the bottom panel.

Dry-assemble the sides, headboard, and footboard, and clamp the assembly. The sides should sit 2" up from the bottom edge of the headboard and footboard.

   Measure the interior span between the sides; add slightly less than ¼" to this dimension to find the width of the bottom panel. Measure between the inside faces of the headboard and footboard to find the length of the bottom panel. Cut the bottom panel to size from ⅜" plywood, using the circular saw and straightedge guide or a table saw.

Before unclamping the assembly, make light pencil marks where the top and bottom edges of the sides meet the headboard and footboard, to facilitate placement during the glue-up.

4. Glue up the crib.

Apply glue to the sides' dadoes, stopping about ¾" from each end of the horizontal (bottom-panel) dadoes. Fit the headboard, footboard, and bottom panel into the dadoes on one side, then add the other side. Clamp the assembly. Check for squareness, and make sure the headboard and footboard sit squarely on a flat surface. Let the glue dry overnight.

5. Finish the piece.

Sand and finish the crib as desired. For a clear finish on the plywood pieces, polyurethane is a good choice for a hard, washable surface. To paint the sides, use a high-gloss, oil-based (alkyd) lacquer for a tough, shiny finish with minimal brush marks.

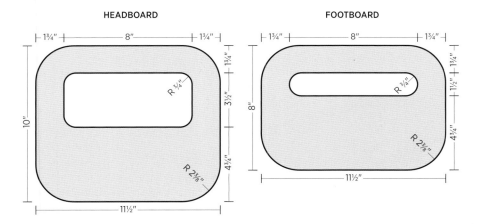

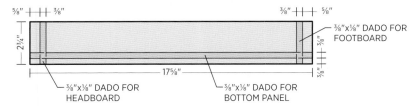

Cutting Diagrams

Donut Table

Designed by Holly Mann and Kerry Mann Sr.

If you have young kids, it shouldn't take you long to see worlds of potential in this clever little table. Originally made for a toy train set — and its engineer, of course — the donut design adapts equally well to arts and crafts, games, theatrical performances, and practical jokes: a tablecloth concealing the hole sets the perfect trap for unsuspecting visitors (the designer is not responsible for this idea). This is a great project for inexpensive or scrap material, and you can easily build the table in a day. You can also modify the dimensions to suit any space or activity or to make the table round, so it looks even more like a donut.

MATERIALS

- One 4 x 5-foot piece ⅝" or ¾" plywood (AC grade)
- Two 8-foot lengths 2 x 6 lumber
- 2½" deck screws or coarse-thread drywall screws
- Nonshrinking wood putty or auto-body filler
- Finish materials (see step 6)

TOOLS

- Straightedge
- Jigsaw
- Homemade compass (page 17)
- Drill with:
  - ⅜" straight bit
  - Combination pilot-countersink bit
- Router with ¼" or ⅜" roundover bit (if available)
- Sandpaper (up to 150 grit or finer) and sanding block
- Circular saw
- Square

1. Cut the plywood top.

Mark the center of the 4 x 5-foot plywood piece by drawing straight lines between opposing corners; the intersection of the lines is the centerpoint. Next, mark the corners of the panel with a 3¼" radius (you can simply trace around a 1-gallon paint can to mark the roundovers). Cut the rounded corners with a jigsaw.

2. Cut the donut hole.

Using a homemade compass, draw a 20"-diameter circle around the centerpoint. Drill a ⅜" or larger starter hole inside the marked circle. Insert the blade of the jigsaw into the starter hole to initiate the cut, then cut out the circle with the jigsaw.

3. Round over the top's edges.

Round over all the edges of the top, including inside the center cutout, with a router and roundover bit or with coarse sandpaper and a sanding block.

Sand the shaped edges and all surfaces with 150-grit sandpaper until they are smooth and free of splinters and sharp edges.

4. Build the legs.

Cut the four legs to length at 24" from the 2 x 6, using a circular saw. Cut the two cross members to length at 36".

Mark one face of each leg 11¼" up from the bottom end, and use a square to draw a horizontal line at the mark. This line represents the bottom face of the cross member.

To assemble each leg pair, position a cross member against each leg, with its bottom face on the marked line. Drill three evenly spaced pilot holes through the outside of the leg and into the end of the cross member, then join the parts with 2½" screws.

5. Assemble the table.

Mark the leg locations on the bottom face of the tabletop, as shown in the plan drawing. The legs are 7¼" from the side (short) edges of the top and 4½" from the front and back (long) edges.

Flip the top over and mark for pilot holes: all of these are 5¼" from the front and back edges of the top. Measuring in from each side edge, mark the holes at 8¼", 10", and 11¾".

Position the top on the legs following the layout marks. Drill the three pilot holes for each leg, and fasten the top to the legs with 2½" screws. Countersink the screw heads slightly below the surface of the tabletop.

6. Paint the table.

Finish-sand the legs so they are smooth and free of splinters. Fill the screw holes in the top and legs with nonshrinking wood putty or auto-body filler, and sand the filler flush after it dries.

Prime and paint the entire table as desired. For the most durable painted finish, use an oil-based (alkyd) high-gloss enamel. Let the paint dry completely before putting the finish to the ultimate test: kids.

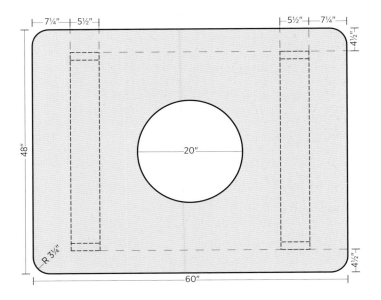

Tabletop Plan

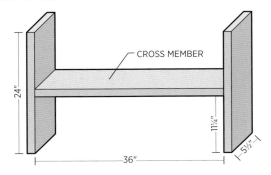

Leg Assembly

Old-School Skateboard

Designed by Philip Schmidt

For anyone whose early days of skateboarding were all about poaching empty swimming pools and carving playground blacktop, the classic boards of the '70s should bring back some priceless (and painful) memories. If you're still up for a ride these days, shaping your own deck is about as much fun as you can have with a sheet of plywood. Think of it as taking a trip down memory lane . . . with speed wobble. For a truly vintage experience, complete the board with some old-school trucks and big, gummy urethane wheels, which are, thanks to the endless California summer, still available today.

MATERIALS

- ☐ One 12" x 30" (or larger) piece heavy paper
- ☐ ½" Baltic birch or similar hardwood plywood (size as needed)
- ☐ Exterior-grade clear polyurethane
- ☐ Grip tape
- ☐ Two skateboard trucks and hardware
- ☐ Four skateboard wheels

TOOLS

- ☐ Straightedge
- ☐ Pencil
- ☐ Square
- ☐ Flexible French curve (drawing tool; if available)
- ☐ X-Acto knife
- ☐ Tape
- ☐ Awl or punch
- ☐ Jigsaw with fine wood blade
- ☐ Sandpaper (60 to 220 grit) and sanding block
- ☐ Clamps
- ☐ Drill with:
    - ☐ ³⁄₁₆" straight bit (or sized for truck mounting bolts)
    - ☐ Countersink bit (sized for truck mounting bolts)
- ☐ Razor blade

Note: Be sure to buy the trucks and wheels before designing the deck; the overall width of the trucks and wheels will guide the sizing and shaping of the deck. Several original skateboard manufacturers have reissued 1970s-era (and later) versions of trucks, wheels, and decks. As of this writing, vintage parts are widely available online, and it's worth spending some time shopping around to find just what you want. Search with key phrases such as vintage skateboards *or* old-school skateboards. *Also check out the websites of original manufacturers of skateboard parts. And though the design calls for ½" plywood stock, you could also use ⅜" plywood, if it's strong enough, which would give you a more flexible deck.*

1. Create a paper template.

Use a straightedge to draw a long, straight line down the middle of a piece of heavy paper; this represents the centerline of the finished deck. Using a square, draw two lines intersecting the centerline at 90 degrees, to represent the ends of the nose and tail of the deck. The distance between the lines is the overall length of the finished deck (minus any necessary sanding). Mark or sketch the approximate locations of the trucks, for reference while shaping the deck.

Begin sketching the deck profile on one side of the centerline. If available, use a flexible French curve tool to create smooth, consistent curves, particularly at the nose and tail. Refine the shape to your liking, using the actual trucks and wheels for reference, if applicable.

Determine the final positions of the trucks, and mark these on the centerline. Use the square to draw a reference line for each truck, as shown in the template layout; each must be precisely perpendicular to the centerline. Position the trucks on the reference lines, and carefully trace inside the four mounting holes. (If you're not planning to ride the deck, you can omit the truck layout and hardware holes.)

Fold the paper in half precisely along the centerline, with the drawn profile facing out. Use an X-Acto knife to cut out the profile through both sides of the paper. Unfold the template and smooth it out flat.

2. Cut out the deck.

Secure the paper template to ½" plywood stock, using small pieces of tape. The length of the deck should parallel the grain of the plywood's face veneer. Trace along the entire perimeter

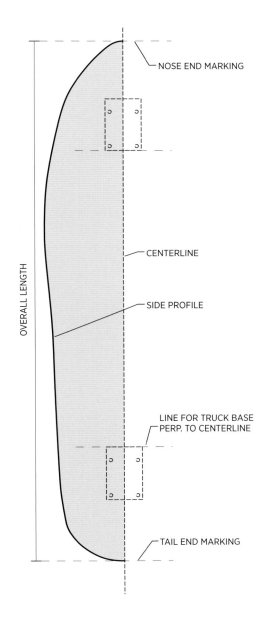

NOSE END MARKING

CENTERLINE

SIDE PROFILE

LINE FOR TRUCK BASE PERP. TO CENTERLINE

TAIL END MARKING

OVERALL LENGTH

Template Layout

of the template with a fine pencil to transfer the outline to the plywood. Then use an awl or punch to mark the exact centers of the truck mounting holes.

Remove the template, and cut out the deck with a jigsaw and a very-fine-tooth wood blade (to minimize splintering). Be careful not to cut inside the line; cutting outside is safer, because you can easily sand the edges down to the line.

Sand the cut edges with coarse sandpaper and a sanding block, smoothing the curves and perfecting the deck's shape, as needed.

3. Drill the hardware holes.

With the deck clamped over a sacrificial surface (to minimize tearout), drill the hardware holes straight through the deck, using a $^3/_{16}$" bit (confirm the proper bit size with your hardware). Then use a countersink bit to countersink the top of each hole just enough to allow the bolt head to sit flush with the deck surface when fully tightened.

4. Finish the deck.

Use medium-grit sandpaper to form a slight roundover along the top and bottom edges of the deck. Then finish-sand the entire deck, working up to 220-grit or finer sandpaper. Make sure that all edges are smooth to the touch.

Finish all surfaces of the deck with three coats of exterior (UV-protected) clear polyurethane or other desired finish, following the manufacturer's directions. Let the final coat cure fully, as directed.

5. Add grip tape.

Self-adhesive grip tape is commonly available in 9- to 12"-wide sheets and lengths of 30" and up, in a range of colors and designs. For the simplest application, you can cover the top of the deck with a solid sheet and trim the tape along the edges. For a custom treatment, you can cut out lettering or decorative shapes from the tape before applying it.

To customize your grip tape, lay the deck upside down on the back film of the grip tape sheet, and trace around the deck with a pencil. Draw or stencil on the film with the desired graphics or lettering. Cut out the graphic with the X-Acto knife. Then rough-cut the grip tape sheet around the deck outline, staying an inch or so outside the line.

For the project as shown, the lettering was printed out full-size via a computer (this required tiling of a few sheets), and the letters were cut out to create a template for tracing onto the grip tape.

To apply the grip tape, carefully cut through the backing across the middle of the deck outline (perpendicular to its length). Position the tape over the top of the deck, using the traced outline as a guide. Then peel the backing away from one side of the center, exposing a small area of the adhesive. Press and smooth the exposed tape onto the deck, being careful to eliminate air bubbles. Peel away more backing, and smooth out the tape, working from the center out to the end. Repeat with the other half of the tape.

Lay the backing film over the top surface of the tape to protect your hands as you give the tape a final, firm smoothing out for a strong bond. Discard the film. Burnish the tape from the top side by rubbing the shaft of a skate tool (or other metal tool you don't mind getting scratched) along the edges of the deck, creating a whitish line and a clean creased edge. Trim the tape flush with the deck's edge, using a new razor blade pulled from underneath the tape, holding the blade at a slight inward angle toward the deck interior. Press down any loose edges of tape.

6. Ride.

Mount the trucks and wheels with the hardware, and get out on the blacktop. (You might want to hold off on the pool riding until you get the "old feel" back.)

Flywood

Designed by Paul Steiner

While this may look like an ordinary handmade boomerang, it is anything but. It's made from a special flying plywood that has amazing aeronautical qualities. First developed by Howard Hughes as a top-secret project . . . All right, we're pulling your leg. There's no such thing as flying plywood. It's just a play on words. The real Flywood is a boomerang that you can make with almost any plywood, from premium stuff like Baltic birch or aircraft plywood (which really does exist) to lowly scrap material salvaged from packing crates. The design is so forgiving that often a slight twist or bow in the material makes the boomerang fly better. Designed for a high school technology class, Flywood is great for a weekend project with teenage kids. And of course you'll make one for yourself.

See page 184 for another work by Paul Steiner.

MATERIALS

- ☐ Photocopier paper (for making paper template)
- ☐ One 11" x 18" (or larger) piece ¼" to ⅜" plywood (with 4 plies min.; see Boomerang Wood on page 279)
- ☐ Glue stick or rubber cement
- ☐ Finish materials (as desired)

TOOLS

- ☐ Tape
- ☐ Scissors
- ☐ Jigsaw with fine wood blade or band saw
- ☐ Sandpaper (from 80 to 220 grit) and sanding block
- ☐ Files and other shaping tools (see step 2)
- ☐ T bevel or other angle guide
- ☐ Mineral spirits or lacquer thinner

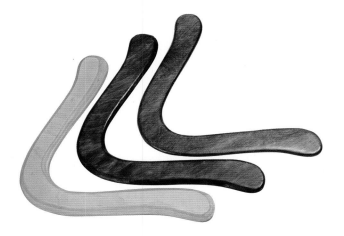

1. Prepare the blank.

The blank is the boomerang body cut and sanded to its shape with square edges. Once the blank is prepared, you will sand and file bevels into the edges to make the piece flyable.

Start by making a full-size copy of each half of the pattern template on a photocopier. Line up the edges of the pattern halves, and tape the two pieces of paper together to create a full pattern. Cut out the pattern with scissors, then adhere the pattern to your plywood stock using glue stick or rubber cement. The pattern will remain in place until the finish-sanding process (step 3).

Cut out the blank in two stages: First rough-cut the shape with a jigsaw or band saw, staying about ½ to 1" outside the pattern outline. With the rough cut complete, make a series of relief cuts — perpendicular to the outline's edge — along the tighter curves, sawing from the outside edge of the blank to ¹⁄₁₆" from the pattern outline. Then carefully cut out the entire profile, staying ¹⁄₃₂" to ¹⁄₁₆" outside the pattern outline.

Finally, use sandpaper and a small sanding block and/or a file to sand the blank's edge down to the pattern outline. The edge should remain square (90 degrees). Finish with fine sandpaper (150 grit and up) to smooth the edge after shaping.

2. Form the bevels.

Starting with files, a Surform tool (rasp), or a block plane, begin beveling the top edges of the blank, following the degree markings on the pattern. The pattern shows where to make the bevel 30 degrees and where to make it 45 degrees. The top of the completed bevels should stop at the inner lines, where the degree markings are; you will file or sand away the outline edge of the pattern to get there. As you create the bevels, check your work frequently with a T bevel (angle finder) to make sure you are maintaining the correct angle. Do your best to sand at 30 and 45 degrees, but don't worry if you deviate slightly from these angles.

Once the bevels are roughed in, begin sanding the edges smooth (see tip below). Also sand the transitions between the different bevel angles by blending the angles together: Start sanding at a 45-degree bevel, increasing the pressure and angle over the transition area until you reach the 30-degree bevel. Follow any machine sanding with hand-sanding, working up to 220-grit sandpaper. Also sand away any sharp or splintered areas.

Tip: Shaping the bevels requires a good deal of sanding, and almost any sanding tool can be helpful. A little creativity and trial and error will help you find ways to sand the contours with the tools you have available. Palm and orbital sanders work well, too, but sanding with them can take some time.

3. Finish the piece.

Peel off the remaining pattern paper, and remove any glue residue with mineral spirits or lacquer thinner. Using fine sandpaper, sand the beveled edges and the top and bottom faces of the boomerang. On the faces, be sure to sand parallel to the grain direction of the face veneers.

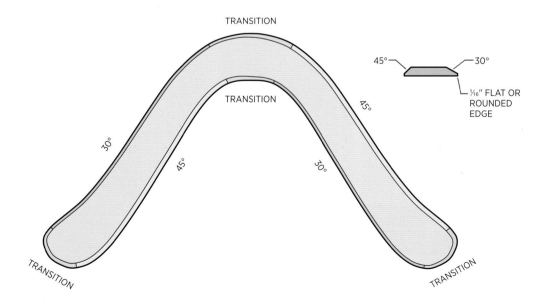

Pattern Template

Apply the finish of your choice. You can apply paint, stain, and/or a clear protective surface finish rated for outdoor exposure. Polyurethane and varnish offer the best protection for outdoor use, while lacquer provides a nicer finish for displaying the piece. To aid in the finishing process, tie a string between two points, like a clothesline. Hold the boomerang on the edges with your hand to finish the majority of the boomerang. Then hang the boomerang on the string and coat the areas where your fingers were holding.

Flying your Flywood

Find a suitable (large) area to throw your boomerang, such as a football, baseball, or soccer field. If there's wind, position yourself so you will be throwing into the wind from one corner of the field. Grip the boomerang with the curved side directed backward, placing the flat face in the palm of your hand and clasping over the bevels with your fingers and thumb. Draw the boomerang back behind your shoulder, then throw it overhand, snapping your wrist and releasing the boomerang level with, or slightly above, your shoulder.

Successful throwing takes some practice, and you'll have to experiment to find the techniques that work best for you — raise or lower your release point, raise or lower your arm, increase or decrease the wrist snap, throw 45 degrees into the wind instead of 90 degrees, and so on. Of course, you'll also learn what does and does not make your boomerang come back to you. In the words of Flywood's designer, "Many happy returns!"

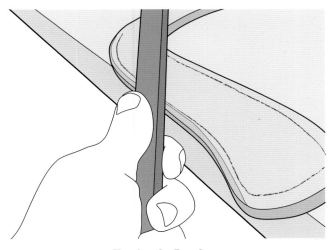

Shaping the Bevels

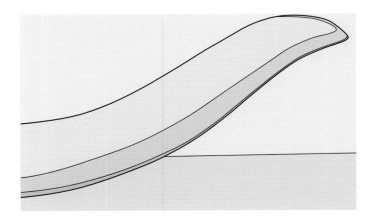

Completed Bevel Edge

Shop Tip

Boomerang Wood

Baltic birch and marine plywood work very well for this project because they have the necessary layers (plies) and a good weight for flying. Another option is to laminate two sheets of ⅛" plywood to gain the minimum four layers. Quarter-inch plywood produces a better-flying boomerang because it allows the piece to flex, helping it to return. Three-eighths-inch plywood doesn't flex, but it does produce a better-looking piece for display. Cabinet shops, manufacturing facilities, and even wood packing crates are good sources for scrap plywood to build a boomerang.

Plywood as . . .
*A showcase of inspired pieces and
the stories behind them*

. . . one sweet ride

Caylee Cruiser

by Marcus Papay

The Caylee Cruiser began as an idea to combine a modern functional aesthetic and an object loaded with playful, innocent associations of that great American toy — a kid's wagon. The design stems from the classic red Radio Flyer designs of the 1920s but has been modified to represent a development in shop materials available to anyone with a lumber supply nearby.

The core material, Baltic birch plywood, is very sturdy, as long as its material properties are taken into consideration. Aluminum is a fine companion to the birch plywood; it is easily worked in a woodshop, provides an effective stabilizing material, and complements the machined wood's light coloring.

Even though a child may haul nothing heavier than stuffed animals in the wagon, the engineering will be put to the test. Connections and mechanical fixtures must withstand some serious stress. When dealing with connections between these two materials, the tighter the better.

For the connections that have movement, I have applied a third material that enables mobility. The yoke of the wagon pivots on a bolt and nut that tighten a nylon washer between wood surfaces. This washer eliminates friction, allowing the bolt to be tightened without freezing the pivoting connection.

The wheels roll on skateboard wheel bearings and a bolt that has been tapped directly into the aluminum axle that runs through the axle mounts. The handle is made with two aluminum pieces that have been formed by hammering over an iron right angle. The handle pull is laminated plywood (two ½" pieces) that has been turned on a lathe. The turned piece sits freely between the two mounting brackets via notching in the edges, preventing it from sliding back and forth.

So far the design has held up, withstanding the impressive pounding a child can inflict, and is still carting the stuffed gang around.

MATERIALS

- ☐ ½" Baltic birch plywood (rails)
- ☐ ¾" Baltic birch plywood (axle assembly)
- ☐ 1" extruded aluminum angle (rail corner hardware)
- ☐ 1" x ½" extruded aluminum tube (handle assembly)
- ☐ 1"-diam. extruded aluminum rod (axles)
- ☐ ¼" aluminum plate stock (various fastener elements)
- ☐ Skateboard wheel bearings

Advanced Projects

A collection of pieces for anyone who's comfortable with biscuits, mortises and tenons, and ripping a $200 panel on a table saw.

Avocado

Designed by Sara Schalliol-Hodge

Described by its creator as "a storage cabinet for the young (and young at heart),"
Avocado is, as a furniture design, equal parts funky and fine. On the funky side
you have the cabinet boxes of OSB (yes, oriented strandboard, also known as
construction-grade sheathing and subflooring). This material is transformed by
a lacquered paint wash and given "windows" glazed with acrylic that's hand-
sanded to offer just enough translucence to reveal shadows of contents within
(they also change with the room's ambient light). On the fine side are the crisp
Baltic birch panels, clear-coated and beautifully mitered at the corners. Supporting
it all is a solid-walnut base with Danish-tapered legs and mortise-and-tenon joinery.
And there you have it: fine, funky furniture.

MATERIALS

- ☐ One 4 x 8-foot sheet ¾" OSB
- ☐ Wood glue
- ☐ Biscuits (for joinery)
- ☐ Acrylic paint
- ☐ One 2 x 4-foot piece ½" Baltic birch plywood
- ☐ One 96" length 1⅛" x 5" solid walnut
- ☐ 1¼" coarse-thread wood screws
- ☐ Clear semigloss lacquer
- ☐ One 14" x 32" sheet ¼"-thick acrylic
- ☐ ⅜" finish screws
- ☐ Two 2" x 13" piano hinges

TOOLS

- ☐ Planer or sanding equipment
- ☐ Table saw or circular saw with straightedge guide
- ☐ Jigsaw
- ☐ Router with ⅜" rabbeting bit
- ☐ Sandpaper (up to 220 grit)
- ☐ Biscuit joiner
- ☐ Sponge (for paint application)
- ☐ Drill and bit set
- ☐ Setup for mortise-and-tenon joints (see step 4)
- ☐ Clamps
- ☐ Hacksaw (if needed for hinges)

1. Prepare the OSB panels.

Using a planer (or the best available sanding equipment), plane the ¾" OSB stock down to ½" in thickness, so the surface is smooth and relatively uniform.

Lay out and cut the panels for the two cabinet boxes, following the OSB cutting diagram. Each box gets a door, a top or bottom panel, one exterior side, and one middle horizontal panel (this becomes the bottom panel on the upper box and the top panel on the lower box). The single middle vertical panel spans the height of both boxes, serving as the inside panel of each carcass. Be sure to follow the miters noted on the diagram.

Cut the door radii and openings with a jigsaw. Rabbet the inside edge of each door opening at ⅜" wide and ¼" deep, to receive the glazing.

Use the jigsaw to cut the acrylic window panels to size, following the acrylic cutting diagram. Sand the cut edges smooth, then sand the faces of the panels with coarse paper until they are evenly cloudy.

2. Assemble and finish the OSB boxes.

Assemble the OSB carcasses with glue and biscuits, checking carefully for squareness. Because of the common middle vertical panel, you have to glue up both carcasses at once.

After the glue cures, finish-sand all surfaces and edges of the assembly, as well as the door frames. Finish all the OSB parts with bright-green acrylic paint (or as desired) diluted with water and applied with a sponge. Be sure to test the paint wash on scrap first. If necessary, add a second coat of paint wash to achieve a uniform color. Let the finish dry completely.

3. Prepare the plywood parts.

Cut the four plywood panels from ½" Baltic birch or similar hardwood plywood, following the plywood cutting diagram. The miter joints on these pieces are an important element in the look of the finished piece, so cut them carefully on the table saw.

Glue up the two L-assemblies with glue and biscuits, making sure the miters are tight and the pieces are perfectly square. After the glue dries, finish-sand the parts, keeping the edges crisp but smooth.

4. Build the walnut base.

The legs and stretchers of the base are assembled with mortise-and-tenon joints using loose tenons. The single main stretcher spans across the inside of the leg pairs and is roughly centered under the cabinet unit. The completed base is fastened to the lower OSB box and lower plywood L with screws driven up through the bottom edges of the three stretchers. All the base parts are cut from solid walnut stock planed to a uniform 1" thickness.

Plane the faces of the walnut stock to bring it to 1" in thickness, then joint the edges, as needed. Cut the main stretcher, right and left stretchers, and four legs to size, following the walnut cutting diagram.

Drill counterbored pilot holes for the cabinet unit, as shown in the diagram; the hole placement isn't critical, as long as the screws are evenly spaced so the legs will attach firmly to the OSB and plywood pieces. Also make sure the holes won't interfere with the tenons on the stretchers. Finish-sand the walnut parts.

Cut and shape the loose tenons to size. The tenons should be at least half the width of each piece they are entering. Cut the mortises to match the tenons. Test-fit the entire base assembly, and make any necessary adjustments. Glue up and clamp the base, checking carefully for squareness.

After the glue cures, finish-sand all of the walnut surfaces and edges.

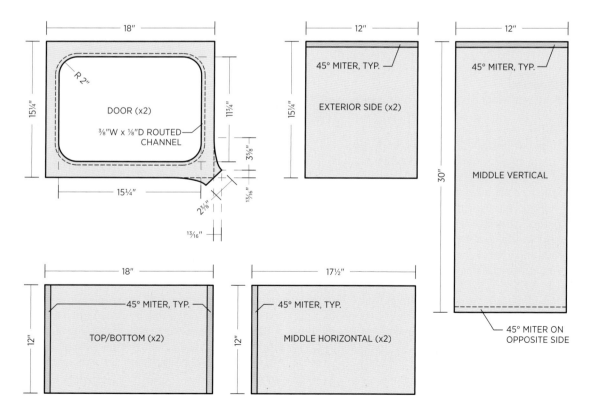

OSB Cutting Diagram

5. Assemble the piece.

Dry-assemble the entire unit. Mark and cut biscuit slots for joining the plywood Ls to the OSB boxes. Attach the plywood Ls to the OSB unit with biscuits and glue; clamp, and check for squareness. After the glue cures, fasten the base to the OSB and plywood assembly, using 1¼" wood screws. The base should be centered under the cabinet assembly.

6. Finish the piece.

Spray the entire unit (and unattached OSB door frames) with clear, semigloss lacquer. After the finish dries, sand it lightly and add a second coat, as directed by the manufacturer.

Fit the acrylic panels into the rabbets of the door frames, and secure the panels with ⅜" finish screws. Cut the two piano hinges to length at 13", if necessary, using a hacksaw. Install the hinges on the boxes and door frames so they are centered from top to bottom and the hinge barrels are on the outsides of the boxes.

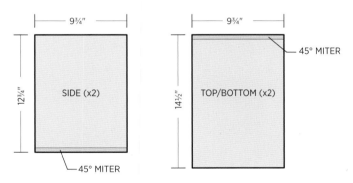

Plywood Cutting Diagram

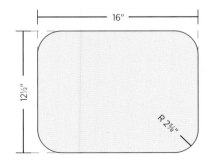

Acrylic Cutting Diagram

MAIN STRETCHER

PREDRILLED HOLES, TYP.

MORTISE HOLES, TYP.

LEFT LEG (x2)

RIGHT LEG (x2)

MORTISE HOLES, TYP.

RIGHT STRETCHER

LEFT STRETCHER

Walnut Cutting Diagram

modBOX 2010

Designed by Steven Ewoldt

If you've ever dreamed of getting your house into *Metropolitan Home* or *Architectural Digest* but then screwed it all up by having kids, modBOX 2010 might just be your salvation. It is, in the words of its designer, "a modernist toy box for the hipster tyke." Yet as cool as it looks on the outside, modBOX is all about the kid experience. It has a big catchall chest (perfect for emergency cleanups), plus two drawers that pull out, two book niches, and, best of all, two *secret* compartments. And if there's anything a kid likes, it's little, private places to put things. So even if you never see your living room featured in a shelter magazine, at least your hipster tyke can have an architect-designed toy box for hosting chic play dates.

MATERIALS

- ☐ Two 5 x 5-foot sheets ¾" apple or Baltic birch plywood
- ☐ Finish materials (see steps 2 and 9)
- ☐ One 3 x 3-foot piece ½" apple or Baltic birch plywood
- ☐ Wood glue
- ☐ #20 biscuits (for joinery)
- ☐ Two torsion hinges (see step 6)
- ☐ Four metal corner braces with screws (for foot)

TOOLS

- ☐ Table saw
- ☐ Circular saw with straightedge guide (for crosscuts)
- ☐ Sandpaper
- ☐ Biscuit joiner
- ☐ Router and bits (for dadoes, pull holes, and hinge mortises)
- ☐ Clamps
- ☐ Drill

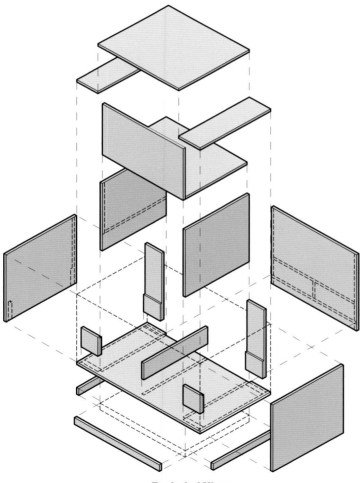

Exploded View

1. Cut the main box panels.

Following the plan illustrations, lay out and cut the following parts from ¾" plywood:

- Box bottom
- Niche sides (2)
- Niche backs (2)
- Compartment fronts (2)
- Niche tops (2)
- Chest sides (2)
- Chest back
- Chest front
- Chest base
- Center support
- Foot front
- Foot sides (2)

Label all the parts as shown in the plan and arrange them for easy reference. Sand all faces and edges smooth, and slightly ease any exposed corners; do not sand any edges that will join with other pieces (including butt/biscuit, dado, and rabbet joints).

2. Finish the chest parts (optional).

To create the distinctive two-tone look of the project shown here, stain the parts of the chest and foot; these are indicated in the plan with dark gray coloring and include the chest sides, front, and back, as well as all foot pieces. Don't stain any surfaces that will be joined with other parts.

3. Prepare the joints.

Start laying out the project on the box bottom. Locate the chest sides first by drawing reference lines on the top face of the box bottom.

Cut the biscuit joints that will connect the box bottom to the niche sides and the chest sides, as shown in the plans. Also cut the biscuit joints that will connect the niche sides and chest sides to the niche tops.

Cut the biscuit joints between the center support (drawer divider) and box bottom, then cut the joints between the box bottom and the front foot piece.

At this point, the box bottom should have five lines of biscuit joints cut into its top face (parallel to the short side) and three biscuits (in one line) on its bottom face for the front of the foot (parallel to the long side).

Cut horizontal dadoes into the inside faces of the chest sides to receive the chest base. Cut vertical dadoes into the inside faces of the niche sides to receive the niche back pieces.

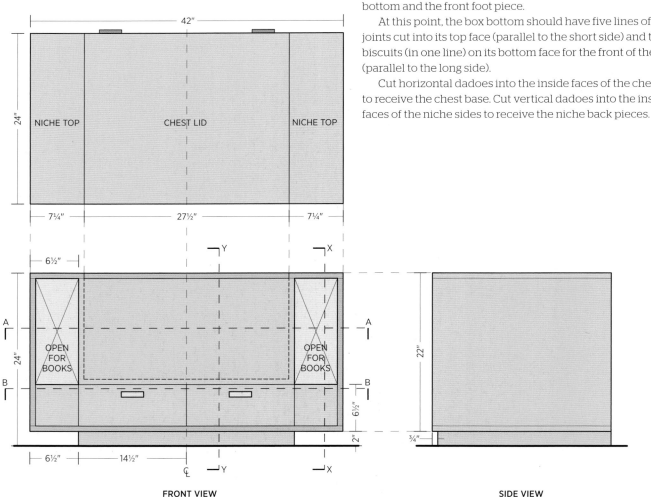

MODBOX - TOP VIEW

FRONT VIEW

SIDE VIEW

Assembly Plan

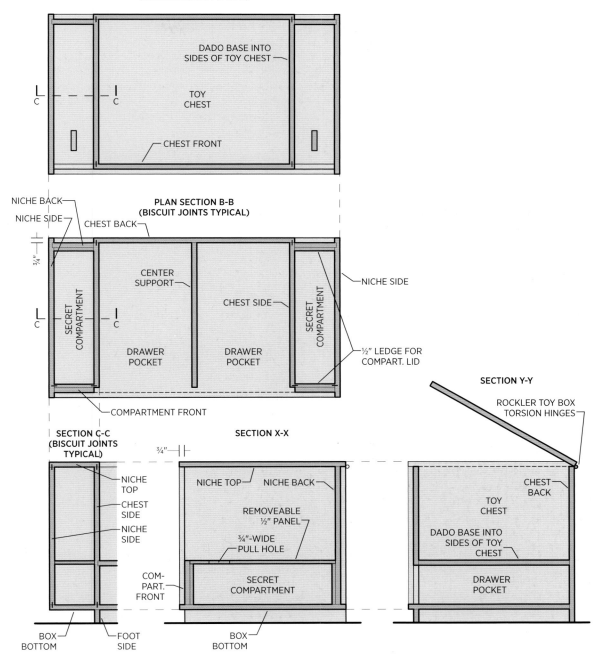

PLAN SECTION A-A
(BISCUIT JOINTS TYPICAL)

DADO BASE INTO
SIDES OF TOY CHEST

TOY
CHEST

CHEST FRONT

PLAN SECTION B-B
(BISCUIT JOINTS TYPICAL)

NICHE BACK

NICHE SIDE

CHEST BACK

NICHE SIDE

CENTER
SUPPORT

CHEST SIDE

SECRET
COMPARTMENT

SECRET
COMPARTMENT

DRAWER
POCKET

DRAWER
POCKET

½" LEDGE FOR
COMPART. LID

COMPARTMENT FRONT

SECTION C-C
(BISCUIT JOINTS
TYPICAL)

NICHE
TOP

CHEST
SIDE

NICHE
SIDE

BOX
BOTTOM

FOOT
SIDE

SECTION X-X

NICHE TOP   NICHE BACK

REMOVEABLE
½" PANEL

¾"-WIDE
PULL HOLE

COM-
PART.
FRONT

SECRET
COMPARTMENT

BOX
BOTTOM

SECTION Y-Y

ROCKLER TOY BOX
TORSION HINGES

CHEST
BACK

TOY
CHEST

DADO BASE INTO
SIDES OF TOY
CHEST

DRAWER
POCKET

Section View

4. Prepare the compartment fronts and ledges.

Cut the four ledge pieces to size at 5¾" wide and 5½" tall from ½" plywood; these will serve as ledges to support the compartment lids.

Cut biscuit joints between the ledges and the chest sides and niche sides. Glue one ledge to the inside face of each compartment front so their side and bottom edges are flush. Glue the remaining two ledges to the inside face of the niche backs so their inside and bottom edges are flush.

5. Glue up the main structure.

With all the dadoes and biscuit joints cut, you're ready to dry-fit the complete chest and niche assemblies and the box bottom to make sure everything fits snugly and squarely.

Glue up the assemblies, starting with the niches (sides, backs, and compartment fronts) and the chest sides. Then glue the chest base into the dadoes on the chest sides. Glue the chest front and back to the chest sides, install the center support and box bottom, and add the foot front to the underside of the box bottom. Clamp the entire assembly and let the glue dry.

6. Mortise for the hinges.

The toy chest lid must have some type of safety hardware to hold the lid open and ensure that it closes slowly. For the project shown, both safety features are accomplished with torsion hinges (available from Rockler Woodworking Hardware; see Resources).

Mortise the top edge of the chest back panel to receive the two hinges, so the lid will fit flush with all edges of the chest. The hinge knuckles are fully exposed at the back of the lid (no lid overlay).

7. Build the drawers.

Measure the drawer pockets and front openings to verify all dimensions for the drawer boxes and fronts. Cut the side, back, and bottom pieces for each drawer from ½" plywood, as shown in the drawer plan. Cut the drawer fronts from ¾" plywood, then mill a ¾"-wide slot into each face to serve as a pull hole.

Glue up the drawers as shown in the plan, using dadoes for the front-side joints and rabbets for the side-back joints; the bottom should fit inside the box frame with dadoes or rabbets, as desired.

8. Complete the final details.

Measure and cut each compartment lid to fit its space, using ½" plywood. Mill a ¾"-wide slot into each lid, centered near the front, matching the pull holes in the drawer fronts.

Cut the chest lid to size, allowing for a small clearance at each side edge.

Use corner braces to attach the two side foot pieces to the foot front.

9. Finish the project.

Finish-sand all surfaces of the project, and slightly ease all edges and corners. Wipe all surfaces clean and finish the entire piece with the desired finish (clear polyurethane was used for the project shown).

Install the hinges and chest lid. Fit the drawers and compartment lids into place to complete the job.

Note: Mirror the plan below for left drawer; verify dimensions of finished drawer pocket.

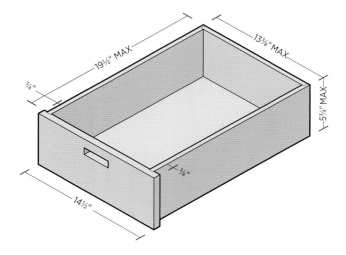

19½" MAX   13⅜" MAX   ¾"   5¾" MAX   ⅝"   14½"

Right Drawer Plan

store + explore

Designed by Anna Parrella

Like its name, everything about this piece is dual-function. It was designed for a daycare center, with the primary goal of occupying an infant while building strength and curiosity. The sloping panel is both a ramp for crawling up and a slide for zipping down (it's also a lid for a storage compartment). The seat at the top is a landing for the slide and a fun place to perch for reading and games. And the cutout beneath the seat is as good for storing books and toys as it is for crawling through. Aren't you tempted to make one in adult size?

MATERIALS

- [ ] One 4 x 4-foot sheet ¾" hardwood plywood
- [ ] 1¼" coarse-thread drywall or wood screws
- [ ] Two sets soft-close cabinet hardware (see Resources for supplier)
- [ ] Four screw eyes
- [ ] Wood glue
- [ ] 6d (2") finish nails
- [ ] Two roto hinges
- [ ] Tension cable and clamps
- [ ] One 4 x 4-foot sheet $^3/_{16}$" hardboard
- [ ] Finish materials (as desired)

TOOLS

- [ ] Circular saw with straightedge guide or table saw
- [ ] Jig saw
- [ ] Router with:
  - [ ] ⅜" roundover bit
  - [ ] ⅜" cove bit
- [ ] Drill and bit set
- [ ] Sandpaper
- [ ] Bar clamps
- [ ] Wire cutters
- [ ] Nail set

Note: All of this project's main parts can be cut from one 4 x 4-foot sheet of plywood. The back panel is made with two pieces joined with a hidden piece of blocking. If you prefer to have a single piece for the back, you can cut it at full size from a separate piece of plywood. Also, as an option on some of the joinery, you can substitute splines in place of the glued and nailed joints described in the steps; see Spline Joints, on page 295.

1. Cut the parts.

Lay out and cut all the plywood parts, as shown in the cutting diagram. Use a circular saw with a straightedge guide or a table saw to ensure straight cuts. Round off both front corners of the slide panel and the top front corner of each side panel with a 1¾" radius, using a jigsaw. Also round off the corners of the two slide support blocks with a ½" radius.

2. Assemble the back panel.

Cut a 2" x 13" strip from any of the plywood scrap. Set the Back A and Back B pieces facedown, and fit their 13$^7/_{16}$" edges together, with their side edges aligned. Place the scrap strip flat on the back pieces, centered over the seam and between their side edges. Fasten the strip to both pieces with four 1¼" screws, driven through the strip and into the back pieces.

3. Round over the edges.

For safety, ease the edges of the main parts that will be exposed in the finished piece. These include:

- All edges of the sides, except along the back
- All edges of the slide
- The outside rear edges of the back
- All long edges on one of the long supports
- The long edges of the corner blocks

Don't round over any edges that will mate with other pieces. If you discover any missed spots after the final assembly, you can round them over with sandpaper.

4. Drill the hinge holes.

Drill one hole in each side edge at the upper end of the slide for a roto hinge, and drill corresponding holes in the side panels (see the side construction view). Use a bit with the same diameter as the hinge; this will provide a snug fit without glue, which could hinder the hinge movement.

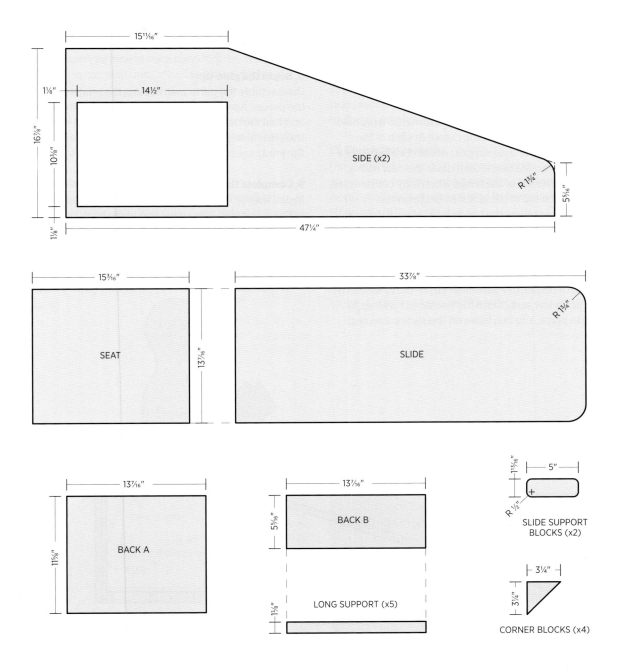

Cutting Diagram

into place. Nail the unfastened parts, clamp the assembly, and let the glue dry. If you have enough clamps, you can glue the corner blocks in place now (one at each corner of the storage compartment), or you can wait until after the assembly dries.

10. Install the slide support blocks.
Mark the position of the slide support blocks so their top edges are on the closing line of the slide. Glue and clamp the blocks in place, and let the glue dry.

11. Add the slide cables.
Install two eye screws on the upper inside face of the slide panel, ⅜" in from each side edge. With a helper holding the slide open just beyond the vertical position, thread a cable through both eye screws on one side, and secure and trim the ends so the cable is taut. Repeat on the remaining side, making sure the cables are equally taut when the slide is resting in the open position. For safety, wrap the cut ends of the cables with tape if they are exposed.

12. Complete the tunnel.
Measure the top and bottom of the tunnel area, and cut hardboard pieces to fit. Holding these in place, measure the sides, and cut hardboard pieces to fit. Glue the hardboard in place with the smooth faces exposed — top and bottom first, then side pieces. Clamp the pieces, using wood blocks as needed for uniform pressure. Let the glue dry.

13. Finish the project.
Use a nail set to set all nail heads slightly below the surface. Sand all surfaces smooth, rounding over any rough or splintery edges. Apply the finish of your choice. In the project shown, the finish is Hope's 100% Tung Oil.

Note: You can line the floor of the tunnel with a custom-cut piece of textured mat, such as a thick yoga mat (textures aid in sensory development). Cut the mat to fit, and secure it with self-adhesive Velcro tabs, or leave it unsecured, as desired. You can also install a lock to keep the lid secured for safety.

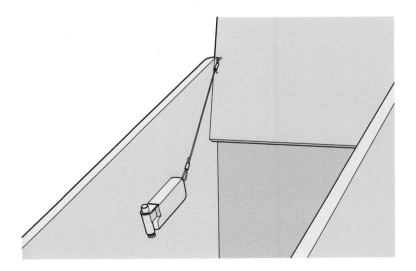

Slide Support Detail

Shop Tip

Spline Joints
For her original prototype of this piece, the designer used ¾"-wide hardboard splines for the joints between the seat and sides, between the back and sides, and between the back-panel pieces. If you know how to make spline joints, this is a desirable option. A glued spline joint is stronger than a glued and nailed butt joint, and splines mean there aren't any nail holes in the exposed surfaces.

Bamboo Ply Wall Unit

Designed by Todd Ouwehand

For anyone unfamiliar with bamboo plywood, this piece is perhaps the best introduction you could ever get. One look speaks volumes about the beauty and versatility of this new breed of sheet material. It's pricey, for sure, but if you're looking for a fine finished product, it's definitely worth consideration.

Now, about this wall unit: it's actually three freestanding pieces set close together to give the illusion of a built-in — and also allowing the designer to build in his studio instead of on-site. Created for a private client, the unit serves as a computer work station, media and storage cabinet, serving counter, and display case. The center credenza and right-side sections have enclosed storage areas with shelves, while the left-side section houses two drawers and a pull-out shelf for a laptop. Clearly, this is a furniture maker's piece — in both design and construction — and it's loaded with nice details, like zebrawood veneer, double laminations (some with full panels, some with material-thrifty strips), walnut elements, and little step-backs (with the vertical panels, doors, and drawers) for added depth and interest.

MATERIALS

- ☐ Seven 4 x 8-foot sheets ¾" bamboo plywood
- ☐ ½" Baltic birch plywood (for spline joints)
- ☐ ¾" Baltic birch plywood (for doors and drawer fronts)
- ☐ ¼" alder plywood (for drawer bottoms)
- ☐ 4/4 cherry lumber (for drawer boxes)
- ☐ 4/4 walnut lumber (for details)
- ☐ Approx. 50 sq. feet zebrawood veneer
- ☐ Biscuits (for joinery)
- ☐ Finish materials (see step 6)
- ☐ Two pairs drawer slides
- ☐ Keyboard slide
- ☐ Two pairs self-closing cabinet hinges
- ☐ Shelf pins

TOOLS

- ☐ Table saw
- ☐ Veneer press
- ☐ Router with bits and edge guide
- ☐ Clamping straightedge guide
- ☐ Biscuit joiner
- ☐ Clamps
- ☐ Chisels
- ☐ Drill with bit set
- ☐ Drill press

Note: This project is suitable for those with advanced woodworking skills and materials experience. The instructions here provide an overview for building the unit as shown. However, given that the unit functions as a built-in, you'll likely want to modify the dimensions of one or more pieces to suit your needs and space.

1. Prepare the laminated panels.

Most of the parts for the wall unit are laminated together into double-thick panels or, where practical, are given the illusion of being double-thick with the addition of a 3"-wide strip along the underside of the leading edge (see note below).

Following the cutting list below, rough-cut the parts ¼" oversize as noted, then trim them to final dimension after lamination. Cut out the parts on a table saw, using the fence and a crosscut sled to ensure square cuts.

- 4 inner shelf-unit uprights at 14" x 36"
- 4 outer shelf-unit uprights at 14" x 44"
- 4 top shelves at 14" x 28"
- 12 cabinet sides at 22" x 32"
- 1 credenza top at 22½" x 84"
- 1 credenza bottom at 22½" x 84"
- 2 cabinet tops at 22½" x 36½"
- 2 cabinet bottoms at 22½" x 36½"

Glue up double-thick panels for the inner and outer shelf-unit uprights, top shelves, and cabinet sides in a veneer press (either a cauls-and-clamps type or a vacuum-bag type). Drive at least two nails through each pair in the waste area to keep them aligned while pressing.

The long horizontal surfaces of the built-in (the tops and bottoms of the credenza and shelf-unit cabinets) are made to look double-thick by adding a 3"-wide strip to the underside of the front edge only. Use a few nails for alignment during glue-up, and fill the holes later.

Note: Bamboo plywood has ⅛"-thick outer veneer with a very regular pattern and can therefore be easily built up into wider panels with biscuit joints to minimize waste — a big plus, because the material is very expensive.

2. Cut the remaining panels.

Cut the remaining panels for the primary assembly, following the cutting list below.

- 5 adjustable shelves (including keyboard tray) at 14" x 22"
- 2 credenza shelves at 18½" x 22"
- 1 credenza shelf at 18½" x 21½"
- 2 credenza internal dividers at 18¾" x 21"

3. Prepare the panel joints.

The panel joints use full-length concealed splines made of ½" Baltic birch plywood set into dadoes that are cut with a handheld router. Use a router and edge guide to create a centered dado that's ½" wide and ⅜" deep on the ends of the panels, and use a 90-degree clamping straightedge guide to cut dadoes ½" wide and ¼" deep across the faces of the panels. Stop the cuts about 1" from the front edges, but cut through the back edges.

4. Assemble the cases.

Assemble the cases one panel at a time, being careful to ensure square joints. First assemble the lower cabinets and upper shelf units, then join the two assemblies together. The credenza has two internal vertical dividers that must be glued up before you can attach the top; see the front view of the credenza in the plan drawings. Also, notch the cabinet sides on the upper front corner to allow for the ¾" x 3" front edge treatment.

After the cabinets are assembled, use a router with a rabbeting bit to cut recesses to receive the back panels. Square the corners of the rabbets with a chisel. Use a portable drill and a shop-made drill guide (see Making a Drilling Guide, page 300) to drill the holes for the adjustable shelves in the upper shelf units and inside the credenza.

5. Build the doors and drawers.

The doors and drawer fronts are veneered with zebrawood on ¾"-thick Baltic birch plywood substrate, edge-banded with ⅛"-thick walnut. Veneer both sides with the same material in order to keep the panels flat and stable. Typically, the striped pattern of the zebrawood looks best when slip-matched.

Make the three sliding doors for the credenza individually. The two hinged doors and drawer fronts can be cut from a single panel after it has been veneered. Cut the parts to size and apply the solid-wood edge banding. Trim the banding flush with a router and flush-trimming bit. Rout full-length dadoes ¼" wide and ¼" deep in the doors and drawer fronts to receive the integrated pulls that mimic the zebrawood stripes. Make these out of walnut and size them to protrude ⅝ to ¾" so they are easy to grasp and pull.

Build separate drawer boxes out of solid cherry, utilizing drawer lock joints cut on a table saw and ¼" plywood bottoms, and attach the fronts with screws. Mount the finished drawers to

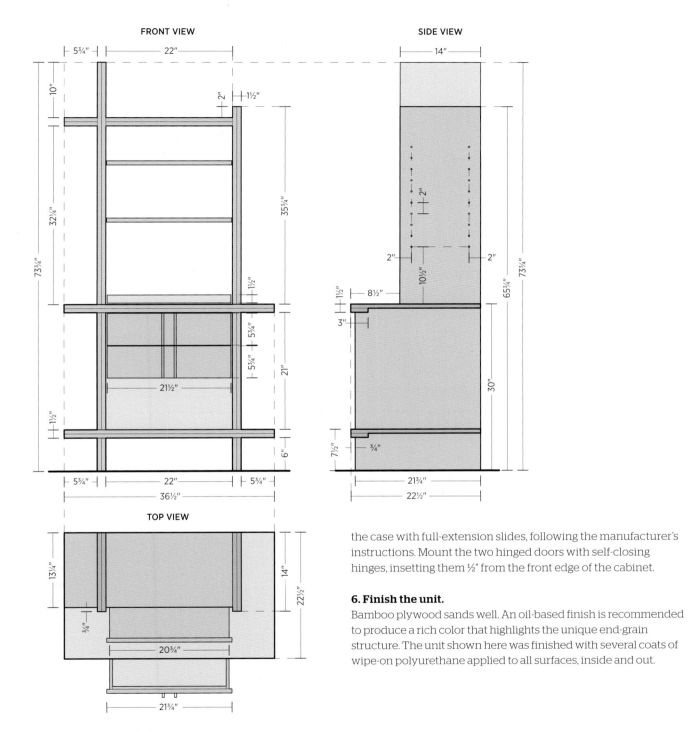

FRONT VIEW

SIDE VIEW

TOP VIEW

Shelf Unit Plans

the case with full-extension slides, following the manufacturer's instructions. Mount the two hinged doors with self-closing hinges, insetting them ½" from the front edge of the cabinet.

6. Finish the unit.

Bamboo plywood sands well. An oil-based finish is recommended to produce a rich color that highlights the unique end-grain structure. The unit shown here was finished with several coats of wipe-on polyurethane applied to all surfaces, inside and out.

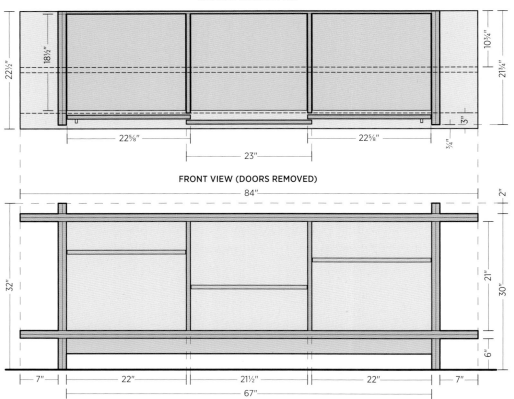

SECTION THROUGH TOP

FRONT VIEW (DOORS REMOVED)

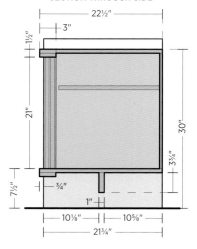

SECTION THROUGH SIDE

Credenza Plan

Shop Tip

Making a Drilling Guide

The shop-made drilling guide for the Bamboo Ply Wall Unit's shelf pin holes is best made with hardwood stock of an appropriate width and length for the number of holes required. Cut the piece about 2" thick, and drill the holes on a drill press so they are precisely spaced, aligned, and square. Trim the bottom end so the first hole in the guide is at the desired height for the lowest shelf, with the guide referenced to the location of the cabinet bottom. Clamp the guide to the panel to be drilled, and use a portable drill with a stop on the bit. The thickness of the guide will ensure straight holes.

Cornhole to Go

Designed by Mark Bradley

For those of you who don't know about cornhole yet, the designer of this customized set explains the game: "Cornhole is a fun lawn game, similar to horseshoes, only portable and safer for kids. In essence, you toss beanbags at a target some 30 feet away. Each target is roughly 2 by 4 feet with a 6"-diameter hole near the top end, which is slightly elevated by short legs. Players toss four bags per round. A bag on the target scores one point; a bag through the hole scores three."

At his family's request, the designer made this set, based on the standard design — with upgrades, of course (master woodworkers don't build standard versions of *anything*). The result is a complete game set that's not only better looking than any you're likely to find, it's also more portable.

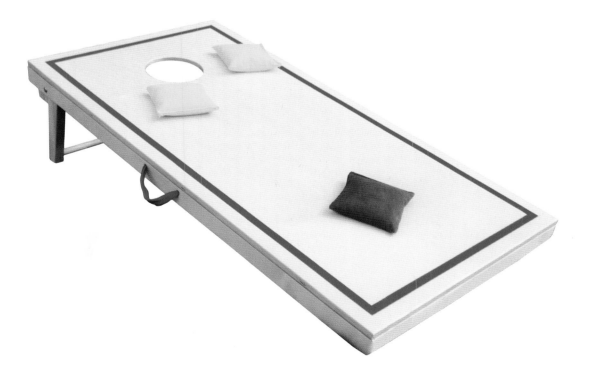

MATERIALS

- One 5 x 5-foot sheet ⅝" Baltic birch plywood
- Wood glue
- Fifty-two #10 biscuits (for joinery)
- One 42" (or longer) length 2 x 4 lumber (free of large knots and splits)
- Eight 2" coarse-thread drywall screws
- Four ¼" x 2½" carriage bolts
- Four ¼" washers (1¼" outside diam.)
- One 48" length ¾"-diam. wood dowel
- Four 1¼" coarse-thread drywall screws
- Two 2¾" draw hasps
- Four landscape staples
- Finish materials (as desired)
- Four ¼" standard washers
- Four ¼" nylon-insert lock nuts
- Eight 1" coarse-thread drywall screws
- One 36" length 1" tubular webbing

TOOLS

- Circular saw
- Compass
- Drill with:
  - ³⁄₃₂" straight bit
  - ⅛" straight bit
  - ³⁄₁₆" straight bit
  - ¼" straight bit
  - ⅜" straight bit
  - ½" straight bit
  - ¾" spade bit
- Jigsaw
- Sandpaper (80- to 150-grit, plus 320-grit for clear finishes)
- Router with:
  - ⅛" rabbeting bit
  - ⅛" roundover bit
- Miter saw
- Biscuit joiner
- Clamps
- Square
- Belt sander with 50-grit belt
- Nickel (coin)
- 6-foot straightedge
- Wire cutters
- Adjustable wrench
- Hammer

CUTTING LIST

Part	Quantity	Material	Width	Length
Top	2	⅝" Baltic birch plywood	23¾"	47¾"
Side	4	⅝" Baltic birch plywood	1⅞"	47¾"
Side	4	⅝" Baltic birch plywood	1⅞"	47¾"
End	4	⅝" Baltic birch plywood	1⅞"	23⅞"
Staple blocks	4	⅝" Baltic birch plywood	1½"	4"
Corner blocks	4	2 x 4	3½"	3½"
Legs	4	2 x 4	2 to 1¼"	13"

1. Cut the tops and sides.

Cut the full 5 x 5-foot plywood panel in half along the direction of the grain. From each half, rip three pieces at 1⅞" wide along the direction of the grain; these will become the sides and ends — leave them long for now. Finally, cut the two tops to width and length, following the cutting list. Save the scrap for use as test pieces later.

2. Cut the holes in the tops.

Mark a centerpoint for a target hole in each top, 9" from one short end and centered side to side; see the plan drawing Set a compass to 3" and draw a 6"-diameter circle around the centerpoint. Drill a ⅜" starter hole inside the circle, then carefully cut the hole with the jigsaw. Smooth the cut edge of the hole with 80-grit paper.

3. Rabbet the sides and ends.

The top outside edge of the side and end pieces get a ⅛" x ⅛" rabbet; see detail A drawing on page 304. The rabbet makes an otherwise difficult joint much more forgiving of slight imperfections, and it accents the beautiful laminations on the edges of the Baltic birch plywood tops.

Using a router and ⅛" rabbeting bit, set the depth for ⅛" and run some test cuts. Then rabbet one square corner from the top outside edge of each side and end piece.

4. Miter the sides and ends.

Set your miter saw to 45 degrees on the right. With the workpiece flat against the saw's back fence (good side out, rabbet up), cut the right-side miters of all the side pieces. Measuring from the long point, mark the length of each side piece and add ¹⁄₁₆". Reset the miter saw to the left and cut the side pieces to length. Repeat the process to miter and trim the end pieces to length. Save the scrap for test pieces.

5. Lay out the biscuit centers.

Biscuits are used for assembling the sides, ends, and top, affording a clean look overall and considerable lateral strength for the sides, which ultimately must carry the weight of each target (about 22 pounds) during transport.

You'll mark the biscuit centers on the top (rabbeted) edge of the side and end pieces, measuring from the long point of the miter. On the side pieces, mark the following distances: 2", 8¼", 14½", and 20¾", first from one end and then from the other. On the end piece, mark the following distances: 2", 7", and 12", first from one end and then the other.

TOP VIEW

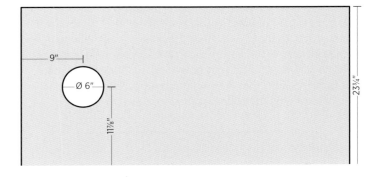

SECTION VIEW

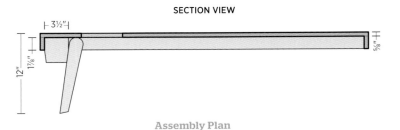

Assembly Plan

6. Cut the biscuit slots in the side and end pieces.

Study the top edge of a side piece: there should be roughly ½" left, as you removed ⅛" with the rabbet. Set the biscuit joiner to cut for a #10 biscuit. The maximum depth should be about ⁷/₁₆".

Set the fence on the biscuit joiner so that the slot cut is centered in the material that remains in the top edge of the side piece; see detail A drawing, below. Practice on a scrap piece and adjust the fence until you get it just right. Clamp one piece at a time, facedown on a work surface, slightly overhanging the edge. Center the biscuit joiner on the marks you made in step 5, and cut each slot.

7. Cut the biscuit slots in the back of the top pieces.

These cuts require folding back or removing (on older models) the fence on the biscuit joiner. The slots will be cut vertically with the biscuit joiner facedown, so the fence would be in the way. You will index the joiner by clamping an edge or side piece onto the back of the top.

The marks made in step 5 will show you where to cut the mating slots. The trick is to know how far from the edge to clamp the piece: Using a reserved scrap top piece, try clamping one of the reserved scrap side pieces parallel to the edge but inset ¾" from the edge. Cut a test slot on a piece of scrap. Try it out with a biscuit and an end or side piece. The idea is to have the plane of the front edge of the side or end in line with the side or end of the top. To achieve this you may have to move the clamped piece in or out slightly. Once you know the exact distance, you can replicate this on the bottom of the actual top pieces.

Clamp the pieces so they lie flat, with the rabbet facing up and the edge with the marks facing out. Be sure to align the side or end piece with the edges of the top piece before you clamp it into place. Use each side and end piece in turn and mark it and its location to ensure proper alignment during assembly later. Cut the biscuits.

8. Fine-tune the miters.

Using dry biscuits (no glue yet), test-fit each side and end piece, and trim the miters as needed until they fit snugly together. Leave the sides and ends in place.

9. Glue the sides and ends to the tops.

Remove one side and its biscuits. Apply enough glue to the sides of the slots in the back of the top so that, when you push the biscuit in, a little glue escapes from each end, but not a lot. Be sure to center the biscuits and push them in, leaving half (⅜") sticking up out of the plywood.

Apply glue to the slots in the side and a modest bead all along the top of the side. Return the side to its proper place, mating glued slots to glued-in biscuits, and clamp the pieces together. The clamps are necessary for only about 30 minutes. Work around the sides and ends of the tops in this fashion, gluing the miters as you go.

10. Prepare the tapered corner blocks.

Using the miter saw, cut two 8" pieces from the 2 x 4 stock. Mark a square line around the blocks 1¾" from each end. On the end grain, mark a rectangle that is ¼" smaller than the sides; see detail B drawing, page 305. Using the belt sander with a 50-grit belt, taper all four sides of each end of both blocks. Finally, cut the corner blocks to length at 3½", yielding four blocks with one square end and one tapered end.

11. Make the legs.

Using the miter saw, cut two 13" pieces from the 2 x 4 stock; each of these will become two legs. The legs taper from 2" at one end to 1¼" at the other; see detail B drawing.

Mark each end of each piece at 1¼" in from the side, measuring from opposing sides at each end. Set the compass to 1". Center the compass in a corner of a leg piece, and mark a 2"-diameter semicircle that touches the end and one adjacent side of the stock, as shown in detail B drawing. Draw a straight line from the

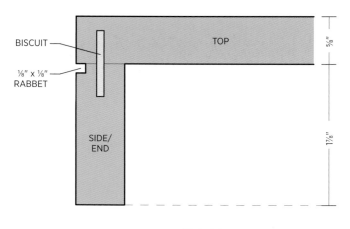

BISCUIT

⅛" x ⅛"
RABBET

SIDE/
END

TOP

⅝"

1⅞"

Detail A

edge of the semicircle to the 1¼" marking at the opposing end of the piece. Repeat to mark the other leg to be cut from the board, and mark the other board in the same way.

Carefully cut out the legs with the jigsaw, and then use the belt sander to smooth your cuts. Mark the center of the semicircle on the opposite face of each leg, to match the first centerpoint. Using a ¼" bit, drill halfway through the leg at this mark. Turn the leg over and complete the hole, starting from the other mark. They should meet in the center and allow you to drill all the way through.

12. Round over all the edges.
Using the router and a ⅛" roundover bit, round over the exposed edges on the target units, plus the edges of the corner blocks and legs; see detail C drawing, below right. Leave the vertical (mitered) corners between the sides and ends square so that the plywood laminations don't show.

13. Attach the corner blocks.
The corner blocks are installed in the inside corners at the upper end of each target, with their square ends flush against the side and end pieces, as shown in the section drawing. Drill pilot holes, and install each block with glue and two 2" drywall screws driven through the block and into the plywood sides. Each target gets two corner blocks.

14. Temporarily mount the legs.
With the target units upside down on a work surface, position a leg against a side piece, aligned with the tapered edge of a corner block. Place a nickel under the leg's semicircular end, to hold it ⅛" off the top piece, which will allow it to pivot without binding. Clamp the leg in place and drill a ¼" hole through the leg and the plywood side. Use a scrap block on the inner face of the side to minimize tearout. Mark this leg and its mated side to indicate that they are matched.

Remove the nickel, and partially insert a carriage bolt through the hole from the outside, placing an oversized washer between the side and the leg; don't drive the bolt home just yet. Repeat these steps for the other legs on each target unit.

15. Cut the legs to length.
Pivot each leg up until it stops on the corner block in the fully open position. On the inside of the leg, measuring from the back of the top, make a mark at 11⅜". Rest one end of the 6-foot straightedge on the front end piece and move the other end up or down until it intersects the mark on the leg. Draw the line described by the straightedge on the inside of the leg. Slide the leg off the bolt, match this angle on the miter saw, and cut the leg. Do the same for the other legs.

16. Connect the legs.
Connecting the legs is a nice touch but isn't absolutely necessary. The advantage is that the two legs move as one. This simplifies setting up and packing up the targets.

Slide the legs back onto their respective bolts on one target unit, in the proper orientation. The oversized washers should be

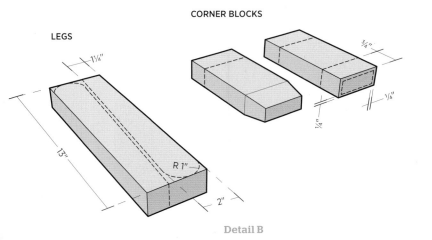

LEGS

CORNER BLOCKS

1¼"

13"

R 1"

2"

¾"

¼"

¼"

Detail B

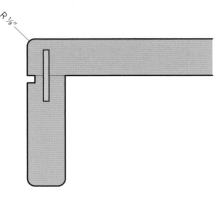

R ⅛"

Detail C

between the legs and the sides. Pivot the legs into their fully open position again. Make a mark on the insides of the legs, 10" above the back of the top. Center this mark across the width of each leg. Push the legs tight against the sides. Measure the distance between the legs near the bolts. Write this distance down. Now slip the legs off again.

Using the ¾" spade bit, drill a hole in each leg at the mark you just made. Drill slowly and keep checking the depth of the hole, stopping at 1". Add 2" to the measurement you wrote down. Cut the ¾" dowel to this length. Dry-fit the dowel into both legs and return the legs to their bolts. The whole leg unit must be able to pivot up and (especially) down between the sides. Trim the dowel a little if the leg unit is too wide. Remove the leg unit one last time. Glue the dowel in place.

Clamp the leg unit together on a flat surface. Predrill with a ³/₃₂" bit through the 1½" side of the leg, through the side of the dowel, and back into the leg on the other side of the ¾" hole. Drive a 1¼" drywall screw into the predrilled hole.

Repeat the process to join the legs for the other target unit.

17. Connect the two target units.

The corner blocks should allow the two units to index into each other, back to back. If they don't, modify the blocks with the belt sander as needed. Mount the draw hasps — centered on the ends — to hold the units together tightly. Attach the longer portion of the draw hasp on the end with the legs, so it won't hit the ground during play.

18. Bore the holes for the webbing handles.

With the hasps holding the units together, choose one side to locate the holes for the webbing handles. Each target unit gets one handle. You will be drilling four holes, two on each target unit, about 4½" apart, and as a pair centered on each end. Drill pilot holes with the ³/₃₂" bit. Open the units up and drill the holes with a ⅜" bit, drilling in turn from each side and meeting in the center to prevent tearout. Finally, countersink both sides of each hole with the ½" bit.

19. Make blocks for the landscape staples.

To prevent the targets from migrating backward during play, each unit gets two landscaping staples located at the inside front end. The staples are secured with two small mounting blocks in each target unit; see detail D drawing, at right.

Cut the four mounting blocks to size at 1½" x 4" from scrap plywood. Measure the distance between the sides of a landscape staple, and mark this on the backs of the blocks. Set your circular saw depth to match the thickness of the staples. Score the back of each block so the kerfs will capture the staple. Using wire cutters, cut each staple to 3½" in length.

20. Sand and finish the targets.

Remove the draw hasps and sand all the wood surfaces with 150-grit paper. If desired, paint a border on the top of each target, as shown in the unit here. Finish the pieces with a durable, exterior-rated clearcoat. The unit here was painted and then finished with three coats of spar urethane.

21. Assemble the targets

After the finish has cured, remount the leg units. Remember to place a large washer between each leg and the adjacent side. Drive the carriage bolts home with a hammer, and secure them with the small washers and lock nuts. Using 1" drywall screws, mount the blocks and landscape staples to the inside front end, no more than about 2½" from each corner.

Cut the webbing in half, and thread it through the holes. Tie knots on the inside, leaving adequate slack to accommodate your hand. Remount the draw hasps.

Make your own beanbags, or order a set online, and start perfecting your game!

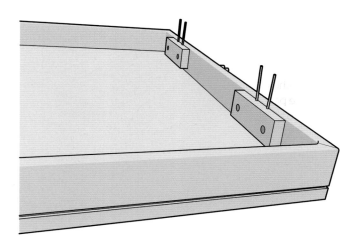

Detail D

Plywood as . . .

*A showcase of inspired pieces and
the stories behind them*

. . . civil disobedience

Tank Man

by Brian Gillis

Created in fall 2010 for an exhibition titled "On Disobedience, Abstraction, and the Opposable Thumb" at the Kirkland Art Center Gallery in Kirkland, Washington, *Tank Man* marks the Tiananmen Square Massacre of 1989. It is a testament to the unknown man who had the audacity to break through the crowds and stand in front of a column of army tanks in mid-victory procession. The now-iconic image of this man has become emblematic not only of the struggle at Tiananmen Square but also of that distinctly human capability of using resistance to demand equity.

My design objective was to use elements of mass production and references to mass media to examine the role of journalism in society as something that informs us of who we are and as an invaluable branch of government in and of itself. As such, it was important for me to use methods and materials that are both common and directly linked to industry and/or mass production.

The element with perhaps the greatest impact in this piece is a 1:3 model of a Type 59 Chinese army tank, the same tank used in the Tiananmen Square victory procession. With the help of a dedicated production team, I rendered a digital model using Rhinoceros (a CAD program) and developed machine operations for a flatbed CNC router to cut the files from ¾" sheets of shop-grade poplar plywood.

Once 80 sheets of plywood were cut and organized, we used an elaborate peg system to register the parts and screw them together into ten 6"-thick sections. Each section was drawn together with threaded rod to hold them in compression, and plywood end caps hide the inner workings. The tank is roughly 12 feet long, 5 feet wide, and 4 feet tall, weighing upward of 700 pounds, and it rolls like a dream on 20 heavy-duty swivel casters. For exhibition, it was engulfed in the armature of a massive billboard.

Contributor Bios

JENNIFER ANDERSON
Doggie Dwelling (page 262)

Jennifer spent two years studying fine woodworking with James Krenov at the College of the Redwoods before earning her MFA in woodworking and furniture design at San Diego State University with Wendy Maruyama. Currently, Jennifer divides her time between teaching design and woodworking classes and building speculative and commission pieces of furniture. Her furniture has been exhibited nationally and internationally and has been featured in a variety of publications, including *Interior Design*, *American Craft*, and *Woodwork Magazine.*

www.jenniferandersonstudio.com

DIETER AMICK
Chalk Back (page 126)

Dieter grew up in Washington State and was interested in design from an early age. He currently is pursuing a degree in industrial design at Western Washington University. Through his studies, Dieter has developed a passion for working and communicating with others to create innovative design solutions that change the way we interact with the world.

www.dankedieter.com

SASCHA AYAD
Mudroom Organizer (page 201)

Sascha is a cabinetmaker with 13 years of experience in commercial casework and store fixtures. He is owner of Boulder Mills, Inc., a custom furniture, cabinetry, and millwork shop in Colorado.

www.bouldermills.com

KATHERINE BELSEY
Type A Coffee Table (page 54)
Light Headboard (page 236)

Katherine has a background in film, writing, and design. She grew up in Switzerland, on the shores of Lake Geneva. Her broad range of studies has included visual arts at the College Voltaire in Geneva, a BA in creative writing from Brown University, and a variety of classes at the Rhode Island School of Design and the DAVI film school in Switzerland. She worked for several years for Woody Allen in New York before retiring from the film business to look after her two sons. When her five-year-old asked her to build a house, she designed one that folded away for storage: a pop-up house. Katherine has also designed and made furniture, light fixtures, clothing, cosmetics, and a sound studio for her husband, John Davis, a film music composer and mixer. She is currently working on a manual, "Make Anything," a handbook for saving money, living green, and having fun with trash.

www.makepopupcards.com
www.makeanything.net

DAN BILLER
File Cabinet Cap (page 244)

Dan has a background in the construction supply trade and currently is a principal in Agristrand Biocomposites, a soy board manufacturing company. He has been married for 30 years to his wife, Helen, and enjoys spending time with family and friends at his lake home and volunteering his time and meager woodworking talents with his church and Habitat for Humanity. Dan will always be looking for new and innovative ways to utilize "scrap," of which he has a seemingly endless supply.

BETH BLAIR
Revue Magazine Table (page 152)

Beth is an industrial designer living in Seattle, Washington. After enjoying a delightful childhood in rural southern Idaho, Beth moved westward and eventually earned a BA in philosophy from Whitman College in Walla Walla as well as a BS in industrial design from Western Washington University in Bellingham. When she isn't scheming up new furniture concepts and designs, she can be found zooming around the streets of Seattle on her vintage green Vespa.

bethblair@gmail.com

HENRY BOYLE
RTA Desk (page 26)

Henry was born in Orange County, California, in 1956, at the peak of the age of modern design. Having watched him build freeways out of wooden blocks, Henry's parents gave him a Euclidean puzzle toy, which stretched his mind in the direction that ultimately inspired his contribution for this book. An industrial designer by training, Henry's early professional experience includes full-time work in factories, creating everything from furniture to electric guitars. He designs products based largely on the experience people will have using them, and their sustainable existence. He holds a BFA in industrial design from the Rhode Island School of Design (RISD) and works and resides in the San Francisco Bay area.

boyleworks@comcast.net
www.creativeshake.com/boyleworks

MARK BRADLEY
Cornhole to Go (page 301)
Mark lives with his wife and daughter in Boulder, Colorado. He has worked as a carpenter for over 20 years, specializing in finish carpentry and custom built-ins.
www.cottonwoodcabinetry.com

FAWN BROKAW
Alliance Table (page 62)
Fawn is a product designer and maker by trade. Her business, FawnRay Designs, aims to equip people with clever, hand-crafted home wares and accessories. Fawn's designs are influenced by her experiences of growing up in the secluded woods of western New York State, studying furniture design in Denmark, and sustainable product design. The Eameses, along with Arne Jacobson and Alvar Aalto, sparked her passion for plywood as an economical, honest, and friendly material that is accessible to nearly everyone. Fawn would like to thank her mom and Brady Doyle for always supporting her design endeavors.
www.fawnraydesigns.etsy.com
www.fawnraydesigns.blogspot.com

GREG BUGEL
Symbiosis Chair (page 122)
Greg is a Brooklyn, New York–based architectural designer with a keen interest in craftsmanship and a cradle-to-grave design approach.

SHAWN CALVIN
Sliding Mirror Shelves (page 206)
Shawn holds a bachelor's degree from the University of Michigan with a concentration in graphic and product design and is currently working toward a master's in interior architecture at Lawrence Technological University. From a young age, Shawn was surrounded by entrepreneurs: her grandfather, William Calvin, was a master wood craftsman, and her mother developed a children's play mat called "Canvas City" for toy cars. Shawn has designed many products with the overall goal of accessibility. She feels that every product should showcase simple elements and encourage an ease for use, as well as sustainability. In an effort toward sustainable practice, she tries to incorporate the use of reclaimed and repurposed materials.

SPIKE CARLSEN
Bowlegged Plant Stand (page 89)
Spike is an editor, author, carpenter, and woodworker who has been immersed in the world of wood and woodworking for over 30 years. He is the former executive editor of *Family Handyman* magazine and the author of *A Splintered History of Wood* (HarperCollins), *Ridiculously Simple Furniture Projects* (Linden), and *Woodworking FAQ* (Storey). He currently is the projects editor for *FreshHome* magazine and serves on the advisory board for *Men's Health* magazine. Prior to becoming an editor, Spike worked as a carpenter for 15 years and ran his own construction and remodeling company. He and his wife, Kat, have five adult children and live in historic Stillwater, Minnesota.
www.asplinteredhistoryofwood.com

ADELE CUARTELON
Indoor Doghouse (page 254)
Born and raised in Dallas, Texas, Adele has worked with MESA Design Group in the Urban Design/Planning Studio and with morrisonseifertmurphy, working for interior designers and architects on hospitality design projects. She holds a bachelor's degree in architecture from the University of Texas at Arlington and is currently attending the School of the Art Institute of Chicago (SAIC) for a master's degree in architecture, with an emphasis on interior architecture. She lives in Chicago with her husband, James, and their dog, Max. Adele would like to thank Billy Batac for his wonderful photographs of Max's house.

STEVEN DE LANNOY
Children's Chair (page 136)
Stephen claims to be far from a professional carpenter and therefore the ideal for this book, because he's living proof that you can do this, too! On weekdays, Steven works in an office and wears a suit, but in his spare time he likes to design and build a wide variety of things, of which the Children's Chair is just one example. You can see more of his projects at the website below. Drop him a line if you made the chair yourself or if you have any questions.
www.instructables.com/member/bertus52x11

STEFFANIE DOTSON
Eclipse Coffee Table (page 84)
Steffanie is a studio furniture maker and educator living in San Diego, California. Her passion for making objects stems from a desire to fuse function and splendor with everyday items.
www.steffaniedotson.com

BRIAN DUBOIS
Cantilever Table (page 80)
TAB-1 Chair (page 108)
Brian's work and experience range from architecture, design/build, and model building to exhibit engineering and furniture. He earned his five-year professional BA in architecture in 1999 at the University of Detroit Mercy, and in 2011 he received his MFA in product/furniture design from Cranbrook Academy of Art.
www.237amstudios.com

JAMES A. DYCK, AIA, LEED AP
Tot Cart & Cradle (page 267)

Jim is an architect, a certified Montessori teacher, and a LEED Accredited Professional. Most of his design activities are directed by his interest in children, learning, and the effects of the built environment on learning. In addition to publishing numerous articles and presenting at national and international conferences, Jim has received national recognition for his designs for learning environments. Some of his most rewarding experiences have been designing and building for his own children.
www.taparch.com

GAVIN ENGEL
Angle Shelf (page 172)

Gavin is an industrial design student at the Rhode Island School of Design (RISD). He entered RISD with a fine arts portfolio but was drawn to ID because it offers a practical and exciting blend of hands-on fabrication skills, problem solving, and creative design thinking. He enjoys woodworking and furniture making as hobbies but would like to focus his future work on attacking social and environmental problems with creative design ideas. Outside the design world, Gavin enjoys playing tennis and basketball and watching movies.

BRIAN EVERETT
Birch Ply Dining Table (page 45)

Brian is an industrial designer, graphic designer, and photographer who creates, among other things, products for the housewares, organization, décor, and gift industries. In his spare time, Brian focuses on his personal design business, EVRT Studio, through which he has designed several pieces of wall art for CB2, as well as his own line of wall art (available through various online retailers). He hopes to develop his own product line under the EVRT Studio brand name, turning it into a full-time career.
www.evrtstudio.com

STEVEN EWOLDT
modBOX 2010 (page 286)

Steve is a practicing architect and adjunct professor in Portland, Oregon. In addition to being the founder and principal architect of artifekt architecture + interiors, Steve runs a personal "idea mill," designing and producing sustainable custom furniture, which has now become a functioning division called artifekt BUILDS. Steve is joined by Joseph Bashaw, a Portland-based architectural designer and cofounder of artifekt BUILDS, who specializes in high-end residential projects and custom furniture design. Together they approach all design with human interaction in mind: He believes that touch is paramount in the engaging of architecture, and furniture is the most immediate channel to touch our built environments.
www.artifekt.com

LARRY FINN
Peninsula Workstation (page 48)
Cantilevered Shelves (page 208)

Larry recalls that his first major woodworking project was a coffin with a glass window in the lid, which he built in his late teens when he was working as a monster-makeup artist. His coffin and Count Dracula outfit won a state contest. Larry spent three years in Germany with the U.S. Army Corps of Engineers before moving with his German wife to Colorado. There the couple has bought and remodeled a number of homes. A lifelong innovator, Larry has always leaned toward fun, custom, hands-on work (just like you).

CEZARY GAJEWSKI
Florence Table (page 23)

Cezary (MFA, MDes) is an associate professor of industrial design and currently resides in Alberta, Canada. He is interested in the application of computer-aided design (CAD) and computer-aided manufacturing (CAM) and their capabilities in enhancing and altering the design process for the modern designer. Entwining technological and traditional methodologies throughout the design process, he emphasizes the designer's central role from sketch to prototype. Using the most innovative computer programs and technology available, Cezary aims to seamlessly integrate hardware and software components of human-computer interaction systems.

RACHEL GANT
Stacked Box (page 156)
Laptop Stand (page 180)

Rachel feels that much of her work reflects her nostalgia for growing up in North Carolina and her strong attachment to the exploration of nature. She strives for a visually minimal and dynamic form, at once simple in construction and lines, yet moving the eye and challenging the state of balance without breaking. The consideration of product life cycles and respect for the systematic and delicate flow of the natural world are extremely influential in her work. Rachel currently studies industrial design at the California College of the Arts (CCA) in San Francisco and previously spent three years as an architecture major at California Polytechnic State University in San Luis Obispo.
www.woodengold.com

BRIAN GILLIS

Tank Man (page 307)

Brian is an artist and educator who lives and works in Eugene, Oregon. Central to his work is the use of atypical processes and storytelling strategies to excavate and chronicle stories that may have fallen on deaf ears, are socially relevant, and have the ability to be personal on a variety of levels. He holds bachelor's degrees in art education and studio art from Humboldt State University and an MFA from NYSCC at Alfred University. Brian currently is an assistant professor of art at the University of Oregon.

www.gillislab.com

BARNABY GUNNING

8 x 4 = 2 Tables (page 31)

Barnaby is principal of Barnaby Gunning Architects, a multidisciplinary practice combining architecture, product design, and 3D-related programming and scripting. He trained under Peter Cook at the Bartlett School of Architecture and has worked in the offices of Renzo Piano, Norman Foster, Atelier One, and Ron Arad. Barnaby's furniture designs have twice been finalists in the *Architects' Journal* "Something to Sit On" competition and have been shortlisted in designboom's premio vico magistretti competition.

www.barnabygunningcom

KRISTIN HARE

Bespoke Chair (page 150)

Kristin graduated from the Georgia Institute of Technology in May 2012 with a major in industrial design and a minor in Spanish. She is interested in furniture and product design. In her free time, Kristin enjoys making pottery and stained glass.

kristin.j.hare@gmail.com

CARL HARRIS

Book of Plies (page 225)

Born in South Wales, UK, Carl studied furniture design at Loughborough University. During that time, he sold the rights to a furniture range he created to NEXT PLC. After traveling to South Africa to work with local artists and teach at schools across township areas, he worked at MJH Architects in Wales before being accepted into the master's program at Design Academy Eindhoven, in 2008. As a designer, Carl is passionate about creating better human-based solutions while constantly striving to question the reason for objects and their impact on daily lives.

www.studiocarlharris.com

CHRIS HEICHEL

Bug Stool (page 118)

Chris currently is an industrial design student at the University of Kansas. He describes his approach to design as user-centered — always keeping the end user in mind. He also strives to include different materials in his designs to enhance the overall design itself.

PHILIPP HERBERT

Candleholders (page 228)
Propeller Bowl (page 252)

Born in 1986, Philipp grew up in southern Germany. He earned a bachelor's degree in transportation interior design from Reutlingen University, during which he completed internships at Opel (GM) and John Deere, designing parts for vehicle interiors. He is currently working toward a master of arts in TID and hopes to work as a professional designer with a car company. He could also imagine working for a furniture designer for a time. Philipp loves to work with wood and is fascinated by the fact that you can give it almost any shape if you use the right technique for the right wood. He can be reached by e-mail.

philipp.herbert@gmx.net

BRIAN HINZ

Striated Ply Table (page 59)

Brian is a master's graduate from the University of Detroit Mercy and currently is working toward licensure in architecture. In his free time, he enjoys designing and constructing furniture.

www.brianhinz.org

WILL HOLMAN

Rubber Hose Chair (page 139)

Will is a designer and writer from Towson, Maryland. He received a degree in architecture from Virginia Tech and completed the postgraduate outreach program at the Rural Studio in Hale County, Alabama. You can see his work and contact him for custom commissions at his website.

www.wholman.com

CHAD KELLY

Mind the Gap Table (page 68)
Pinstriped Console (page 168)

Chad Kelly lives in Austin, Texas, and owns Baldmanmod Design. He has been creating modern furniture, lighting, and other woody decor for several years, specializing in plywood and bentwood laminations. For more information and pictures of additional work, visit his website (below) or contact Chad at baldmanmod@gmail.com. Chad Kelly is also bald.

www.baldmanmod.com

SEAN KELLY

Sto#2 (page 112)

Sean is a native Northwesterner living and designing in Portland, Oregon. As a child, he loved to draw spaceships and creatures. That love led to studying art and architecture as an adult before he finally found a happy medium: product design. In 2011, Sean received a BFA in product design from the University of Oregon. His furniture designs are playful in use and function, with an emphasis in creating unique interactions between user and object. He draws inspiration from the ever-changing relationships between people and their environments, and his designs all have a similar focus on community, using objects to inspire social interactions between users.

MATT KENNEDY, PORT RHOMBUS DESIGN
Paint Chip Modular Bookshelf (page 175)
Matt Kennedy created port rhombus design to create unique, nostalgic objects through a marriage of simple craft methods and technological production.
www.portrhombusdesign.com

JIN KIM
Tea Table (page 93)
Jin originally studied as a painter in her native Korea, where she won numerous awards for her work and was a professor of painting at the Chung-Nam National University. In 2007, Jin came to America to further develop her artistic vision by studying industrial design. She currently works as a furniture designer and lives in Seattle.

PAOLO KORRE
Drunken Monkey (page 182)
Paolo currently is a student at the Institute of Design at the Illinois Institute of Technology, where he is pursuing master of design and MBA degrees. He has spent many years as an industrial designer in Toronto, Ontario, working for a number of product and manufacturing firms. Paolo has a passion for the crafts of fine wood and metalwork but now focuses his attention toward experiential and strategic design.

MAYA LEE
Twinkle Board (page 250)
Originally from Richmond, Virginia, Maya is a graphic designer currently living and working in New York City. She received her BFA from Virginia Commonwealth University and her MFA from the School of Visual Arts. Her goal is to consistently produce meaningful and memorable work no matter what medium. She is also passionate about photography, piano, ping-pong, and kicking back with her beloved Westie, Jemie.
www.mayalee.com

ALEXIS LIU
Flat Pack Stool (page 106)
Originally from the San Francisco Bay area, Alexis moved to New York City at age 17. She received her bachelor's degree in marketing from NYU and worked in the fashion industry for a number of years before pursuing her master's degree in industrial design at Pratt Institute. She is passionate about making, building, and learning new types of craft.
www.alexisliu.com

RYAN MAHAN
Gather (page 196)
Ryan is an industrial designer living in Seattle, Washington. His work focuses on truly understanding the user's needs and the language of form. In addition to design, Ryan focuses on his photography and builds cameras to suit his needs.

JOHN MALINOSKI
Dollhouse (page 261)
John has a BA in studio arts from the State University of New York in Fredonia and an MFA in graphic design from the Rochester Institute of Technology. He teaches graphic

design, design theory, and typography at Virginia Commonwealth University's department of graphic design. Professor Malinoski maintains a steady practice catering to the needs of nonprofits and benevolent businesses and currently teaches in his school's Design Center, an honors studio that works for nonprofit and community organizations. John's design work includes graphic design, typography, exhibition design, furniture, hand puppets, constructions, photographs, poetry, and recontextualized articles of clothing.

HOLLY MANN
Donut Table (page 272)
Holly's Donut Table plan was a collaborative effort with Kerry Mann Sr., an experienced hobby builder who enjoys carpentry and constructing anything from a small piece of furniture to a bed or even a garage. Holly's experience with carpentry is limited, but she enjoys do-it-yourself projects, crafts, sewing, and photography. She works as a writer, web designer, and marketer. Her latest website (below) is geared toward anyone who enjoys making their own items.
www.howtomakeityourself.com

PATRICK MCAFFREY
Three's Company (page 132)
Patrick hails from Denver, Colorado, and studies architecture and product design at the University of Oregon, in Eugene. He has always been fascinated by the harmonious relationship between these two fields of design and is really excited to be able to experiment with that relationship in a place so enamored with sustainable practices and ideas.

BRYCE MOULTON
Capsa (page 158)

Bryce is a student at Western Washington University, studying industrial design with a minor in sustainable design. Bryce, raised in the mountains of central Idaho, surrounded by national forest, feels that Idaho's combination of art and engineering is a perfect fit for his interests and creative mind-set. His goal as a designer is to create products with ease-of-use and greater understandability while also being more sustainable — recycled, recyclable, and repairable.

CHRISTIE MURATA
Kidnetic (page 233)

Christie grew up in Barrington, Illinois, and earned a degree in architecture from Cornell University in Ithaca, New York. It was during college that she got her first taste of international travel, in both the Middle East and Honduras, and she continues her journeys today. Christie raised her children in Denver, Colorado, where, when not making wooden toys, she practiced as a freelance architect and later found her passion with preservation architecture. She worked for many years as a preservation architect for the Landmark Preservation Commission and is presently on the board of Historic Denver, Inc.

REBECCA MUYAL
Tank Table (page 73)

By profession, Rebecca is a registered interior designer working in facilities management in an educational environment. She holds a degree in interior design from Mount Royal College and a BA in interior design from Ryerson University in Toronto, and is currently pursuing a master's in interior design at the University of Manitoba while working full-time in Toronto. Her hobbies, other than sports, are centered in the arts, with acrylic painting currently at the forefront. Bright, vivid colors are the foundation in her paintings; they are a bold statement of life and what life has to offer.
www.rebeccamuyal.ca

CHRISTY OATES
Telephone Book Chair (page 143)

Christy started working in the furniture industry at age five, in her mother's basement upholstery shop in her childhood home. After earning an associate's degree in interior design and working as a kitchen designer, she went back to school and earned her BFA in furniture design from the Minneapolis College of Art and Design, in 2006. Christy graduated with an MFA from the furniture design program at San Diego State University in 2010. She specializes in laser-cut furniture.
www.christyoatesdesign.com

JUSTIN ORTON
Ribbed Bench (page 146)

Justin is an accomplished artist and designer, based in Nashville, Tennessee, who holds a BFA in interior design from Watkins College of Art and Design. Justin balances his time between his family and career. He has a loving wife and son and enjoys spending as much time as he can with them. He is co-owner of Line Design Studio, which focuses on creating renderings and presentation drawings for architects and designers.
www.justinorton.com
www.linedesignstudio.com

TODD OUWEHAND
Bamboo Ply Wall Unit (page 297)

Todd Ouwehand is a designer/craftsman based in Los Angeles who creates unique pieces through a symbiosis of graceful forms and solid functionalism. He works closely with each client to marry their vision with his, while focusing on the harmony of materials, including cherry, lacewood, walnut, and zebrawood. Todd received his MA and BA in art from California State University at Long Beach and is an adjunct professor of woodworking at Cerritos College. Todd's work has been published in the books 500 Tables and 500 Chairs and in three Fine Woodworking publications: Furniture: 102 Contemporary Designs; Design Book Eight: Original Furniture from the World's Finest Craftsmen; and Design Book Five.
www.toddouwehand.com

MARCUS PAPAY
Incurvated (page 102)
Caylee Cruiser (page 280)

Marcus is a furniture designer/maker and artist. His current work responds to the rapid changes in design and how these affect the perceived history of functional objects. By providing a basic function in living environments, his pieces suggest an alternative to the obsessive discarding of material goods in today's society. The driving idea is the bond between user and object that develops through use. His current approach is to reconstruct broken, discarded furniture in unique ways, embracing the history of the once beloved object, as well as retrofitting the damaged structure. Marcus believes that the true beauty in a functional object lies in its use and history.
www.marcuspapay.com

ANNA PARRELLA
store + explore (page 291)

Anna is a student in industrial design at Western Washington University in Bellingham, Washington.

JORIE RUUD
Desk Coverlet (page 230)
A product design student at the University of Oregon, Jorie is particularly interested in furniture and housewares. Her Desk Coverlet is one of the many pieces she made for her first apartment, where she lives with four of her closest friends. Jorie looks forward to continuing in her studies and becoming established in the design industry.

SARA SCHALLIOL-HODGE
Avocado (page 282)
Sara grew up in Georgia with a do-it-yourself attitude that was thoroughly encouraged by her parents. Her love of making led her to the Savannah College of Art and Design, where she received a BFA in Industrial Design. Sara has designed a broad range of products, from furniture and lighting to backpacking coffeemakers and airplane lavatories. Lately she's been into printmaking — exploring themes of production and consumption, the origin of things, and the last frontier, while adding in some kitsch and humor for good measure. Sara spends her free time sawing, sanding, painting, reading, baking, and sewing. She has a great love of cats, chocolate, thrift stores, tea, and good books.
www.saraschalliol.com

JAMES SCHEIFLA
Super Shelves (page 188)
James is a material and product studies major at the University of Oregon's School of Architecture and Allied Arts.

KATHY SCHMIDT
Groovy Headboard (page 240)
Kathy is a stay-at-home mom with a great deal of opinions about how things should look. She is also the wife of this book's author and his collaborator/critic on several of his projects herein. She holds a BA in art history from St. Lawrence University and has worked at the Isabella Stewart Gardner Museum and the Museum of Fine Arts Boston. Claiming to possess no creative ability whatsoever, Kathy is one of those annoying people who sits down to a casual craft project and almost invariably creates a masterpiece.

PHILIP SCHMIDT
Lap Desk (page 40)
Reluctance Sofa Table (page 96)
Light Within (page 216)
Groovy Headboard (page 240)
Repair-a-Chair (page 246)
Jumbo Eames Cards (page 259)
Old-School Skateboard (page 274)
Philip is the author of 18 books (including this one) about houses and the stuff we put in them. He's an ardent fan of good design in everything from skyscrapers to silverware but readily admits that on the day they were handing out artistic talent he spent all of his time waiting in the Good Grammar line.
www.philipschmidt.net

ASHLEY SCHWEBEL
One-Sheet Table & Benches (page 37)
An all-around creative person with a background in architecture, a degree in industrial design, and a keen sense of the world around her, Ashley explains that she deals less in slick and polished computer-generated designs and more in designs that manifest an idea; designs that have a je ne sais qoui feeling about them, often a sculptural one-off rather than mass-produced aesthetic; and designs not necessarily worried about production or marketing, but rather are concerned only with the idea driving the design and the environment in which the idea exists.
www.designwhathaveyou.com

RALPH STAMPONE
Swing Table (page 76)
Ralph graduated from the Rhode Island School of Design (RISD) with a BFA in industrial design. With an emphasis in furniture design, he has experience working in custom metal and wood shops.
www.coroflot.com/ralphstampone

PAUL STEINER
Toolboxes (page 184)
Flywood (page 277)
Paul currently is a technology education teacher at Woodbridge Senior High School in Woodbridge, Virginia. A Virginia Tech graduate, he enjoys woodworking, home improvement, and designing unique and challenging projects for his students. You can reach him by e-mail.
paul@steinerwoodwork.com

NORMAN STUBY
Hardwareless Shelf (page 192)
Norm is a sculptor/fabricator in the business of props, models, and exhibits. He came up with the concept for his Hardwareless Shelf in design school several years ago and finally got around to building it one summer when work was slow.
www.normanstuby.com

LAUREN VON DEHSEN
Chaise (page 100)
Lauren graduated from Carnegie Mellon University in May 2010 with a degree in industrial design and human-computer interaction. As a design student she was given the opportunity to create work as

a means of investigating her curiosities. Therefore, she sees the resulting artifacts not as completed pieces but as unfinished experiments. Currently, Lauren is working as an interaction designer at R/GA in New York, designing web experiences for brands.
www.laurenvondehsen.com

CAMDEN WHITEHEAD
Dyed MDF Storage Cabinet (page 163)
Whitewashed Ply Paneling (page 222)
Camden is an architect in Richmond, Virginia, who has taught at Virginia Commonwealth University's VCUArts for 25 years. His architecture is characterized by work that is sensitive to the site and demonstrates a thoughtful, responsible use of materials. Taking seriously his stewardship of the earth and its resources, he meditates design solutions on a range of scales, from neighborhood planning to furniture design and from houses to additions to watercolors. Along with his wife, Mimi Sadler, Camden practices architecture as Sadler & Whitehead Architects PLC.
www.sadlerandwhitehead.com
www.vcu.edu/arts/interiordesign/dept/

ANDREW WILLIAMS
Resin Art Panels (page 219)
Andrew is a furniture design student at the University of Kansas in Lawrence. He has always been a maker, bringing his designs to life with his hands. His primary focus is to push materials into new and unseen applications in the world of furniture design.
www.coroflot.com/andrew-williams

ELISA WILLIAMS
Bubbles (Desk & Drinks Trolley) (page 34)
Elisa is an Alameda, California–based writer and marketing consultant whose work has appeared in *Newsweek*, *Real Simple*, *Budget Travel*, and *Better Homes & Gardens*, as well as many trade publications. She is an avid knitter, cook, and sailor, and the Bubbles desk was her first woodworking project. It was designed and produced at the Crucible, in Oakland, California, under the expert tutelage of Matt Wolpe and Kevin Hoelscher, in their "One Sheet of Plywood" class.
www.thecrucible.org

ANTON WILLIS AND KATE LYDON, CIVIL TWILIGHT
Built-In Hutch (page 210)
Civil Twilight is a design studio committed to brilliant simplicity. With work spanning architecture and interiors, branding, and product design and development, they're a group of keen observers, smart listeners, creative thinkers, and skilled makers. Their work is driven by curiosity rather than ideology, and their projects are inspired by the intersection of natural and built environments. Civil Twilight has been recognized by awards including Metropolis magazine's Next Generation Prize and the I.D. Annual Design Review.

MATT WOLPE
Plane Table (page 64)
Matt makes furniture and teaches furniture making at the Crucible in Oakland, California. One of his classes is called "One Sheet of Plywood: Design/Build."
www.justfinedesignbuild.com

MEGAN WRIGHT
Bent-Wood Table and Chair (page 43)
Megan holds a bachelor's degree in industrial design from the College of Creative Studies in Detroit. While in school, she concentrated on furniture design. Toward the end of her senior year, she took her love of molds for bent furniture and turned in the direction of ceramic molds. She is currently working on dinnerware and serving pieces from her home in Michigan. To see any of her other work, send her an e-mail.
design.meganelizabeth@gmail.com.

IGOR ZEMSKOV
Flip Chair (page 214)
Igor was born in St. Petersburg, Russia, and raised in Columbus, Ohio. A student of industrial design at the Columbus College of Art & Design, he believes that ID can change the world for the better, asserting that the more intelligence we gain through technology and understanding, the more solutions we discover to improve life. To Igor, ID is a very powerful, emotional field, where teamwork and ideation play important roles. One of his favorite parts of design work is the way people interact with a simple object, and their emotional attachment to a product they've worked on.
www.igorzemskovdesign.com

Resources

GREEN BUILDING ADVISOR

Taunton Press, Inc.
866-325-2558
www.greenbuildingadvisor.com
Comprehensive resource for green building issues and materials suppliers, including a list of companies that offer certified and/or low- or no-added-formaldehyde sheet goods

HAIRPINLEGS.COM

614-949-6918
www.hairpinlegs.com
Custom metal fabrication shop offering midcentury-style legs.

MCMASTER-CARR

330-995-5500
www.mcmaster.com
Online supplier of a vast range of fittings, fasteners, and other hardware.

ROCKLER WOODWORKING AND HARDWARE

800-279-4441
www.rockler.com
National store and online retailer of tools, materials, and hardware for all things woodworking.

SIENNA PRODUCTS, LLC

800-516-4729
www.soft-close-cabinet.com
Supplier of soft-close cabinet hardware.

Photography credits

Interior photography

Chapter opener photos by © Arthur Koch
© 2008 China Photos/Getty Images: 8
© 2010 Free Stock Textures: plywood texture throughout
© Adele Cuartelon: 255
© Alexis Liu: 106
© Anna Parrella: 291
© Arthur Koch: 7, 21, 26, 53, 64, 101, 151, 156, 180, 211, 215, 253, and 281
© Ashley Schwebel: 37
© Barnaby Gunning: 31
© Bernard Wolf: 296
© Beth Blair: 152
© Brian DuBois: 109
© Brian Everett: 44
© Brian Gillis: 307
© Brian Hinz: 59
© Bryce Moulton: 158
© Camden Whitehead: 163 and 223
© Carl Harris: 225
© Cezary Gajewski: 22
© Chad Kelly: 68 and 169
© Chris Heichel: 118
© Christy Oates: 144
© Dieter Amick: 126
© Eric Bishoff Photography: 113, 133, 175, and 230
© Greg Bugel: 122
© Igor Zemskov: 214
© James Scheifla: 188
© Jennifer Anderson: 262
© Jin Kim: 92
© John Malinoski: 261

© Justin Orton: 146
© Kristin Hare: 150
© Lauren Von Dehsen: 100
© Lightbox Images Photography, images by Thomas Cooper: 10 bottom, 11, 12, 15, 16, 20, 40, 49, 96, 208, 216, 232, 240, 246 right, 259, 267, and 274
Marcelino Vilaubi: 10 top, 89, 192, 206, 219, and 221
© Marcus Papay: 103 and 280
© Mark Bradley: 301
© Martin Besko: 73
© Maya Lee: 250
© Nathalie Schueller: 54 and 237
© Paul Steiner: 184 and 277
© Paolo Korre: 182
© Philip Schmidt: 246 left
© Philipp Herbert: 228 and 252
© Ralph Stampone: 76
© Ryan Mahan: 197
© Sara Schalliol-Hodge: 282
© Sascha Ayad: 201
© Steffanie Dotson: 84
© Steven De Lannoy: 136
© Steven Ewoldt: 286
© Will Holman: 139

Index

Other Storey Titles You Will Enjoy

Compact Cabins, by Gerald Rowan.
Simple living in 1,000 square feet or less — includes 62 design interpretations for every taste.
216 pages. Paper. ISBN 978-1-60342-462-2.

HomeMade, by Ken Braren & Roger Griffith.
An ideabook of 101 easy-to-make projects for your garden, home, or farm.
176 pages. Paper. ISBN 978-0-88266-103-2.

The Kids' Building Workshop, by J. Craig & Barbara Roberston.
These projects bring parents and children together to teach essential skills and build 15 fun and useful items.
144 pages. Paper. ISBN 978-1-58017-488-6.

Rustic Retreats: A Build-It-Yourself Guide, by David and Jeanie Stiles.
Illustrated, step-by-step instructions for more than 20 low-cost, sturdy, beautiful outdoor structures.
160 pages. Paper. ISBN 978-1-58017-035-2.

The Vegetable Gardener's Book of Building Projects.
Simple-to-make projects include cold frames, compost bins, planters, rasied beds, outdoor furniture, and more.
152 pages. Paper. ISBN 978-1-60342-526-1.

Woodworking FAQ, by Spike Carlsen.
Practical answers to common woodworking questions, plus insider tips on how to be successful in every project.
304 pages. Paper with partially concealed wire-o. ISBN 978-1-60342-729-6.

These and other books from Storey Publishing are available wherever quality books are sold or by calling 1-800-441-5700.
Visit us at *www.storey.com*.